business solutions

VBA
for the
2007 Microsoft®
Office System

Paul McFedries

800 E. 96th Street
Indianapolis, Indiana 46240

GW00360279

VBA for the 2007 Microsoft ® Office System

International Standard Book Number: 0-7897-3667-5

Library of Congress Cataloging-in-Publication Data

McFedries, Paul.
  VBA for the 2007 Microsoft Office system / Paul McFedries.
    p. cm.
  ISBN 0-7897-3667-5
1. Microsoft Office. 2. Microsoft Visual Basic for applications. 3. Business—Computer programs. 4. Integrated software. I. Title.
  HF5548.4.M525M395 2007
  005.5—dc22
                              2007004121

Printed in the United States of America

First Printing: April 2007

10   09   08   07   4   3   2   1

Trademarks

Warning and Disclaimer

Bulk Sales

Que Publishing offers excellent discounts on this book when ordered in quantity for bulk purchases or special sales. For more information, please contact

U.S. Corporate and Government Sales
1-800-382-3419
corpsales@pearsontechgroup.com

For sales outside of the U.S., please contact

International Sales
international@pearsoned.com

This Book Is Safari Enabled

The Safari® Enabled icon on the cover of your favorite technology book means the book is available through Safari Bookshelf. When you buy this book, you get free access to the online edition for 45 days. Safari Bookshelf is an electronic reference library that lets you easily search thousands of technical books, find code samples, download chapters, and access technical information whenever and wherever you need it.

To gain 45-day Safari Enabled access to this book:

- Go to http://www.quepublishing.com/safarienabled
- Complete the brief registration form
- Enter the coupon code 2WDR-VVBC-6Y4V-WTCG-TKYP

If you have difficulty registering on Safari Bookshelf or accessing the online edition, please e-mail customer-service@safaribooksonline.com.

Associate Publisher
Greg Wiegand

Acquisitions Editor
Loretta Yates

Development Editor
Todd Brakke

Managing Editor
Gina Kanouse

Project Editor
Betsy Harris

Copy Editor
Margo Catts

Indexer
Erika Millen

Proofreader
Paula Lowell

Technical Editor
Greg Perry

Publishing Coordinator
Cindy Teeters

Book Designer
Anne Jones

Senior Compositor
Gloria Schurick

Contents

I   GETTING STARTED WITH VBA

III GETTING THE MOST OUT OF VBA

IV   APPENDIXES

About the Author

Paul McFedries is well-known as a teacher of Office, Windows, and programming, particularly VBA. He is the president of Logophilia Limited, a technical writing company. Paul started programming when he was a teenager in the mid-1970s and has worked with everything from mainframes to desktops to bar code scanners. He has programmed in many different languages, including Fortran, assembly language, C++, Java, JavaScript, Visual Basic, and VBScript. He has been writing programs for PCs for more than 25 years, and has been developing VBA applications since Microsoft first added VBA to the Office suite in 1994. Now primarily a writer, Paul has written more than 50 books that have sold more than three million copies worldwide. These books include *Access 2007 Forms, Reports, and Queries* (Que, 2007), *Formulas and Functions with Excel 2007* (Que, 2007), *Tricks of the Office 2007 Gurus* (Que, 2007), and *Windows Vista Unleashed* (Sams, 2006).

Dedication

To Karen and Gypsy.

Acknowledgments

Robert Pirsig, in *Zen and the Art of Motorcycle Maintenance*, wrote that "a person who sees Quality and feels it as he works, is a person who cares." If this book is a quality product (and I immodestly think that it is), it's because the people at Que editorial cared enough to make it so.

So a round of hearty thanks is in order for all the good people who worked on this project. You'll find them all listed near the front of the book, but I'd like to extend special kudos to the folks I worked with directly: Acquisitions Editor Loretta Yates, Development Editor Todd Brakke, Production Editor Betsy Harris, Copy Editor Margo Catts, and Tech Editor Greg Perry.

We Want to Hear from You!

As the reader of this book, you are our most important critic and commentator. We value your opinion and want to know what we're doing right, what we could do better, what areas you'd like to see us publish in, and any other words of wisdom you're willing to pass our way.

As an associate publisher for Que Publishing, I welcome your comments. You can email or write me directly to let me know what you did or didn't like about this book—as well as what we can do to make our books better.

Please note that I cannot help you with technical problems related to the topic of this book. We do have a User Services group, however, where I will forward specific technical questions related to the book.

When you write, please be sure to include this book's title and author as well as your name, email address, and phone number. I will carefully review your comments and share them with the author and editors who worked on the book.

Email: feedback@quepublishing.com

Mail: Greg Wiegand
           Associate Publisher
           Que Publishing
           800 East 96th Street
           Indianapolis, IN 46240 USA

Reader Services

Visit our website and register this book at www.quepublishing.com/register for convenient access to any updates, downloads, or errata that might be available for this book.

INTRODUCTION

Visual Basic for Applications is a mouthful to say (which is why I'll use the standard short form— VBA—from now on), but it also seems like it would be a real handful to learn. After all, this is a *programming language* we're talking about, right?

True, but VBA was designed to be easy to learn and straightforward to apply. I've learned a couple of dozen programming languages over the past 30 years or so, and I can tell you that VBA is, hands down, the easiest language I've ever worked with.

Okay, but isn't this stuff just for power users and the staff of the Information Technology department?

Yes, VBA is a useful tool for hardcore users and those who need to design major projects. But VBA can be immensely useful for *every* user. As a writer, I use Word constantly, and over the years I've developed dozens of small macros, functions, and forms that streamline or automate repetitive chores. Most of these routines consist of only a few lines of code, and each one saves me only about 30 seconds to a minute, depending on the task. But I use these routines 50 or 100 times a day, so I end up saving myself anywhere from 30 to 90 minutes a day! That's pretty remarkable, but the proof is in the pudding: I can now write far more pages in a day than I used to. (Don't tell my editor!)

Whether your concern is ease-of-use or personal productivity, there's little doubt VBA can make working with the Office applications a better experience. So now all you have to do is learn how to use it, and that's where this book comes in. My goal in writing this book was to give you an introduction to the VBA language, and to give you plenty of examples for putting the language to good use. Even if you've never even programmed your VCR, this book will teach you VBA programming from the ground up. The first six chapters, in particular, give you all the know-how you'll need to be a competent and productive programmer.

What Is a Macro?

It doesn't matter in which Office program you're working—it could be Word, it could be Excel, it could be PowerPoint. A few times a day you probably find yourself performing some chore that either you've done dozens of times in the past, or that you have to repeat a number of times in a row. It could be typing and formatting a section of text, running a series of menu commands, or editing a document in a particular way. If you're like most people, when faced with these repetitive chores, you probably find yourself wishing there was some way to ease the drudgery and reduce the time taken by this mindless but necessary work.

Sure, most of the Office applications have a Repeat button on the Quick Access Toolbar that lets you repeat your most recent action. That's handy, but it repeats only a single action. If you need to repeat two or more actions, this solution doesn't work.

What's a person to do about this? Well, what if I told you that it was possible to *automate* just about any routine and repetitive task? What if I told you that it was possible to take this automated task and run it immediately simply by selecting a command or even by just pressing a key or clicking a button?

It sounds too good to be true, I know, but that's just what Visual Basic for Applications (VBA) can do for you. You use VBA to create something called a *macro*, which is really just a series of tasks that you want a program to perform. So a macro is not unlike a recipe, which is a set of instructions that tells you what tasks to perform to cook or bake something. A macro, too, is a set of instructions, but in this case it tells a program (such as Word or Excel) what tasks to perform to accomplish some goal.

The big difference, however, is that a macro combines all these instructions into a single script that you can invoke with a keystroke or just a few mouse clicks. In this sense, then, a macro isn't so much like a recipe for, say, how to bake bread, but is more akin to a bread machine, which, after it has been loaded with ingredients, bakes a loaf with the push of a button.

This list of instructions is composed mostly of *macro statements*. Some of these statements perform specific macro-related tasks, but most correspond to the underlying application's commands and dialog box options. For example, in any application, you can close the current (active) window by selecting the Office menu's Close command. In a VBA macro, the following statement does the same thing:

```
ActiveWindow.Close
```

What Does VBA Have to Do with Macros?

VBA is a programming language designed specifically for creating application macros. That sounds intimidating, I'm sure, but VBA's biggest advantage is that it's just plain easier to use than most programming languages. If you don't want to do any programming, VBA enables you to record macros and attach them to buttons either inside a document or on the Quick Access Toolbar (as you'll see in Chapter 1). You also can create your own dialog boxes by "drawing" the appropriate controls onto a document. Other visual tools enable you to customize the Ribbon as well, so you have everything you need to create simple scripts without writing a line of code.

Of course, if you want to truly unleash VBA's capabilities, you'll need to augment your interface with programming code. That sounds pretty fancy, but the VBA language is constructed in such a way that it's fairly easy to get started and to figure things out as you go along. More than any other programming language, VBA enables you to do productive things without climbing a huge learning curve.

What You Should Know Before Reading This Book

First and foremost, this book does *not* assume that you've programmed before. VBA beginners are welcome here and will find the text to their liking.

I've tried to keep the chapters focused on the topic at hand and unburdened with long-winded theoretical discussions. For the most part, each chapter gets right down to brass tacks without much fuss and bother. To keep the chapters uncluttered, I've made a few assumptions about what you know and don't know:

- I assume you have knowledge of rudimentary computer concepts such as files and folders.
- I assume you're familiar with Windows and that you know how to launch applications and work with tools such as menus, dialog boxes, and the Help system.
- I assume you can operate peripherals attached to your computer, such as the keyboard, mouse, printer, and modem.
- This book's examples use the Office 2007 applications, although most of them also work with Office 2000, Office XP, and Office 2003. Therefore, I assume you've used these Office programs for a while and are comfortable working with these programs.

What's in the Book

This book isn't meant to be read from cover to cover, although you're certainly free to do just that if the mood strikes you. Instead, most of the chapters are set up as self-contained units that you can dip into at will to extract whatever nuggets of information you need. However, if you're a beginning VBA programmer, I recommend working through Chapters 1 to 6 to ensure that you have a thorough grounding in the fundamentals of the VBA editor and the VBA language.

The book is divided into four main parts. To give you the big picture before diving in, here's a summary of what you'll find in each part:

>   **Part 1, "Getting Started with VBA"**—The half dozen chapters in Part 1 give you a thorough grounding in VBA. You start off easy by learning how to create and run recorded macros, which doesn't require any programming (Chapter 1). In Chapters 2 though 6, you learn the basics of the VBA language, which you'll use in earnest throughout the rest of the book.

>   **Part 2, "Putting VBA to Work"**—The five chapters in Part 2 enable you to put your VBA programming knowledge to good and practical use by showing you how to program the five main Office applications: Word (Chapter 7), Excel (Chapter 8), PowerPoint (Chapter 9), Access (Chapter 10), and Outlook (Chapter 11).

>   **Part 3, "Getting the Most Out of VBA"**—The five chapters in Part 3 augment your VBA toolkit with lots of useful techniques. You learn how to interact with users (Chapter 12), how to create custom dialog boxes (Chapter 13), how to create custom Ribbon tabs and buttons (Chapter 14), how to debug your VBA code (Chapter 15), and how to use VBA to control other applications (Chapter 16).

>   **Appendixes**—The book finishes with two appendixes that you can use as a reference. Appendix A lists all the VBA statements, and Appendix B lists all the VBA functions.

This Book's Special Features

VBA for the 2007 Microsoft Office System is designed to give you the information you need without making you wade through ponderous explanations and interminable technical background. To make your life easier, this book includes various features and conventions that help you get the most out of the book and VBA itself.

- **Things you type:** Whenever I suggest that you type something, what you type appears in a **bold** font.

- **Commands:** I use the following style for Ribbon commands: View, Macros. This means that you click the Ribbon's View tab, and then click the Macros button.

- **Dialog box controls:** Dialog box controls have underlined accelerator keys: Close.

- **Visual Basic keywords:** Keywords reserved in the VBA language appear in monospace type.
- **Code-continuation character (➥):** When a statement is too long to fit on one line of this book, I break it at a convenient place, and add the code-continuation character at the beginning of the next line.

This book also uses the following boxes to draw your attention to important (or merely interesting) information.

> **NOTE**
> The Note box presents asides that give you more information about the topic under discussion. These tidbits provide extra insights that give you a better understanding of the task at hand.

> **TIP**
> The Tip box tells you about VBA methods that are easier, faster, or more efficient than the standard methods.

> **CAUTION**
> The all-important Caution box tells you about potential accidents waiting to happen. There are always ways to mess things up when you're working with computers. These boxes help you avoid at least some of the pitfalls.

→ These cross-reference elements point you to related material elsewhere in the book.

Getting Started with VBA

I

Creating and Running Recorded Macros

This book is about programming, but for certain tasks you may not need to do any programming at all. That's because VBA in Word and Excel lets you create a macro automatically by *recording* a set of steps you perform in the program. (Unfortunately, the other programs in the 2007 Office suite don't have macro recording capabilities.) This is by far the easiest way to create a macro. With this method, you start the macro recording feature and then run through the operations you want to automate—which can include selecting text, running commands from the Ribbon (the Office 2007 replacement for the menus and toolbars in previous versions of Office), and choosing dialog box options. The macro recorder takes note of everything you do, translates everything into the appropriate VBA programming statements, and stores them where you can easily rerun the macro later on. If you're just starting out with VBA (or programming in general), recording macros is a great way to get your feet wet because you never have to work with or even *see* a single line of programming code.

1

> **TIP**
> Even if you're an experienced programmer and plan only to write your own VBA code, you should still know how to record macros. That's because it's often easiest to begin a VBA procedure by recording some of the actions you need. This way, VBA does much of the work for you, and you can then tweak the resulting code by hand.

What kinds of things should you record? Just about any operation that's lengthy—it could be either a single complex task or multiple, related tasks—or tedious, and that you perform relatively often. You can probably think of several operations right off the bat. Here are four common ideas:

- **Multiple find and replace actions**—It's common in business to get a document that requires a number of adjustments throughout: converting one style to another, removing formatting, deleting extra line breaks, changing two spaces after each sentence to one space, and so on. Each of these operations requires a separate Replace command. That's fine for one document, but if you have a number of documents or documents that you receive regularly, the task becomes inefficient and tedious. You can avoid the drudgery by recording all the Replace operations to a single macro, and then running that macro each time you receive a document that requires those adjustments.

- **Automate repetitive steps**—Working with certain documents, you may find that you need to run certain steps to fix or adjust text. For example, the paragraphs in a document may all be indented by, say, five spaces rather than a First Line Indent marker on the Ruler. If the document consists of dozens of paragraphs, adjusting them all by hand is no one's idea of fun. However, it would be easy to record a macro that moves to the start of the paragraph, deletes the five spaces, and then applies the first line indent. If you assign a shortcut key or Quick Access toolbar button to the macro, you can run through all the paragraphs very quickly.

- **Window adjustments**—Unless you run all your documents maximized, you probably have a certain spot on the screen where you like to work. For example, you might want your document windows adjusted so that you can see your Outlook window and monitor incoming email while you work. Similarly, you might prefer that your documents use the most vertical room possible, which means adjusting the size so that the top is flush with the top of the screen, and the bottom is flush with the Windows taskbar. These position and size adjustments aren't difficult, but if you regularly work with dozens of documents during the day, it can be a pain to be constantly tweaking the window as you open each document. A better idea is to record the window adjustments to a macro and then run that macro each time you open a document.

- **Common steps for new documents**—It's quite common to have to run several steps with some or all of the new documents you create. In Word, for example, when you create a new document you might always insert a certain cover page, activate the Document Map, switch to Draft view, and display the Document Properties information panel so you can set the document's Title, Subject, and Keywords. Depending on the number of tasks you run, all this can take a number of minutes. By recording the same steps to a macro, however, you can perform them in seconds and with just a few mouse clicks or a single keystroke.

Recording macros is endlessly useful, and after you get the hang of it, you'll likely find yourself recording all kinds of routine operations (and therefore saving yourself tons of time, to boot).

Recording a VBA Macro

As I mentioned earlier, only Word and Excel come with the Record Macro command, which is a shame. (In Office 2003, you could record macros in PowerPoint, too.) However, these two programs are the most suited to recording macros, so it's not all that surprising that Microsoft has restricted the Office macro recording capabilities. The next two sections show you how to record a macro in Word and Excel.

Recording a Word Macro

Before getting started, make sure that Word is set up so that it's ready to record. If you want to perform your actions on a specific document, for example, make sure that document is open. Similarly, if you want to record a series of formatting options, select the text you want to work with. Here are the steps to follow to record a macro in Word:

1. Choose View, pull down the Macros menu, and then choose <u>R</u>ecord Macro. (You can also click the Macro Recording button in the status bar. If you don't see the Macro Recording button, right-click the status bar and then click Macro Recording.) The Record Macro dialog box appears, as shown in Figure 1.1.

Figure 1.1
Use Word's version of the Record Macro dialog box to name and describe your macro.

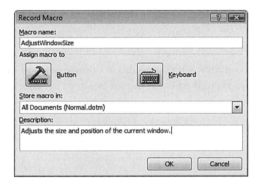

2. Word proposes a name for the macro (such as Macro1), but you should use the <u>M</u>acro Name text box to change the name to something more meaningful. However, you must follow a few naming conventions:
   - No more than 255 characters. (That sounds like a lot, and it is. Because you may occasionally have to type macro names, I recommend keeping the names relatively short to save wear and tear on your typing fingers.)
   - The first character must be a letter or an underscore (_).
   - No spaces or periods are allowed.

You'll see later on that one way to run a recorded macro is to select it from a list of all your recorded macros. If you create a lot of macros this way, that list will get long in a hurry. Therefore, when naming your recorded macros, make sure you assign names that will make it easy to differentiate one macro from another. Names such as `Macro1` and `Macro2` tell you nothing, but names such as `AdjustWindowSize` and `NewDocumentTasks` are instantly understandable.

3. Use the <u>S</u>tore Macro In drop-down list to specify where the macro will reside. I recommend keeping the default All Documents (Normal.dotm) option. This saves the macro in the Normal template, which makes it available all the time. (You can also store the macro in any open template, which makes the macro available to any document that uses the template, or in any open document, which makes the macro available only to that document.)

4. Enter an optional description of the macro in the <u>D</u>escription text box.

5. Click OK. The application returns you to the document and starts the recorder.

6. Perform the tasks you want to include in the macro. Here are some things to bear in mind during the recording:

   - Word gives you two indications that a recording is in progress (see Figure 1.2): the mouse pointer includes what looks like a cassette tape icon, and the status bar's Record Macro button changes to a blue square.

   - The mouse works only for selecting Ribbon commands and dialog box options. If you need to change the document cursor position or select text, you need to use the keyboard.

   - Because the macro recorder takes note of *everything* you do, be careful not to perform any extraneous keyboard actions or mouse clicks during the recording.

Figure 1.2
Word indicates that you're recording a macro by changing the mouse pointer and Record Macro button.

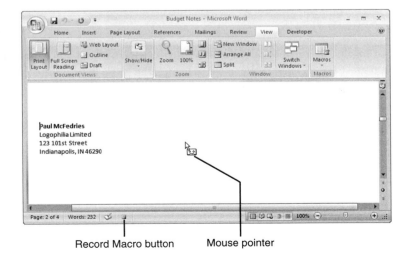

Record Macro button   Mouse pointer

7. When you finish the tasks, choose View, pull down the Macros menu, and then choose Stop Recording (or click the Macro Recording button in the status bar).

Recording an Excel Macro

Before launching your recording in Excel, make sure the program is set up as required. For example, open the workbook and select the worksheet you want to use during the recording. Here are the steps to follow to record a macro in Excel:

1. Choose View, pull down the Macros menu, and then choose Record Macro. (You can also click the Macro Recording button in the status bar.) The Record Macro dialog box appears. Figure 1.3 shows the Excel version.

Figure 1.3
Use Excel's Record Macro dialog box to name and describe your macro.

2. Use the Macro Name text box to change the name to something memorable or descriptive. (Follow the same naming conventions as I outlined in the previous section.)

3. In Excel, you can use the Shortcut Key: Ctrl+ text box to assign a shortcut key to the macro. Note, however, that this is optional because VBA offers other ways to run your recorded macros (see "Running a Recorded Macro," later in this chapter).

4. Use the Store Macro In drop-down list to specify where the macro will reside. You can store the macro in the current workbook, a new workbook, or in the Personal Macro Workbook. If you use the Personal Macro Workbook, your macros will be available to all your workbooks.

> **NOTE**
> Excel's Personal Macro Workbook doesn't exist until you assign at least one recorded macro to it. After you do that, the Personal Macro Workbook (its filename is PERSONAL.XLSB) opens automatically every time you start Excel. This is useful because any macros contained in this file will be available to all your workbooks, which makes them easy to reuse. Note, however, that you don't see the Personal Macro Workbook when you start Excel because the file is hidden. If you want to see this workbook, you have to first unhide it: Choose the View, Unhide command, select Personal in the Unhide dialog box, and then click OK.

5. Enter an optional description of the macro in the Description text box.

6. Click OK. Excel returns you to the workbook and starts recording.

7. Perform the tasks you want to include in the macro. Here are some things to bear in mind during the recording:

    • Excel gives you just one indication that a recording is in progress: The status bar's Record Macro button changes to a blue square (see Figure 1.2, earlier).

    • Unlike Word, Excel makes the mouse available for all actions.

    • Because the macro recorder takes note of *everything* you do, be careful not to perform any extraneous keyboard actions or mouse clicks during the recording.

8. When you finish the tasks, choose View, pull down the Macros menu, and then choose Stop Recording (or click the Macro Recording button in status bar).

Running a Recorded Macro

In almost all cases, you record a macro so that you can run it again in the future, probably a number of times depending on the tasks you recorded. (The exception would be, as I mentioned earlier, if you record a macro to use as a starting point for writing your own code.) So after you record a macro, how do you get it to run again? There are three main methods you can use: the Macro Name list, a shortcut key, and a Quick Access toolbar button.

Using the Macro Name List

The Macro Name list is a listing of all your recorded macros. (It also contains macros you create by hand, as discussed in the next chapter.) This means that all your recorded macros are as little as four mouse clicks away, as you see in the following steps:

1. Set up the document so that it's ready to handle the tasks that the recorded macro will run (for example, open a document, move the cursor into position, or select text).

2. Choose View, Macros (or press Alt+F8). Word displays the Macros dialog box (see Figure 1.4), although in Excel it's called the Macro dialog box.

3. (Optional) Use the Macros In list to click the template or document that contains the macro.

4. In the Macro Name list, click the macro you want to run.

5. Click Run. The program runs the macro.

Figure 1.4
Use the Macro Name list to select the macro you want to run.

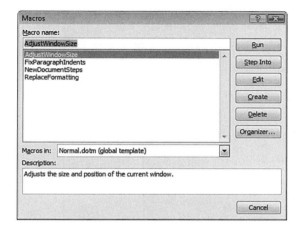

Assigning Shortcut Keys to Recorded Word Macros

If you have a recorded macro that you'll be using frequently, even the few mouse clicks required to run the macro from the Macro Name list can seem excessive. A faster alternative is to assign a shortcut key to the macro, which means you can run the macro by pressing the shortcut key.

To assign a shortcut key in Word, follow these steps:

1. You have two ways to get started:
   - If you haven't recorded the macro yet, choose View, pull down the Macros list, and then choose Record Macro. Fill in the macro details (name, storage location, and description) first, and then click Keyboard. Skip to step 4.
   - If you've already recorded the macro, choose Office, Word Options, click Customize, and then click the Customize button beside the Keyboard Shortcuts text.
2. In the Customize Keyboard dialog box, use the Categories list to click Macros. Word displays your macros in the Macros list.
3. In the Macros list, click the macro you want to work with.
4. Click inside the Press New Shortcut Key box and then press the shortcut key you want to use. One of two things will happen:
   - Word displays Currently Assigned To, followed by [unassigned], as shown in Figure 1.5. This means no other command is using the shortcut key, so proceed to step 5.

Figure 1.5
Use Word's
Customize Keyboard
dialog box to assign
a shortcut key to a
macro.

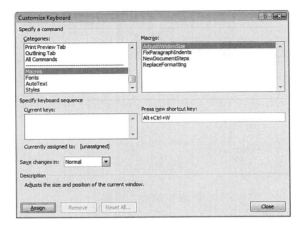

- Word displays Currently Assigned To, followed by the name of a command. This means that another Word command (or macro) is already using the shortcut key. Repeat step 4 until you find an unassigned shortcut key.

> **CAUTION**
>
> It's best to avoid overwriting any of Word's built-in shortcuts because you may use them now or in the future. By using key combinations that include some or all of the Shift, Ctrl, and Alt keys, you can almost always find an unassigned shortcut for your macros.

> **TIP**
>
> If you have trouble remembering your keyboard shortcuts, you can get Word to print out a list of them. Choose Office, Print to open the Print dialog box. In the Print What list, click Key Assignments, and then click OK.

5. Click Assign.
6. Click Close.
7. If you opening the Word Options dialog box earlier, click OK.

Assigning Shortcut Keys to Recorded Excel Macros

If you want to assign a shortcut key to a recorded Excel macro, you have two ways to get started:

- If you haven't recorded the macro yet, choose View, pull down the Macros list, and then choose Record Macro. Fill in the macro details (name, storage location, and description) first, and then click Keyboard. Skip to step 4.

■ If you've already recorded the macro, choose View, Macros (or press Alt+F8) to display the Macro dialog box. Click the macro you want to work with and then click Options to display the Macro Options dialog box shown in Figure 1.6.

Figure 1.6
Use the Macro Options dialog box to assign a shortcut key to a macro.

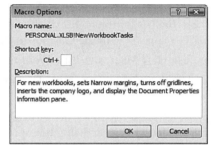

In the Shortcut Key Ctrl+ text box, type the letter you want to use with Ctrl for the key combination. For example, if you type **e**, you can run the macro by pressing Ctrl+E. Click OK.

> **NOTE**
> Excel shortcut keys are case sensitive, meaning you can create separate shortcuts with uppercase and lowercase letters. For example, if you type **e** into the Ctrl+ text box, you have to press Ctrl+E (or, to be precise, Ctrl+e) to run the macro. However, if you type **E** into the Ctrl+ text box, you have to press Ctrl+Shift+E to run the macro.

> **CAUTION**
> Make sure you don't specify a shortcut key that conflicts with Excel's built-in shortcuts (such as Ctrl+B for Bold or Ctrl+C for Copy). If you use a key that clashes with an Excel shortcut, Excel over-rides its own shortcut and runs your macro instead (provided that the workbook containing the macro is open).
>
> There are only four letters not assigned to Excel commands that you can use with your macros: e, j, m, and q. You can get extra shortcut keys by using uppercase letters. Note, however, that Excel uses four built-in Ctrl+Shift shortcuts: A, F, O, and P.

Creating a Quick Access Toolbar Button for a Recorded Macro

The only problem most people have with assigning shortcut keys to macros is remembering which shortcut runs which macro! The more shortcuts you assign, the harder it gets to remember them all and the more likely it is that you'll press an incorrect shortcut key by mistake. What many VBA veterans do is assign just a few shortcut keys to their most frequently used macros, and other macros that they need handy they assign to the Quick

Access toolbar. This is a great way to run oft-used macros because they're only a click away and you can assign different icons to each macro to help you differentiate them.

Follow these steps in either Word or Excel to create a Quick Access toolbar button for a macro:

1. Click the Customize Quick Access Toolbar button and then choose <u>M</u>ore Commands. The application's Options dialog box appears with the Customize tab displayed.

2. In the <u>C</u>hoose Commands From list, click Macros. A list of your macros appears.

3. Click the macro you want to work with and then click <u>A</u>dd. The program adds the macro to the list of Quick Access toolbar buttons.

4. To change the macro button's icon, click the macro in the list of Quick Access toolbar buttons and then click <u>M</u>odify. The Modify Button dialog box appears, as shown in Figure 1.7.

Figure 1.7
Use the Modify Button dialog box to assign an icon and display name to your macro button.

5. Use the Symbol list to click the icon you want to use for the macro button.

6. Use the Display Name text box to type the name you want to appear when you hover the mouse pointer over the button.

7. Click OK.

8. Repeat steps 3–7 to assign other macros to buttons.

9. Click OK.

Figure 1.8 shows a macro button added to the Quick Access toolbar.

Macro button

Figure 1.8
A macro button added to the Quick Access toolbar.

TIP In its default position above the Ribbon, the Quick Access toolbar can display only so many buttons. If you want to add lots of buttons for your macros (or other program commands), move the Quick Access toolbar below the Ribbon. Click the Customize Quick Access Toolbar button and then choose Show Below the Ribbon.

From Here

- You'll learn more about the Visual Basic Editor as well as how to create your own procedures and enter your own VBA statements in Chapter 2, "Writing Your Own Macros."

- You won't get too far writing VBA code without learning about variables, and you'll do that in Chapter 3, "Understanding Program Variables."

- Your procedures will also rely heavily on operators and expressions. Turn to Chapter 4, "Building VBA Expressions," to learn more.

- Objects are one of the most important concepts in VBA. You'll find out how they work in Chapter 5, "Working with Objects." Also, see Part II, "Putting VBA to Work," to get the specifics on the objects used in Word, Excel, and other Office applications.

- VBA, like any programming language worth its salt, contains a number of statements that control program flow. I discuss these statements in Chapter 6, "Controlling Your VBA Code."

Writing Your Own Macros

2

Letting VBA do all the work by recording your macros is an easy way to automate tasks, and it's a technique you'll use often. However, to get the most out of VBA you need to do some full-fledged programming, which means writing your own macros, either from scratch or by using a recorded macro as a starting point.

Why go to all that trouble? Here are just a few of the advantages you gain by doing this:

- If you make a mistake while recording a macro, particularly one that requires a large number of steps, you can make a simple edit to the macro's VBA code to fix the mistake rather than re-record the whole thing from scratch.

- You get full control over each macro, which means you ensure that your macros do exactly what you need them to do.

- You can take advantage of the hidden power of VBA to manipulate the Office programs and to perform some impressive programming feats that are simply not available via the recording process.

To help you realize these advantages and many more, this chapter introduces you to the basics of writing simple procedures and functions, as well as how to get around in the Visual Basic Editor, which is the tool that VBA provides for writing macros by hand. This sets the stage for the next few chapters, where I take a closer look at the specifics of the VBA language.

Activating the Ribbon's Developer Tab

If you'll be writing VBA code regularly, you can make some coding chores a bit more efficient by displaying the new Developer tab in the Office 2007 Ribbon. This tab gives you one-click access to many VBA-related features, so it's worth displaying. Follow these steps:

1. Choose Office, *Application* Options (where *Application* is the name of the current Office program, such as Word or Excel).

2. In the Popular tab, click to activate the Show Developer Tab in Ribbon check box.

3. Click OK.

Note that displaying the Developer tab in one Office program displays it in all of them. Figure 2.1 shows the Developer tab displayed in Excel.

Figure 2.1
Display the Developer tab for easier access to some VBA features.

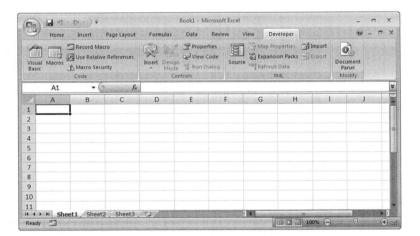

Displaying the Visual Basic Editor

To get the Visual Basic Editor onscreen in any Office program, choose Developer, Visual Basic. (Note, however, that for simplicity's sake, I use a single Office application—Excel—for the examples throughout this chapter.) Figure 2.2 shows the new window that appears (although bear in mind that the window you see may be slightly different).

> **TIP**
> You can also get to the Visual Basic Editor by pressing Alt+F11. In fact, this key combination is a toggle that switches you between the Visual Basic Editor and the current Office program.

Figure 2.2
You use the Visual Basic Editor to craft and edit your macros.

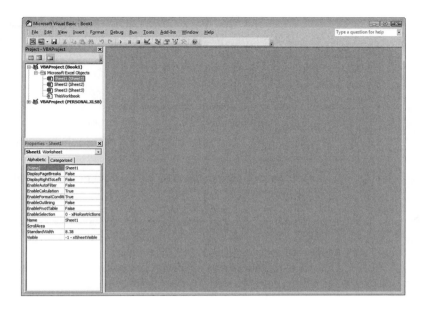

Touring the Visual Basic Editor

The idea behind the Visual Basic Editor is simple: It's a separate program that's designed to do nothing else but help you create and edit VBA macros. (In professional programming circles, the Visual Basic Editor is called an *integrated development environment* or *IDE*.)

When you open the Visual Basic Editor for the first time, you don't see much. The left side of the editor has two windows labeled Project and Properties. The latter you don't need to worry about right now. (I'll talk about it in Chapter 5, "Working with Objects.") The Project window (technically, it's called the Project Explorer) shows you the contents of the current VBA project. In simplest terms, a *project* is an Office file and all its associated VBA items, including its macros and its user forms. (You learn about user forms in Chapter 12, "Creating Custom VBA Dialog Boxes.")

Creating a New Module

You do most of your work in the Visual Basic Editor within one or more *modules*, which are windows designed to hold programming code. You may already have an existing module if you recorded some macros in the previous chapter. Just in case, here are the steps to follow to create a new module:

1. In the Project Explorer on the left side of the Visual Basic Editor window, click the project into which you want to insert the new module. Here are some notes to bear in mind:

   • In Word, if you want the new module's macros to be available all the time, click the Normal project (this adds the module to the Normal template).

- In Excel, if you want the new module's macros to be available all the time, click the PERSONAL.XLSB project (this adds the module to the PERSONAL workbook).

→ Remember that you won't see PERSONAL.XLSB until you store at least one recorded macro in the Personal Macro Workbook; **see** "Recording an Excel Macro," **p. 7**.

- In any program, if you want the new module's macros available only when a particular document is open, click that document or one of its objects.

2. Choose Insert, Module. The Visual Basic Editor creates the new module and opens it, as shown in Figure 2.3.

3. (Optional) In the Properties window, use the (Name) property to edit the module name, and then press Enter.

→ To learn techniques such as renaming, exporting, and deleting modules, **see** "Working with Modules," **p.299**.

The new module appears
in the Modules branch   The new module window appears

Figure 2.3
A new module
added to a project.

Use the (Name)
property to rename
the module

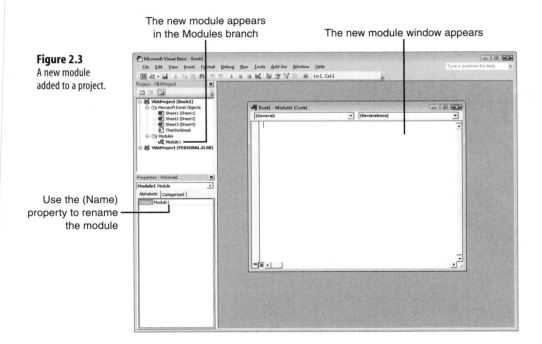

Opening an Existing Module

If you already have an existing module in the Project window, here are the steps to follow to open it:

1. In the Project window, open a project by clicking the plus sign (+) to its left.

2. In the project you just opened, open the Modules branch by clicking the plus sign (+) to its left.

3. Double-click the name of the module you want to open. The Visual Basic Editor opens the module window and displays its VBA code.

Understanding VBA Procedures

Before you get to the nitty-gritty of writing your own macros, let's take a second to understand what exactly you'll be writing. When you create VBA code by hand (or when you create a recorded macro, as described in Chapter 1), what you're creating is something called a *procedure*. In VBA, a procedure is, broadly speaking, a collection of related statements that forms a unit and performs some kind of task. (A *statement* is an instruction that tells VBA to perform a specific task.) For the purposes in this book, VBA procedures come in two flavors: command macros and user-defined functions. Here's a summary of the differences:

- *Command macros* are the most common types of procedures; they usually contain statements that are the equivalent of Ribbon options and other program commands. The distinguishing feature of command macros is that, like regular application commands, they have an effect on their surroundings. (In Word, for example, this means the macro affects the current document, a section of text, and so on.) Whether it's opening a document, formatting some text, or inserting a paragraph, command macros *change* things. See "Creating a Command Macro," next.

- *User-defined functions* work just like a program's built-in functions. Their distinguishing characteristic is that they accept input values and then manipulate those values and return a result. See "Creating a User-Defined Function," later in this chapter.

Creating a Command Macro

As I mentioned at the start of this chapter, recording macros is limiting because there are plenty of macro features that you can't access with mouse or keyboard actions or by selecting menu options. In Excel, for example, VBA has a couple dozen information macro functions that return data about cells, worksheets, workspaces, and more. Also, the VBA control functions enable you to add true programming structures such as looping, branching, and decision-making (see Chapter 6, "Controlling Your VBA Code").

To access these macro elements, you need to write your own VBA routines from scratch. This is easier than it sounds because all you really need to do is enter a series of statements in a module.

Although this section tells you how to create VBA macros, I realize there's an inherent paradox here: How can you write your own macros when you haven't learned anything about them yet? The goal of the next four chapters is to familiarize you with VBA's statements and functions. This section will get you started, and you can use this knowledge as a base on which to build your VBA skills in the chapters that follow.

Writing a Command Macro

With a module window open and active, follow these steps to write your own command macro:

1. Open the module you want to use for the function.

2. Place the insertion point where you want to start the macro. (Make sure the insertion point isn't inside an existing macro.)

3. Choose Insert, Procedure. The Visual Basic Editor displays the Add Procedure dialog box (see Figure 2.4).

Figure 2.4
Use the Add Procedure dialog box to name your new procedure and select the type of procedure you want to insert.

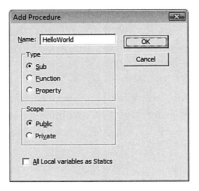

4. Use the Name text box to type the name of the macro. Here are some general guidelines you need to follow:

   • The name must be 255 characters or fewer.

   • The first character must be a letter or an underscore (_).

   • You cannot use spaces or periods.

5. In the Type group, make sure the Sub option is activated.

6. Click OK. VBA adds the following code to the module (where *ProcedureName* is the name you typed in step 3):

```
Public Sub ProcedureName()

End Sub
```

7. Between the `Public Sub` and `End Sub` lines, type the VBA statements you want to include in the macro. Press Enter after each statement to start a new line.

Figure 2.5 shows a simple example where I've added just a single VBA statement:

`MsgBox "Hello World!"`

In this example, the statement contains VBA's `MsgBox` function, which is used to display a simple dialog box (the name `MsgBox` is short for "message box") to the user. (To enhance readability, I pressed Tab once before typing the statement. I talk about indenting statements in more depth a bit later in this chapter.)

> **NOTE** The code for the examples used in this chapter can be found on my website at www.mcfedries.com/Office2007VBA.

→ For the `MsgBox` details, **see** "Getting Input Using `MsgBox`," **p.45**.

Figure 2.5
The example macro, ready for execution.

Running a Command Macro

The Office applications offer several methods for running your VBA command macros, but you'll use two most often:

■ In a module, click anywhere inside the macro, and then either select Run, Run Sub/UserForm or press the F5 key.

■ In the Office application, choose Developer, Macros (or press Alt+F8) to display the Macro dialog box. If necessary, use the Macros In list to choose the document that contains the macro with which you want to work. Now use the Macro Name list to click the macro; then click the Run button.

> **NOTE** You can also use the Macro dialog box to jump directly to any command macro that you want to edit using the Visual Basic Editor. In the Macro Name list, click the macro and then click Edit.

If you try this on the example macro shown in Figure 2.5, you see the dialog box shown in Figure 2.6. Click OK to close the dialog box.

Figure 2.6
When you run the macro shown in Figure 2.5, you see this dialog box.

Entering VBA Statements

As I mentioned earlier, entering VBA statements is, on the surface, a straightforward matter: You type the code and then press Enter after each line. I also recommend that when you're beginning a command macro, press Tab before starting the first line. This indents your code, which makes it easier to read. (Don't do this for the `Public Sub` and `End Sub` lines, just the statements that go between them.) Conveniently, VBA preserves the indentation on subsequent lines, so you have to indent only the first line.

A *comment* is a special type of VBA statement that you use to describe something about your procedure. For example, many people add a few lines of comments before a procedure to describe what the procedure does. Most programmers (and *all* good programmers) augment their code with comments throughout the procedure to describe what statements are doing, the logical flow of the procedure, and so on. VBA does not execute comments; instead, you add them for your own or other people's benefit to clarify or make it possible to follow what a procedure does. Figure 2.7 shows a simple example of a commented procedure. The comments are the statements that begin with an apostrophe (').

> **NOTE**
> At this early stage of your VBA programming career, I'd like to impress upon you the advantages to taking a neat, orderly approach to your programming. Humans can and do thrive in messy environments, but we're many times smarter and infinitely more intuitive than any macro. Procedures live in a world of strict and unyielding logic, and programming is always much easier if you supplement that logic with a sense of order. Fortunately, there are only two things you need to do to achieve most of the order you need to be a successful programmer: Indent your code and don't skimp on the comments. The latter is particularly important. Any procedure will be much easier to read (especially if you haven't looked at the code for a few months) if it's sprinkled liberally with comments throughout the code. Also, adding comments as you go is a great way of getting a grip on your own thoughts and logical leaps as you go.

Figure 2.7
A VBA procedure with comments that describe the procedure and its code.

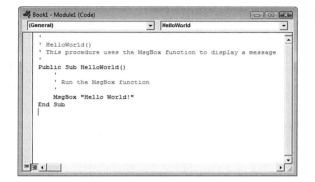

Each time you press Enter to start a new line, VBA analyzes the line you just entered and performs three chores:

- It formats the color of each word in the line: By default, VBA keywords are blue, comments are green, errors are red, and all other text is black.
- VBA keywords are converted to their proper case. For example, if you type **msgbox "Hello World!"**, VBA converts this to `MsgBox "Hello World!"` when you press Enter.
- It checks for *syntax errors*, which are errors when a word is misspelled, a function is entered incorrectly, and so on. VBA signifies a syntax error either by displaying a dialog box to let you know what the problem is, or by not converting a word to its proper case or color.

> **TIP**
> If you always enter VBA keywords in lowercase letters, you'll be able to catch typing errors by looking for those keywords that VBA doesn't recognize (in other words, the ones that remain in lowercase).

Creating a User-Defined Function

The Office applications come with a large number of built-in functions. Excel, for example, has hundreds of functions—one of the largest function libraries of any spreadsheet package. However, even with this vast collection, you'll still find plenty of situations that are not covered. For example, you might need to calculate the area of a circle of a given radius, or the gravitational force between two objects. You could, of course, easily calculate these things on a worksheet, but if you need such calculations frequently, it makes sense to define your own functions that you can use anytime. The next three sections show you how it's done.

Understanding User-Defined Functions

As I mentioned earlier, the defining characteristic of user-defined functions is that they return a result. They can perform any number of calculations on numbers, text, logical values, or whatever, but they generally don't affect their surroundings. In a worksheet, for example, they usually don't move the active cell, format a range, or change the workspace settings.

So, what *can* you put in a user-defined function? Most user-defined functions consist of one or more *expressions*. An expression is some combination of values (such as numbers), operators (such as + and *), variables (see Chapter 3), VBA functions, or application functions that, together, produce a result. (I discuss expressions in detail in Chapter 4, "Building VBA Expressions.")

All user-defined functions have the same basic structure:

```
Function ProcedureName (argument1, argument2, ...)
    [VBA statements]
    ProcedureName = returnValue
End Function
```

Here's a summary of the various parts of a user-defined function:

- **Function**—This keyword identifies the procedure as a user-defined function. The Function keyword is the reason that user-defined functions also are also known as *function procedures*.

- ***ProcedureName***—This is a unique name for the function.

- ***argument1, argument2,*** ...—Just as many application functions accept arguments, so do user-defined functions. Arguments (or parameters, as they're sometimes called) are typically one or more values that the function uses as the raw material for its calculations. You always enter arguments between parentheses after the function name, and you separate multiple arguments with commas. (If the function doesn't require arguments, you still need to include the parentheses after the function name.)

- ***VBA statements***—This is the code that actually performs the calculations, and it's usually a series of VBA statements and expressions that lead toward an overall result for the function.

- ***returnValue***—This is the final result calculated by the function.

- **End Function**—These keywords indicate the end of the function.

All your user-defined functions will have this basic structure, so you need to keep three things in mind when designing these kinds of macros:

- What arguments will the function take?
- What expressions will you use within the function?
- What value will be returned?

Writing a User-Defined Function

When you record a macro, VBA always puts the code inside a command macro. Unfortunately, there is no way to record a user-defined function; you have to write them out by hand. Fortunately, the process is very similar to creating a command macro from scratch. Here are the general steps to follow to write a user-defined function:

1. Open the module you want to use for the function.

2. Place the insertion point where you want to start the function. (Make sure the insertion point isn't inside an existing macro.)

3. Choose Insert, Procedure to open the Add Procedure dialog box.

4. Use the Name text box to type the function's name. The guidelines you must follow are the same as those for a command macro: The name must be 255 characters or fewer; the first character must be a letter or an underscore (_); and you can't use spaces or periods.

5. In the Type group, click the Function option.

6. Click OK. VBA adds the following code to the module (where *ProcedureName* is the name you typed in step 3):

```
Public Function ProcedureName()

End Function
```

7. Between the `Public Function` and `End Function` lines, type the VBA statements you want to include in the function. Press Enter after each statement to start a new line.

8. Be sure to include a statement that defines the return value. That statement should consist of the function name, followed by an equals sign (=), followed by the return value.

Figure 2.8 shows an example user-defined function that calculates and returns a result, using a single VBA statement:

```
GrossMargin = (Sales - Expenses) / Sales
```

Here, `Sales` and `Expenses` are the arguments that get passed to the function. The function subtracts the `Expenses` value from the `Sales` value, and then divides by `Sales` to return the gross margin.

Figure 2.8
The example function, ready for use in other procedures.

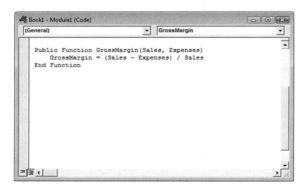

Using a Function

You can't "run" a user-defined function in the same way that you run a command macro. Instead, you use the function either as part of a command macro (or even as part of another function), or within the application itself.

To use a function in a command macro, you create a separate VBA statement that includes the function name as well as any arguments it requires. (This is known as *calling* the function.) Here's a simple example:

```
Public Sub GrossMarginTest1()
    MsgBox GrossMargin (100000, 90000)
End Sub
```

This Sub procedure calls the GrossMargin function and supplies it with the values 100000 and 90000 for the Sales and Expenses arguments, respectively. The MsgBox function displays the result in a dialog box.

To use a function in an application, you include it as part of some other calculation. This is most useful in Excel, where you can employ a user-defined function within a worksheet formula.

The easiest way to do this is to enter the function into the cell the same way you would any of Excel's built-in functions. In other words, enter the name of the function and then the necessary arguments enclosed in parentheses. Here's a sample formula that uses the GrossMargin function and assumes the Sales and Expenses values are in cells B1 and B2, respectively (see Figure 2.9):

```
=GrossMargin(B1, B2)
```

Figure 2.9
The GrossMargin function used in an Excel worksheet formula.

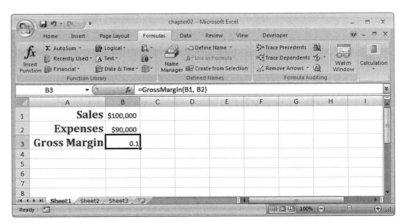

You can also use the Function wizard to insert a user-defined function. Here are the steps to follow:

1. Click the cell into which you want to insert the user-defined function.

2. Choose Formulas, Insert Function to display the Insert Function dialog box.

3. In the Or Select a Category list, click User Defined. Excel displays a list of your user-defined functions, as shown in Figure 2.10.

Figure 2.10
In the Insert Function
dialog box, choose the
User Defined category to
see a list of your user-
defined functions.

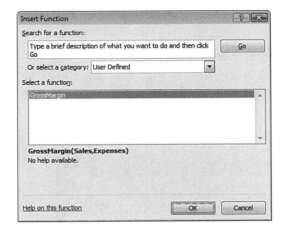

4. Click the function you want to insert and then click OK. The Function Arguments dialog box appears.
5. Specify values or cell addresses for the function arguments and then click OK. Excel inserts the function.

Taking Advantage of IntelliSense

VBA's IntelliSense feature is like a mini version of the VBA Help system. It offers you assistance with VBA syntax, either on the fly or on demand. You should find this an incredibly useful tool because, as you'll see as you work through this book, VBA contains dozens of statements and functions and VBA-enabled programs offer hundreds of objects to work with. Few people are capable of committing all this to memory, and it's a pain to be constantly looking up the correct syntax. IntelliSense helps by giving you hints and alternatives as you type. To see what I mean, let's look at the four most useful types of IntelliSense help available.

List Properties/Methods

In Chapter 4, you'll learn how to work with the objects that each VBA-enabled application makes available. In particular, you'll learn about *properties* and *methods* which, put simply, define the characteristics of each object. (In broad terms, properties describe an object's appearance or behavior and methods describe what you can do with an object.)

As you'll see, however, each object can have dozens of properties and methods. To help you code your procedures correctly, IntelliSense can display a list of the available properties and methods as you type your VBA statements. To try this out, activate a module in the Visual

Basic Editor and type **application** followed by a period (**.**). As shown in Figure 2.11, VBA displays a pop-up menu. The items on this menu are the properties and methods that are available for the **Application** object. Use the following methods to work with this menu:

- Keep typing to display different items in the list. In Excel, for example, if you type **cap**, VBA highlights Caption in the list.
- Double-click an item to insert it in your code.
- Highlight an item (by clicking it or by using the up and down arrow keys) and then press Tab to insert the item and continue working on the same statement.
- Highlight an item and then press Enter to insert the item and start a new line.
- Press Esc to remove the menu without inserting an item.

Figure 2.11
IntelliSense displays the available properties and methods as you type.

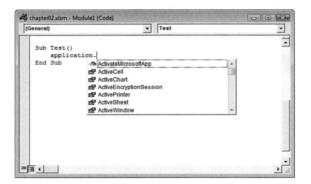

Note that if you press Esc to remove the pop-up menu, VBA won't display it again for the same object. If you would like to display the menu again, choose Edit, List Properties/Methods (or press Ctrl+J).

List Constants

IntelliSense has a List Constants feature that's similar to List Properties/Methods. In this case, you get a pop-up menu that displays a list of the available constants for a property or method. (A *constant* is a fixed value that corresponds to a specific state or result. See Chapter 3 to learn more about them.) For example, type the following in a module:

Application.ActiveWindow.WindowState=

Figure 2.12 shows the pop-up menu that appears in Excel. This is a list of constants that correspond to the various settings for a window's WindowState property. For example, you would use the xlMaximized constant to maximize a window. You work with this list using the same techniques that I outlined for List Properties/Methods.

If you need to display this list by hand, choose Edit, List Constants (or press Ctrl+Shift+J).

Figure 2.12
The List Constants feature in action.

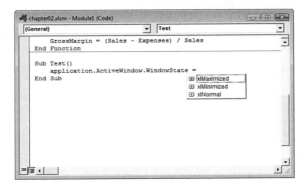

Parameter Info

You learned earlier that a user-defined function typically takes one or more arguments (or parameters) to use in its internal calculations. Many of the functions and statements built into VBA also use parameters, and some have as many as a dozen separate arguments! The syntax of such statements is obviously very complex, so it's easy to make mistakes. To help you out when entering a user-defined function or one of VBA's built-in functions or statements, IntelliSense provides the Parameter Info feature. As its name implies, this feature displays information on the parameters that you can utilize in a function. To see an example, enter the following text in any Excel module:

```
activecell.formula=pmt(
```

As soon as you type the left parenthesis, a banner pops up that tells you the available arguments for (in this case) VBA's Pmt function (see Figure 2.13). Here are the features of this banner:

- The current argument is displayed in boldface. When you enter an argument and then type a comma, VBA displays the next argument in boldface.
- Arguments that are optional are surrounded by square brackets ([ ]).
- The various As statements (for example, As Double) tell you the *data type* of each argument. I'll explain data types in the next chapter but, for now, think of them as defining what kind of data is associated with each argument (text, numeric, and so on).
- To remove the banner, press Esc.

As usual, IntelliSense also enables you to display this information by hand by choosing Edit, Parameter Info (or pressing Ctrl+Shift+I).

Figure 2.13
The Parameter Info
feature shows you
the defined argu-
ments for the cur-
rent function or
statement.

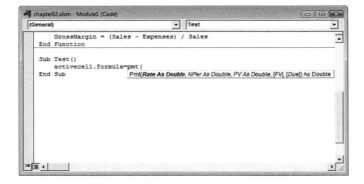

Complete Word

The last of the IntelliSense features that I'll discuss is Complete Word. You use this feature to get VBA to complete a keyword that you've started typing, and thus save some wear-and-tear on your typing fingers. To use Complete Word, type in the first few letters of a keyword and then choose <u>E</u>dit, Complete <u>W</u>ord (or press Ctrl+Space).

If the letters you typed are enough to define a unique keyword, IntelliSense fills in the rest of the word. For example, if you type **appl** and run Complete Word, IntelliSense changes your typing to **Application**. However, if there are multiple keywords that begin with the letters you typed, IntelliSense displays a pop-up menu that you can use to select the word you want.

Shutting Down the Visual Basic Editor

When you've completed your VBA chores, you can shut down the Visual Basic Editor by using either of the following techniques:

- Pull down the File menu and select the Close and Return to *Application* command, where *Application* is the name of the program you're running (such as Microsoft Excel).
- Press Alt+Q.

From Here

- To learn about using variables in your VBA code, **see** Chapter 3, "Understanding Program Variables," **p. 33**.
- For a complete look at the MsgBox function, **see** "Getting Input Using MsgBox," **p. 45**.
- To get the details on expressions, **see** Chapter 4, "Building VBA Expressions," **p. 53**.

- For information on object properties, **see** "Working with Object Properties," **p. 73**.
- For information on object methods, **see** "Working with Object Methods," **p. 75**.
- To learn techniques such as renaming, exporting, and deleting modules, **see** "Working with Modules," **p. 299**.

2

Understanding Program Variables

3

Your VBA procedures often need to store temporary values for use in statements and calculations that come later in the code. For example, you might want to store values for total sales and total expenses to use later in a gross margin calculation. Although you probably could get away with using the underlying application to store these values (in, say, a cell in an Excel worksheet), this almost always isn't very practical. Instead, VBA (like all programming languages) lets you store temporary values in special memory locations called *variables*. This chapter explains this important topic and shows you how to use variables in your VBA procedures.

Declaring Variables

Declaring a variable tells VBA the name of the variable you're going to use. (It also serves to specify the *data type* of the variable, which I'll explain later in this chapter.) Note that at this point you're not assigning a value to the variable. That comes later. All you're doing now is telling VBA that the variable exists. You declare variables by including Dim statements (Dim is short for *dimension*) at the beginning of each Sub or Function procedure.

> **NOTE**
> Technically, you can put variable declarations anywhere you like within a procedure and VBA won't complain. The only real restriction is that the Dim statement must precede the first use of the variable in a procedure. Having said all that, however, it's not only traditional, but also clearer, to list all your Dim statements together at the top of a procedure.

In its simplest form, a `Dim` statement has the following syntax:

```
Dim variableName
```

Here, `variableName` is the name of the variable. You make up these names yourself, but you need to bear a few restrictions in mind:

- The name must begin with a letter.
- The name can't be longer than 255 characters.
- The name can't be a VBA keyword (such as `Dim` or `Sub` or `End`).
- The name can't contain a space or any of the following characters: . ! # $ % & @.

For example, the following statement declares a variable named `totalSales`:

```
Dim totalSales
```

> **NOTE**
>
> To avoid confusing variable names with the names of things that are built into the VBA language, many programmers begin their variable names with a lowercase letter. If the name contains multiple "words," then each subsequent word should use an uppercase first letter (for example, `totalSales` or `newFileName`). This is the style I use in this book. (Programming types call it *camel style*, thanks to the "humps" created by the uppercase letters.)
>
> Also, note that VBA preserves the case of your variable names throughout a procedure. For example, if you declare a variable named `totalSales` and you later enter this variable name as, say, `totalsales`, VBA will convert the name to `totalSales` automatically as part of its syntax checking. This means two things:
>
> - If you want to change the case used in a variable, change the *first* instance of the variable (usually the `Dim` statement).
> - After you've declared a variable, you should enter all subsequent references to the variable entirely in lowercase. Not only is this easier to type, but you'll immediately know whether you've misspelled the variable name if you see that VBA doesn't change the case of the variable name after you enter the line.

Most programmers set up a declaration section at the beginning of each procedure and use it to hold all their `Dim` statements. Then, after the variables have been declared, you can use them throughout the procedure. Listing 3.1 shows a `Function` procedure that declares two variables—`totalSales` and `totalExpenses`—and then uses Excel's `Sum` function to store a range sum in each variable. Finally, the `GrossMargin` calculation uses each variable to return the function result.

> **TIP**
>
> The code for the examples used in this chapter can be found on my website at www.mcfedries.com/Office2007VBA.

Listing 3.1	**A Function That Uses Variables to Store the Intermediate Values of a Calculation**

```
Function GrossMargin()
    '
    ' Declarations
    '
    Dim totalSales
    Dim totalExpenses
    '
    ' Code
    '
    totalSales = Application.Sum(Range("Sales"))
    totalExpenses = Application.Sum(Range("Expenses"))
    GrossMargin = (totalSales - totalExpenses) / totalSales
End Function
```

In the `GrossMargin` function, notice that you store a value in a variable with a simple assignment statement of the following form:

```
variableName = value
```

3

> **TIP** To conserve space, you can declare multiple variables on a single line. In the `GrossMargin` function, for example, you could declare `totalSales` and `totalExpenses` using the following statement:
>
> ```
>     Dim totalSales, totalExpenses
> ```

→ Listing 3.1 gets its values from the Excel worksheet by using the `Range` method. For the details, **see** "Using the Range Method," **p. 153**.

Avoiding Variable Errors

One of the most common errors in VBA procedures is to declare a variable and then later misspell the name. For example, suppose I had entered the following statement in the `GrossMargin` procedure from Listing 3.1:

```
totlExpenses = Application.Sum(Range("Expenses"))
```

Here, `totlExpenses` is a misspelling of the variable named `totalExpenses`. VBA supports *implicit declarations*, which means that if it sees a name it doesn't recognize, it assumes that the name belongs to a new variable. In this case, VBA would assume that `totlExpenses` is a new variable, proceed normally, and calculate the wrong answer for the function.

To avoid this problem, you can tell VBA to generate an error whenever it comes across a name that hasn't been declared explicitly with a `Dim` statement. There are two ways to do this:

- For an individual module, enter the following statement at the top of the module:
```
Option Explicit
```
- To force VBA to add this statement automatically to all your modules, in the Visual Basic Editor select Tools, Options, display the Editor tab in the Options dialog box that appears, and activate the Require Variable Declaration check box.

> **NOTE** Activating the Require Variable Declaration check box forces VBA to add the `Option Explicit` statement at the beginning of each new module. However, it *doesn't* add this statement to any existing modules; you need to do that by hand.

Variable Data Types

The *data type* of a variable determines the kind of data the variable can hold. You specify a data type by including the As keyword in a Dim statement. Here is the general syntax:

```
Dim variableName As DataType
```

variableName is the name of the variable and *DataType* is one of the data types. Here's a rundown of the most useful VBA data types:

- String—This type holds *strings*, which are simple text values. Here's a sample declaration and assignment statement (note the use of quotation marks in the assignment statement value; this tells VBA that the value is a string):
```
Dim newFileName As String
newFileName = "Budget Notes.doc"
```
- Date—This type holds *date* values, which refers to dates and/or times. Here are a few examples (note the use of the # character around the values; this tells VBA that the values are dates and/or times):
```
Dim myBirthDate As Date
Dim myBirthTime As Date
Dim anotherDate As Date
myBirthDate = #8/23/59#
myBirthTime = #3:02 AM#
anotherDate = #4/27/07 16:05#
```
- Object—You use this type to hold generic *objects*, which I discuss in detail in Chapter 5, "Working with Objects."
- Byte—This rarely used type holds small, positive integer values (from 0 to 255).
- Integer—This type holds *integer* values, which VBA defines as whole numbers between –32,768 and 32,767. Here's an example:
```
Dim paragraphNumber As Integer
paragraphNumber = 1
```

■ Long—This type holds *long integer* values, which VBA defines as whole numbers between –2,147,483,648 and 2,147,483,647. Here's an example (note that you don't include commas—or periods, if you're in Europe—in numbers that would normally use one or more thousands separators):

```
Dim wordCount As Long
wordCount = 100000
```

■ Boolean—This type holds *Boolean* values, which take one of two values: True or False. Here's an example:

```
Dim documentSaved As Boolean
documentSaved = False
```

■ Currency—This type holds monetary values. The value range is from –922,337,203,685,477.5808 to 922,337,203,685,477.5807.

■ Single—This type holds *single-precision floating point* values, which are numbers that have a decimal component. Here's an example:

```
Dim averageUnitSales As Single
averageUnitSales = 50.3
```

■ Double—This type holds *double-precision floating point* values, which can accommodate much larger or smaller numbers than the Single type. Note, however, that the range available with the Single type should be more than enough for your VBA macros, so you'll probably never use the Double type. Here's an example:

```
Dim atomsInTheUniverse As Double
atomsInTheUniverse = 2.0E+79
```

> **NOTE**
> Double values often use *exponential notation*, such as the value 2.0E+79 used in the Double example. A positive number, say X, after the E symbol means that you move the decimal point X positions to the right to get the actual number. So, for example, 2.0E+3 is the same thing as 2000. A negative number, say $-X$, after the E means that you move the decimal point X positions to the left. So 3.14E-4 is the equivalent of 0.000314.

Here are a few notes to keep in mind when using data types:

■ If you don't include a data type when declaring a variable, VBA assigns the Variant data type. This enables you to store any kind of data in the variable. However, this isn't a good idea because Variant variables use more memory and are much slower than the other data types. Therefore, always give your variables a specific data type. Note, however, that you may on occasion need a variable that can assume different data types. In that case, you should declare the variable using the Variant type.

→ For an example of a situation in which declaring a variable as a Variant is a good idea, **see** "Getting Input Using InputBox," **p. 50**.

- If you declare a variable to be one data type and then try to store a value of a different data type in the variable, VBA often displays an error. For example, if you declare a variable using the `Single` type and you try to assign a value that's outside the `Single` type's allowable range, VBA displays an "Overflow" error message when you attempt to run the procedure.

- To specify the data type of a procedure argument, use the `As` keyword in the argument list. For example, the following `Function` statement declares variables `Sales` and `Expenses` to be `Currency`:

  ```
  Function GrossMargin(Sales As Currency, Expenses As Currency)
  ```

- To specify the data type of the return value for a `Function` procedure, use the `As` keyword at the end of the `Function` statement:

  ```
  Function GrossMargin(Sales, Expenses) As Single
  ```

TIP

Many programmers remind themselves of each variable's data type by applying *data type prefixes* to the variable names. For example, the data type prefix for a `String` variable is `str`, so the declaration for such a variable might look like this:

```
Dim strName As String
```

This helps you avoid programming errors because you're less likely to try and store, say, an `Integer` value in a `String` variable if that variable's name begins with `str`. Here are some other common data type prefixes:

Data Type	Prefix
String	str or s
Date	dte or dtm
Object	obj
Byte	byt
Integer	int or i
Long	lng
Boolean	bln or b
Currency	cur
Single	sgl or sng
Double	dbl
Variant	vnt

Changing the Default Data Type

I mentioned in the preceding section that VBA assigns the `Variant` type to a variable if you don't specify a data type. However, VBA supports a number of `DefType` statements that let you redefine the default data type. These statements all use the following syntax:

```
DefType letter1[-letter2]
```

Here, `Type` is a three- or four-letter code that specifies the data type, and `letter1` and `letter2` define a range of letters. Note that this is a module-level statement, so you must place it at the top of a module, before any procedures or functions.

The idea is that any variable (or function argument or function result) that begins with one of these letters will be assigned the specified data type by default. For example, the `DefInt` keyword is used to set the default data type to `Integer`. If you want VBA to assign, say, the `Integer` data type to any variables that begin with the letters X through Z, you would add the following statement at the module level:

```
DefInt X-Z
```

Table 3.1 lists the various `DefType` keywords and the data types they represent.

Table 3.1. VBA's `DefType` keywords.

DefType	Data Type
DefBool	Boolean
DefByte	Byte
DefInt	Integer
DefLng	Long
DefCur	Currency
DefSng	Single
DefDbl	Double
DefDate	Date
DefStr	String
DefObj	Object
DefVar	Variant

Creating User-Defined Data Types

VBA's built-in data types cover a lot of ground and should be sufficient to meet most of your needs. However, VBA also lets you set up *user-defined data types*. These are handy for storing similar types of data in a single structure. For example, suppose your program is working with car makes and models. In this case, you might need to work with values for the manufacturer, the model, the year the car was made, and the purchase price. One way to go about this would be to set up variables for each item of data, like so:

```
Dim carMake As String
Dim carModel As String
Dim yearMade As Integer
Dim carPrice As Currency
```

This approach works, but what if you need to work with the data from multiple cars at once? You could set up new variables for each car, but that seems too inefficient. A better way is to define a "CarInfo" data type that holds all the required information. Here's how you would do it:

```
Type CarInfo
    make As String
    model As String
    made As Integer
    price As Currency
End Type
```

The Type keyword tells VBA that you're creating a user-defined data type. In this example, the new data type is named CarInfo. The statements between Type and End Type define the various elements within the new data type. Note that you need to place this definition at the module level; VBA doesn't let you define new data types within a procedure.

Now you use the data type as you would any other. For example, the following statement declares a new variable named myCar to be of type CarInfo:

```
Dim myCar As CarInfo
```

From here, you refer to the various elements within the data type by separating the variable name and the element name with a period (.), like so:

```
myCar.make = "Porsche"
myCar.model = "911 Turbo"
myCar.made = 2007
myCar.price = 122000
```

Using Array Variables

In VBA, an *array* is a group of variables of the same data type. Why would you need to use an array? Well, suppose you wanted to store twenty employee names in variables to use in a procedure. One way to do this would be to create 20 variables named, say, employee1, employee2, and so on. However, it's much more efficient to create a single employees array variable that can hold up to 20 names. VBA creates a single variable with 20 different "slots" into which you can add data (such as employee names). Such an array variable is akin to an Excel range that consists of 20 cells in a row or column: the range is a single entity, but it contains 20 slots (cells) into which you can insert data. The major difference is that you almost always use an array variable to hold data of a single type, such as String. When you declare an array variable you specify the data type, as shown here:

```
Dim employees(19) As String
```

As you can see, this declaration is very similar to one you would use for a regular variable. The difference is the 19 enclosed in parentheses. The parentheses tell VBA that you're declaring an array, and the number tells VBA how many elements you'll need in the array. Why 19 instead of 20? Well, each element in the array is assigned a *subscript*, where the first element's subscript is 0, the second is 1, and so on up to, in this case, 19. Therefore, the total number of elements in this array is 20.

You use a subscript to refer to any element simply by enclosing its index number in the parentheses, like so:

```
employees(0) = "Ponsonby"
```

By default, the subscripts of VBA arrays start at 0 (this is called the *lower bound* of the array) and run up to the number you specify in the Dim statement (this is called the *upper bound* of the array). If you would prefer your array index numbers to start at 1, include the following statement at the top of the module (in other words, before declaring your first array and before your first procedure):

```
Option Base 1
```

Note, too, that after resetting the lower bound in this way, if you want to declare an array with the same number of elements, then you need to adjust the upper bound in the Dim statement accordingly. For example, with the lower bound set to 1, if you want to declare an array variable named employees and you want it to hold up to 20 names, then you need to declare it like so:

```
Dim employees(20) As String
```

Dynamic Arrays

What do you do if you're not sure how many subscripts you'll need in an array? You could guess at the correct number, but that will almost always leave you with one of the following problems:

- If you guess too low and try to access a subscript higher than the array's upper bound, VBA will generate an error message.
- If you guess too high, VBA will still allocate memory to the unused portions of the array, so you'll waste precious system resources.

To avoid both of these problems, you can declare a *dynamic* array by leaving the parentheses blank in the Dim statement:

```
Dim myArray() As Double
```

Then, when you know the number of elements you need, you can use a `ReDim` statement to allocate the correct number of subscripts (notice that you don't specify a data type in the `ReDim` statement):

```
ReDim myArray(52)
```

The following is a partial listing of a procedure named `PerformCalculations`. The procedure declares `calcValues` as a dynamic array and `totalValues` as an integer. Later in the procedure, `totalValues` is set to the result of a function procedure named `GetTotalValues`. The `ReDim` statement then uses `totalValues` to allocate the appropriate number of subscripts to the `calcValues` array.

```
Sub PerformCalculations()
    Dim calcValues() As Double, totalValues as Integer
    .
    .
    .
    totalValues = GetTotalValues()
    ReDim calcValues(totalValues)
    .
    .
    .
End Sub
```

> **NOTE**   The `ReDim` statement reinitializes the array so that any values stored in the array are lost. If you want to preserve an array's existing values, use `ReDim` with the `Preserve` option, as follows:
>
> ```
> ReDim Preserve myArray(52)
> ```

Listing 3.2 presents a more concrete example. (Note that this procedure uses lots of VBA code that you haven't seen yet, so don't be discouraged if you don't fully understand what's happening here.)

Listing 3.2   A Procedure That Stores the Names of the Worksheets in a Dynamic Array

```
Sub StoreWorksheetNames()
    Dim sheetNames() As String
    Dim totalSheets As Integer
    Dim sheet As Worksheet
    Dim i As Integer
    Dim strMessage As String
    '
    ' Store the total number of worksheets
    ' that are in the current workbook
    '
    totalSheets = ActiveWorkbook.Worksheets.Count
    '
    ' Now redimension the dynamic array
    '
    ReDim sheetNames(totalSheets)
    '
    ' Loop through the worksheets to store the names in the array
    '
```

```
    For i = 1 To totalSheets
        sheetNames(i - 1) = ActiveWorkbook.Worksheets(i).Name
    Next 'i
    '
    ' Loop through the array to add the names to a string
    '
    strMessage = "Here are the worksheet names:" & vbCrLf
    For i = 0 To totalSheets - 1
        strMessage = strMessage & sheetNames(i) & vbCrLf
    Next 'i
    '
    ' Display the worksheet names
    '
    MsgBox strMessage
End Sub
```

This procedure begins by declaring `sheetNames` as a dynamic array. It then uses the `totalSheets` variable to store the total number of worksheets that are in the current workbook. The procedure then sets the size of the array based on the `totalSheets` value:

```
ReDim sheetNames(totalSheets)
```

The procedure then uses one loop (see Chapter 6, "Controlling Your VBA Code") to store the worksheet names in the array and a second loop to add the worksheet names to the `strMessage` variable, which is a `String` value. Finally, the procedure uses the `MsgBox` function to display the string, as shown in Figure 3.1.

Figure 3.1
The results of the dynamic array procedure in Listing 3.2.

> **NOTE**
>
> If your program needs to know the lower bound and the upper bound of an array, VBA provides a couple of functions that can do the job:
>
> | `LBound(arrayName)` | Returns the lower bound of the array given by *arrayName*. |
> |---|---|
> | `UBound(arrayName)` | Returns the upper bound of the array given by *arrayName*. |

Multidimensional Arrays

If you enter a single number between the parentheses in an array's `Dim` statement, VBA creates a *one-dimensional* array. But you also can create arrays with two or more dimensions (60 is the maximum). For example, suppose you wanted to store both a first name and a last name in your `employee` array. To store two sets of data with each element, you would declare a two-dimensional array, like so:

```
Dim employees(19,1) As String
```

The subscripts for the second number work like the subscripts you've seen already. In other words, they begin at 0 and run up to the number you specify. So this `Dim` statement sets up a "table" (or a *matrix*, as it's usually called) with 20 "rows" (one for each employee) and two "columns" (one for the first name and one for the last name). So if a one-dimensional array is like an Excel range consisting of cells in a single row or column, a multidimensional array is like an Excel range consisting of cells in multiple rows or columns.

Here are two statements that initialize the data for the first employee:

```
employees(0,0) = "Biff"
employees(0,1) = "Ponsonby"
```

Working with Constants

Constants are values that don't change. They can be numbers, strings, or other values, but, unlike variables, they keep their value throughout your code. VBA recognizes two types of constants: built-in and user-defined.

Using Built-In Constants

Many properties and methods have their own predefined constants. For Excel objects, these constants begin with the letters `xl`. For Word objects, the constants begin with `wd`. For VBA objects, the constants begin with `vb`.

For example, Excel's `Window` object has a `WindowState` property that recognizes three built-in constants: `xlNormal` (to set a window in its normal state), `xlMaximized` (to maximize a window), and `xlMinimized` (to minimize a window). To maximize the active window, for example, you would use the following statement:

```
ActiveWindow.WindowState = xlMaximized
```

> **NOTE** If you want to see a list of all the built-in constants for an application, open the Visual Basic Editor, choose <u>V</u>iew, <u>O</u>bject Browser (or click F2), use the Project/Library list to click the application name (such as Word or Excel), and then click <globals> at the top of the Classes list. Scroll down the Members list until you get to the items that begin with the application's constant prefix (`xl` for Excel, `wd` for Word, `pp` for PowerPoint, and `ac` for Access).

Creating User-Defined Constants

To create your own constants, use the `Const` statement:

```
Const CONSTANTNAME [As type] = expression
```

- *CONSTANTNAME*—The name of the constant. Most programmers use all-uppercase names for constants, which helps distinguish them from your regular variables as well as the VBA keywords.

- `As` *type*—Use this optional expression to assign a data type to the constant.

- *expression*—The value (or a formula that returns a value) that you want to use for the constant. You must use either a literal value or an expression that combines literal values and one or more other constants (as long as those constants have been declared before the current constant).

For example, the following statement creates a constant named `DISCOUNT` and assigns it the value 0.4:

```
Const DISCOUNT As Single = 0.4
```

3

Storing User Input in a Variable

Your VBA programs will usually be self-contained and run just fine on their own. However, you'll likely come across situations where you'll require some kind of custom input. For example, you might have a procedure that adjusts various aspects of a Word document. You could insert the name and location of a Word document into the procedure (this is called *hard-coding* the data), but that's not very flexible if your procedure is capable of working with different documents. A better idea is to have your procedure prompt for the name and location of a document. Your procedure could then take that data and use it to work on the specified document.

Whatever type of input you ask for, the result needs to be stored in a variable so that the rest of your procedure can access it. The next couple of sections take you through some VBA techniques that enable you to prompt for data and then store that data in a variable.

Getting Input Using `MsgBox`

You've seen a couple of times already in this book that you can display information by using the `MsgBox` function. This is a very useful function, so let's take a closer look at it. Here is the full syntax of this function:

```
MsgBox(Prompt[, Buttons][, Title][, HelpFile][, Context])
```

Prompt	The message you want to display in the dialog box. (You can enter a string up to 1,024 characters long.)
Buttons	A number or constant that specifies, among other things, the command buttons that appear in the dialog box. (See the next section.) The default value is 0.

Title	The text that appears in the dialog box title bar. If you omit the title, VBA uses the name of the current program (for example, Microsoft Excel).
HelpFile	The text that specifies the Help file that contains the custom help topic. (I don't discuss custom help topics in this book.) If you enter *HelpFile*, you also have to include *Context*. If you include *HelpFile*, a Help button appears in the dialog box.
Context	A number that identifies the help topic in *HelpFile*.

> **NOTE** There are a number of tutorials online that show you how to create a Help file. Type "creating help files" into your favorite search engine.

For example, the following statement displays the message dialog box shown in Figure 3.2:

```
MsgBox "You must enter a number between 1 and 100!",,"Warning"
```

Figure 3.2
A simple message dialog box produced by the MsgBox function.

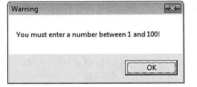

> **NOTE** The MsgBox function, like all VBA functions, needs parentheses around its arguments only when you use the function's return value. See the section later in this chapter called "Getting Return Values from the Message Dialog Box" to learn about the return values produced by the MsgBox function.

> **TIP** For long prompts, VBA wraps the text inside the dialog box. If you'd prefer to create your own line breaks, use VBA's vbCrLf constant to insert a carriage-return and line-feed between each line:
> ```
> MsgBox "First line" & vbCrLf & "Second line"
> ```

Setting the Style of the Message

The default message dialog box displays only an OK button. You can include other buttons and icons in the dialog box by using different values for the *Buttons* parameter. Table 3.2 lists the available options.

Table 3.2 The MsgBox **Buttons Parameter Options**

Constant	Value	Description
Buttons		
vbOKOnly	0	Displays only an OK button. (This is the default.)
vbOKCancel	1	Displays the OK and Cancel buttons.
vbAbortRetryIgnore	2	Displays the Abort, Retry, and Ignore buttons.
vbYesNoCancel	3	Displays the Yes, No, and Cancel buttons.
vbYesNo	4	Displays the Yes and No buttons.
vbRetryCancel	5	Displays the Retry and Cancel buttons.
Icons		
vbCritical	16	Displays the Critical Message icon.
vbQuestion	32	Displays the Warning Query icon.
vbExclamation	48	Displays the Warning Message icon.
vbInformation	64	Displays the Information Message icon.
Default Button		
vbDefaultButton1	0	The first button is the default (that is, the button selected when the user presses Enter).
vbDefaultButton2	256	The second button is the default.
vbDefaultButton3	512	The third button is the default.
Modality		
vbApplicationModal	0	The user must respond to the message box before continuing work in the current application.
vbSystemModal	4096	All applications are suspended until the user responds to the message box.

You derive the *Buttons* argument in one of two ways:

- By adding up the values for each option. For example, if you want the OK and Cancel buttons (value 1) and the Warning Message icon (value 48), then you specify the value 49.

- By using the VBA constants separated by plus signs (+). This is the better way to go because it makes your code much easier to read.

For example, Listing 3.3 shows a procedure named `ButtonTest`, and Figure 3.3 shows the resulting dialog box. Here, three variables—`msgPrompt`, `msgButtons`, and `msgTitle`—store the values for the `MsgBox` function's *Prompt*, *Buttons*, and *Title* arguments, respectively. In particular, the following statement derives the *Buttons* argument:

```
msgButtons = vbYesNo + vbQuestion + vbDefaultButton2
```

You also could derive the *Buttons* argument by adding up the values that these constants represent (4, 32, and 256, respectively), but the procedure becomes less readable that way.

Listing 3.3   A Procedure That Creates a Message Dialog Box

```
Sub ButtonTest()

    Dim msgPrompt As String, msgTitle As String
    Dim msgButtons As Integer, msgResult As Integer

    msgPrompt = "Are you sure you want to display " & vbCrLf & _
                "the worksheet names?"
    msgButtons = vbYesNo + vbQuestion + vbDefaultButton2
    msgTitle = "Display Worksheet Names"

    msgResult = MsgBox(msgPrompt, msgButtons, msgTitle)

End Sub
```

Figure 3.3
The dialog box that's displayed when you run the code in Listing 3.3.

Getting Return Values from the Message Dialog Box

A message dialog box that displays only an OK button is straightforward. The user either clicks OK or presses Enter to remove the dialog from the screen. The multibutton styles are a little different, however; the user has a choice of buttons to select, and your procedure should have a way to find out which button the user chose.

You do this by storing the `MsgBox` function's return value in a variable. Table 3.3 lists the seven possible return values.

Table 3.3   The MsgBox **Function's Return Values**

Constant	Value	Button Selected
vbOK	1	OK
vbCancel	2	Cancel
vbAbort	3	Abort
vbRetry	4	Retry
vbIgnore	5	Ignore
vbYes	6	Yes
vbNo	7	No

To process the return value, you test the value in the variable and have your procedure take appropriate action. You learn how to do this in Chapter 6. Listing 3.4 shows a revised version of ButtonTest that uses an If statement to see whether the msgResult value equals vbYes. If so, it means the user clicked Yes in the dialog box, so the procedure runs the StoreWorksheetNames procedure (see Listing 3.4); otherwise, it does nothing.

➔ To learn about the If statement, **see** "Using If...Then to Make True/False Decisions," **p. 92**.

➔ For MsgBox functions that use three buttons, you need to use the Select Case statement to process the result; **see** "Using the Select Case Statement," **p. 97**.

Listing 3.4   A Procedure that Handles the Return Value of the MsgBox **Function**

```
Sub ButtonTest2()

    Dim msgPrompt As String, msgTitle As String
    Dim msgButtons As Integer, msgResult As Integer

    msgPrompt = "Are you sure you want to display " & vbCrLf & _
                "the worksheet names?"
    msgButtons = vbYesNo + vbQuestion + vbDefaultButton2
    msgTitle = "Display Worksheet Names"

    msgResult = MsgBox(msgPrompt, msgButtons, msgTitle)

    If msgResult = vbYes Then
        StoreWorksheetNames
    End If

End Sub
```

Getting Input Using InputBox

As you've seen, the MsgBox function lets your procedures interact with the user and get some feedback. Unfortunately, this method limits you to simple command-button responses. For more varied user input, you need to use a more sophisticated technique. The rest of this chapter shows you just such a method: prompting the user for input using the InputBox function.

The InputBox function displays a dialog box with a message that prompts the user to enter data, and it provides a text box for the data itself. Here's the syntax for this function:

InputBox(*Prompt*[, *Title*][, *Default*][, *Xpos*][, *Ypos*][, *HelpFile*][, *Context*])

Prompt	The message you want to display in the dialog box (1,024-character maximum).
Title	The text that appears in the dialog box title bar. The default value is the null string (nothing).
Default	The default value displayed in the text box. If you omit *Default*, the text box is displayed empty.
Xpos	The horizontal position of the dialog box from the left edge of the screen. The value is measured in points (there are 72 points in an inch). If you omit *Xpos*, the dialog box is centered horizontally.
Ypos	The vertical position, in points, from the top of the screen. If you omit *Ypos*, the dialog is centered vertically in the current window.
HelpFile	The text specifying the Help file that contains the custom help topic. (Again, I don't cover Help files in this book.) If you enter *HelpFile*, you also have to include *Context*. If you include *HelpFile*, a Help button appears in the dialog box.
Context	A number that identifies the help topic in *HelpFile*.

For example, Listing 3.5 shows a procedure called InputBoxText that uses the InputBox method to prompt the user for data. Figure 3.4 shows the dialog box that appears. The result is stored in the inputData variable. If the user didn't enter data, the function returns nothing, which is represented in VBA by the string value "" (this is called the *null string*). The procedure uses the If statement to check whether the value stored in inputData is "" and, if it's not, it runs MsgBox to display the entered data.

Listing 3.5   A Procedure That Prompts the User for Input and Then Displays the Data

```
Sub InputBoxTest()
    Dim inputData As String
    '
    ' Get the data
    '
    inputData = InputBox("Enter some text:", "Input Box Text")
    '
    ' Check to see if any data was entered
    '
    If inputData <> "" Then
        '
        ' If so, display it
        '
        MsgBox inputData
    End If
End Sub
```

Figure 3.4
A dialog box generated by the `InputBox` function in Listing 3.5.

From Here

- You often use operators and expressions to assign values to variables. I discuss this in detail in Chapter 4, "Building VBA Expressions."

- Objects have a separate variable type. I talk about it, as well as about assigning objects to variables, in Chapter 5, "Working with Objects."

- To learn about the `If` statement for processing `MsgBox` and `InputBox` results, **see** "Using `If...Then` to Make True/False Decisions," **p. 92.**

- For `MsgBox` functions that use three buttons, you need to use the `Select Case` statement to process the result; **see** "Using the `Select Case` Statement," **p. 97.**

Building VBA Expressions

4

The VBA variables you learned about in the Chapter 3, "Understanding Program Variables," don't amount to a hill of beans unless you do something with them. In other words, a procedure or function is merely a lifeless collection of Dim statements until you define some kind of relationship among the variables and your program objects. (I'll talk about the latter in Chapter 5, "Working with Objects.")

To establish these relationships, you need to create *expressions* that perform calculations and produce results. This chapter takes you through some expression basics and shows you a number of techniques for building powerful expressions using not only variables, but also VBA's built-in functions.

Understanding Expressions

You can think of an expression as being like a compact version of a user-defined function. In other words, in the same way that a function takes one or more arguments, combines them in various ways, and returns a value, so too does an expression take one or more inputs (called *operands*) combines them with special symbols (called *operators*) and produces a result. The main difference, though, is that an expression must do all its dirty work in a single VBA statement.

For example, consider the following statement:

```
frequency = "Monthly"
```

Here, the left side of the equation is a variable named frequency. The right side of the equation is the simplest of all expressions: a text string. So, in other words, a string value is being stored in a variable.

Here's a slightly more complex example:

```
energy = mass * (speedOfLight ^ 2)
```

Again, the left side of the equation is a variable (named energy) and the right side of the equation is an expression. For the latter, a variable named speedOfLight is squared, and then this result is multiplied by another variable named mass. In this example, you see the two main components of any expression:

- **Operands**—These are the "input values" used by the expression. They can be constants, variables, object properties, function results, or literals. (A *literal* is a specific value, such as a number or text string. In the first expression example, "Monthly" is a string literal.)
- **Operators**—These are symbols that combine the operands to produce a result. Common operators are the familiar + (addition) and - (subtraction). In the example just shown, the * symbol represents multiplication and the ^ symbol represents exponentiation.

Combining operands and operators produces a result that conforms to one of the variable data types outlined in the previous chapter: String, Date, Boolean, or one of the numeric data types (Integer, Long, Currency, Single, or Double). When building your expressions, the main point to keep in mind is that you must maintain *data type consistency* throughout the expression. This means you must watch for three things:

- The operands must use compatible data types. Although it's okay to combine, say, an Integer operand with a Long operand (because they're both numeric data types), it wouldn't make sense to use, say, a Double operand and a String operand.
- The operators you use must match the data types of the operands. For example, you wouldn't want to multiply two strings together.
- If you're storing the expression result in a variable, make sure the variable's data type is consistent with the type of result produced by the expression. For example, don't use a Boolean variable to store the result of a string expression.

VBA divides expressions into four groups: numeric, string, date, and logical. I discuss each type of expression later in this chapter, but let's first run through all the available VBA operators.

Working with VBA Operators

You've already seen the first of VBA's operators: the *assignment operator*, which is just the humble equals sign (=). You use the assignment operator to assign the result of an expression to a variable (or, as you'll see in Chapter 5, to an object property).

Bear in mind that VBA always derives the result of the right side of the equation (that is, the expression) before it modifies the value of the left side of the equation. This seems like obvious behavior, but it's the source of a handy trick that you'll use quite often. In other words, you can use the current value of whatever is on the left side of the equation *as part of the expression* on the right side. For example, consider the following code fragment:

```
currentYear = 2007
currentYear = currentYear + 1
```

The first statement assigns the value 2007 to the currentYear variable. The second statement also changes the value stored in the currentYear, but it uses the expression currentYear + 1 to do it. This looks weird until you remember that VBA always evaluates the expression first. In other words, it takes the current value of currentYear, which is 2007, and adds 1 to it. The result is 2008 and *that* is what's stored in currentYear when all is said and done.

VBA has a number of different operators that you use to combine functions, variables, and values in a VBA expression. These operators work much like the operators—such as addition (+) and multiplication (*)—that you use to build formulas in Excel worksheets and Word tables. VBA operators fall into five general categories: arithmetic, concatenation, comparison, logical, and miscellaneous.

Arithmetic Operators

VBA's arithmetic operators are similar to those you use to build Excel formulas. Table 4.1 lists each of the arithmetic operators you can use in your VBA statements.

Table 4.1   The VBA Arithmetic Operators

Operator	Name	Example	Result
+	Addition	10+5	15
-	Subtraction	10-5	5
-	Negation	-10	-10
*	Multiplication	10*5	50
/	Division	10/5	2
\	Integer division	11\5	2
^	Exponentiation	10^5	100000
Mod	Modulus (remainder)	10 Mod 5	0

The Mod operator works like Excel's MOD() worksheet function. In other words, it divides one number by another and returns the remainder. Here's the general form to use:

```
result = dividend Mod divisor
```

Here, *dividend* is the number being divided; *divisor* is the number being divided into *dividend*; and *result* is the remainder of the division. For example, 16 Mod 5 returns 1 because 5 goes into 16 three times with a remainder of 1.

The Concatenation Operator

You use the concatenation operator (&) to combine text strings within an expression. One way to use the concatenation operator is to combine string literals. For example, consider the following expression:

```
"soft" & "ware"
```

The result of this expression is the following string:

```
software
```

Here's a less trivial example:

```
Dim strFirst As String
Dim strLast As String
strFirst = "Paul"
strLast = "McFedries"
MsgBox strFirst & " " & strLast
```

This code declares two String variables names strFirst and strLast, and then assigns them the string literals "Paul" and "McFedries", respectively. A MsgBox function uses & to combine the two strings with a space in between. Figure 4.1 shows the result.

Figure 4.1
The result of a MsgBox function that uses & to combine two text strings with a space between them.

You can also use & to combine not just String operands, but also numeric and Date operands, too. Just remember that the result will always be of the String data type. For more information on the concatenation operator, check out the section "Working with String Expressions" later in this chapter.

Comparison Operators

You use the comparison operators in an expression that compares two or more numbers, text strings, variables, or function results. If the statement is true, the result of the formula is given the logical value True (which is equivalent to any nonzero value). If the statement is false, the formula returns the logical value False (which is equivalent to 0). Table 4.2 summarizes VBA's comparison operators.

Table 4.2	The VBA Comparison Operators		
Operator	**Name**	**Example**	**Result**
=	Equal to	10=5	False
>	Greater than	10>5	True
<	Less than	10<5	False
>=	Greater than or equal to	"a">="b"	False
<=	Less than or equal to	"a"<="b"	True
<>	Not equal to	"a"<>"b"	True

Logical Operators

You use the logical operators to combine or modify true/false expressions. Table 4.3 summarizes VBA's logical operators. I provide more detail about each operator later in this chapter (see "Working with Logical Expressions").

Table 4.3	The VBA Logical Operators	
Operator	**General Form**	**What It Returns**
And	*Expr1* And *Expr2*	True if both *Expr1* and *Expr2* are true; False otherwise.
Or	*Expr1* Or *Expr2*	True if at least one of *Expr1* and *Expr2* are true; False otherwise.
Xor	*Expr1* Xor *Expr2*	False if both *Expr1* and *Expr2* are true or if both *Expr1* and *Expr2* are false; True otherwise.
Not	Not *Expr*	True if *Expr* is false; False if *Expr* is true.

4

Understanding Operator Precedence

You'll often use simple expressions that contain just two values and a single operator. In practice, however, many expressions you use will have a number of values and operators. In these more complex expressions, the order in which the calculations are performed becomes crucial. For example, consider the expression 3+5^2. If you calculate from left to right, the answer you get is 64 (3+5 equals 8 and 8^2 equals 64). However, if you perform the exponentiation first and then the addition, the result is 28 (5^2 equals 25 and 3+25 equals 28). As this example shows, a single expression can produce multiple answers depending on the order in which you perform the calculations.

To control this problem, VBA evaluates an expression according to a predefined *order of precedence*. This order of precedence lets VBA calculate an expression unambiguously by determining which part of the expression it calculates first, which part second, and so on.

The Order of Precedence

The order of precedence that VBA uses is determined by the various expression operators I outlined in the preceding section. Table 4.4 summarizes the complete order of precedence used by VBA.

Table 4.4   The VBA Order of Precedence

Operator	Operation	Order of Precedence
^	Exponentiation	First
—	Negation	Second
* and /	Multiplication and division	Third
\	Integer division	Fourth
Mod	Modulus	Fifth
+ and —	Addition and subtraction	Sixth
&	Concatenation	Seventh
= < > <= >= <>	Comparison	Eighth
And Eqv Imp Or Xor Not	Logical	Ninth

From this table, you can see that VBA performs exponentiation before addition. Therefore, the correct answer for the expression 3+5^2 (just discussed) is 28.

Notice, as well, that some operators in Table 4.4 have the same order of precedence (for example, multiplication and division). This means that it doesn't matter in which order these operators are evaluated. For example, consider the expression 5*10/2. If you perform the multiplication first, the answer you get is 25 (5*10 equals 50, and 50/2 equals 25). If you perform the division first, you also get an answer of 25 (10/2 equals 5, and 5*5 equals 25). By convention, VBA evaluates operators with the same order of precedence from left to right.

Controlling the Order of Precedence

Sometimes you want to override the order of precedence. For example, suppose you want to create an expression that calculates the pre-tax cost of an item. If you bought something for $10.65, including 7 percent sales tax, and you wanted to find the cost of the item less the tax, you'd use the expression 10.65/1.07, which gives you the correct answer of $9.95. In general, the expression to use is given by the formula shown in Figure 4.2.

Figure 4.2
A formula for calculating the pre-tax cost of an item.

$$Pre - Tax\ Cost = \frac{Total\ Cost}{1 + Tax\ Rate}$$

Listing 4.1 shows a function that attempts to implement this formula.

Listing 4.1   A First Attempt at Calculating the Pre-Tax Cost

```
Function PreTaxCost(totalCost As Currency, taxRate As Single) As Currency
    PreTaxCost = totalCost / 1 + taxRate
End Function
```

Figure 4.3 shows an Excel worksheet that uses this function. The value in cell B4 is passed to the `totalCost` argument and the value in cell B1 is passed to the `taxRate` argument.

Figure 4.3
A function that attempts to calculate the pre-tax cost of an item.

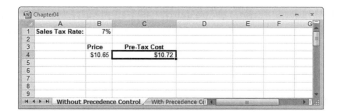

As you can see, the result is incorrect. What happened? Well, according to the rules of precedence, VBA performs division before addition, so the `totalCost` value first is divided by 1 and then is added to the `taxRate` value, which isn't the correct order.

To get the correct answer, you have to override the order of precedence so the addition 1 + `taxRate` is performed first. You do this by surrounding that part of the expression with parentheses, as in Listing 4.2. Using this revised function, you get the correct answer, as shown in Figure 4.4.

Listing 4.2   The Correct Way to Calculate the Pre-Tax Cost

```
Function PreTaxCost2(totalCost As Currency, taxRate As Single) As Currency
    PreTaxCost2 = totalCost / (1 + taxRate)
End Function
```

Figure 4.4
The revised function calculates the pre-tax cost correctly.

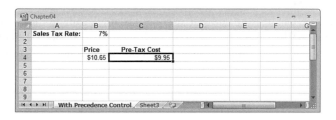

4

In general, you can use parentheses to control the order that VBA uses to calculate expressions. Terms inside parentheses are always calculated first; terms outside parentheses are calculated sequentially (according to the order of precedence). To gain even more control over your expressions, you can place parentheses inside one another; this is called *nesting* parentheses, and VBA always evaluates the innermost set of parentheses first. Here are a few sample expressions:

Expression	First Step	Second Step	Third Step	Result
3^(15/5)*2–5	3^3*2–5	27*2–5	54–5	49
3^((15/5)*2–5)	3^(3*2–5)	3^(6–5)	3^1	3
3^(15/(5*2–5))	3^(15/(10–5))	3^(15/5)	3^3	27

Notice that the order of precedence rules also hold within parentheses. For example, in the expression (5*2–5), the term 5*2 is calculated before 5 is subtracted.

Using parentheses to determine the order of calculations gives you full control over VBA expressions. This way, you can make sure that the answer given by an expression is the one *you* want.

> **CAUTION**
>
> One of the most common mistakes when using parentheses in expressions is to forget to close a parenthetic term with a right parenthesis. If you do this, VBA displays an `Expected:  )` message. To make sure you've closed each parenthetic term, count all the left parentheses and count all the right parentheses. If these totals don't match, you know you've either left out a parenthesis or included too many.

Working with Numeric Expressions

Numeric expressions are what I normally think of when I use the generic term "expression." Whether it's calculating gross margin, figuring out commissions, or determining the monthly payment on a loan, many expressions perform some kind of number crunching. You saw VBA's arithmetic operators earlier in this chapter. This section adds to that by giving you a quick look at VBA's built-in math and financial functions.

VBA's Math Functions

The operands you use in your numeric expressions are usually numeric literals or variables declared as one of VBA's numeric data types. However, VBA also boasts quite a few built-in math functions that your expressions can use as operands. These functions are outlined in Table 4.5.

Table 4.5 VBA's Math Functions

Function	What It Returns
Abs(*number*)	The absolute value of *number*.
Atn(*number*)	The arctangent of *number*.
Cos(*number*)	The cosine of *number*.
Exp(*number*)	*e* (the base of the natural logarithm) raised to the power of *number*.
Fix(*number*)	The integer portion of *number*. If *number* is negative, Fix returns the first negative integer greater than (that is, closer to 0) or equal to *number*.
Hex(*number*)	The hexadecimal value, as a Variant, of *number*.
Hex$(*number*)	The hexadecimal value, as a String, of *number*.
Int(*number*)	The integer portion of *number*. If *number* is negative, Int returns the first negative integer less than (that is, further from 0) or equal to *number*.
Log(*number*)	The natural logarithm of *number*.
Oct(*number*)	The octal value, as a Variant, of *number*.
Oct$(*number*)	The octal value, as a String, of *number*.
Rnd(*number*)	A random number between 0 and 1, as a Single. You use the optional *number* as a "seed" value, as follows:

number	*What It Generates*
Less than 0	The same number every time (varies with *number*).
Equal to 0	The most recently generated number.
Greater than 0	The next random number in the sequence.

Function	What It Returns
Sgn(*number*)	The sign of *number*.
Sin(*number*)	The sine of *number*.
Sqr(*number*)	The square root of *number*.
Tan(*number*)	The tangent of *number*.

NOTE: The random numbers generated by Rnd are only pseudo-random. In other words, if you use the same seed value, you get the same sequence of numbers. If you need truly random numbers, run the Randomize statement just before using Rnd. This initializes the random number generator with the current system time. Here's an example:

```
Randomize
myRandomNumber = Rnd()
```

The need for random numbers comes up quite a bit in programming. However, instead of random numbers between 0 and 1, you might need to generate numbers within a larger range. Here's the general formula to use to get Rnd to generate a random number between a lower bound and an upper bound:

```
Int((upper - lower) * Rnd + lower)
```

For example, here's some code that generates a random 8-digit integer:

```
Randomize
fileName = Int((99999999 - 10000000) * Rnd + 10000000)
```

VBA's Financial Functions

VBA has quite a few financial functions that offer you powerful tools for building applications that manage both business and personal finances. You can use these functions to calculate such things as the monthly payment for a loan, the future value of an annuity, or the yearly depreciation of an asset.

Although VBA has a baker's dozen financial functions that use many different arguments, the following list covers the arguments you'll use most frequently:

- *rate*—The fixed rate of interest over the term of the loan or investment.
- *nper*—The number of payments or deposit periods over the term of the loan or investment.
- *pmt*—The periodic payment or deposit.
- *pv*—The present value of the loan (the principal) or the initial deposit in an investment.
- *fv*—The future value of the loan or investment.
- *type*—The type of payment or deposit. Use 0 (the default) for end-of-period payments or deposits and 1 for beginning-of-period payments or deposits.

For most financial functions, the following rules apply:

- The underlying unit of both the interest rate and the period must be the same. For example, if the *rate* is the annual interest rate, you must express *nper* in years. Similarly, if you have a monthly interest rate, you must express *nper* in months.
- You enter money you receive as a positive quantity, and you enter money you pay as a negative quantity. For example, you always enter the loan principal as a positive number because it's money you receive from the bank.
- The *nper* argument should always be a positive integer quantity.

Table 4.6 lists all VBA's financial functions.

Table 4.6   The Built-In Financial Functions in VBA

Function	What It Returns
DDB(*cost,salvage,life,period,factor*)	The depreciation of an asset over a specified period, using the double-declining balance method.
FV(*rate,nper,pmt,pv,type*)	The future value of an investment or loan.
IPmt(*rate,per,nper,pv,fv,type*)	The interest payment for a specified period of a loan.
IRR(*values,guess*)	The internal rate of return for a series of cash flows.
MIRR(*values,finance_rate,reinvest_rate*)	The modified internal rate of return for a series of periodic cash flows.
NPer(*rate,pmt,pv,fv,type*)	The number of periods for an investment or loan.
NPV(*rate,value1,value2...*)	The net present value of an investment based on a series of cash flows and a discount rate.
Pmt(*rate,nper,pv,fv,type*)	The periodic payment for a loan or investment.
PPmt(*rate,per,nper,pv,fv,type*)	The principal payment for a specified period of a loan.
PV(*rate,nper,pmt,fv,type*)	The present value of an investment.
Rate(*nper,pmt,pv,fv,type,guess*)	The periodic interest rate for a loan or investment.
SLN(*cost,salvage,life*)	The straight-line depreciation of an asset over one period.
SYD(*cost,salvage,life,period*)	Sum-of-years' digits depreciation of an asset over a specified period.

4

Working with String Expressions

A *string expression* is an expression that returns a value that has a String data type. String expressions can use as operands string literals (one or more characters enclosed in double quotation marks), variables declared as String, or any of VBA's built-in functions that return a String value. Table 4.7 summarizes most of the VBA functions that deal with strings.

Table 4.7   VBA's String Functions

Function	What It Returns
Asc(*string*)	The ANSI character code of the first letter in *string*.
Chr(*charcode*)	The character, as a Variant, that corresponds to the ANSI code given by *charcode*.
Chr$(*charcode*)	The character, as a String, that corresponds to the ANSI code given by *charcode*.
CStr(*expression*)	Converts *expression* to a String value.
Format(*expression, format*)	The *expression*, as a Variant, in the specified *format*.
Format$(*expression, format*)	The *expression*, as a String, in the specified *format*.
FormatCurrency(*expression*)	The *expression* formatted as currency.
FormatDateTime(*expression*)	The *expression* formatted as a date or time.
FormatPercent(*expression*)	The *expression* formatted as a percentage.
FormatCurrency(*expression*)	The *expression* formatted as currency.
InStr(*start,string1,string2*)	The character position of the first occurrence of *string2* in *string1*, starting at *start*.
InStrRev(*string1,string2, start*)	The character position of the final occurrence of *string2* in *string1*, starting at *start*.
LCase(*string*)	*string* converted to lowercase, as a Variant.
LCase$(*string*)	*string* converted to lowercase, as a String.
Left(*string,length*)	The leftmost *length* characters from *string*, as a Variant.
Left$(*string,length*)	The leftmost *length* characters from *string*, as a String.
Len(*string*)	The number of characters in *string*.
LTrim(*string*)	A string, as a Variant, without the leading spaces in *string*.
LTrim$(*string*)	A string, as a String, without the leading spaces in *string*.
Mid(*string,start,length*)	*length* characters, as a Variant, from *string* beginning at *start*.
Mid$(*string,start,length*)	*length* characters, as a String, from *string* beginning at *start*.
Replace(*expression,find,replace*)	The *expression* with every instance of *find* replaced by *replace*.

Function	What It Returns
Right(*string*)	The rightmost *length* characters from *string*, as a Variant.
Right$(*string*)	The rightmost *length* characters from *string*, as a String.
RTrim(*string*)	A string, as a Variant, without the trailing spaces in *string*.
RTrim$(*string*)	A string, as a String, without the trailing spaces in *string*.
Trim(*string*)	A string, as a Variant, without the leading and trailing spaces in *string*.
Trim$(*string*)	A string, as a String, without the leading and trailing spaces in *string*.
Space(*number*)	A string, as a Variant, with *number* spaces.
Space$(*number*)	A string, as a String, with *number* spaces.
Str(*number*)	The string representation, as a Variant, of *number*.
Str$(*number*)	The string representation, as a String, of *number*.
StrComp(*string2,string2,compare*)	A value indicating the result of comparing *string1* and *string2*.
StrConv(*string, conversion*)	The *string* converted into another format, as specified by *conversion* (such as vbUpperCase, vbLowerCase, and vbProperCase).
String(*number,character*)	*character*, as a Variant, repeated *number* times.
String$(*number,character*)	*character*, as a String, repeated *number* times.
UCase(*string*)	*string* converted to uppercase, as a Variant.
UCase$(*string*)	*string* converted to uppercase, as a String.
Val(*string*)	All the numbers contained in *string*, up to the first nonnumeric character.

Listing 4.3 shows a procedure that uses some of these string functions.

Listing 4.3   A Procedure That Uses a Few String Functions

```
Function ExtractLastName(fullName As String) As String
    Dim spacePos As Integer
    spacePos = InStr(fullName, " ")
    ExtractLastName = Mid$(fullName, _
                      spacePos + 1, _
                      Len(fullName) - spacePos)
End Function
```

continues

Listing 4.3   Continued

```
Sub TestIt()
    MsgBox ExtractLastName("Millicent Peeved")
End Sub
```

> **NOTE**
>
> Note the use of the underscore (_) in Listing 4.3. This is VBA's *code continuation character*—it's useful for breaking up long statements into multiple lines for easier reading. One caveat, though: Make sure you add a space before the underscore or VBA will generate an error.

The purpose of this procedure is to take a name (first and last, separated by a space, as shown in the `TestIt` procedure) and extract the last name. The full name is brought into the function as the `fullName` argument. After declaring an `Integer` variable named `spacePos`, the procedure uses the `InStr` function to check `fullName` and find out the position of the space that separates the first and last names. The result is stored in `spacePos`:

```
spacePos = InStr(fullName, " ")
```

The real meat of the function is provided by the `Mid$` string function, which uses the following syntax to extract a substring from a larger string:

```
Mid$(string,start,length)
```

string	The string from which you want to extract the characters. In the `ExtractLastName` function, this parameter is the `fullName` variable.
start	The starting point of the string you want to extract. In `ExtractLastName`, this parameter is the position of the space, plus 1 (in other words, `spacePos + 1`).
length	The length of the string you want to extract. In the `ExtractLastName` function, this is the length of the full string—`Len(fullName)`—minus the position of the space.

Working with Logical Expressions

A logical expression is an expression that returns a Boolean result. A Boolean value is almost always either `True` or `False`, but VBA also recognizes some Boolean equivalents:

- A `False` result can be used in an expression as though it were 0. Similarly, you can use 0 in a logical expression as though it were `False`.

- A `True` result can be used in an expression as though it were –1. However, *any* nonzero value can be used in a logical expression as though it were `True`.

In Chapter 6, "Controlling Your VBA Code," I'll show you various VBA statements that let your procedures make decisions and loop through sections of code. In most cases, the mechanism that controls these statements will be a logical expression. For example, if x is a logical expression, you can tell VBA to run one set of statements if x returns True and a different set of statements if x returns False.

You'll see that these are powerful constructs, and they'll prove invaluable in all your VBA projects. To help you prepare, let's take a closer look at VBA's logical operators.

The And Operator

You use the And operator when you want to test two Boolean operands to see whether they're both true. For example, consider the following generic expression (where *Expr1* and *Expr2* are Boolean values):

Expr1 And *Expr2*

- If both *Expr1* and *Expr2* are true, this expression returns True.
- If either or both *Expr1* and *Expr2* are false, the expression returns False.

The Or Operator

You use the Or operator when you want to test two Boolean operands to see whether one of them is true:

Expr1 Or *Expr2*

- If either or both *Expr1* and *Expr2* are true, this expression returns True.
- If both *Expr1* and *Expr2* are false, the expression returns False.

The Xor Operator

Xor is the exclusive Or operator. It's useful when you need to know whether two operands have the opposite value:

Expr1 Xor *Expr2*

- If one of the values is true and the other is false, the expression returns True.
- If *Expr1* and *Expr2* are both true or are both false, the expression returns False.

The Not Operator

The Not operator is the logical equivalent of the negation operator. In this case, Not returns the opposite value of an operand. For example, if *Expr* is true, Not *Expr* returns False.

Working with Date Expressions

A *date expression* is an expression that returns a `Date` value. For operands in date expressions, you can use either a variable declared as `Date` or a date literal. For the latter, you enclose the date in pound signs, like so:

```
dateVar = #8/23/2007#
```

When working with dates, it helps to remember that VBA works with dates internally as *serial numbers*. Specifically, VBA uses December 31, 1899 as an arbitrary starting point and then represents subsequent dates as the number of days that have passed since then. So, for example, the date serial number for January 1, 1900 is 1, January 2, 1900 is 2, and so on. Table 4.8 displays some sample date serial numbers.

Table 4.8   Examples of Date Serial Numbers

Serial Number	Date
366	December 31, 1900
16229	June 6, 1944
39317	August 23, 2007

Similarly, VBA also uses serial numbers to represent times internally. In this case, though, VBA expresses time as a fraction of the 24-hour day to get a number between 0 and 1. The starting point, midnight, is given the value 0, noon is 0.5, and so on. Table 4.9 displays some sample time serial numbers.

Table 4.9   Examples of Time Serial Numbers

Serial Number	Time
0.25	6:00:00 AM
0.375	9:00:00 AM
0.70833	5:00:00 PM
.99999	11:59:59 PM

You can combine the two types of serial numbers. For example, 39317.5 represents 12 noon on August 23, 2007.

The advantage of using serial numbers in this way is that it makes calculations involving dates and times very easy. Because a date or time is really just a number, any mathematical operation you can perform on a number can also be performed on a date. This is invaluable for procedures that track delivery times, monitor accounts receivable or accounts payable aging, calculate invoice discount dates, and so on.

VBA also comes equipped with quite a few date and time functions. Table 4.10 summarizes them all.

Table 4.10   VBA's Date and Time Functions

Function	Returns
CDate(*expression*)	Converts *expression* into a Date value.
Date	The current system date, as a Variant.
Date$()	The current system date, as a String.
DateAdd(*interval*,*number*,*date*)	A Date value derived by adding the specified *number* of *intervals* (days, months, years, and so on) to *date*.
DateDiff(*interval*,*date1*,*date2*)	A numeric value that represents the number of *intervals* (days, months, years, and so on) between *date1* and *date2*.
DatePart(*interval*,*date*)	A numeric value that corresponds to the part of *date* specified by *interval* (the day, month, year, and so on).
DateSerial(*year*,*month*,*day*)	A Date value for the specified *year*, *month*, and *day*.
DateValue(*date*)	A Date value for the *date* string.
Day(*date*)	The day of the month given by *date*.
Hour(*time*)	The hour component of *time*.
Minute(*time*)	The minute component of *time*.
Month(*date*)	The month component of *date*.
MonthName(*month*)	The name of the *month*.
Now	The current system date and time.
Second(*time*)	The second component of *time*.
Time	The current system time, as a Variant.
Time$	The current system time, as a String.
Timer	The number of seconds since midnight.
TimeSerial(*hour*,*minute*,*second*)	A Date value for the specified *hour*, *minute*, and *second*.
TimeValue(*time*)	A Date value for the *time* string.
Weekday(*date*)	The day of the week, as a number, given by *date*.
WeekdayName(*weekday*)	The name of the *weekday*.
Year(*date*)	The year component of *date*.

Listing 4.4 shows a couple of procedures that take advantage of a few of these date functions.

Listing 4.4   A Function Procedure That Uses Various Date Functions to Calculate a Person's Age

```
Function CalculateAge(birthDate As Date) As Byte
    Dim birthdayNotPassed As Boolean
    birthdayNotPassed = CDate(Month(birthDate) & "/" & _
                              Day(birthDate) & "/" & _
                              Year(Now)) > Now
    CalculateAge = Year(Now) - Year(birthDate) + birthdayNotPassed
End Function
'
' Use this procedure to test CalculateAge.
'
Sub TestIt2()
    MsgBox CalculateAge(#8/23/59#)
End Sub
```

The purpose of the `CalculateAge` function is to figure out a person's age given the date of birth (as passed to `CalculateAge` through the `Date` variable named `birthDate`). You might think the following formula would do the job:

```
Year(Now) - Year(birthDate)
```

This works, but only if the person's birthday has already passed this year. If the person hasn't had his or her birthday yet, this formula reports the person's age as being one year greater than it really is.

To solve this problem, you need to take into account whether or not the person's birthday has occurred. To do this, `CalculateAge` first declares a Boolean variable `birthdayNotPassed` and then uses the following expression to test whether or not the person has celebrated his or her birthday this year:

```
CDate(Month(birthDate) & "/" & Day(birthDate) & "/" & Year(Now)) > Now
```

This expression uses the `Month`, `Day`, and `Year` functions to construct the date of the person's birthday this year, and uses the `CDate` function to convert this string into a date. The expression then checks to see whether this date is greater than today's date (as given by the `Now` function). If it is, the person hasn't celebrated his or her birthday, so `birthdayNotPassed` is set to `True`; otherwise, `birthdayNotPassed` is set to `False`.

The key is that to VBA a `True` value is equivalent to -1, and a `False` value is equivalent to 0. Therefore, to calculate the person's correct age, you need only add the value of `birthdayNotPassed` to the expression `Year(Now) - Year(birthDate)`.

From Here

- Objects will play a big part in your expressions. For example, you'll use expressions to set the values of object properties. **See** Chapter 5, "Working with Objects," **p. 71**.
- To put your newfound knowledge of logical expressions to good use, **see** "Code That Makes Decisions," **p. 91**.
- For a complete list of VBA functions, see "VBA Functions," **p. 361**.

Working with Objects

5

Many of your VBA procedures will perform calculations using simple combinations of numbers, operators, and the host application's built-in functions. You'll probably find, however, that most of your code manipulates the application environment in some way, whether it's formatting document text, entering data in a worksheet range, or setting application options. Each of these items—the document, the range, the application—is called an *object* in VBA. Objects are perhaps the most crucial concept in VBA programming, and I'll explain them in detail in this chapter.

What Is an Object?

The dictionary definition of an object is "anything perceptible by one or more of the senses, especially something that can be seen and felt." Now, of course, you can't *feel* anything in an Office application, but you can *see* all kinds of things. To VBA, an object is anything in an application that you can see *and* manipulate in some way.

For example, a paragraph in a Word document is something you can see, and you can manipulate it by inserting text, changing the style, setting the font, and so on. A paragraph, therefore, is an object.

What isn't an object? The Office programs are so customizable that most things you can see qualify as objects, but not everything does. For example, the Maximize and Minimize buttons in document windows aren't objects. Yes, you can operate them, but you can't change them. Instead, the window itself is the object, and you manipulate it so that it's maximized or minimized.

You can manipulate objects in VBA in any of the following three ways:

- You can make changes to the object's *properties*.
- You can make the object perform a task by activating a *method* associated with the object.
- You can define a procedure that runs whenever a particular *event* happens to the object.

To help you understand properties, methods, events, and objects, I'll put things in real-world terms. First, let's consider a simple analogy using a car. A car is an object, to be sure, but what does it mean to say that it has its own "properties, methods, and events"? Let's see:

- The car's "properties" would be its physical characteristics: its model, color, engine size, and so on.
- The car's "methods" define what you can do with the car: accelerate, brake, turn, and so on.
- The car's "events" are the actions that happen to the car that generate an automatic response from the car. For example, on most modern cars, if you exit the vehicle with the key still in the ignition (the event), a warning bell will sound (the response).

Let's run through a more detailed example. Specifically, let's look at your computer as though it were an object. For starters, you can think of your computer in one of two ways: as a single object or as a *collection* of objects (such as the monitor, the keyboard, the system unit, and so on).

If you wanted to describe your computer as a whole, you would mention things such as the name of the manufacturer, the price, the color, and so on. Each of these items is a *property* of the computer. You also can use your computer to perform tasks, such as writing letters, crunching numbers, and playing games. These are the *methods* associated with your computer. There are also a number of things that happen to the computer that cause it to respond in predefined ways. For example, when you press the On button, the computer runs through its Power On Self-Test, initializes its components, and so on. The actions to which the computer responds automatically are its *events*.

The sum total of all these properties, methods, and events gives you an overall description of your computer.

But your computer is also a collection of objects, each with its own properties, methods, and events. The DVD drive, for example, has various properties, including its speed and data rate. Its methods would be actions such as inserting and ejecting a disc. A DVD drive event might be the insertion of a disc that contains a file that causes the disc's program to run automatically.

In the end, you have a complete description of the computer: what its distinguishing features are (its properties), how you interact with it (its methods), and to what actions it responds (its events).

The Object Hierarchy

As you've seen, your computer's objects are arranged in a hierarchy with the most general object (the computer as a whole) at the top. Lower levels progress through more specific objects (such as the system unit, the motherboard, and the processor).

Each Office application's objects are arranged in a hierarchy also. The most general object—the `Application` object—refers to the program itself. In Word, for example, the `Application` object contains more than 30 objects, including the `Documents` object (the collection of all open documents, each one being a `Document` object), the `Options` object (the settings available in the Options dialog box), and the `RecentFiles` object (the names of the files that have been used most recently).

Many of these objects have objects beneath them in the hierarchy. A `Document` object, for example, contains objects that represent the document's characters, words, sentences, paragraphs, bookmarks, and much more. Similarly, a `Paragraph` object contains objects for the paragraph format and the tab stops.

To specify an object in the hierarchy, you usually start with the uppermost object and add the lower objects, separated by periods. For example, here's one way you could refer to the first word in the second paragraph in a document named `Memo.doc`:

```
Application.Documents("Memo.doc").Paragraphs(2).Range.Words(1)
```

As you'll see, there are ways to shorten such long-winded "hierarchical paths."

5

Working with Object Properties

Every object has a defining set of characteristics. These characteristics are called the object's *properties*, and they control the appearance and position of the object. For example, each `Window` object has a `WindowState` property you can use to display a window as maximized, minimized, or normal. Similarly, a Word `Document` object has a `Name` property to hold the filename, a `Saved` property that tells you whether or not the document has changed since the last save, a `Type` property to hold the document type (regular or template), and many more.

When you refer to a property, you use the following syntax:

```
Object.Property
```

For example, the following expression refers to the `ActiveWindow` property of the `Application` object:

```
Application.ActiveWindow
```

> **NOTE**
>
> You'll come across the word "active" quite often in your VBA travels, so let's make sure you know what it means. In the VBA world, *active* describes the item with which you're currently working. In Word, for example, the document you're currently using is the active document. Similarly, in Excel the worksheet cell that you're editing or formatting is the active cell. In programming lingo, the active item is said to have the *focus*.

One of the most confusing aspects of objects and properties is that some properties do double-duty as objects. Figure 5.1 uses an Excel example to illustrate this. The `Application` object has an `ActiveWindow` property that tells you the name of the active window. However, `ActiveWindow` is also a `Window` object. Similarly, the `Window` object has an `ActiveCell` property that specifies the active cell, but `ActiveCell` is also a `Range` object. Finally, a `Range` object has a `Font` property, but a font is also an object with its own properties (`Italic`, `Name`, `Size`, and so on).

Figure 5.1

Some Excel properties also can be objects.

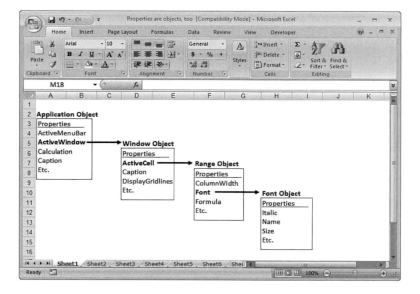

In other words, lower-level objects in the object hierarchy are really just properties of their parent objects. This idea will often help you to reduce the length of a hierarchical path (and thus reduce the abuse your typing fingers must bear). For example, consider the following object path:

```
Application.ActiveWindow.ActiveCell.Font.Italic
```

Here, an object such as `ActiveCell` implicitly refers to the `ActiveWindow` and `Application` objects, so you can knock the path down to size, as follows:

```
ActiveCell.Font.Italic
```

Setting the Value of a Property

To set a property to a certain value, you use the following syntax:

```
Object.Property=value
```

Here, `value` is an expression that returns the value to which you want to set the property. As such, it can be any of VBA's recognized data types, including the following:

- **A numeric value**—For example, the following statement sets the size of the font in the active cell to 14:
  ```
  ActiveCell.Font.Size = 14
  ```

- **A string value**—The following example sets the font name in the active cell to Times New Roman:
  ```
  ActiveCell.Font.Name = "Times New Roman"
  ```

- **A logical value** (in other words, `True` or `False`)—The following statement turns on the `Italic` property in the active cell:

  ```
  ActiveCell.Font.Italic = True
  ```

Returning the Value of a Property

Sometimes you need to know a property's current setting before changing the property or performing some other action. You can find out a property's current value by using the following syntax:

```
variable = Object.Property
```

Here, `variable` is a variable or another property. For example, the following statement stores the contents of the active cell in a variable named `cellContents`:

```
cellContents = ActiveCell.Value
```

Working with Object Methods

An object's properties describe what the object is, whereas its *methods* describe what you can do with the object. For example, in Word you can spell check a `Document` object by using the `CheckSpelling` method. Similarly, you can sort a `Table` object by using the `Sort` method.

How you refer to a method depends on whether or not the method uses any arguments. If it doesn't, the syntax is similar to that of properties:

```
Object.Method
```

For example, the following statement saves the active document:

```
ActiveDocument.Save
```

If the method requires arguments, you use the following syntax:

```
Object.Method (argument1, argument2, ...)
```

Technically, the parentheses around the argument list are necessary only if you'll be storing the result of the method in a variable or object property:

```
variable = Object.Method (argument1, argument2, ...)
```

For example, Word's `Document` object has a `Close` method that you can use to close a document programmatically. Here's the syntax:

```
Object.Close(SaveChanges, OriginalFormat, RouteDocument)
```

`Object`	The `Document` object you want to work with.
`SaveChanges`	A constant that specifies whether or not the file is saved before closing.
`OriginalFormat`	A constant that specifies whether or not the file is saved in its original format.
`RouteDocument`	A True or False value that specifies whether or not the document is routed to the next recipient.

For example, the following statement prompts the user to save changes, saves the changes (if applicable) in the original file format, and routes the document to the next recipient:

```
ActiveDocument.Close wdPromptToSaveChanges, wdOriginalFormat, True
```

For many VBA methods, not all the arguments are required. For the `Close` method, for example, only the `SaveChanges` argument is required. Throughout this book, I differentiate between required and optional arguments by displaying the required arguments in bold type.

To skip a non-required argument (and thus use its default value), leave it blank, although you still need to enter all the commas that separate the arguments. For example, to exclude the `OriginalFormat` argument in the `Close` method, you use a statement like this:

```
ActiveDocument.Close wdPromptToSaveChanges, , True
```

To make your methods clearer to read, you can use VBA's predefined *named arguments*. For example, the syntax of the `Close` method has three named arguments: `SaveChanges`, `OriginalFormat`, and `RouteDocument`. Here's how you would use them in the preceding example:

```
ActiveDocument.Close SaveChanges:=wdPromptToSaveChanges, _
   OrignalFormat:=wdOriginalFormat, _
   RouteDocument:=True
```

Notice how the `:=` operator assigns values to the named arguments.

Named arguments make your code easier read, but they also bring two other advantages to the table:

- You can enter the arguments in any order you like.

- You can ignore any arguments you don't need (except arguments that are required by the method, of course).

 TIP How did I know to use the constants `wdPromptToSaveChanges` and `wdOriginalFormat` in the `Close` method example? They're all listed in the VBA Help system. To see them, type the method name in a module and then press F1. The Visual Basic Editor launches the Help system and displays the Help topic for the method.

Handling Object Events

In simplest terms, an *event* is something that happens to an object. For example, the opening of an Excel workbook would be an event for that workbook. Don't confuse a method with an event, however. Yes, Word has an `Open` method that you can use to open a document, but this method only *initiates* the procedure; the actual process of the file being opened is the event. Note, too, that events can happen either programmatically (if the appropriate method is included in your code, such as `Documents.Open`) or by user intervention (if a command is selected, such as Office, Open).

In VBA, the event itself isn't as important as how your procedures *respond* to the event. In other words, you can write special procedures called *event handlers* that run every time a particular event occurs. In a Word document, for example, you can specify event handlers for both opening the file and closing the file. (Excel's `Workbook` object has an even larger list of events, including not just opening the file, but also activating the workbook window, saving the file, inserting a new worksheet, closing the file, and much more.)

For example, Figure 5.2 shows a module window for a document. (Specifically, it's the module window for the project's `ThisDocument` object.) Notice that the module window has two drop-down lists just below the title bar:

- **Object list**—This is the list on the left and it tells you what kind of object you're working with. If you select (General) in this list, you can use the module window to enter standard VBA procedures and functions. If you select an object from this list, however, you can enter event handlers for the object.

- **Procedure list**—This is the list on the right and it tells you which procedure is active in the module. If you select (General) in the Object list, the Procedure list contains all the standard VBA procedures and functions in the module. If you select an object in the Object list, however, the Procedure list changes to show all the events recognized by the object.

5

Figure 5.2
An example of an event procedure. Here, this procedure runs each time the document is opened.

Object list   Procedure list

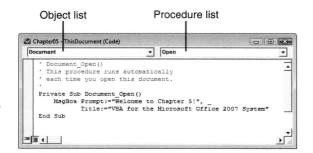

In Figure 5.2, I've selected Document in the Object list, so the Procedure list contains all the events recognized by the Document object. For the Open event, I've inserted a MsgBox statement into the Document_Open event handler. This statement will display a message each time the document is opened.

→ To learn how the MsgBox function works, **see** "Getting Input Using MsgBox," **p. 45**.

Working with Object Collections

A *collection* is a set of similar objects. For example, Word's Documents collection is the set of all the open Document objects. Similarly, the Paragraphs collection is the set of all Paragraph objects in a document. Collections are objects, too, so they have their own properties and methods, and you can use these properties and methods to manipulate one or more objects in the collection.

The members of a collection are called the *elements* of the collection. You can refer to individual elements by either the object's name or an *index*. For example, the following statement closes a document named Budget.doc:

```
Documents("Budget.doc").Close
```

On the other hand, if the Budget.doc document was the first document opened in the current Word session, then you could also use its index value in the following statement to close the document:

```
Documents(1).Close
```

If you don't specify an element, VBA assumes you want to work with the entire collection.

> **NOTE**
> It's important to understand that you often can't refer to objects by themselves. Instead, you must refer to the object as an element in a collection. For example, when referring to the Budget.doc document, you can't just use Budget.doc. You have to use Documents("Budget.doc") or Documents(1) (or whatever the correct index is) so that VBA knows you're talking about a currently open document.

Assigning an Object to a Variable

As I mentioned at the end of Chapter 3, "Understanding Program Variables," objects have their own data types. You can declare a variable as an object by using the following form of the `Dim` statement:

```
Dim variableName As ObjectType
```

Here, `ObjectType` is the data type of the object you want to work with. For example, if you want to work with a `Document` object, you'd use a `Dim` statement similar to this:

```
Dim currentDocument As Document
```

It's a good idea to use object variables whenever you can because it enables you to use the Visual Basic Editor's handy IntelliSense features that I described in detail in Chapter 1 (see "Taking Advantage of IntelliSense"). Using the preceding example, if I type `currentDocument` and then a period (.), VBA displays a list of all the properties and methods associated with that object, as shown in Figure 5.3.

> **NOTE**
> In the list, the items that have the green blocks with motion lines are the methods, whereas the items that have the rectangles with a pointing finger are the properties.

Figure 5.3
Using specific object variable types saves you time because VBA displays a list of the available properties and methods for the object.

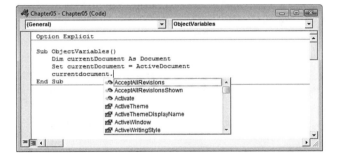

After you've set up your object variable, you can assign an object to it by using the `Set` statement. `Set` has the following syntax:

```
Set variableName = ObjectName
```

> `variableName` The name of the variable.
>
> `ObjectName` The object you want to assign to the variable.

For example, the following statements declare a variable named `budgetSheet` to be a `Worksheet` object and then assign it to the 2008 Budget worksheet in the `Budget.xls` workbook:

```
Dim budgetSheet As Worksheet
Set budgetSheet = Workbooks("Budget.xls").Worksheets("2008 Budget")
```

> **NOTE**
> Object variables take up memory. For optimum code performance, you can reclaim the memory used by unneeded object variables by setting the variable equal to Nothing, like so:
> ```
> Set budgetSheet = Nothing
> ```

The Is Operator

When you looked at comparison operators in the last chapter, the operands you used were simple numbers and strings. Indeed, most of the comparison operators don't make sense in the context of objects (for example, it's absurd to think of one object being "greater than" another). However, VBA does have a comparison operator specifically for objects—the Is operator:

```
result = Object1 Is Object2
```

Here, *Object1* and *Object2* are objects or Object variables. If they're the same object, *result* takes the value True; otherwise, *result* is False.

Working with Multiple Properties or Methods

Because most objects have many different properties and methods, you'll often need to perform multiple actions on a single object. This is accomplished easily with multiple statements that set the appropriate properties or run the necessary methods. However, this can be a pain if you have a long object name.

For example, take a look at the FormatParagraph procedure shown in Listing 5.1. This procedure uses six statements to format a paragraph. Note that the Paragraph object name—ThisDocument.Paragraphs(1)—is quite long and is repeated in all six statements.

Listing 5.1   A Procedure That Formats a Range

```
Sub FormatParagraph()
    ThisDocument.Paragraphs(1).Style = "Heading 1"
    ThisDocument.Paragraphs(1).Alignment = wdAlignParagraphCenter
    ThisDocument.Paragraphs(1).Range.Font.Size = 16
    ThisDocument.Paragraphs(1).Range.Font.Bold = True
    ThisDocument.Paragraphs(1).Range.Font.Color = RGB(255, 0, 0) ' Red
    ThisDocument.Paragraphs(1).Range.Font.Name = "Times New Roman"
End Sub
```

> **NOTE**
> When you want to specify colors in VBA, use the RGB function:
> ```
> RGB(red, green, blue)
> ```
> | | |
> |---|---|
> | *red* | An integer value between 0 and 255 that represents the red component of the color. |
> | *green* | An integer value between 0 and 255 that represents the green component of the color. |
> | *blue* | An integer value between 0 and 255 that represents the blue component of the color. |

To shorten this procedure, VBA provides the With statement. Here's the syntax:

```
With object
    [statements]
End With
```

> object   The name of the object.
>
> statements The statements you want to execute on object.

The idea is that you strip out the common object and place it on the With line. Then all the statements between With and End With need only reference a specific method or property of that object. In the FormatParagraph procedure, the common object in all six statements is ThisDocument.Paragraphs(1). Listing 5.2 shows the FormatParagraph2 procedure, which uses the With statement to strip out this common object and make the previous macro more efficient.

Listing 5.2   A More Efficient Version of FormatParagraph()

```
Sub FormatParagraph2()
    With ThisDocument.Paragraphs(1)
        .Style = "Heading 1"
        .Alignment = wdAlignParagraphCenter
        .Range.Font.Size = 16
        .Range.Font.Bold = True
        .Range.Font.Color = RGB(255, 0, 0)  ' Red
        .Range.Font.Name = "Times New Roman"
    End With
End Sub
```

> **NOTE**
>
> You can make the FormatParagraph2 procedure even more efficient when you realize that the Font object also is repeated several times. In this case, you can *nest* another With statement inside the original one. The new With statement would look like this:
>
> ```
> With .Range.Font
>     .Size = 16
>     .Bold = True
>     .Color = RGB(255, 0, 0)
>     .Name = "Times New Roman"
> End With
> ```

Example: The Application Object

You'll be seeing plenty of objects when you turn your attention to the Microsoft Office programs in Part 2, "Putting VBA to Work." For now, though, let's take a look at an object that is common to all programs: the Application object. The Application object refers to the application as a whole; therefore, it acts as a container for all the program's objects. However, the Application object does have a few useful properties and methods of its own, and many of these members are applicable to all the Office applications.

The next few sections take you through examples of some of the most useful `Application` object properties and methods.

Displaying a Message in the Status Bar

Most applications have a status bar at the bottom of the screen that's used for displaying messages and indicating the progress of the current operation. For Word and Excel, you can use the `Application` object's `StatusBar` property to display text messages in the status bar at the bottom of the screen. This gives you an easy way to keep the user informed about what a procedure is doing or how much is left to process.

Listing 5.3 demonstrates the `StatusBar` property

Listing 5.3   A Procedure That Displays a Message in the Status Bar

```
Sub StatusBarProperty()
    ActiveDocument.Save
    Application.StatusBar = ActiveDocument.Name & " was saved."
End Sub
```

This procedure saves the active document and then uses the `StatusBar` property to display a message telling the user that the document (specified with the `Name` property) was saved.

> **TIP**
> To clear any messages from the status bar, set the `StatusBar` property to the null string (" "):
> ```
> Application.StatusBar = ""
> ```

Changing the Title Bar Caption

The `Application` object's `Caption` property returns or sets the name that appears in the title bar of the main application window. In Excel, for example, to change the title bar caption from "Microsoft Excel" to "ACME Coyote Supplies," you would use the following statement:

```
Application.Caption = "ACME Coyote Supplies"
```

> **TIP**
> To reset the title bar to the default application name, set the `Caption` property to the null string (" "):
> ```
> Application.Caption = ""
> ```

Working with the Application Window

The application's window contains the interface elements such as the Ribbon and the status bar, as well as an area for displaying a document. In Word, PowerPoint, and Access the application window can have multiple instances (one for each open document, presentation, or database), whereas in Excel there is always just one application window (possibly with multiple open workbooks). You can wield seven `Application` object properties to control the application window:

- `Application.Height`—Returns or sets the height, in points, of the application window.

- `Application.Left`—Returns or sets the distance, in points, of the left edge of the application window from the left edge of the screen.

- `Application.Top`—Returns or sets the distance, in points, of the top of the application window from the top of the screen.

- `Application.UsableHeight`—The maximum height, in points, that a window can occupy within the application's window. In other words, this is the height of the application window less the vertical space taken up by the title bar, menu bar, toolbars, status bar, and so on.

- `Application.UsableWidth`—The maximum width, in points, that a window can occupy within the application's window. This is the width of the application window less the horizontal space taken up by items such as the vertical scroll bar.

- `Application.Width`—Returns or sets the width, in points, of the application window.

- `Application.WindowState`—Returns or sets the state of the main application window. This property is controlled via three built-in constants that vary between applications:

Window State	Excel	Word	PowerPoint
Maximized	xlMaximized	wdWindowStateMaximize	ppWindowMaximized
Minimized	xlMinimized	wdWindowStateMinimize	ppWindowMinimized
Normal	xlNormal	wdWindowStateNormal	ppWindowNormal

Accessing an Application's Built-In Dialog Boxes

Many VBA methods are known as *dialog box equivalents* because they let you select the same options that are available in an application's built-in dialog boxes. Using dialog box equivalents works fine if your procedure knows which options to select, but there are times when you might want the user to specify some of the dialog box options.

For example, if your procedure prints a document (using the `Application` object's `PrintOut` method), you might need to know how many copies the user wants or how many pages to print. You could use the `InputBox` method to get this data, but it's usually easier to just display the Print dialog box.

The `Application` object has a `Dialogs` property, which represents the collection of all the built-in dialog boxes, each of which is a `Dialog` object. Note that these objects are implemented only in Word and Excel.

To reference a particular dialog box, use one of the predefined application constants. Table 5.1 lists a few of the more common ones from Word and Excel.

5

Table 5.1 Some Word and Excel Built-in Dialog Box Constants

Word Constant	Excel Constant	Dialog Box
wdDialogFormatFont	xlDialogFont	Font
wdDialogFileNew	xlDialogNew	New
wdDialogFileOpen	xlDialogOpen	Open
wdDialogFilePageSetup	xlDialogPageSetup	Page Setup
wdDialogEditPasteSpecial	xlDialogPasteSpecial	Paste Special
wdDialogFilePrint	xlDialogPrint	Print
wdDialogFilePrintSetup	xlDialogPrinterSetup	Printer Setup
wdDialogFileSaveAs	xlDialogSaveAs	Save As
wdDialogInsertObject	xlDialogObject	Object
wdDialogFormatStyle	xlDialogStyle	Style
wdDialogTableSort	xlDialogSort	Sort

NOTE To see a complete list of constants for Word and Excel's built-in dialog boxes, first open the Object Browser by selecting View, Object Browser (or by pressing F2). In the list of libraries, select the application (such as Excel or Word), and highlight <globals> in the Classes list. In the Member list, look for the *xx*Dialog constants, where *xx* varies between applications: wdDialog for Word and xlDialog for Excel.

NOTE The Object Browser is a handy tool that shows you the objects available for your procedures as well as the properties, methods, and events for each object. To display the Object Browser in the Visual Basic Editor, select View, Object Browser (you can also press F2). In the Object Browser dialog box that appears, use the Classes list to select the object you want to see and its properties, methods, and events appear in the Members list on the right.

To display any of these dialog boxes, use the Dialog object's Show method. For example, the following statement displays Excel's Print dialog box:

```
Application.Dialogs(xlDialogPrint).Show
```

If the user clicks Cancel to exit the dialog box, the `Show` method returns False. This means that you can use `Show` inside an `If` statement to determine what the user did:

→ To get the details on the `If` statement, **see** "Using `If . . . Then` to Make True/False Decisions," **p. 92**.

```
If Not Application.Dialogs(xlDialogPrint).Show Then
    MsgBox "File was not printed"
End If
```

Note, too, that the `Show` method can take arguments. For example, Word's `Show` method uses the following syntax:

Dialog.Show(*Timeout*)

> *Dialog*   The `Dialog` object you want to show.
>
> *Timeout*   The time, in thousandths of a second, after which the dialog box is dismissed. (Changes made by the user are accepted.)

For example, the following statement shows the Font dialog box, and then dismisses it after approximately 10 seconds:

```
Application.Dialogs(wdDialogFormatFont).Show 10000
```

Here's the syntax for Excel's `Show` method:

Dialog.Show(*Arg1, Arg2....*)

> *Dialog*   The Dialog object you want to show.
>
> *Arg1, Arg2,...*   These arguments represent specific controls in the dialog box, and they enable you to set the value of the controls in advance.

For example, here's the syntax for Excel's Font dialog box:

```
Application.Dialogs(xlDialogFont).Show name_text, size_num
```

Here, *name_text* and *size_num* represent the Face and Size controls, respectively, in the Font dialog box. The following statement shows Excel's Font dialog box, and it sets the Face list to Garamond and the Size list to 16:

```
Application.Dialogs(xlDialogFont).Show "Garamond", 16
```

To do the same thing in Word, you use the predefined argument names as though they were properties of the specified `Dialog` object. For example, you use `Font` to return or set the Font control value in the Font dialog box:

```
With Dialogs(wdDialogFormatFont)
    .Font = "Garamond"
    .Show
End With
```

5

NOTE
To see a complete list of the control arguments used by Word and Excel, see the following Microsoft websites:

Word:

http://msdn.microsoft.com/library/default.asp?url=/library/en-us/vbawd11/html/wohowDialog Arguments1_HV05210109.asp

Excel:

http://msdn.microsoft.com/library/default.asp?url=/library/en-us/vbaxl11/html/ xlmscDialog ArgLists1_HV05199604.asp

Word's `Dialog` object is much more flexible and powerful than Excel's in that it supports extra properties and methods. For example, the `DefaultTab` property enables you to specify which dialog box tab has the focus when you display a dialog box. Here's an example that displays the Layout tab in the Page Layout dialog box:

```
With Application.Dialogs(wdDialogFilePageSetup)
    .DefaultTab = wdDialogFilePageSetupTabLayout
    .Show
End With
```

Word's `Dialog` object also has a `Display` method that uses a syntax similar to that of the `Show` method:

Dialog.Display(*Timeout*)

> *Dialog*   The `Dialog` object you want to show.
>
> *Timeout*   The time, in thousandths of a second, after which the dialog box is dismissed.

The difference is that if you specify a *Timeout* value, Word does *not* accept the user's changes when the dialog box is dismissed after the specified time.

Another useful `Dialog` object method is `Execute`, which runs the dialog box without showing it to the user. Listing 5.4 shows an example.

Listing 5.4   A Function Procedure That Uses Word's Word Count Dialog Box to Get the Total Number of Words in the Active Document

```
Function CountDocumentWords() As Long
    With Dialogs(wdDialogToolsWordCount)
        .Execute
        CountDocumentWords = .Words
    End With
End Function

Sub DisplayWordCount()
    MsgBox "This document contains " & CountDocumentWords & " words."
End Sub
```

This procedure uses `Execute` to run the Word Count dialog box, and then uses the `Words` argument to return the number of words in the document. (Note, however, that if you have text selected before running this procedure, it will return the number of words in the selection.)

Checking Spelling

When used with the Word or Excel `Application` object, the `CheckSpelling` method checks the spelling of a single word using the following syntax (note that Word's method has a few extra arguments):

`Application.CheckSpelling(word,customDictionary,ignoreUppercase)`

word	The word you want to check.
customDictionary	The filename of a custom dictionary that the application can search if *word* wasn't found in the main dictionary.
ignoreUppercase	Set to `True` to tell the application to ignore words entirely in uppercase.

For example, the code shown in Listing 5.5 gets a word from the user, checks the spelling, and tells the user whether or not the word is spelled correctly. (You also can use this property with a `Document`, `Worksheet`, or `Range` object, as described in Chapter 7, "Programming Word," and 8, "Programming Excel.")

→ To learn about the `InputBox` function, **see** "Getting Input Using `InputBox`," **p. 50**.

Listing 5.5   A Procedure That Checks the Spelling of an Entered Word

```
Sub SpellCheckTest()
    '
    ' Get the word from the user
    '
    word2Check = InputBox("Enter a word:")
    '
    ' Spell-check it
    '
    result = Application.CheckSpelling(word2Check)
    '
    ' Display the result to the user
    '
    If result = True Then
        MsgBox "'" & word2Check & "' is spelled correctly!"
    Else
        MsgBox "Oops! '" & word2Check & "' is spelled incorrectly."
    End If
End Sub
```

5

Example: The `Window` Object

Another object that's common to almost all applications is the `Window` object, which represents an open window in an application. Note that this isn't the same as an open document. Rather, the `Window` object is just a container for a document, so the associated properties and methods have no effect on the document data. You can use VBA to change the window state (maximized or minimized), size and move windows, navigate open windows, and much more. In the next three sections you learn how to specify a `Window` object in your code, how to open a new window, and how to activate a window.

Specifying a `Window` Object

If you need to perform some action on a window or change a window's properties, you need to tell the application which window you want to use. VBA gives you two ways to do this:

- **Use the `Windows` object**—The `Windows` object is the collection of all the open windows in the application. To specify a window, either use its index number (as given by the numbers beside the windows on the application's Windows menu) or enclose the window caption (in other words, the text that appears in the window's title bar) in quotation marks. For example, if the `Budget.doc` window is listed first in the Window menu, the following two statements would be equivalent:

```
Windows(1)
Windows("Budget.doc")
```

- **Use the `ActiveWindow` object**—The `ActiveWindow` object represents the window that currently has the focus. For example, the following statement uses the `WindowState` property (common to all `Window` objects) to maximize the active Word window:

```
ActiveWindow.WindowState = wdWindowStateMaximize
```

Opening a New Window

If you need to create a new window, use the `Window` object's `NewWindow` method:

```
Window.NewWindow
```

    Window   The `Window` object from which you want to create the new window.

Note that this argument is optional in some applications. In Word, for example, if you omit *Window*, the active window is used.

Activating a Window

If your code needs to switch from one window to another, you need to activate the other window. You do that by running the `Window` object's `Activate` method, which activates the specified open window. For example, the following statement activates the `Finances.xls` window:

```
Windows("Finances.xls").Activate
```

From Here

- To learn how the MsgBox function works, **see** "Getting Input Using MsgBox," **p. 45**.

- To learn about the InputBox function, **see** "Getting Input Using InputBox," **p. 50**.

- To get the details on the If statement, **see** "Using If...Then to Make True/False Decisions," **p. 92**.

- You use a For Each...Next loop to run through all the objects in a collection; **see** "Using For Each...Next Loops," **p. 109**.

- Part 2, "Putting VBA to Work," is a veritable "object fest" as I examine the object hierarchies in the main Office applications.

5

Controlling Your VBA Code

6

One of the advantages of writing your own VBA procedures instead of simply recording them is that you end up with much more control over what your code does and how it performs its tasks. In particular, you can create procedures that make *decisions* based on certain conditions and that can perform *loops*—the running of several statements repeatedly. The statements that handle this kind of processing—*control structures*—are the subject of this chapter.

Code That Makes Decisions

A smart procedure performs tests on its environment and then decides what to do next based on the results of each test. For example, suppose you've written a Function procedure that uses one of its arguments as a divisor in a formula. You should test the argument before using it in the formula to make sure that it isn't 0 (to avoid producing a "Division by zero" error). If it is, you could then display a message that alerts the user of the illegal argument.

Similarly, a well-designed application will interact with the user and ask for feedback in the form of extra information or a confirmation of a requested action. The program can then take this feedback and redirect itself accordingly.

Using If . . . Then **to Make True/False Decisions**

The most basic form of decision is the simple true/false decision (which could also be seen as a yes/no or an on/off decision). In this case, your program looks at a certain condition, determines whether it is currently true or false, and acts accordingly. As you might expect from the discussion of expressions in Chapter 4, "Building VBA Expressions," logical expressions (which, you'll recall, always return a `True` or `False` result) play a big part here.

In VBA, simple true/false decisions are handled by the `If...Then` statement. You can use either the *single-line* syntax:

```
If condition Then statement
```

or the *block* syntax:

```
If condition Then
    [statements]
End If
```

condition	You can use either a logical expression that returns `True` or `False`, or you can use any expression that returns a numeric value. In the latter case, a return value of zero is functionally equivalent to `False`, and any nonzero value is equivalent to `True`.
statement(s)	The VBA statement or statements to run if *condition* returns `True`. If *condition* returns `False`, VBA skips over the statements.

Whether you use the single-line or block syntax depends on the statements you want to run if the *condition* returns a `True` result. If you have only one statement, you can use either syntax. If you have multiple statements, you must use the block syntax.

Listing 6.1 shows a revised version of the `GrossMargin` procedure from Chapter 3, "Understanding Program Variables" (see Listing 3.1). This version—called `GrossMargin2`— uses `If...Then` to check the `totalSales` variable. The procedure calculates the gross margin only if the value of `totalSales` isn't zero.

Listing 6.1 An If...Then **Example**

```
Function GrossMargin2()
    Dim totalSales
    Dim totalExpenses
    totalSales = Application.Sum(Range("Sales"))
    totalExpenses = Application.Sum(Range("Expenses"))
    If totalSales <> 0 Then
        GrossMargin2 = (totalSales - totalExpenses) / totalSales
    End If
End Function
```

> **NOTE**
> The code for this chapter is available on my website at the following address:
> http://www.mcfedries.com/Office2007VBA/Chapter06.xlsm

> **TIP**
> You can make the If...Then statement in the GrossMargin2 procedure slightly more efficient by taking advantage of the fact that in the condition, zero is equivalent to False and any other number is equivalent to True. This means you don't have to explicitly test the totalSales variable to see whether it's zero. Instead, you can use the following statements:
>
> ```
> If totalSales Then
>
>         GrossMargin = (totalSales-totalExpenses)/totalSales
>
> End If
> ```
>
> On the other hand, many programmers feel that including the explicit test for a nonzero value (totalSales <> 0) makes the procedure easier to read and more intuitive. Because, in this case, the efficiency gained is only minor, you're probably better off leaving in the full expression.

Using If...Then...Else to Handle a False Result

Using the If...Then statement to make decisions adds a powerful new weapon to your VBA arsenal. However, this technique suffers from an important drawback: A False result only bypasses one or more statements; it doesn't execute any of its own. This is fine in many cases, but there will be times when you need to run one group of statements if the condition returns True and a different group if the result is False. To handle this, you need to use an If...Then...Else statement:

```
If condition Then
    [TrueStatements]
Else
    [FalseStatements]
End If
```

condition	The logical expression that returns True or False.
TrueStatements	The statements to run if condition returns True.
FalseStatements	The statements to run if condition returns False.

If the condition returns True, VBA runs the group of statements between If...Then and Else. If it returns False, VBA runs the group of statements between Else and End If.

Let's look at an example. Suppose you want to calculate the future value of a series of regular deposits, but you want to differentiate between monthly deposits and quarterly deposits. Listing 6.2 shows a Function procedure called FutureValue that does the job.

6

Listing 6.2 A Procedure That Uses If...Then...Else

```
Function FutureValue(Rate As Single, Nper As Integer, Pmt As Currency,
➥Frequency As String) As Currency
    If Frequency = "Monthly" Then
        FutureValue = FV(Rate / 12, Nper * 12, Pmt / 12)
    Else
        FutureValue = FV(Rate / 4, Nper * 4, Pmt / 4)
    End If
End Function
```

The first three arguments—Rate, Nper, and Pmt—are, respectively, the annual interest rate, the number of years in the term of the investment, and the total deposit available annually. The fourth argument—Frequency—is either "Monthly" or "Quarterly." The idea is to adjust the first three arguments based on Frequency. To do that, the If...Then...Else statement runs a test on the Frequency argument:

```
If Frequency = "Monthly" Then
```

If the logical expression Frequency = "Monthly" returns True, the procedure runs the following statement:

```
FutureValue = FV(Rate / 12, Nper * 12, Pmt / 12)
```

This statement divides the interest rate by 12, multiplies the term by 12, and divides the annual deposit by 12. Otherwise, if the logical expression returns False, then a quarterly calculation is assumed and the procedure executes the following statement:

```
FutureValue = FV(Rate / 4, Nper * 4, Pmt / 4)
```

This statement divides the interest rate by 4, multiplies the term by 4, and divides the annual deposit by 4. In both cases, VBA's FV function (see Chapter 4) is used to return the future value.

> **TIP**
> If...Then...Else statements are much easier to read when you indent the expressions between If...Then, Else, and End If, as I've done in Listing 6.2. This lets you easily identify which group of statements will be run if there is a True result and which group will be run if the result is False. Pressing the Tab key once at the beginning of the first line in the block does the job. See also "Indenting for Readability," later in this chapter.

Making Multiple Decisions

The problem with If...Then...Else is that normally you can make only a single decision. The statement calculates a single logical result and performs one of two actions. However, plenty of situations require multiple decisions before you can decide which action to take.

For example, the FutureValue procedure discussed in the preceding section probably should test the Frequency argument to make sure it's either Monthly or Quarterly and not something else. The next few sections show you three solutions to this problem.

Using the And **and** Or **Operators**

One solution to the multiple-decision problem is to combine multiple logical expressions in a single If...Then statement. From Chapter 4, you'll recall that you can combine logical expressions by using VBA's And and Or operators. In the example, we want to calculate the future value only if the Frequency argument is either Monthly *or* Quarterly. The following If...Then statement uses the Or operator to test this:

```
If Frequency = "Monthly" Or Frequency = "Quarterly" Then
```

As shown in Listing 6.3, if Frequency equals either of these values, the entire condition returns True and the procedure runs the calculation in the usual way; otherwise, if Frequency doesn't equal either value, then the procedure returns a message to the user.

Listing 6.3   A Procedure That Uses the Or **Operator to Perform Multiple Logical Tests**

```
Function FutureValue2(Rate As Single, Nper As Integer, Pmt As Currency,
➥Frequency As String) As Currency
    If Frequency = "Monthly" Or Frequency = "Quarterly" Then
        If Frequency = "Monthly" Then
            FutureValue2 = FV(Rate / 12, Nper * 12, Pmt / 12)
        Else
            FutureValue2 = FV(Rate / 4, Nper * 4, Pmt / 4)
        End If
    Else
        MsgBox "The Frequency argument must be either " & _
               """Monthly"" or ""Quarterly""!"
    End If
End Function
```

Note that this procedure isn't particularly efficient because you end up testing the Frequency argument in two places. However, that just means that this example isn't the best use of the And and Or operators. The overall principle of using these operators to perform multiple logical tests is a useful one, however, and you should keep it in mind when constructing your decision-making code.

> **TIP**
>
> In Listing 6.3, if Frequency equals either Monthly or Quarterly, the result of the first If...Then...Else is true and the procedure then executes a *second* If...Then...Else structure. This is called *nesting* one control structure within another. This is very common in VBA procedures, but it can also get very confusing very quickly. To help you keep things straight, not only indent the statements within the first If...Then...Else, but *double-indent* the statements within the second If...Then...Else (refer to Listing 6.3 for an example).

Using Multiple If...Then...Else **Statements**

There is a third syntax for the If...Then...Else statement that lets you string together as many logical tests as you need:

6

```
If condition1 Then
    [condition1 TrueStatements]
ElseIf condition2 Then
    [condition2 TrueStatements]
<etc.>
Else
    [FalseStatements]
End If
```

`condition1`	A logical expression.
`condition1 TrueStatements`	The statements to run if `condition1` returns `True`.
`condition2`	A different logical expression.
`condition1 TrueStatements`	The statements to run if `condition2` returns `True`.
`FalseStatements`	The statements to run if both `condition1` and `condition2` return `False`.

VBA first tests `condition1`. If this returns `True`, VBA runs the group of statements between `If...Then` and `ElseIf...Then`. If it returns `False`, VBA then tests `condition2`. If this test is `True`, VBA runs the group of statements between `ElseIf...Then` and `Else`. Otherwise, VBA runs the statements between `Else` and `End If`. Here are two things you should note about this structure:

- You can have as many `ElseIf` conditions as you need.
- You don't have to use the `Else` part if you don't need it.

Listing 6.4 shows `FutureValue3`, a revised version of `FutureValue` that makes allowances for an improper `Frequency` argument.

Listing 6.4   A Procedure That Uses Multiple `If...Then...Else` **Statements**

```
Function FutureValue3(Rate As Single, Nper As Integer, Pmt As Currency,
➥Frequency As String) As Currency
    If Frequency = "Monthly" Then
        FutureValue3 = FV(Rate / 12, Nper * 12, Pmt / 12)
    ElseIf Frequency = "Quarterly" Then
        FutureValue3 = FV(Rate / 4, Nper * 4, Pmt / 4)
    Else
        MsgBox "The Frequency argument must be either " & _
               """Monthly"" or ""Quarterly""!"
    End If
End Function
```

As before, the `If...Then` statement checks to see whether `Frequency` equals `Monthly` and, if it does, calculates the future value accordingly. If it doesn't, the `ElseIf...Then` statement checks to see whether `Frequency` equals `Quarterly` and calculates the future value if the expression returns `True`. If it returns `False`, the user entered the `Frequency` argument incorrectly, so a warning message is displayed.

Using the `Select Case` **Statement**

Performing multiple tests with `If...ElseIf` is a handy technique—it's a VBA tool you'll reach for quite often. However, it quickly becomes unwieldy as the number of tests you need to make gets larger. It's okay for two or three tests, but any more than that makes the logic harder to follow.

For these situations, VBA's `Select Case` statement is a better choice. The idea is that you provide a logical expression at the beginning and then list a series of possible results. For each possible result—called a *case*—you provide one or more VBA statements to execute should the case prove to be true. Here's the syntax:

```
Select Case TestExpression
    Case FirstCaseList
        [FirstStatements]
    Case SecondCaseList
        [SecondStatements]
    <etc>
    Case Else
        [ElseStatements]
End Select
```

`TestExpression`	This expression is evaluated at the beginning of the structure. It must return a value (logical, numeric, string, and so on).
`CaseList`	A list of one or more possible results for `TestExpression`. These results are values or expressions separated by commas. VBA examines each element in the list to see whether one matches the `TestExpression`. The expressions can take any one of the following forms:
	`Expression`
	`Expression To Expression`
	`Is LogicalOperator Expression`
	The `To` keyword defines a range of values (for example, `1 To 10`). The `Is` keyword defines an open-ended range of values (for example, `Is >= 100`).
`Statements`	These are the statements VBA runs if any part of the associated `CaseList` matches the `TestExpression`. VBA runs the optional `ElseStatements` if no `CaseList` contains a match for the `TestExpression`.

> **NOTE**
> If more than one `CaseList` contains an element that matches the `TestExpression`, VBA runs only the statements associated with the `CaseList` that appears *first* in the `Select Case` structure.

6

Listing 6.5 shows how you would use Select Case to handle the Frequency argument problem.

Listing 6.5   A Procedure That Uses Select Case **to Test Multiple Values**

```
Function FutureValue4(Rate As Single, Nper As Integer, Pmt As Currency,
➡Frequency As String) As Currency
    Select Case Frequency
        Case "Monthly"
            FutureValue4 = FV(Rate / 12, Nper * 12, Pmt / 12)
        Case "Quarterly"
            FutureValue4 = FV(Rate / 4, Nper * 4, Pmt / 4)
        Case Else
            MsgBox "The Frequency argument must be either " & _
                    """Monthly"" or ""Quarterly""!"
    End Select
End Function
```

A Select Case **Example: Converting Test Scores to Letter Grades**

To help you get a better feel for the Select Case statement, let's take a look at another example that better showcases the unique talents of this powerful structure. Suppose you want to write a procedure that converts a raw test score into a letter grade according to the following table:

Raw Score	Letter Grade
90 and over	A
Between 80 and 89	B
Between 70 and 79	C
Between 60 and 69	D
Less than 60	F

Listing 6.6 shows the LetterGrade procedure, which uses a Select Case statement to make the conversion.

Listing 6.6   A Procedure That Uses Select Case **to Convert a Raw Test Score into a Letter Grade**

```
Function LetterGrade(rawScore As Integer) As String
    Select Case rawScore
        Case Is < 0
            LetterGrade = "ERROR! Score less than 0!"
        Case Is < 60
            LetterGrade = "F"
        Case Is < 70
            LetterGrade = "D"
        Case Is < 80
            LetterGrade = "C"
```

```
        Case Is < 90
            LetterGrade = "B"
        Case Is <= 100
            LetterGrade = "A"
        Case Else
            LetterGrade = "ERROR! Score greater than 100!"
    End Select
End Function
```

The rawScore argument is an integer value between 0 and 100. The Select Case structure first checks to see whether rawScore is negative and, if so, the function returns an error message. The next Case statement checks to see whether the score is less than 60, and the function returns the letter grade "F" if it is. The next Case statement looks for a score that is less than 70. If we get this far, we already know (thanks to the preceding Case statement) that the score is at least 60. Therefore, this case is really checking to see whether the score is between 60 and 70 (including 60, but not including 70). If so, the letter grade "D" is returned. The rest of the Case statements proceed in the same manner. The Case Else checks for a score greater than 100 and returns another error message if it is.

Another Example: Taming the RGB Function

In Chapter 5, "Working with Objects," I mentioned briefly that you can use the RGB (*red,green,blue*) VBA function anytime you need to specify a color for a property. Each of the three named arguments (*red*, *green*, and *blue*) are integers between 0 and 255 that determine how much of each component color is mixed into the final color. In the *red* component, for example, 0 means no red is present and 255 means that pure red is present. If all three values are the same, you get a shade of gray.

Here are some sample values for each component that produce common colors:

Red	Green	Blue	Result
0	0	0	Black
0	0	255	Blue
0	255	0	Green
0	255	255	Cyan
255	0	0	Red
255	0	255	Magenta
255	255	0	Yellow
255	255	255	White

However, rather than memorize these combinations, let's put VBA and Select Case to work to make choosing colors easier. Listing 6.7 shows the VBAColor function, which lets you use names (for example, "red" or "blue") rather than cryptic number combinations to set 16 of the most common colors.

Listing 6.7   A Function That Accepts a Color Name as a String and Returns the Corresponding RGB Value

```
Function VBAColor(colorName As String) As Long

    Select Case LCase(Trim(colorName))
        Case "black"
            VBAColor = RGB(0, 0, 0)
        Case "white"
            VBAColor = RGB(255, 255, 255)
        Case "gray"
            VBAColor = RGB(192, 192, 192)
        Case "dark gray"
            VBAColor = RGB(128, 128, 128)
        Case "red"
            VBAColor = RGB(255, 0, 0)
        Case "dark red"
            VBAColor = RGB(128, 0, 0)
        Case "green"
            VBAColor = RGB(0, 255, 0)
        Case "dark green"
            VBAColor = RGB(0, 128, 0)
        Case "blue"
            VBAColor = RGB(0, 0, 255)
        Case "dark blue"
            VBAColor = RGB(0, 0, 128)
        Case "yellow"
            VBAColor = RGB(255, 255, 0)
        Case "dark yellow"
            VBAColor = RGB(128, 128, 0)
        Case "magenta"
            VBAColor = RGB(255, 0, 255)
        Case "dark magenta"
            VBAColor = RGB(128, 0, 128)
        Case "cyan"
            VBAColor = RGB(0, 255, 255)
        Case "dark cyan"
            VBAColor = RGB(0, 128, 128)
    End Select
End Function

Sub ColorTester()
    ActiveCell.Font.Color = VBAColor("red")
End Sub
```

VBAColor takes a single argument, colorName, which is the name of the color you want to work with. Notice how the Select Case statement massages the argument to prevent errors:

```
Select Case LCase(Trim(colorName))
```

The Trim function removes any extraneous spaces at the beginning and end of the argument, and the LCase function converts colorName to lowercase. This ensures that the function is not case sensitive, which means it doesn't matter whether you send *black*, *BLACK*, or *Black*: The function will still work.

The rest of the function uses `Case` statements to check for the various color names and return the appropriate RGB value. You can use the `ColorTester` procedure to give `VBAColor` a whirl. This procedure just formats the font color of the currently selected worksheet cell.

> **NOTE** VBA also defines eight color constants that you can use when you just need the basic colors: `vbBlack`, `vbBlue`, `vbCyan`, `vbGreen`, `vbMagenta`, `vbRed`, `vbWhite`, and `vbYellow`.

Functions That Make Decisions

Much of what we're talking about in this chapter involves ways to make your procedures cleaner and more efficient. These are laudable goals for a whole host of reasons, but the following are the main ones:

- Your code will execute faster.
- You'll have less code to type.
- Your code will be easier to read and maintain.

This section looks at three powerful VBA functions that can increase the efficiency of your procedures.

The `IIf` Function

You've seen how the decision-making prowess of the `If...Then...Else` structure lets you create "intelligent" procedures that can respond appropriately to different situations. However, sometimes `If...Then...Else` just isn't efficient. For example, suppose you're writing a document that can't be longer than 1,000 words and you want to devise a test that will alert you when the document's word count exceeds that number. Here's a code fragment that includes an `If...Then...Else` structure that performs this test:

```
Dim DocTooLong As Boolean
If ActiveDocument.Range.Words.Count > 1000 Then
    DocTooLong = True
Else
    DocTooLong = False
End If
```

In Word, the `ActiveDocument.Range.Words.Count` property tells you the total number of words in the active document. As it stands, there's nothing wrong with this code. However, it seems like a lot of work to go through just to assign a value to a variable. For these types of situations, VBA has an `IIf` function that's more efficient. `IIf`, which stands for "inline If," performs a simple `If` test on a single line:

```
IIf (condition, TrueResult, FalseResult)
```

condition	A logical expression that returns `True` or `False`.
TrueResult	The value returned by the function if *condition* is `True`.
FalseResult	The value returned by the function if *condition* is `False`.

6

Listing 6.8 shows a function procedure that checks the word count by using `IIf` to replace the `If...Then...Else` statement shown earlier.

Listing 6.8   A Function That Uses `IIf` to Test a Document's Word Count

```
Function DocTooLong() As Boolean
    DocTooLong = IIf(ActiveDocument.Range.Words.Count > 1000, True, False)
End Function
```

If the number of words exceeds 1000, `IIf` returns `True`; otherwise, the function returns `False`.

The `Choose` Function

In the previous section, I showed you how the `IIf` function is an efficient replacement for `If...Then...Else` when all you need to do is assign a value to a variable based on the results of the test. Suppose now you have a similar situation with the `Select Case` structure. In other words, you want to test a number of possible values and assign the result to a variable.

For example, you saw in Chapter 4 that VBA's `Weekday` function returns the current day of the week as a number. Here's a procedure fragment that takes the day number and uses a `Select Case` structure to assign the name of the deity associated with that day to the `dayDeity` variable:

```
Dim dayDeity As String
Select Case Weekday(Now)
    Case 1
        dayDeity = "Sun"
    Case 2
        dayDeity = "Moon"
    Case 3
        dayDeity = "Tiw"
    Case 4
        dayDeity = "Woden"
    Case 5
        dayDeity = "Thor"
    Case 6
        dayDeity = "Freya"
    Case 7
        dayDeity = "Saturn"
End Select
```

Again, this seems like *way* too much effort for a simple variable assignment. And, in fact, it *is* too much work thanks to VBA's `Choose` function. `Choose` encapsulates the essence of the preceding `Select Case` structure—the test value and the various possible results—into a single statement. Here's the syntax:

```
Choose(index, value1, value2,...)
```

index	A numeric expression that determines which of the values in the list is returned. If *index* is 1, *value1* is returned. If *index* is 2, *value2* is returned (and so on). Note that if *index* is less than 1 or greater than the number of values in the list, the function returns `Null`.
value1, value2...	A list of values from which `Choose` selects the return value. The values can be any valid VBA expression.

Listing 6.9 shows a function called `DayDeity` that returns the name of a day's deity by using `Choose` to replace the `Select Case` structure shown earlier.

Listing 6.9   A Function That Uses the `Choose` Function to Select from a List of Values

```
Function DayDeity(weekdayNum As Integer) As String
    DayDeity = Choose(weekdayNum, "Sun", "Moon", _
        "Tiw", "Woden", "Thor", "Freya", "Saturn")
End Function
```

The `Switch` Function

`Choose` is a welcome addition to the VBA function library, but its use is limited because of two constraints:

- You can use `Choose` only when the *index* argument is a number or a numeric expression.
- `Choose` can't handle logical expressions.

To illustrate why the last point is important, consider the `Select Case` structure used earlier in this chapter to convert a test score into a letter grade:

```
Select Case rawScore
    Case Is < 0
        LetterGrade = "ERROR! Score less than 0!"
    Case Is < 60
        LetterGrade = "F"
    Case Is < 70
        LetterGrade = "D"
    Case Is < 80
        LetterGrade = "C"
    Case Is < 90
        LetterGrade = "B"
    Case Is <= 100
        LetterGrade = "A"
    Case Else
        LetterGrade = "ERROR! Score greater than 100!"
End Select
```

At first blush, this structure seems to satisfy the same inefficiency criteria that I mentioned earlier for `If...Then...Else` and `Select Case`. In other words, each `Case` runs only a single statement and that statement serves only to assign a value to a variable. The difference, though, is that the `Case` statements use logical expressions, so we can't use `Choose` to make this code more efficient.

6

However, you *can* use VBA's Switch function to do the job:

```
Switch(expr1, value1, expr2, value2,...)
```

expr1, expr2...	These are logical expressions that determine which of the values in the list is returned. If *expr1* is True, *value1* is returned. If *expr2* is True, *value2* is returned (and so on).
value1, value2...	A list of values from which Switch selects the return value. The values can be any valid VBA expression.

Switch trudges through the logical expressions from left to right. When it comes across the first True expression, it returns the value that appears immediately after the expression. Listing 6.10 puts Switch to work to create a more efficient version of the LetterGrade function.

Listing 6.10 A Procedure That Uses the Switch Function to Convert a Test Score into a Letter Grade

```
Function LetterGrade2(rawScore As Integer) As String
    LetterGrade2 = Switch( _
        rawScore < 0, "ERROR! Score less than 0!", _
        rawScore < 60, "F", _
        rawScore < 70, "D", _
        rawScore < 80, "C", _
        rawScore < 90, "B", _
        rawScore <= 100, "A", _
        rawScore > 100, "ERROR! Score greater than 100!")
End Function
```

Code That Loops

You've seen in this chapter and in previous chapters that it makes sense to divide up your VBA chores and place them in separate procedures or functions. That way, you need to write the code only once and then call it any time you need it. This is known in the trade as *modular programming*, and it saves time and effort by helping you avoid reinventing too many wheels.

There are also wheels to avoid reinventing *within* your procedures and functions. For example, consider the following code fragment:

```
MsgBox "The time is now " & Time
Application.Wait Now + TimeValue("00:00:05")
MsgBox "The time is now " & Time
Application.Wait Now + TimeValue("00:00:05")
MsgBox "The time is now " & Time
Application.Wait Now + TimeValue("00:00:05")
```

> **NOTE**
> This code fragment uses the Excel Application object's Wait method to produce a delay. The argument Now + TimeValue("00:00:05") pauses the procedure for about five seconds before continuing.

This code does nothing more than display the time, delay for five seconds, and repeat this two more times. Besides being decidedly useless, this code just reeks of inefficiency. It's clear that a far better approach would be to take just the first two statements and somehow get VBA to repeat them as many times as necessary.

The good news is that not only is it possible to do this, but VBA also gives you a number of different methods to perform this so-called *looping*. I spend the rest of this chapter investigating each of these methods.

Using Do...Loop **Structures**

What do you do when you need to loop but you don't know in advance how many times to repeat the loop? This could happen if, for example, you want to loop only until a certain condition is met, such as encountering a blank cell in an Excel worksheet. The solution is to use a Do...Loop.

The Do...Loop has four different syntaxes:

`Do While condition`
`[statements]`
`Loop`
	Checks *condition* before entering the loop. Executes the *statements* only while *condition* is True.

`Do`
`[statements]`
`Loop While condition`
	Checks *condition* after running through the loop once. Executes the *statements* only while *condition* is True. Use this form when you want the loop to be processed at least once.

`Do Until condition`
`[statements]`
`Loop`
	Checks *condition* before entering the loop. Executes the *statements* only while *condition* is False.

`Do`
`[statements]`
`Loop Until condition`
	Checks *condition* after running through the loop once. Executes the *statements* only while *condition* is False. Again, use this form when you want the loop to be processed at least once.

Listing 6.11 shows a procedure called BigNumbers that runs down a worksheet column and changes the font color to magenta whenever a cell contains a number greater than or equal to 1,000.

Listing 6.11   A Procedure That Uses a Do...Loop **to Process Cells Until It Encounters a Blank Cell**

```
Sub BigNumbers()
    Dim rowNum As Integer, colNum As Integer, currCell As Range
    '
    ' Initialize the row and column numbers
    '
```

continues

6

Listing 6.11   Continued

```
      rowNum = ActiveCell.Row
      colNum = ActiveCell.Column
      '
      ' Get the first cell
      '
      Set currCell = ActiveSheet.Cells(rowNum, colNum)
      '
      ' Loop while the current cell isn't empty
      '
      Do While currCell.Value <> ""
          '
          ' Is it a number?
          '
          If IsNumeric(currCell.Value) Then
              '
              ' Is it a big number?
              '
              If currCell.Value >= 1000 Then
                  '
                  ' If so, color it magenta
                  '
                  currCell.Font.Color = VBAColor("magenta")
              End If
          End If
          '
          ' Increment the row number and get the next cell
          '
          rowNum = rowNum + 1
          Set currCell = ActiveSheet.Cells(rowNum, colNum)
      Loop
End Sub
```

The idea is to loop until the procedure encounters a blank cell. This is controlled by the following Do While statement:

```
Do While currCell.Value <> ""
```

currCell is an object variable that is set using the Cells method (which I describe in Chapter 8, "Programming Excel"). Next, the first If...Then uses the IsNumeric function to check whether the cell contains a number, and the second If...Then checks whether the number is greater than or equal to 1,000. If both conditions are True, the font color is set to magenta by the VBAColor function described earlier in this chapter.

Using For...Next Loops

The most common type of loop is the For...Next loop. Use this loop when you know exactly how many times you want to repeat a group of statements. The structure of a For...Next loop looks like this:

```
For counter = start To end [Step increment]
    [statements]
Next [counter]
```

counter	A numeric variable used as a *loop counter*. The loop counter is a number that counts how many times the procedure has gone through the loop.
start	The initial value of *counter*. This is usually 1, but you can enter any value or you can use a variable.
end	The final value of *counter*. You can also use a variable here, if it's appropriate.
increment	This optional value defines an increment for the loop counter. If you leave this out, the default value is 1. Use a negative value to decrement *counter*.
statements	The statements to execute each time through the loop.

The basic idea is simple. When VBA encounters the For...Next statement, it follows this five-step process:

1. Set *counter* equal to *start*.
2. Test *counter*. If it's greater than *end*, exit the loop (that is, process the first statement after the Next statement). Otherwise, continue. If *increment* is negative, VBA checks to see whether *counter* is less than *end*.
3. Execute each statement between the For and Next statements.
4. Add *increment* to *counter*. Add 1 to *counter* if *increment* isn't specified.
5. Repeat steps 2 through 4 until done.

Listing 6.12 shows a simple Sub procedure—LoopTest—that uses a For...Next statement. Each time through the loop, the procedure uses the Application object's StatusBar property to display the value of counter (the loop counter) in the status bar. When you run this procedure, *counter* gets incremented by 1 each time through the loop, and the new value gets displayed in the status bar.

6

Listing 6.12   A Simple For...Next **Loop**

```
Sub LoopTest()
    Dim counter
    For counter = 1 To 10
        '
        'Display the message
        '
        Application.StatusBar = "Counter value: " & counter
        '
        ' Wait for 1 second
        '
```

continues

Listing 6.12   Continued

```
        Application.Wait Now + TimeValue("00:00:01")
    Next counter
    Application.StatusBar = False
End Sub
```

> **NOTE**
>
> The `LoopTest` procedure works fine in Excel, but it will fail in the other Office applications because they don't implement the `Wait` method. If you need to get your code to delay for a short while, here's a simple procedure that does the trick:
>
> ```
>     Sub VBAWait(delay As Integer)
>         Dim startTime As Long
>         startTime = Timer
>         Do While Timer - startTime < delay
>             DoEvents
>         Loop
>     End Sub
> ```
>
> Note the use of the `DoEvents` function inside the `Do While...Loop` structure. This function yields execution to the operating system so that events such as keystrokes and application messages are processed while the procedure delays.

Here are some notes on `For...Next` loops:

- If you use a positive number for *increment* (or if you omit *increment*), *end* must be greater than or equal to *start*. If you use a negative number for *increment*, *end* must be less than or equal to *start*.
- If *start* equals *end*, the loop will execute once.
- As with `If...Then...Else` structures, indent the statements inside a `For...Next` loop for increased readability.
- To keep the number of variables defined in a procedure to a minimum, always try to use the same name for all your `For...Next` loop counters. The letters *i* through *n* traditionally are used for counters in programming. For greater clarity, you might want to use names such as "counter."
- For the fastest loops, don't use the counter name after the `Next` statement. If you'd like to keep the counter name for clarity (which I recommend), precede the name with an apostrophe (') to comment out the name, like this:

```
For counter = 1 To 10
    [statements]
Next 'counter
```

- If you need to break out of a `For...Next` loop before the defined number of repetitions is completed, use the `Exit For` statement, described in the section "Using `Exit For` or `Exit Do` to Exit a Loop."

Using For Each...Next Loops

A useful variation of the For...Next loop is the For Each...Next loop, which operates on a collection of objects. You don't need a loop counter because VBA just loops through the individual elements in the collection and performs on each element whatever operations are inside the loop. Here's the structure of the basic For Each...Next loop:

```
For Each element In collection
    [statements]
Next [element]
```

element	A variable used to hold the name of each element in the collection.
collection	The name of the collection.
statements	The statements to be executed for each element in the collection.

As an example, let's create a command procedure that converts a range of text into proper case (that is, the first letter of each word is capitalized). This function can come in handy if you import mainframe text into your worksheets because mainframe reports usually appear entirely in uppercase. This process involves three steps:

1. Loop through the selected range with For Each...Next.

2. Convert each cell's text to proper case. Use Excel's Proper() worksheet function to handle this:

   ```
   WorksheetFunction(Proper(text))
   ```

text	The text to convert to proper case.

3. Enter the converted text into the selected cell. This is the job of the Range object's Formula method:

   ```
   object.Formula = expression
   ```

object	The Range object in which you want to enter expression.
expression	The data you want to enter into object.

Listing 6.13 shows the resulting procedure, ConvertToProper. Note that this procedure uses the Selection object to represent the currently selected range.

Listing 6.13   A Sub Procedure That Uses For Each...Next **to Loop Through a Selection and Convert Each Cell to Proper Text**

```
Sub ConvertToProper()
    Dim cellObject As Range
    For Each cellObject In Selection
        cellObject.Formula = WorksheetFunction(Proper(cellObject.Formula))
    Next
End Sub
```

How would you use this procedure in practice? You'd highlight the cells you want to convert and then choose the Developer, Macros command to find and run the ConvertToProper procedure.

6

Using `Exit For` or `Exit Do` to Exit a Loop

Most loops run their natural course and then the procedure moves on. There might be times, however, when you want to exit a loop prematurely. For example, you might come across a certain type of cell, or an error might occur, or the user might enter an unexpected value. To exit a For...Next loop or a For Each...Next loop, use the `Exit For` statement. To exit a Do...Loop, use the `Exit Do` statement.

Listing 6.14 shows a revised version of the `BigNumbers` procedure, which exits the Do...Loop if it comes across a cell that isn't a number.

Listing 6.14   Version of the `BigNumbers` Procedure That Terminates with the `Exit Do` Statement If the Current Cell Isn't a Number

```
Sub BigNumbers2()
    Dim rowNum As Integer, colNum As Integer, currCell As Range
    '
    ' Initialize the row and column numbers
    '
    rowNum = ActiveCell.Row
    colNum = ActiveCell.Column
    '
    ' Get the first cell
    '
    Set currCell = ActiveSheet.Cells(rowNum, colNum)
    '
    ' Loop while the current cell isn't empty
    '
    Do While currCell.Value <> ""
        '
        ' Is it a number?
        '
        If IsNumeric(currCell.Value) Then
            '
            ' Is it a big number?
            '
            If currCell.Value >= 1000 Then
                '
                ' If so, color it magenta
                '
                currCell.Font.Color = VBAColor("magenta")
            End If
        '
        ' Otherwise, exit the loop
        '
        Else
            Exit Do
        End If
        '
        ' Increment the row number and get the next cell
        '
        rowNum = rowNum + 1
        Set currCell = ActiveSheet.Cells(rowNum, colNum)
    Loop
End Sub
```

Indenting for Readability

For beginning programmers, one of the most common causes of confusion when using these control structures is keeping track of which statements belong to which `If...Then` test or `Do...While` loop. This is particularly true if you end up with control structures nested within other control structures (see, for example, Listings 6.3, 6.11, and 6.14). I've stressed indenting your code throughout this book, and I want to underline this programming principle once again here:

- In the main test or loop, indent the statements once (press Tab at the beginning of the first statement).

- In a secondary (that is, nested) test or loop, double-indent the statements (press Tab again at the beginning of the first statement).

- In a tertiary (that is, nested within a nested structure) test or loop, triple-indent the statements (press Tab again at the beginning of the first statement).

Here's a general example of how this indenting looks:

```
If MainExpression Then
    If SecondaryExpression Then
        If TertiaryExpression Then
            [TertiaryTrueStatements]
        Else
            [TeriaryFalseStatements]
        End If
    Else
        [SecondaryFalseStatements]
    EndIf
Else
    [MainFalseStatements]
End If
```

From Here

- This chapter used a few Word objects as examples. To get the full scoop on other objects available in Word, **see** Chapter 7, "Programming Word," **p. 115**.

- For the details on Excel's objects, **see** Chapter 8, "Programming Excel," **p. 139**.

- Controlling code often depends on interaction with the user. For example, you might use `If...Then...Else` to test the value of a check box, or `Select Case` to process a group of option buttons. To find out more about these topics, **see** Chapter 12, "Creating Custom VBA Dialog Boxes," **p. 237**.

- A big part of procedure control involves anticipating potential user errors. To learn more about this topic, **see** Chapter 16, "Debugging VBA Procedures," **p. 337**.

6

Putting VBA to Work

II

Programming Word

7

Microsoft Word is a large, complex program, so it will come as no surprise that its list of objects is equally big and complicated. Fortunately, just as most people use only a tiny subset of Word's features, so too will you probably only use just a few of Word's objects in your VBA programming. In fact, with Word there are only really three levels of objects you'll need to worry about most of the time: Word itself, which is represented by the `Application` object; Word documents, which are represented by the `Document` object; and the text within those documents, which are represented by various objects, including `Range`, `Selection`, `Sentence`, and `Paragraph`. In this chapter you'll focus on programming these basic objects.

Working with Documents

In Word, the `Document` object appears directly below the `Application` object in the object hierarchy. As you'll see in the sections that follow, you can use VBA to create new documents, open or delete existing documents, save and close open documents, and much more.

Specifying a `Document` Object

If you need to do something with a document, or if you need to work with an object contained in a specific document (such as a section of text), you need to tell Word which document to use. VBA gives you three ways to do this:

- **Use the `Documents` object**—The `Documents` object is the collection of all open document files. To specify a particular document, either use its index number (where 1 represents the first document opened) or enclose the document name in quotation marks. For example, if `Memo.docx` was the first document opened, the following two expressions would be equivalent:

```
Documents("Memo.docx")
Documents(1)
```

- Use the `ActiveDocument` object—The `ActiveDocument` object represents the document that currently has the focus.

- Use the `ThisDocument` object—The `ThisDocument` object represents the document where the VBA code is executing. If your code deals only with objects residing in the same document as the code itself, you can use the `ActiveDocument` object. However, if your code deals with other documents, use `ThisDocument` whenever you need to make sure that the code affects only the document containing the procedure.

Opening a Document

To open a document file, use the `Open` method of the `Documents` collection. The `Open` method has a dozen arguments you can use to fine-tune your document openings, but only one of these is mandatory. Here's the simplified syntax showing the one required argument (for the rest of the arguments, look up the `Open` method in the VBA Help system):

```
Documents.Open(FileName)
```

    FileName   The name of the document file, including the drive and folder where the file is located.

For example, to open a document named `Letter.docx` in the `C:\Users\Paul\Documents` folder, you would use the following statement:

```
Documents.Open "C:\Users\Paul\Documents\Letter.docx"
```

>
> Rather than hard-coding the path to your user profile's Documents folder in Windows Vista, you can use the expression `Environ("UserProfile")`, which returns the path to your user profile's main folder. So, in Vista, you'd use the following expression to return your Documents folder:
>
>   `Environ("UserProfile") & "\Documents"`
>
> If you're using Windows XP, instead, replace `Documents` with `My Documents`. The `Environ` function (it's short for *environment*) returns the value of the Windows built-in environment variables. To see a list of these variables, choose Start, All Programs, Accessories, Command Prompt, type **set** at the command prompt, and then press Enter.

The `RecentFiles` Object

Another way to open Word documents is to use the `RecentFiles` object, which is the collection of the most recently used files displayed on Word's Office menu. Each item on this list is a `RecentFile` object.

You specify a `RecentFile` object by using `RecentFiles(Index)`, where *Index* is an integer that specifies the file you want to work with. The most-recently used file is 1, the second most-recently used file is 2, and so on.

> **TIP**
>
> The maximum value of *Index* is given by the `RecentFiles.Maximum` property. Note, too, that you can set this property. For example, the following statement sets the maximum value to 50 (the highest Word allows for this value):
>
>   RecentFiles.Maximum = 50

> **CAUTION**
>
> Be careful you don't specify an *Index* value that's greater than the number of items in the recent documents list. To check the maximum possible value for *Index*, use `RecentFiles.Count`.

Each `RecentFile` object comes with a `Name` property that returns the file's name, as well as a `Path` property that returns the file's path. Here's some code that uses these two properties to tell Word to open the most recently used file:

```
With RecentFiles(1)
    Documents.Open .Path & "\" & .Name
End With
```

That's useful, but it would be handy to have Word open the most recently used file each time you start the program. If you want Word to run some code each time it's started, follow these steps:

1. Open the Normal project in the Visual Basic Editor's Project Explorer.
2. Create a new module and rename it as `AutoExec`.
3. In this module, create a `Sub` procedure named `Main`.
4. Enter your code in that procedure.

Listing 7.1 shows a sample `Main` procedure that opens the most recently used file at startup.

Listing 7.1   A Procedure to Open the Most Recently Used Document at Startup

```
Sub Main()
    With RecentFiles(1)
        Documents.Open .Path & "\" & .Name
    End With
End Sub
```

7

> **NOTE**
>
> The code used in this chapter's listings can be found on my website at the following address:
>
> http://www.mcfedries.com/Office2007VBA/Chapter07.docm

Creating a New Document

If you need to create a new document, use the Documents collection's Add method:

```
Documents.Add([Template][, NewTemplate][, DocumentType][, Visible])
```

Template	This optional argument specifies the template file to use as the basis for the new document. Enter a string that spells out the path and name of the .DOT file. If you omit this argument, Word creates the new document based on the Normal template.
NewTemplate	If you set this optional argument to True, Word creates a new template file.
DocumentType	This optional argument determines the type of document that's created. Use one of the following constants:

wdNewBlankDocument	Creates a new, blank Word document (this is the default).
wdNewEmailMessage	Creates a new email message.
wdNewFrameset	Creates a new web frameset page.
wdNewWebPage	Creates a new web page.
wdNewXMLDocument	Creates a new XML document.

Visible	This is an optional Boolean value that determines whether Word displays the new document in a visible window. True is the default; use False to create the document without displaying it in a visible window.

Because all the Add method's arguments are optional, you can create a basic Word document based on the Normal template with the following simple statement:

```
Documents.Add
```

> **NOTE** After you create a new document, it automatically becomes the active document in the Word window, so you can use the ActiveDocument property to work with the new document (for example, to save it, as discussed in the next section).

Saving a Document

The worst nightmare of any Word user is a power failure or glitch that shuts down Word or even the computer itself while you have one or more documents open with unsaved changes. I know people who have lost *hours* of work when this has happened. We tell ourselves to save more often, but it's easy to forget in the heat of battle. Even Word's AutoRecover feature doesn't always work as advertised, so it can't be relied upon.

Using the Save **Method**

Fortunately, VBA proves very useful in solving this problem because it's easy to set up a procedure that takes the guesswork out of saving. Before you get to that, however, let's look at a few fundamental properties and methods of Document objects.

First up is the Save method:

```
Document.Save
```

      Document   This is a reference to the document you want to save.

For example, the following statement saves the active document:

```
ActiveDocument.Save
```

If you're dealing with a large document, you might not want to save it unnecessarily because the save operation may take a while. You can avoid that by first checking the document's Saved property. If this returns False, it means the document has unsaved changes. Here's an example:

```
If ActiveDocument.Saved = False Then
    ActiveDocument.Save
End If
```

The Save method will fail if the document is a new one that has never been saved before. How can you tell? There are two ways to tell whether a document is new and unsaved:

- You've just created the document using the Add method.
- Check the document's Path property. For a document that has been saved, Path returns the drive and folder in which the document is stored. (Note that the string returned by the Path property does not have a trailing backslash; for example, "C:\My Documents".) However, if the document has never been saved the Path property returns an empty string ("").

Here's a bit of code that checks the Path property before trying to save the active document:

```
If ActiveDocument.Path <> "" Then
    ActiveDocument.Save
End If
```

Listing 7.2 presents a procedure named SafeSave that combines these two checks so that it avoids saving new or unchanged documents.

Listing 7.2   A Procedure That Avoids Saving New or Unchanged Documents

```
Sub SafeSave()
    With ActiveDocument
        If .Path <> "" And .Saved = False Then
            .Save
        End If
    End With
End Sub
```

7

Using the SaveAs Method

If the document is new, use the SaveAs method instead.

```
Document.SaveAs([FileName][, FileFormat])
```

Document	The Document object you want to save to a different file.
FileName	(optional) The full name of the new document file, including the drive and folder where you want the file to reside. If you don't specify this value, Word uses the current folder and a default name (such as Doc1.docx).
FileFormat	(optional) The file format to which the document should be saved. You can either use a predefined wdSaveFormat constant or an integer that specifies the format (wdWordDocument is the default):

File Format	Constant	Integer Value
Word Document	wdFormatDocument	0
Document Template	wdFormatTemplate	1
Text Only	wdFormatText	2
Text Only with Line Breaks	wdFormatTextLineBreaks	3
MS-DOS Text	wdFormatDOSText	4
MS-DOS Text with Line Breaks	wdFormatDOSTextLineBreaks	5
Rich Text Format	wdFormatRTF	6
Unicode Text	wdFormatUnicodeText	7
Web Page	wdFormatHTML	8
Web Archive	wdFormatWebArchive	9
XML Document	wdFormatXML	12
PDF	wdFormatPDF	17
XPS	wdFormatXPS	18

> **NOTE** This is the simplified syntax for the SaveAs method. To see all 16 arguments in their full syntax, look up the SaveAs method in the VBA Help system.

Both of the following statements are equivalent (that is, they both save the active document as a web page):

```
ActiveDocument.SaveAs "index.html", wdFormatHTML
ActiveDocument.SaveAs "index.html", 8
```

Closing a Document

When you no longer need a document, you can reduce clutter on the screen and within Word by using the `Close` method to close the corresponding `Document` object:

```
Document.Close([SaveChanges][, OriginalFormat][, RouteDocument])
```

Document	The `Document` object you want to close.
SaveChanges	(optional) If the document has been modified, this argument determines whether Word saves those changes:

`wdSaveChanges`	Saves changes before closing.
`wdDoNotSaveChanges`	Doesn't save changes.
`wdPromptToSaveChanges`	Asks the user whether he or she wants to save changes (this is the default).

OriginalFormat	Specifies the format to use when saving the document:

`wdOriginalFormat`	Saves the document in its original format (this is the default).
`wdWordDocument`	Saves the document in Word format.
`wdPromptUser`	Asks the user whether he wants to save the document in its original format.

RouteDocument	If set to `True`, this argument tells Word to route the document to the next recipient.

For example, the following statement closes the active document and saves any changes:

```
ActiveDocument.Close wdSaveChanges
```

Closing All Open Documents

Later in this book you'll learn how to create *workspaces*—collections of Word documents that you open as a unit. Before you open a workspace, it's a good idea to close all your open documents. You might also want to close all your open documents to get a fresh start with Word. In previous versions of Word you could do this by holding down the Shift key, pulling down the File menu, and then selecting the Close All command. Unfortunately, that trick no longer works in Word 2007. The other alternative is to shut down and restart Word, but that's often time-consuming. A faster method is to use the macro in Listing 7.3.

> **TIP**
>
> The Close All command still exists in Word, but it's not part of the Ribbon. To add it to the Quick Access Toolbar, pull down the Customize Quick Access toolbar list and click More Commands. In the Choose Commands From list, click All Commands, scroll down the list of commands, and click Close All. Click Add and then click OK.

7

Listing 7.3   A Macro That Closes All Open Documents

```
Sub CloseAllOpenDocuments()
    Dim doc As Document
    For Each doc In Documents
        doc.Close
    Next 'doc
End Sub
```

This macro uses a `For Each...Next` loop to run through all the `Document` objects in the `Documents` collection. For each document, the macro runs the `Close` method without any arguments, which means that Word prompts you to save changes.

Example: Making Document Backups

Let's put the `Document` object to work by creating a procedure that not only saves a document, but also makes a backup copy to another location. Listing 7.4 shows a procedure named `MakeBackup` that does all this by using the `SaveAs` method as well as a few other methods and properties of the `Document` object.

Listing 7.4   A Procedure That Creates a Backup Copy of the Active Document on a Floppy Disk

```
Sub MakeBackup()
    Dim currFile As String
    Dim backupFile As String
    Const BACKUP_FOLDER = "G:\Backups\"
    With ActiveDocument
        '
        ' Don't bother if the document is unchanged or new
        '
        If .Saved Or .Path = "" Then Exit Sub
        '
        ' Mark current position in document
        '
        .Bookmarks.Add Name:="LastPosition"
        '
        ' Turn off screen updating
        '
        Application.ScreenUpdating = False
        '
        ' Save the file
        '
        .Save
        '
        ' Store the current file path, construct the path for the
        ' backup file, and then save it to the backup drive
        '
        currFile = .FullName
        backupFile = BACKUP_FOLDER & .Name
        .SaveAs FileName:=backupFile
    End With
    '
    ' Close the backup copy (which is now active)
    '
```

```
        ActiveDocument.Close
        '
        ' Reopen the current file
        '
        Documents.Open FileName:=currFile
        '
        ' Return to the pre-backup position
        '
        Selection.GoTo What:=wdGoToBookmark, Name:="LastPosition"
        '
        ' Turn screen updating back on
        '
        Application.ScreenUpdating = True
End Sub
```

The procedure opens by declaring some variables, including a constant called BACKUP_ FOLDER that stores the folder to which the backup copy will be saved. (If you plan on using this macro, you'll almost certainly need to modify the value of this constant.) The procedure then checks to see whether the backup operation is necessary. In other words, if the document has no unsaved changes (the Saved property returns True) or if it's a new, unsaved document (the Path property returns ""), bail out of the procedure (by running Exit Sub).

Otherwise, a new Bookmark object is created to save the current position in the document. (This ensures that when the procedure re-opens the document after running SaveAs later on, you'll be returned to your place in the document.) Bookmarks is a collection that holds all the defined bookmarks in a specified Document object. Each element of this collection is a Bookmark object. To add a bookmark, use the Add method, as follows:

Document.Bookmarks.Add Name:= *BookmarkName*

Document	The Document object with which you want to work.
BookmarkName	A string that specifies the name of the bookmark.

Then the following statement turns off screen updating, which means you won't see the opening and closing of files that occurs later in the code:

Application.ScreenUpdating = False

Then the Save method is used to save the file. You're now ready to perform the backup. First, the currFile variable is used to stored the document's full pathname (that is, the document's drive, folder, and filename), which is given by the FullName property. Then the pathname of the backup file is built with the following statement:

backupFile = BACKUP_FOLDER & .Name

This is used to save the file to the folder specified by BACKUP_FOLDER.

The actual backup takes place via the SaveAs method, which saves the document to the path given by backupFile. From there, the procedure closes the backup file, reopens the original file, and uses the GoTo method to return to the original position within the document.

7

Automating the Backup Procedure

Rather than running the MakeBackup procedure by hand, it would be better to schedule backups at specific times or at regular intervals. You can do this by using the Application object's OnTime method, which runs a procedure at a specified time, using the following syntax:

```
Application.OnTime(When, Name[, Tolerance])
```

When	The time (and date, if necessary) you want the procedure to run. Enter a date/time serial number.
Name	The name (entered as text) of the procedure to run when the time given by *When* arrives.
Tolerance	If Word isn't ready to run the procedure at *When*, it keeps trying for the number of seconds specified by *Tolerance*. If you omit *Tolerance*, VBA waits until Word is ready.

The easiest way to enter a time serial number for the *When* argument is to use the TimeValue function:

```
TimeValue(Time)
```

Time	A string representing the time you want to use (such as "5:00PM" or "17:00").

For example, the following formula runs the MakeBackup procedure at 5:00 p.m.:

```
Application.OnTime _
    When:=TimeValue("5:00PM"), _
    Name:="MakeBackup"
```

That's fine, but what we really want is the OnTime method to run after a specified time interval (for example, a half hour from now). To make this happen, use Now + TimeValue(*Time*) for *When* (where *Time* is the interval you want to use). For example, the following statement schedules the MakeBackup procedure to run in 5 minutes:

```
Application.OnTime _
    When:=Now + TimeValue("00:05:00"), _
    Name:="MakeBackup"
```

Add this code to the end of the MakeBackup procedure, and Word will automatically run the backup every five minutes.

Working with Text

Although you can add lines, graphics, and other objects to a document, text is what Word is all about. So it won't come as any surprise to you that Word has a truckload of objects that give you numerous ways to work with text. Five of these objects are quite useful: Range, Selection, Words, Sentences, and Paragraphs. The next few sections take you through each of these objects.

Working with the Range **Object**

If you've used VBA with Excel, you probably know that Excel has no separate object to represent a cell. Instead, a cell is considered to be just an instance of the generic Range class.

Along similar lines, Word has no separate objects for its most fundamental text units: the character and the word. Like Excel, Word considers these items to be instances of a generic class, which is also called the Range object. A Range object is defined as a continuous section of text in a document: a few characters in a row, a few words in a row, and few paragraphs in a row, or whatever. A range can be anything from a single character to an entire document, as long as the text within the range is continuous.

There are two basic methods for returning a Range object: the Document object's Range method and the Range property.

The Range **Method**

The Document object has a Range method that lets you specify starting and ending points for a range. Here's the syntax:

```
Document.Range(Start,End)
```

Document	The Document object with which you want to work.
Start	The starting character position. Note that the first character in a document is at position 0.
End	The ending character position. Note that this character is *not* included in the range.

For example, the following statements use the myRange object variable to store the first 100 characters (0 through 99) in the active document:

```
Dim myRange As Range
myRange = ActiveDocument.Range(0, 100)
```

The Range **Property**

Many Word objects have a Range property that returns a Range object, including the Paragraph and Selection objects (discussed later). This is important because these objects lack certain properties and methods that are handy for manipulating text. For example, the Paragraph object doesn't have an Italic property. The Range object does, however, so you format a paragraph's font as italic programmatically by referring to its Range property, like so:

```
ActiveDocument.Paragraphs(1).Range.Italic = True
```

This statement formats the first paragraph in the active document with italic text. (I discuss the Paragraphs collection in a moment.)

7

Reading and Changing Range Text

The Range object has a Text property that returns the text in the specified range. You can also use the Text property to set the text within the specified range. For example, the following code fragment checks the text in a document called letter.docx to see whether the first four characters equal the string "Dear"; if so, the text is replaced with "Greetings":

```
With Documents("letter.docx").Range.(0,4)
    If .Text = "Dear" Then
        .Text = "Greetings"
    End If
End With
```

Formatting Text

The Range object's properties also include many of the standard text formatting commands. For example, the Bold property returns True if the Range object is formatted entirely as bold, returns False if no part of the range is bold, and returns wdUndefined if only part of the range is formatted as bold. You can also set this property by using True (for bolding), False (to remove bolding), or wdToggle (to toggle the current setting between True and False).

A similar property is Italic, which returns True if the specified range is formatted entirely as italic, returns False if no part of the range is italic, and returns wdUndefined if only part of the range is formatted as italic. You can also set this property by using True (for italics), False (to remove italics), or wdToggle (to toggle the current setting between True and False).

Another useful property is Case, which returns or sets the case of the specified range. This property uses various wdCharacterCase constants, including wdLowerCase, wdTitleSentence, wdTitleWord, wdToggleCase, and wdUpperCase.

For example, the following code fragment takes the Range object of the active document's first paragraph, and then sets Bold to True, Italic to True, and the case to wdTitleWord:

```
With ActiveDocument.Paragraphs(1).Range
    .Bold = True
    .Italic = True
    .Case = wdTitleWord
End With
```

If you want maximum control over the character formatting in a range, use the Font property, which returns a Font object. From there you can manipulate not only the Bold and Italic properties, but also the type size (the Size property), the color (Color), strikethrough (StrikeThrough and DoubleStrikeThrough), small caps (SmallCaps), and much more. Here's an example:

```
With ActiveDocument.Range.Font
    .Color = RGB(0, 0, 255)
    .Size = 12
    .SmallCaps = True
End With
```

Inserting Text

If you need to insert text into a document, Word offers several `Range` object methods. In most cases, you start by inserting a paragraph into the document, which you do by running the `InsertParagraphAfter` method. For example, the current cursor position is given by the `Selection` object (which I discuss in detail later). To insert a new paragraph after the current cursor position, you'd use the following statement:

```
Selection.InsertParagraphAfter
```

You can also run the `InsertParagraphBefore` method to insert a paragraph before the specified range, or the `InsertParagraph` method, which inserts a paragraph that replaces the specified range.

With your new paragraph ready, you can then insert text using the `InsertAfter` method, which inserts text after the specified range:

```
Range.InsertAfter(Text)
```

> *Range*   The `Range` object after which you want to insert the text.
>
> *Text*   The text to insert.

For example, the following statement inserts the current date at beginning of the active document:

```
ActiveDocument.Range(0, 0).InsertAfter Date
```

Alternatively, you can use the `InsertBefore` method, which inserts text before the specified *Range*:

```
Range.InsertBefore(Text)
```

> *Range*   The `Range` object before which you want to insert the text.
>
> *Text*   The text to insert.

One common Word task is to start a new document and then populate it with some kind of repeated text. For example, when I start a new chapter of a book, I create a separate document that holds copies of all the chapter's figures, which I then annotate as I go along. Under each image, I add captions such as Figure 7.1, Figure 7.2, and so on. Rather than insert these numbers by hand, I use a macro that prompts me for the chapter number and the total number of figures I think I'll need. The macro then inserts the figure numbers automatically. Listing 7.5 shows a version of this macro.

Listing 7.5   A Procedure That Inserts Paragraphs and Text

```
Public Sub InsertParagraphsAndText()
    Dim nChapter As Integer
    Dim nFigures As Integer
    Dim i As Integer
    '
    ' Get the chapter number
    '
```

7

continues

Listing 7.5   Continued

```
    nChapter = InputBox("What's the chapter number?")
    '
    ' Get the total number of figures
    '
    nFigures = InputBox("How many figures?")
    '
    ' Insert the figure numbers
    '
    For i = 1 To nFigures
        Selection.InsertParagraphAfter
        Selection.InsertAfter "Figure " & nChapter & "." & i
    Next 'i
End Sub
```

This procedure uses the InputBox function to prompt for the chapter number (stored in the nChapter variable) and the total number of figures (stored in the nFigures variable). It then uses a For loop to add the figure numbers, first by inserting a paragraph and then by inserting the figure text. Figure 7.1 shows an example document with some figure numbers added by this macro.

Figure 7.1
Figure numbers
inserted into a docu-
ment by the code in
Listing 7.5.

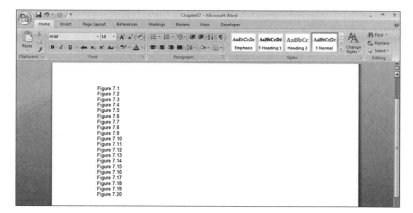

Deleting Text

Range.Delete—If used without arguments, this method deletes the entire Range. However, you can fine-tune your deletions by using the following syntax:

Range.Delete([Unit][, Count])

Range	The Range object containing the text you want to delete.
Unit	(optional) A constant that specifies whether you're deleting characters (use wdCharacter) or entire words (use wdWord). If you omit this argument, VBA assumes you're deleting characters.
Count	(optional) The number of units to delete. Use a positive number to delete forward; use a negative number to delete backward. (The default is 1.)

For example, the following statement deletes five characters, starting at the current cursor position:

```
Selection.Delete Unit:=wdCharacter, Count:=5
```

Using the Selection Object

The Selection object always references one of two things:

- The selected text.
- The position of the insertion point cursor.

Because much of what you do in Word involves one of these two items (formatting text, inserting text at the insertion point, and so on), the Selection object is one of the most important in Word. (I'm simplifying things a bit for this discussion because the Selection object can also refer to a selected shape, inline shape, or block. I'll deal only with text-related selections in this section.)

You reference the currently selected text or insertion point by using the Selection property without an object qualifier. For example, the following statement formats the selected text as bold:

```
Selection.Range.Bold = True
```

To create a Selection object, use the Select method, which is available with a number of Word objects, including Document, Range, Bookmark, and Table. For example, the following statement selects the first paragraph in the active document:

```
ActiveDocument.Paragraphs(1).Range.Select
```

The Selection object offers many of the same methods as does the Range object, including Delete, InsertAfter, InsertBefore, InsertParagraphAfter, and InsertParagraphBefore.

Checking the Selection Type

The Selection object has a number of properties, including many that you've seen already with the Document and Range objects. The few properties that are unique to the Selection object aren't particularly useful, so I won't discuss them here. The lone exception is the Type property, which returns the type of selection:

wdNoSelection	Nothing is selected.
wdSelectionColumn	A column in a table is selected.
wdSelectionIP	The selection is the insertion point.
wdSelectionNormal	Some text is selected.
wdSelectionRow	A row in a table is selected.

7

Moving the Insertion Point

The insertion point is the simplest form of the `Selection` object. If your code needs to move the insertion point, the easiest way to do this is to use the `Move` method, which collapses the current selection and moves the insertion point by a specified number of units. You can also use the `MoveEnd` method to move the insertion point to the end of the specified unit (such as a paragraph), or the `MoveStart` method to move the insertion point to the beginning of the specified unit. (Note that all three methods return the number of units that the insertion point was moved.) The syntax is the same for each method:

```
Selection.Move([Unit][, Count])
Selection.MoveEnd([Unit][, Count])
Selection.MoveStart([Unit][, Count])
```

Unit	(optional) Specifies the unit by which the insertion point is moved. For regular text, use `wdCharacter` (this is the default), `wdWord`, `wdLine`, `wdSentence`, `wdParagraph`, `wdSection`, or `wdStory`. In a table, use `wdCell`, `wdColumn`, `wdRow`, or `wdTable`.
Count	(optional) The number of units by which the insertion point is moved (the default is 1).

For example, you probably know that Word offers many keyboard shortcuts for navigating characters, words, paragraphs, screens, and so on. You can press Ctrl+left arrow or Ctrl+right arrow to move word by word, Ctrl+up arrow and Ctrl+down arrow to move paragraph by paragraph, and so on. However, Word does *not* have a keyboard shortcut for moving from one sentence to another, which is sorely missed. To implement this useful shortcut yourself, use the macros in Listing 7.6 to navigate forward and backward one sentence.

Listing 7.6   Macros to Navigate from One Sentence to Another

```
Sub GoToNextSentence()
    Selection.Move wdSentence, 1
End Sub
Sub GoToPreviousSentence()
    Selection.Move wdSentence, -1
End Sub
```

> **TIP** For maximum convenience, assign shortcut keys to the macros in Listing 7.6. Choose Office, Word Options, click Customize, and then click the Customize button. In the Categories list, click Macros, click the procedure name in the Macros list, and then click inside the Press New Shortcut Key box. Press the shortcut key (for example, Ctrl+Alt+Shift+left arrow for `GoToNextSentence` and Ctrl+Alt+Shift+right arrow for `GoToPreviousSentence`), and then click Assign.

Extending the Selection

When you use the Selection object, it's important to know how to manipulate the currently selected text by extending the selection. The simplest way to extend the selection is with the various Move commands that either move the insertion point or extend the selection in a particular direction:

```
Selection.MoveDown([Unit][, Count][, Extend])
Selection.MoveLeft([Unit][, Count][, Extend])
Selection.MoveRight([Unit][, Count][, Extend])
Selection.MoveUp([Unit][, Count][, Extend])
```

Unit	(optional) Specifies the unit by which the insertion point is moved or the selection is extended. For regular text, use wdCharacter, wdWord, wdLine (this is the default), wdSentence, wdParagraph, wdSection, or wdStory. In a table, use wdColumn, or wdRow.
Count	(optional) The number of units by which the insertion point is moved or the selection is extended (the default is 1).
Extend	(optional) Specifies what happens to the selection. To extend the selection to the end of the specified number of Units, use wdExtend; to collapse the selection to the insertion point, use wdMove (this is the default).

Listing 7.7 offers a procedure that puts a couple of these methods to the text.

Listing 7.7   A Procedure That Uses Selection Extension to Format Different Aspects of a Paragraph

```
Sub FormatFirstParagraph()
    '
    ' Select the first word in the first paragraph
    '
    ActiveDocument.Paragraphs(1).Range.Words(1).Select
    With Selection
        '
        ' Extend the select to the first three words
        '
        .MoveRight wdWord, 2, wdExtend
        '
        ' Convert the selection to uppercase
        '
        .Range.Case = wdUpperCase
        '
        ' Extend the selection to the entire paragraph
        '
        .MoveDown wdParagraph, 1, wdExtend
        '
        ' Set the paragraph font size to 14
        '
        .Range.Font.Size = 14
        '
```

7

continues

Listing 7.7 Continued

```
        ' Move the insertion point to the next paragraph
        '
        .Move wdParagraph, 1
    End With
End Sub
```

This procedure begins by selecting the first word in the first paragraph. Using the `Selection` object, the procedure then applies the `MoveRight` method to select the next two words, and then formats those words as uppercase. The procedure then uses the `MoveDown` method to extend the selection to the entire paragraph, which is then formatted with a 14-point font.

Collapsing the Selection

When you no longer want text selected, you can use the `Move`, `MoveEnd`, or `MoveStart` methods to automatically collapse the selection and move the insertion point. Sometimes, however, you might prefer to place the insertion point either at the beginning or the end of the current selection. To so that, use the `Collapse` method:

```
Selection.Collapse [Direction]
```

> `Direction` (optional) Specifies where you want the insertion point to end up. Use `wdCollapseStart` to position the cursor at the beginning of the `Selection` (this is the default). Use `wdCollapseEnd` to position the cursor at the end of the `Selection`.

For example, in Listing 7.7 (presented in the previous section), the procedure ends by using the `Move` method to move the insertion point to the next paragraph. If you prefer to leave the insertion point at the end of the selected paragraph, you need to do two things: extend the selection to the left by one character to remove the paragraph mark from the selection, and then perform the collapse:

```
.MoveLeft wdCharacter, 1, wdExtend
.Collapse wdCollapseEnd
```

Using the Words Object

The `Words` object is a collection that represents all the words in whatever object is specified. For example, `ActiveDocument.Words` is the collection of all the words in the active document. Other objects that have the `Words` property are `Paragraph`, `Range`, and `Selection`.

You refer to individual words by using an index number with the Words collection. As I mentioned earlier, however, this doesn't return a "Word" object; there is no such thing in Microsoft Word's VBA universe. Instead, individual words are classified as `Range` objects (see "Working with the `Range` Object" earlier in this chapter).

The following statement formats the first word in the active document as bold:

```
ActiveDocument.Words(1).Font.Bold = True
```

To count the number of words in the specified object, use the Count property:

```
totalWords = Documents("Article.docx").Words.Count
```

Note, however, that the Words object includes the punctuation and paragraph marks inside the object, which is certainly bizarre behavior, and serves to render the Words.Count property more or less useless. If you want to know the number of real words in an object, use the CountWords function shown in Listing 7.8.

Listing 7.8   A Function That Counts the Number of "Real" Words in an Object, Ignoring Punctuation Marks and Paragraph Marks

```
Function CountWords(countObject As Object) As Long
    Dim i As Long, word As Range
    i = 0
    For Each word In countObject.Words
        Select Case Asc(Left(word, 1))
            Case 48 To 57, 65 To 90, 97 To 122
                i = i + 1
        End Select
    Next 'word
    CountWords = i
End Function

Sub TestCountWords()
    With ActiveDocument
        MsgBox "Words.Count reports " & .Words.Count & Chr(13) & _
               "CountWords reports " & CountWords(.Range)
    End With
End Sub
```

This function takes a generic object as an argument (because the function can work with a Document, Range, or Selection object). It then uses a For Each loop to run through each word in the object. With each loop, the ASCII value of the leftmost character is plugged into a Select Case statement. If that value is between 48 and 90 or between 97 and 122, it means the character is either a number or a letter. If so, the function counts the word as a "real" word and increments the counter (the variable named i).

Working with the Sentences **Object**

The next rung on Word's text object ladder is the Sentences object. This is a collection of all the sentences in whatever object you specify, be it a Document, Range, or Selection.

As with Words, you refer to specific members of the Sentences collection by an index number, and the resulting object is a Range. For example, the following statement stores the active document's first sentence in the firstSentence variable:

7

```
firstSentence = ActiveDocument.Sentences(1)
```

Again, the `Count` property can be used to return the total number of sentences in an object. In the following procedure fragment, the `Count` property is used to determine the last sentence in a document:

```
With Documents("Remarks.docx")
    totalSentences = .Sentences.Count
    lastSentence = .Sentences(totalSentences)
End With
```

Displaying Sentence Word Counts

You can configure Word's grammar checker to show the average number of words per sentence in a document. That's useful because you don't want a document to have many long sentences. However, in a long document it's also important to have a variety of sentence lengths, but the grammar checker can't help you with this.

> **NOTE** To configure the grammar checker to show the average number of words per sentence, choose Office, Word Options, click Proofing, and activate the Show Readability Statistics check box.

To see the lengths of the sentences in a document, use the code in Listing 7.9.

Listing 7.9   A Macro That Displays the Lengths of Sentences in the Active Document

```
Sub DisplaySentenceLengths()
    Dim s As Range
    Dim maxWords As Integer
    Dim i As Integer
    Dim sentenceLengths() As Integer
    Dim str As String

    With ActiveDocument
        '
        ' Run through all the sentences to find the longest
        '
        maxWords = 0
        For Each s In .Sentences
            If CountWord(s) > maxWords Then
                maxWords = CountWord(s)
            End If
        Next 's
        '
        ' Redimension the array of sentence lengths
        '
```

```
        ReDim sentenceLengths(maxWords)
        '
        ' Run through the sentences again to count
        ' the number of sentences for each length
        '
        For Each s In .Sentences
            '
            ' Get the word count for the sentence
            '
            j = CountWords(s)
            '
            ' If it's not empty, add it to the array
            '
            If j > 0 Then
                sentenceLengths(j - 1) = sentenceLengths(j - 1) + 1
            End If
        Next 's
        '
        ' Construct the string that displays the sentence lengths
        ' and their frequencies
        '
        str = "Sentence Length:" & vbTab & "Frequency:" & vbCrLf & vbCrLf
        '
        ' The UBound() function tells you the upper bound of an array.
        ' In this case, it tells you the largest value in sentenceLengths.
        '
        For i = 0 To UBound(sentenceLengths) - 1
            '
            ' Build the string
            '
            str = str & IIf(i + 1 < 10, "  ", "") & i + 1 & _
                IIf(i = 0, " word:  ", " words: ") & _
                vbTab & vbTab & sentenceLengths(i) & vbCrLf
        Next 'i
        '
        ' Display the string
        '
        MsgBox str
    End With
End Sub
```

Using the `ActiveDocument` object, the macro makes a first pass through all the sentences to find the one with the most words. Notice that the procedure uses the `CountWords` function from Listing 7.8 to get accurate word counts for each `Sentence` object. The macro then uses this maximum word count to redimension the `sentenceLengths` array, which is used to hold the number of occurrences of each sentence length within the document. To calculate these frequencies, the macro then runs through all the sentences again and increments the array values for each length. The macro finishes by constructing and then displaying a string that holds the sentence lengths and frequencies. Figure 7.2 shows an example.

7

Figure 7.2
The `Display Sentence Lengths` macro displays a message box such as this to show you the document's sentence lengths and the frequency with which each length occurs.

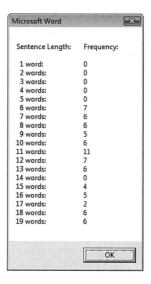

```
Microsoft Word                        ✕

    Sentence Length:    Frequency:

    1 word:             0
    2 words:            0
    3 words:            0
    4 words:            0
    5 words:            0
    6 words:            7
    7 words:            6
    8 words:            6
    9 words:            5
    10 words:           6
    11 words:           11
    12 words:           7
    13 words:           6
    14 words:           0
    15 words:           4
    16 words:           5
    17 words:           2
    18 words:           6
    19 words:           6


              [    OK    ]
```

> **TIP**
>
> To display word count data for each paragraph, replace `.Sentences` in Listing 7.2 with `.Paragraphs`.

Programming the `Paragraph` **Object**

From characters, words, and sentences, you make the next logical text leap: paragraphs. A `Paragraph` object is a member of the `Paragraphs` collection, which represents all the paragraphs in the specified `Document`, `Range`, or `Selection`. As with the other text objects, you use an index number with the `Paragraphs` object to specify an individual paragraph.

One common scenario is to run through all the paragraphs in a document and either modify each paragraph in some way or check for some kind of paragraph property. Here's a code snippet that shows the general procedure for doing this:

```
Dim p As Paragraph
For Each p In ActiveDocument.Paragraphs
    [VBA statements]
Next 'p
```

For example, it's often useful to add a set of hyperlinks to a document that enable the reader to jump to a particular heading. Listing 7.10 presents a macro that does just that.

7

Listing 7.10   A Procedure That Inserts Hyperlinks for a Specified Style of Heading

```
Sub InsertHyperlinks(heading As String)
    Dim b As Bookmark
    Dim p As Paragraph
    Dim lastParagraph As Paragraph
    Dim totalParagraphs As Integer
```

```
        Dim i As Integer
        i = 0
        With ActiveDocument
            '
            ' Delete the existing "Anchor" bookmarks
            '
            For Each b In .Bookmarks
                If InStr(b.Name, "Anchor") Then b.Delete
            Next 'b
            '
            ' Run through the paragraphs
            '
            totalParagraphs = .Paragraphs.Count
            For Each p In .Paragraphs
                '
                ' Look for the specified style
                '
                If p.Style = heading Then
                    '
                    ' Create a bookmark (Anchor1, Anchor2, etc.)
                    '
                    i = i + 1
                    .Bookmarks.Add "Anchor" & i, p.Range
                End If
            Next 'p
            '
            ' Run through the bookmarks
            '
            For Each b In .Bookmarks
                '
                ' Work only with the "Anchor" bookmarks
                '
                If InStr(b.Name, "Anchor") <> 0 Then
                    '
                    ' Add a paragraph at the end of the document
                    '
                    Set lastParagraph = .Paragraphs(.Paragraphs.Count)
                    lastParagraph.Range.InsertParagraphAfter
                    '
                    ' Turn the last paragraph into a
                    ' hyperlink to the bookmarked header
                    '
                    lastParagraph.Range.Hyperlinks.Add _
                        Anchor:=lastParagraph.Range, _
                        Address:="", _
                        SubAddress:=b.Name, _
                        ScreenTip:=b.Range.Text, _
                        TextToDisplay:=b.Range.Text
                End If
            Next 'b
        End With
    End Sub
```

The idea here is that given a style name represented by the `heading` variable, the procedure will look for paragraphs that have that style, and then set up bookmarks for each paragraph, each of which will have the name Anchor*n*, where *n* is an integer (Anchor1, Anchor2, and so on). So the procedure begins by running through all the active document's bookmarks and deleting those that have a name that includes Anchor. (This enables you to run this procedure multiple times without generating errors.) Then the procedure runs through every paragraph in the active document, and looks for those paragraphs that use whatever style is specified as the heading argument. When it finds such a paragraph, it creates a new Bookmark object for the paragraph. Then the procedure runs through all the bookmarks once again, and each time it comes across an Anchor bookmark it inserts a paragraph at the end of the document and adds a hyperlink that points to the bookmark.

> NOTE I don't discuss programming hyperlinks in this book, but the text in the example file (Chapter07.docm) contains a tutorial on creating and working with hyperlinks via VBA.

From Here

- To learn how to use the InputBox function, **see** "Getting Input Using InputBox," **p. 50**.
- For a general discussion of VBA objects, **see** Chapter 5, "Working with Objects," **p. 71**.
- You use For Each...Next loops quite often when dealing with the Words, Sentences, and Paragraphs collections; **see** "Using For Each...Next Loops," **p. 109**.

7

Programming Excel

8

If you're using VBA in Excel, most of your procedures will eventually do something to the Excel environment. They might open a workbook, rename a worksheet, select a cell or range, enter a formula, or even set some of Excel's options. Therefore, knowing how VBA interacts with Excel is crucial if you ever hope to write useful routines. This chapter looks closely at that interaction. You learn how to work with all the most common Excel objects, including the Workbook, Worksheet, and Range objects.

Excel's Application Object

You begin, however, with the Application object. Recall that in Chapter 5, "Working with Objects," you learned a few Application object properties and methods that are common to all VBA applications. As you can imagine, though, each application has its own unique set of properties and methods for the Application object. Excel is no exception, as you'll see in this section.

Accessing Worksheet Functions

VBA has dozens of functions of its own, but its collection is downright meager compared to the hundreds of worksheet functions available with Excel. If you need to access one of these worksheet functions, VBA makes them available via a property of the Application object called WorksheetFunction. Each function works exactly as it does on a worksheet—the only difference being that you have to append Application. to the name of the function.

For example, to run the SUM() worksheet function on the range named Sales and store the result in a variable named totalSales, you'd use the following statement:

```
totalSales = Application.WorksheetFunction.Sum(Range("Sales"))
```

> **CAUTION**
>
> The WorksheetFunction object includes only those worksheet functions that don't duplicate an existing VBA function. For example, VBA has a UCase function that's equivalent to Excel's UPPER() worksheet function (both convert a string into uppercase). In this case, you must use VBA's UCase function in your code. If you try to use Application.WorksheetFunction. Upper, you'll receive an error message. For a complete list of VBA functions, see Appendix B, "VBA Functions."

Recalculating Workbooks

The Application object features a couple of methods that enable you to recalculate the open workbooks if you've turned off automatic recalculation:

- Calculate—Calculates all the open workbooks. Specifically, this method recalculates only those formulas with cell precedents that have changed values. (This is equivalent to pressing F9, or clicking Calculate Now in the Ribbon's Formulas tab.) Note that you don't need to specify the Application object. You can just enter Calculate by itself.

> **NOTE** A *precedent* is a cell that is directly or indirectly referenced in a formula.

- Application.CalculateFull—Runs a full calculation of all the open workbooks. Specifically, this method recalculates every formula in each workbook, even those with cell precedents that haven't changed values. (This is equivalent to pressing Ctrl+Alt+F9.) Note that for this method you must specify the Application object.

Converting a String into an Object

Excel's Application object comes with an Evaluate method that converts a string into an Excel object, using the following syntax:

```
Evaluate(Name)
```

Name   A string that specifies a cell address, a range, or a defined name.

For example, Evaluate("A1") returns a Range object (that is, a cell or groups of cells; see "Working with Range Objects," later in this chapter) that represents cell A1 in the active worksheet. Listing 8.1 shows a more elaborate example that takes the value in cell A1 (the value is "A") and the value in cell B1 (the value is "2"), concatenates them, and then uses Evaluate to display the value from cell A2.

Listing 8.1   A Procedure That Tests the Evaluate **Function**

```
Sub EvaluateTest()
    Dim columnLetter As String
    Dim rowNumber As String
    Dim cellAddress As String
    '
    ' Activate the "Test Data" worksheet
    '
    Worksheets("Test Data").Activate
    '
    ' Get the value in cell A1
    '
    columnLetter = [A1].Value
    '
    ' Get the value in cell B1
    '
    rowNumber = [B1].Value
    '
    ' Concatenate the two values and then display the message
    '
    cellAddress = columnLetter & rowNumber
    MsgBox "The value in cell " & cellAddress & " is " & _
            Application.Evaluate(cellAddress)
End Sub
```

> **NOTE**   The code used in this chapter's examples can be found on my website at the following address:
> http://www.mcfedries.com/Office2007VBA/Chapter08.xlsm

Pausing a Running Macro

The Application object comes with a Wait method that pauses a running macro until a specified time is reached. Here's the syntax:

```
Application.Wait(Time)
```

Time   The time you want to macro to resume running.

For example, if you wanted your procedure to delay for about five seconds, you would use the following statement:

```
Application.Wait Now + TimeValue("00:00:05")
```

See "Running a Procedure at a Specific Time," later in this chapter, to learn more about the TimeValue function.

Some Event-Like Methods

Excel's Application object comes with several methods that are "event-like." In other words, they respond to outside influences such as the press of a key. This section looks at four of these methods: OnKey, OnTime, OnRepeat, and OnUndo.

Running a Procedure when the User Presses a Key

When recording a macro, Excel enables you to assign a Ctrl+*key* shortcut to a procedure. However, there are two major drawbacks to this method:

- Excel uses some Ctrl+*key* combinations internally, so your choices are limited.
- It doesn't help if you would like your procedures to respond to "meaningful" keys such as Delete and Esc.

To remedy these problems, use the `Application` object's `OnKey` method to run a procedure when the user presses a specific key or key combination:

```
Application.OnKey(Key[, Procedure])
```

> *Key*   The key or key combination that runs the procedure. For letters, numbers, or punctuation marks, enclose the character in quotes (for example, "a"). For other keys, see Table 8.1.
>
> *Procedure*   The name (entered as text) of the procedure to run when the user presses a key. If you enter the null string ("") for *Procedure*, a key is disabled. If you omit *Procedure*, Excel resets the key to its normal state.

Table 8.1   Key Strings to Use with the `OnKey` Method

Key	What to Use
Backspace	"{BACKSPACE}" or "{BS}"
Break	"{BREAK}"
Caps Lock	"{CAPSLOCK}"
Delete	"{DELETE}" or "{DEL}"
Down arrow	"{DOWN}"
End	"{END}"
Enter (keypad)	"{ENTER}"
Enter	"~" (tilde)
Esc	"{ESCAPE}" or "{ESC}"
Help	"{HELP}"
Home	"{HOME}"
Insert	"{INSERT}"
Left arrow	"{LEFT}"
Num Lock	"{NUMLOCK}"
Page Down	"{PGDN}"
Page Up	"{PGUP}"

Key	What to Use
Right arrow	`"{RIGHT}"`
Scroll Lock	`"{SCROLLLOCK}"`
Tab	`"{TAB}"`
Up arrow	`"{UP}"`
F1 through F12	`"{F1}"` through `"{F15}"`

You also can combine these keys with the Shift, Ctrl, and Alt keys. You just precede these codes with one or more of the codes listed in Table 8.2.

Table 8.2   Symbols That Represent Alt, Ctrl, and Shift in OnKey

Key	What to Use
Alt	% (percent)
Ctrl	^ (caret)
Shift	+ (plus)

For example, pressing Delete normally wipes out only a cell's contents. If you would like a quick way of deleting everything in a cell (contents, formats, comments, and so on), you could set up (for example) Ctrl+Delete to do the job. Listing 8.2 shows three procedures that accomplish this:

■ SetKey—This procedure sets up the Ctrl+Delete key combination to run the DeleteAll procedure. Notice how the *Procedure* argument includes the name of the workbook where the DeleteAll procedure is located; therefore, this key combination will operate in any workbook.

■ DeleteAll—This procedure runs the Clear method on the currently selected cells.

■ ResetKey—This procedure resets Ctrl+Delete to its default behavior.

Listing 8.2   Procedures That Use the OnKey **Method to Set and Reset a Key Combination**

```
Sub SetKey()
    Application.OnKey _
        Key:="^{Del}", _
        Procedure:="Chaptr08.xlsm!DeleteAll"
End Sub

Sub DeleteAll()
    Selection.Clear
End Sub

Sub ResetKey()
    Application.OnKey _
        Key:="^{Del}"
End Sub
```

Running a Procedure at a Specific Time

If you need to run a procedure at a specific time, use the OnTime method:

```
Application.OnTime(EarliestTime, Procedure[, LatestTime][, Schedule])
```

EarliestTime	The time (and date, if necessary) you want the procedure to run. Enter a date/time serial number.
Procedure	The name (entered as text) of the procedure to run when the EarliestTime arrives.
LatestTime	If Excel isn't ready to run the procedure at EarliestTime (in other words, if it's not in Ready, Cut, Copy, or Find mode), it will keep trying until LatestTime arrives. If you omit LatestTime, VBA waits until Excel is ready. Enter a date/time serial number.
Schedule	A logical value that determines whether the procedure runs at EarliestTime or not. If Schedule is True or omitted, the procedure runs. Use False to cancel a previous OnTime setting.

The easiest way to enter the time serial numbers for EarliestTime and LatestTime is to use the TimeValue function:

```
TimeValue(Time)
```

Time	A string representing the time you want to use (such as "5:00PM" or "17:00").

For example, the following formula runs a procedure called Backup at 5:00 p.m.:

```
Application.OnTime _
    EarliestTime:=TimeValue("5:00PM"), _
    Procedure:="Backup"
```

> **TIP** If you want the OnTime method to run after a specified time interval (for example, an hour from now), use Now + TimeValue(Time) for EarliestTime (where Time is the interval you want to use). For example, the following statement schedules a procedure to run in 30 minutes:
>
> ```
> Application.OnTime _
>     EarliestTime:=Now + TimeValue("00:30"), _
>     Procedure:="Backup"
> ```

Running a Procedure when the User Selects Repeat or Undo

Excel has a couple of event-like methods that run procedures when the user selects the Undo or Repeat commands.

> **TIP** The Repeat command (shortcut key: Ctrl+Y) doesn't appear in the Ribbon or the Quick Access toolbar (which holds the Undo command). To add the Repeat command to the Quick Access toolbar, pull down the Customize Quick Access Toolbar list and then click More Commands. Make sure Popular Commands appears in the Choose Commands From list, click Repeat, click Add, and then click OK.

The `OnRepeat` method customizes the name of the Repeat command (that is, the text that appears when you hover the mouse pointer over the Repeat button) and specifies the procedure that runs when the user clicks Repeat. Set this property at the end of a procedure so the user can easily repeat the procedure just by clicking Repeat. Here's the syntax:

```
Application.OnRepeat(Text, Procedure)
```

Text	The name of the Repeat command.
Procedure	The procedure to run when the user clicks Repeat (this is usually the name of the procedure that contains the `OnRepeat` statement).

The `OnUndo` method is similar to `OnRepeat`, except that it sets the name of the Undo command and specifies the procedure that runs when the user clicks Undo:

```
Application.OnUndo(Text, Procedure)
```

Text	The name of the Undo command.
Procedure	The procedure to run when the user clicks Undo.

Listing 8.3 shows an example that uses both `OnRepeat` and `OnUndo`. The `currCell` variable stores the address of the active cell. Notice that it's declared at the module level—that is, at the top of the module, above all the procedures— to make it available to all the procedures in the module. The `BoldAndItalic` procedure makes the font of the active cell bold and italic and then sets the `OnRepeat` property (to run `BoldAndItalic` again) and the `OnUndo` property (to run the procedure named `UndoBoldAndItalic`).

Listing 8.3   Procedures That Set the `OnRepeat` **and** `OnUndo` **Properties**

```
Dim currCell As String   ' The module-level variable
Sub BoldAndItalic()
    With ActiveCell
        .Font.Bold = True
        .Font.Italic = True
        currCell = .Address
    End With
    Application.OnRepeat _
        Text:="Repeat Bold and Italic", _
        Procedure:="BoldAndItalic"
    Application.OnUndo _
        Text:="Undo Bold and Italic", _
        Procedure:="UndoBoldAndItalic"
```

continues

8

Listing 8.3 Continued

```
End Sub

Sub UndoBoldAndItalic()
    With Range(currCell).Font
        .Bold = False
        .Italic = False
    End With
End Sub
```

Manipulating Workbook Objects

Workbook objects appear directly below the Application object in Excel's object hierarchy. You can use VBA to create new workbooks, open or delete existing workbooks, save and close open workbooks, and much more. The next section takes you through various techniques for specifying workbooks in your VBA code; then you'll look at some Workbook object properties and methods.

Specifying a Workbook Object

If you need to perform some action on a workbook, or if you need to work with an object contained in a specific workbook (such as a worksheet), you need to tell Excel which workbook you want to use. VBA gives you no fewer than three ways to do this:

- **Use the Workbooks object**—The Workbooks object is the collection of all the open workbook files. To specify a workbook, either use its index number (where 1 represents the first workbook opened) or enclose the workbook name in quotation marks. For example, if the Budget.xlsx workbook was the first workbook opened, the following two statements would be equivalent:

```
Workbooks(1)
Workbooks("Budget.xlsx")
```

- **Use the ActiveWorkbook object**—The ActiveWorkbook object represents the workbook that currently has the focus.

- **Use the ThisWorkbook object**—The ThisWorkbook object represents the workbook where the VBA code is executing. If your code deals only with objects residing in the same workbook as the code itself, you can use the ActiveWorkbook object. However, if your code deals with other workbooks, use ThisWorkbook whenever you need to make sure that the code affects only the workbook containing the procedure.

Opening a Workbook

To open a workbook file, use the Open method of the Workbooks collection. The Open method has a dozen arguments you can use to fine-tune your workbook openings, but only one of these is mandatory. Here's the simplified syntax showing the one required argument (for the rest of the arguments, look up the Open method in the VBA Help system):

```
Workbooks.Open(FileName)
```

FileName   The full name of the workbook file, including the
                                       drive and folder that contain the file.

For example, to open a workbook named `Data.xlsx` in your user profile's Documents
folder, you would use the following statement:

```
Workbooks.Open Environ("UserProfile") & "\Documents\Data.xlsx"
```

→ To learn about the `Environ` function, **see** the tip in the section "Opening a Document," **p. 116**.

Creating a New Workbook

If you need to create a new workbook, use the `Workbooks` collection's `Add` method:

```
Workbooks.Add(Template)
```

Template is an optional argument that determines how the workbook is created. If *Template*
is a string specifying an Excel file, VBA uses the file as a template for the new workbook.
You also can specify one of the following constants:

xlWBATWorksheet   Creates a workbook with a single worksheet.

xlWBATChart   Creates a workbook with a single chart sheet.

Here's a sample statement that uses the `Add` method to open a new workbook based on
Excel's `ExpenseReport.xltx` template file:

```
Workbooks.Add "C:\Program Files\Microsoft Office" & _
    "\Templates\1033\ExpenseReport.xltx"
```

Specifying the Number of Sheets in a New Workbook

When you create a new workbook in Excel, the file comes with three worksheets by
default. Most people just use one worksheet, but leave the other two sheets in the workbook, just in case. If you use several sheets in many or all of your workbooks, you should
consider increasing the default number of sheets that Excel includes in new workbooks.
Follow these steps:

1. Choose Office, Excel Options to open the Excel Options dialog box.
2. Click Popular.
3. Use the Include This Many Sheets spin box to set the number of sheets you want by
   default.
4. Click OK.

That's fine if you *always* use lots of sheets, but what if you use lots of sheets only occasionally? In that case, it would be nice to be able to specify the number of sheets you want as
you're creating a new workbook. The macro in Listing 8.4 enables you to do just that.

Listing 8.4   A Procedure That Prompts You to Specify the Number of Sheets You Want in a New Workbook

```
Sub NewWorkbookWithCustomSheets()
    Dim currentSheets As Integer
    With Application
        '
        ' Save the current value of SheetsInNewWorkbook
        '
        currentSheets = .SheetsInNewWorkbook
        '
        ' Ask how many sheets to include in the new workbook
        ' and store the result in SheetsInNewWorkbook
        '
        .SheetsInNewWorkbook = InputBox( _
            "How many sheets do you want " & _
            "in the new workbook?", , 3)
        '
        ' Create the new workbook
        '
        Workbooks.Add
        '
        ' Restore the original value of SheetsInNewWorkbook
        '
        .SheetsInNewWorkbook = currentSheets
    End With
End Sub
```

The value of the Include This Many Sheets setting is given by the Application object's SheetsInNewWorkbook property. The macro first stores the current SheetsInNewWorkbook value in the currentSheets variable. Then the macro runs the InputBox function to get the number of required sheets (with a default value of 3), and this value is assigned to the SheetsInNewWorkbook property. Then the Workbooks.Add statement creates a new workbook (which will have the specified number of sheets) and the SheetsInNewWorkbook property is returned to its original value.

Saving Every Open Workbook

If you often work with multiple workbooks at once, you may find yourself moving from one workbook to another, making changes to each one as you go. Unless you remember to save all along, you probably end up with some or all of your open workbooks with unsaved changes. Unfortunately, Excel doesn't tell you which workbooks have unsaved changes, so you have no choice but to trudge through each open workbook and run the Save command.

You can avoid this drudgery by using the SaveAll macro shown in Listing 8.5.

Listing 8.5   A Procedure That Saves Every Open Workbook

```
Sub SaveAll()
    Dim wb As Workbook
    Dim newFilename As Variant
    '
    ' Run through all the open workbooks
    '
    For Each wb In Workbooks
        '
        ' Has the workbook been saved before?
        '
        If wb.Path <> "" Then
            '
            ' If so, save it
            '
            wb.Save
        Else
            '
            ' If not, display the Save As dialog box
            ' to get the workbook's path & filename
            '
            With Application
                newFilename = .GetSaveAsFilename( _
                    FileFilter:="Microsoft Office " & _
                    "Excel Workbook " & _
                    "(*.xlsx), *.xlsx")
            End With
            '
            ' Did the user click Cancel?
            '
            If newFilename <> False Then
                '
                ' If not, save the workbook using the
                ' specified path and filename
                '
                wb.SaveAs fileName:=newFilename
            End If
        End If
    Next 'wb
End Sub
```

The main loop in the SaveAll macro uses the Workbooks collection and a For Each...Next loop to run through all the open workbooks. For each workbook (given by the wb Workbook variable), the loop first checks the Path property to see whether it returns the null string (""). If not, it means the workbook has been saved previously, so the macro runs the Save method to save the file. If Path does return the null string, it means you're saving the workbook for the first time. In this case, the macro runs the GetSaveAsFilename method, which displays the Save As dialog box so that you can select a save location and filename, which are stored in the newFilename variable. If this variable's value is False, it means you clicked Cancel in the Save As dialog box, so the macro skips the file; otherwise, the macro uses the SaveAs method to save the workbook, using the specified path and filename.

8

Closing a Workbook

To close a Workbook object, use the Close method, which uses the following syntax:

`Workbook.Close([SaveChanges][, FileName][, RouteWorkbook])`

Workbook	The Workbook object you want to close.
SaveChanges	If the workbook has been modified, this argument determines whether or not Excel saves those changes:

SaveChanges	Action
True	Saves changes before closing.
False	Doesn't save changes.
Omitted	Asks the user whether changes should be saved.

FileName	Save the workbook under this filename.
RouteWorkbook	Routes the workbook according to the following values:

RouteWorkbook	Action
True	Sends the workbook to the next recipient.
False	Doesn't send the workbook.
Omitted	Asks the user whether the workbook should be sent.

Dealing with Worksheet Objects

Worksheet objects contain a number of properties and methods you can exploit in your code. These include options for activating and hiding worksheets, adding new worksheets to a workbook, and moving, copying, and deleting worksheets. The next few sections discuss these and other worksheet operations.

Specifying a Worksheet Object

If you need to deal with a worksheet in some way, or if your code needs to specify an object contained in a specific worksheet (such as a range of cells), you need to tell Excel which worksheet you want to use. To do this, use the Worksheets object. Worksheets is the collection of all the worksheets in a particular workbook. To specify a worksheet, either use its index number (where 1 represents the first worksheet tab, 2 the second worksheet tab, and so on) or enclose the worksheet name in quotation marks. For example, if Sheet1 is the first worksheet, the following two statements would be equivalent:

```
Worksheets(1)
Worksheets("Sheet1")
```

Alternatively, if you want to work with whichever worksheet is currently active in a specified Workbook object, use the ActiveSheet property, as in this example:

```
currentWorksheet = Workbooks("Budget.xlsx").ActiveSheet
```

If you need to work with multiple worksheets (say, to set up a 3D range), use VBA's Array function with the Worksheets collection. For example, the following statement specifies the Sheet1 and Sheet2 worksheets:

```
Worksheets(Array("Sheet1","Sheet2"))
```

Creating a New Worksheet

The Worksheets collection has an Add method you can use to insert new sheets into the workbook. Here's the syntax for this method:

```
Worksheets.Add([Before][, After][, Count][, Type])
```

Before	The sheet before which the new sheet is added. If you omit both *Before* and *After*, the new worksheet is added before the active sheet.
After	The sheet after which the new sheet is added. Note that you can't specify both the *Before* and *After* arguments.
Count	The number of new worksheets to add. VBA adds one worksheet if you omit *Count*. If you set *Count* greater than 1, all the sheets are added in the same location, as specified by either *Before* or *After*.
Type	The type of worksheet. You have three choices—xlWorksheet (the default) and two constants that create Excel 4 macro sheets (which, therefore, you'll never use, because Excel 4 macros are long obsolete): xlExcel4MacroSheet and xlExcel4IntlMacroSheet.

In the following statement, a new worksheet is added to the active workbook before the Sales sheet:

```
Worksheets.Add Before:=Worksheets("Sales")
```

Properties of the Worksheet Object

Let's take a tour through some of the most useful properties associated with Worksheet objects:

- *Worksheet*.Name—Returns or sets the name of the specified *Worksheet*. For example, the following statement renames the Sheet1 worksheet to 2007 Budget:

  ```
  Worksheets("Sheet1").Name = "2007 Budget"
  ```

- *Worksheet*.StandardHeight—Returns the standard height of all the rows in the specified *Worksheet*.

8

- *Worksheet*.StandardWidth—Returns the standard width of all the columns in the specified *Worksheet*.

- UsedRange—Returns a *Range* object that represents the used range in the specified *Worksheet*.

- *Worksheet*.Visible—Controls whether or not the user can see the specified *Worksheet*. Setting this property to False is equivalent to selecting Format, Sheet, Hide. For example, to hide a worksheet named Expenses, you would use the following statement:

```
Worksheets("Expenses").Visible = False
```

To unhide the sheet, set its Visible property to True.

Methods of the Worksheet Object

Here's a list of some common Worksheet object methods:

- *Worksheet*.Activate—Makes the specified *Worksheet* active (so that it becomes the ActiveSheet property of the workbook). For example, the following statement activates the Sales worksheet in the Finance.xlsx workbook:

```
Workbooks("Finance.xlsx").Worksheets("Sales").Activate
```

- *Worksheet*.Calculate—Calculates the specified *Worksheet*. For example, the following statement recalculates the Budget 2007 worksheet:

```
Worksheets("Budget 2007").Calculate
```

- *Worksheet*.Copy—Copies the specified *Worksheet* to another location in the same workbook using the following syntax:

```
Worksheet.Copy([Before][, After])
```

Worksheet	The worksheet you want to copy.
Before	The sheet before which the sheet will be copied. If you omit both *Before* and *After*, VBA creates a new workbook for the copied sheet.
After	The sheet after which the new sheet is added. You can't specify both the *Before* and *After* arguments.

In the following statement, the Budget 2007 worksheet is copied to a new workbook:

```
Worksheets("Budget 2007").Copy
```

- *Worksheet*.Delete—Deletes the specified *Worksheet*. For example, the following statement deletes the active worksheet:

```
ActiveSheet.Delete
```

- *Worksheet*.Move—Moves the specified *Worksheet* to another location in the same workbook using the following syntax:

```
Worksheet.Move([Before][, After])
```

`Worksheet`	The worksheet you want to move.
`Before`	The sheet before which the sheet will be moved. If you omit both `Before` and `After`, VBA creates a new workbook for the moved sheet.
`After`	The sheet after which the new sheet is added. You can't specify both the `Before` and `After` arguments.

In the following statement, the Budget 2007 worksheet is moved before the Budget 2006 worksheet:

```
Worksheets("Budget 2007").Move Before:=Worksheets("Budget 2006")
```

- `Worksheet.Select`—Selects the specified `Worksheet`.

Working with Range Objects

Mastering cell and range references is perhaps the most fundamental skill to learn when working with spreadsheets. After all, most worksheet chores involve cells, ranges, and range names. However, this skill takes on added importance when you're dealing with VBA procedures. When you're editing a worksheet directly, you can easily select cells and ranges with the mouse or the keyboard, or you can paste range names into formulas. In a procedure, though, you always have to describe—or even calculate—the range with which you want to work.

What you describe is the most common of all Excel VBA objects: the `Range` object. A `Range` object can be a single cell, a row or column, a selection of cells, or a 3D range. The following sections look at various techniques that return a `Range` object, as well as a number of `Range` object properties and methods.

Returning a Range Object

Much of your VBA code will concern itself with `Range` objects of one kind or another. Therefore, you need to be well versed in the various techniques that are available for returning range objects, whether they're single cells, rectangular ranges, or entire rows and columns. This section takes you through each of these techniques.

Using the Range Method

The `Range` method is the most straightforward way to identify a cell or range. It has two syntaxes. The first requires only a single argument:

```
Worksheet.Range(Name)
```

`Worksheet`	The `Worksheet` object to which the `Range` method applies. If you omit `Worksheet`, VBA assumes the method applies to the `ActiveSheet` object.
`Name`	A range reference or name entered as text.

For example, the following statements enter a date in cell B2 and then create a data series in the range B2:E10 of the active worksheet:

```
Range("B2").Value = #01/01/2008#
Range("B2:B13").DataSeries Type:=xlChronological, Date:=xlMonth
```

→ For information on the `Value` property and `DataSeries` method, **see** "Inserting Data into a Range," **p. 162.**

The `Range` method also works with named ranges. For example, the following statement clears the contents of a range named `Criteria` in the Data worksheet:

```
Worksheets("Data").Range("Criteria").ClearContents
```

The second syntax for the `Range` method requires two arguments:

```
Worksheet.Range(Cell1, Cell2)
```

Worksheet	The `Worksheet` object to which the `Range` method applies. If you omit *Worksheet*, VBA assumes that the method applies to the `ActiveSheet` object.
Cell1, Cell2	The cells that define the upper-left corner (*Cell1*) and lower-right corner (*Cell2*) of the range. Each can be a cell address as text, a `Range` object consisting of a single cell, or an entire column or row.

The advantage of this syntax is that it separates the range corners into individual arguments. This lets you modify each corner under procedural control. For example, you could set up variables named `upperLeft` and `lowerRight` and then return `Range` objects of different sizes:

```
Range(upperLeft,lowerRight)
```

Using the `Cells` Method

The `Cells` method returns a single cell as a `Range` object. Here's the syntax:

```
Object.Cells(RowIndex, ColumnIndex)
```

Object	A `Worksheet` or `Range` object. If you omit *Object*, the method applies to the `ActiveSheet` object.
RowIndex	The row number of the cell. If *Object* is a worksheet, a *RowIndex* of 1 refers to row 1 on the sheet. If *Object* is a range, *RowIndex* 1 refers to the first row of the range.
ColumnIndex	The column of the cell. You can enter a letter as text or a number. If *Object* is a worksheet, a *ColumnIndex* of A or 1 refers to column A on the sheet. If *Object* is a range, *ColumnIndex* A or 1 refers to the first column of the range.

For example, the following procedure fragment loops five times and enters the values Field1 through Field5 in cells A1 through E1:

```
For colNumber = 1 To 5
    Cells(1, colNumber).Value = "Field" & colNumber
Next colNumber
```

> **TIP** You also can refer to a cell by enclosing an A1-style reference in square brackets ([]). For example, the following statement clears the comments from cell C4 of the active worksheet:
>
> ```
> ActiveSheet.[C4].ClearComments
> ```

Returning a Row

If you need to work with entire rows or columns, VBA has several methods and properties you can use. In each case, the object returned is a Range.

The most common way to refer to a row in VBA is to use the Rows method. This method uses the following syntax:

```
Object.Rows([Index])
```

Object	The Worksheet or Range object to which the method applies. If you omit *Object*, VBA uses the ActiveSheet object.
Index	The row number. If *Object* is a worksheet, an *Index* of 1 refers to row 1 on the sheet. If *Object* is a range, an *Index* of 1 refers to the first row of the range. If you omit *Index*, the method returns a collection of all the rows in *Object*.

For example, Listing 8.6 shows a procedure named InsertRangeRow. This procedure inserts a new row before the last row of whatever range is passed as an argument (rangeObject). This would be a useful subroutine in programs that need to maintain ranges.

Listing 8.6   A Procedure That Uses the Rows Method to Insert a Row Before the Last Row of a Range

```
Sub InsertRangeRow(rangeObject As Range)
    Dim totalRows As Integer, lastRow As Integer
    With rangeObject
        totalRows = .Rows.Count          ' Total rows in the range
        lastRow = .Rows(totalRows).Row   ' Last row number
        .Rows(lastRow).Insert            ' Insert before last row
    End With
End Sub

Sub InsertTest()
    InsertRangeRow ThisWorkbook.Worksheets(1).Range("Test")
End Sub
```

After declaring the variables, the first statement uses the Rows method without the *Index* argument to return a collection of all the rows in rangeObject and uses the Count property to get the total number of rangeObject rows:

```
totalRows = rangeObject.Rows.Count
```

The second statement uses the `totalRows` variable as an argument in the `Rows` method to return the last row of `rangeObject`, and then the `Row` property returns the row number:

```
lastRow = rangeObject.Rows(totalRows).Row
```

Finally, the last statement uses the `Insert` method to insert a row before `lastRow`.

To use `InsertRangeRow`, you need to pass a `Range` object to the procedure. For example, the `InsertRange` procedure shown at the end of Listing 8.4 inserts a row into a range named `Test`.

> **NOTE** You also can use the `EntireRow` property to return a row. The syntax `Range.EntireRow` returns the entire row or rows that contain the `Range` object. This is most often used to mimic the Shift+Spacebar shortcut key that selects the entire row that includes the active cell. To do this, you use the following statement:
>
> ```
> ActiveCell.EntireRow.Select
> ```

Returning a Column

To return a column, use the `Columns` method. The syntax for this method is almost identical to the `Rows` method:

```
Object.Columns([Index])
```

Object	The `Worksheet` or `Range` object to which the method applies. If you omit *Object*, VBA uses the `ActiveSheet` object.
Index	The column number. If *Object* is a worksheet, an *Index* of A or 1 refers to column A on the sheet. If *Object* is a range, *Index* A or 1 refers to the first column of the range. If you omit *Index*, the method returns a collection of all the columns in *Object*.

For example, the following statement sets the width of column B on the active worksheet to 20:

```
Columns("B").ColumnWidth = 20
```

> **NOTE** The syntax `Range.EntireColumn` returns the entire column or columns that contain the specified `Range` object.

Using the `Offset` **Method**

When defining your `Range` objects, you often won't know the specific range address to use. For example, you might need to refer to the cell that's two rows down and one column to the right of the active cell. You could find out the address of the active cell and then calculate the address of the other cell, but VBA gives you an easier (and more flexible) way: the `Offset` method. `Offset` returns a `Range` object that is offset from a specified range by a certain number of rows and columns. Here is its syntax:

```
Range.Offset([RowOffset][, ColumnOffset])
```

`Range`	The original `Range` object.
`RowOffset`	The number of rows to offset `Range`. You can use a positive number (to move down), a negative number (to move up), or 0 (to use the same rows). If you omit `RowOffset`, VBA uses 0.
`ColumnOffset`	The number of columns to offset `Range`. Again, you can use a positive number (to move right), a negative number (to move left), or 0 (to use the same columns). If you omit `ColumnOffset`, VBA uses 0.

For example, the following statement formats the range B2:D6 as bold:

```
Range("A1:C5").Offset(1,1).Font.Bold = True
```

Listing 8.7 shows a procedure called `ConcatenateStrings` that concatenates two text strings. This is handy, for instance, if you have a list with separate first and last name fields and you want to combine them.

Listing 8.7   A Procedure That Uses the `Offset` Method to Concatenate Two Text Strings

```
Sub ConcatenateStrings()
    Dim string1 As String, string2 As String
    '
    ' Store the contents of the cell 2 to the left of the active cell
    '
    string1 = ActiveCell.Offset(0, -2)
    '
    ' Store the contents of the cell 1 to the left of the active cell
    '
    string2 = ActiveCell.Offset(0, -1)
    '
    ' Enter combined strings (separated by a space) into active cell
    '
    ActiveCell.Value = string1 & " " & string2
End Sub
```

The procedure begins by declaring `String1` and `String2`. The next statement stores in `String1` the contents of the cell two columns to the left of the active cell by using the `Offset` method as follows:

```
String1 = ActiveCell.Offset(0, -2)
```

Similarly, the next statement stores in `String2` the contents of the cell one column to the left of the active cell. Finally, the last statement combines `String1` and `String2` (with a space in between) and stores the new string in the active cell.

Selecting a Cell or Range

VBA lets you access objects directly without having to select them first. This means that your VBA procedures rarely have to select a range. For example, even if, say, cell A1 is currently selected, the following statement sets the font in the range B1:B10 without changing the selected cell:

```
Range("B1:B10").Font.Name = "Times New Roman"
```

However, there are times when you do need to select a range. For example, you might need to display a selected range to the user. To select a range, use the `Select` method:

Range.Select

    Range   The `Range` object you want to select.

For example, the following statement selects the range A1:E10 in the Sales worksheet:

```
Worksheets("Sales").Range("A1:E10").Select
```

> **TIP** To return a `Range` object that represents the currently selected range, use the `Selection` property. For example, the following statement applies the Times New Roman font to the currently selected range:
>
> ```
> Selection.Font.Name = "Times New Roman"
> ```

Selecting A1 on All Worksheets

When you open an Excel file that you've worked on before, the cells or ranges that were selected in each worksheet when the file was last saved remain selected upon opening. This is handy behavior because it often enables you to resume work where you left off previously. However, when you've completed work on an Excel file, you may prefer to remove all the selections. For example, you might run through each worksheet and select cell A1 so that you or anyone else opening the file can start "fresh."

Selecting all the A1 cells manually is fine if the workbook has only a few sheets, but it can be a pain in a workbook that contains many sheets. Listing 8.8 presents a macro that selects cell A1 in all of a workbook's sheets.

Listing 8.8   A Macro That Selects Cell A1 on All the Sheets in the Active Workbook

```
Sub SelectA1OnAllSheets()
    Dim ws As Worksheet
    '
    ' Run through all the worksheets in the active workbook
    '
```

```
    For Each ws In ActiveWorkbook.Worksheets
        '
        ' Activate the worksheet
        '
        ws.Activate
        '
        ' Select cell A1
        '
        ws.[A1].Select
    Next 'ws
    '
    ' Activate the first worksheet
    '
    ActiveWorkbook.Worksheets(1).Activate
End Sub
```

The macro runs through all the worksheets in the active workbook. In each case, the worksheet is first activated (you must activate a sheet before you can select anything on it), and then the Select method is called to select cell A1. The macro finishes by activating the first worksheet.

Selecting the "Home Cell" on All Worksheets

Many worksheets have a "natural" starting point, which could be a model's first data entry cell or a cell that displays a key result. In such a case, rather than selecting cell A1 on all the worksheets, you might prefer to select each of these "home cells."

One way to do this is to add a uniform comment to each home cell. For example, you could add the comment Home Cell. Having done that, you can then use the macro in Listing 8.9 to select all these home cells.

Listing 8.9   A Macro That Selects the "Home Cell" on All the Sheets in the Active Workbook

```
Sub SelectHomeCells()
    Dim ws As Worksheet
    Dim c As Comment
    Dim r As Range
    '
    ' Run through all the worksheets in the active workbook
    '
    For Each ws In ActiveWorkbook.Worksheets
        '
        ' Activate the worksheet
        '
        ws.Activate
        '
        ' Run through the comments
        '
        For Each c In ws.Comments
            '
            ' Look for the "Home Cell" comment
            '
```

continues

8

Listing 8.9   Continued

```
            If InStr(c.Text, "Home Cell") <> 0 Then
                '
                ' Store the cell as a Range
                '
                Set r = c.Parent
                '
                ' Select the cell
                '
                r.Select
            End If
        Next 'c
    Next 'ws
    '
    ' Activate the first worksheet
    '
    ActiveWorkbook.Worksheets(1).Activate
End Sub
```

The `SelectHomeCells` procedure is similar to the `SelectA1OnAllSheets` procedure from Listing 8.8. That is, the main loop runs through all the sheets in the active workbook and activates each worksheet in turn. In this case, however, another loop runs through each worksheet's `Comments` collection. The `Text` property of each `Comment` object is checked to see whether it includes the phrase `Home Cell`. If so, the cell containing the comment is stored in the `r` variable (using the `Comment` object's `Parent` property) and then the cell is selected.

Selecting the Named Range That Contains the Active Cell

It's often handy to be able to select the name range that contains the current cell (for example, to change the range formatting). If you know the name of the range, you need only select it from the Name box. However, in a large model or a workbook that you're not familiar with, it may not be obvious which name to choose. Listing 8.10 shows a function and procedure that will handle this chore for you.

Listing 8.10   A Function and Procedure That Determine and Select the Named Range Containing the Active Cell

```
Function GetRangeName(r As Range) As String
    Dim n As Name
    Dim rtr As Range
    Dim ir As Range
    '
    ' Run through all the range names in the active workbook
    '
    For Each n In ActiveWorkbook.Names
        '
        ' Get the name's range
        '
        Set rtr = n.RefersToRange
        '
```

```
        ' See whether the named range and the active cell's range intersect
        '
        Set ir = Application.Intersect(r, rtr)
        If Not ir Is Nothing Then
            '
            ' If they intersect, then the active cell is part of a
            ' named range, so get the name and exit the function
            '
            GetRangeName = n.Name
            Exit Function
        End If
    Next 'n
    '
    ' If we get this far, the active cell is not part of a named range,
    ' so return the null string
    '
    GetRangeName = ""
End Function

Sub SelectCurrentNamedRange()
    Dim r As Range
    Dim strName As String
    '
    ' Store the active cell
    '
    Set r = ActiveCell
    '
    ' Get the name of the range that contains the cell, if any
    '
    strName = GetRangeName(r)
    If strName <> "" Then
        '
        ' If the cell is part of a named range, select the range
        '
        Range(strName).Select
    End If
End Sub
```

The heart of Listing 8.10 is the GetRangeName function, which takes a range as an argument. The purpose of this function is to see whether the passed range—r—is part of a named range and if so, to return the name of that range. The function's main loop runs through each item in the active workbook's Names collection. For each name, the RefersToRange property returns the associated range, which the function stores in the rtr variable. The function then uses the Intersect method to see whether the ranges r and rtr intersect. If they do, it means that r is part of the named range (because, in this case, r is just a single cell), so GetRangeName returns the range name. If no intersection is found for any name, the function returns the null string (""), instead.

The SelectCurrentNamedRange procedure makes use of the GetRangeName function. The procedure stores the active cell in the r variable and then passes that variable to the GetRangeName function. If the return value is not the null string, the procedure selects the returned range name.

Defining a Range Name

In Excel VBA, range names are `Name` objects. To define them, you use the `Add` method for the `Names` collection (which is usually the collection of defined names in a workbook). Here is an abbreviated syntax for the `Names` collection's `Add` method (this method has eleven arguments; see the VBA Reference in the Help system):

```
Names.Add(Text, RefersTo)
```

Text	The text you want to use as the range name.
RefersTo	The item to which you want the name to refer. You can enter a constant, a formula as text (such as `"=Sales-Expenses"`), or a worksheet reference (such as `"Sales!A1:C6"`).

For example, the following statement adds the range name `SalesRange` to the `Names` collection of the active workbook:

```
ActiveWorkbook.Names.Add _
    Text:="SalesRange", _
    RefersTo:="=Sales!$A$1$C$6"
```

Inserting Data into a Range

If your VBA procedure needs to add data to a range, VBA offers several properties that can do this. (Note that all these properties also return the current data that resides in a range.)

If you just want to add a simple value such as a number, string, date, or time to a range, use the `Range` object's `Value` property. For example, the following statement inserts the current date and time into cell A1 on the active worksheet:

```
ActiveSheet.Range("A1").Value = Now
```

Similarly, the following statement fills the range A2:D20 with zeroes:

```
ActiveSheet.Range("A2:D20").Value = 0
```

If you want to add a formula to a range, use the `Range` object's `Formula` property. For example, the following statement adds a formula to cell E15:

```
ActiveWorkbook.Worksheets("Budget").Range("E15").Formula = "=E5 - E14"
```

If you need to enter an array formula into a cell, use the `Range` object's `FormulaArray` property. Note that you don't include the braces, as shown in the following example:

```
ActiveCell.FormulaArray = "=SUM(IF(A2:C5 > 0, 1, 0))"
```

> **NOTE** If you're not sure how to work with those tricky array formulas, I explain them in detail in my book *Formulas and Functions with Microsoft Office Excel 2007* (Que, 2007; ISBN: 0-7897-3668-3).

Excel also enables you to enter a data series into a range by using the `Range` object's `DataSeries` method. The `DataSeries` method uses the following syntax:

```
Range.DataSeries(Range[, Rowcol][, Type][, Date][, Step][, Stop][, Trend])
```

Range	The range to use for the data series.
Rowcol	Use `xlRows` to enter the data in rows, or `xlColumns` to enter the data in columns. If you omit *Rowcol*, Excel uses the size and shape of *Range*.
Type	The type of series. Enter `xlLinear` (the default), `xlGrowth`, `xlChronological`, or `xlAutoFill`.
Date	The type of date series, if you used `xlChronological` for the *Type* argument. Your choices are `xlDay` (the default), `xlWeekday`, `xlMonth`, or `xlYear`.
Step	The step value for the series (the default value is 1).
Stop	The stop value for the series. If you omit *Stop*, Excel fills the range.
Trend	Use `True` to create a linear or growth trend series. Use `False` (the default) to create a standard series.

For example, the following statements insert a date into cell B2 and then create a data series in the range B2:B13:

```
ActiveSheet.Range("B2").Value = #01/01/2008#
ActiveSheet.Range("B2:B13").DataSeries Type:=xlChronological, Date:=xlMonth
```

Returning Data About a Range

Here's a list of some `Range` object properties that return data about a range:

- `Range.Address`—Returns the address, as text, of the specified *Range*.
- `Range.Column`—Returns the number of the first column in the specified *Range*.
- `Range.Count`—Returns the number of cells in the specified *Range*.
- `Range.CurrentRegion`—Returns a `Range` object that represents the entire region in which the specified *Range* resides. A range's "region" is the area surrounding the range that is bounded by at least one empty row above and below, and at least one empty column to the left and right.
- `Range.Row`—Returns the number of the first row in the specified *Range*.

Resizing a Range

When you need to resize a range, use the `Range` object's `Resize` method. Here's the syntax for this method:

```
Range.Resize(RowSize, ColSize)
```

Range	The range to resize.
RowSize	The number of rows in the new range.
ColSize	The number of columns in the new range.

For example, suppose you use the `InsertRangeRow` procedure from Listing 8.6 to insert a row into a named range. In most cases, you'll want to redefine the range name so that it includes the extra row you added. Listing 8.11 shows a procedure that calls `InsertRangeRow` and then uses the `Resize` method to adjust the named range.

Listing 8.11   A Procedure That Uses `Resize` to Adjust a Named Range

```
Sub InsertAndRedefineName()
    With ThisWorkbook.Worksheets("Test Data")
        InsertRangeRow .Range("Test")
        With .Range("Test")
            Names.Add _
                Name:="Test", _
                RefersTo:=.Resize(.Rows.Count + 1)
        End With
        .Range("Test").Select
End Sub
```

In the `Names.Add` method, the new range is given by the expression `.Resize(.Rows.Count + 1)`. Here, the `Resize` method returns a range that has one more row than the `Test` range.

From Here

- For a general discussion of VBA objects, **see** Chapter 5, "Working with Objects," **p. 71**.
- Some VBA functions perform the same tasks as some Excel worksheet functions. To find out which ones, **see** Appendix B, "VBA Functions," **p. 361**.

Programming PowerPoint

This chapter shows you how to leverage your VBA knowledge in the PowerPoint environment by examining a few PowerPoint objects and their associated properties, methods, and events. To illustrate these items, I'll build an example presentation strictly by using VBA code.

PowerPoint's Presentation Object

In PowerPoint, the Presentation object represents a presentation file that is open in the PowerPoint application window. You can use VBA to create new presentations, open or delete existing presentations, save and close presentations, and more. The next section takes you through various techniques for specifying presentations in your VBA code; then we'll look at some Presentation object properties and methods.

Specifying a Presentation Object

If you need to do something with a presentation, or if you need to work with an object contained in a specific presentation (such as a slide), you need to tell PowerPoint which presentation you want to use. VBA gives you three ways to do this:

- Use the Presentations object—The Presentations object is the collection of all open presentation files. To specify a particular presentation, either use its index number (where 1 represents the first presentation opened) or enclose the presentation filename in quotation marks. For example, if Proposal.pptx were the first presentation opened, the following two statements would be equivalent:

```
Presentations(1)
Presentations("Proposal.pptx")
```

- **Use the `ActivePresentation` object**—The `ActivePresentation` object represents the presentation that currently has the focus.

- **Use the `Presentation` property**—Open slide show windows have a `Presentation` property that returns the name of the underlying presentation. For example, the following statement uses the `currPres` variable to store the `Presentation` object associated with the first slide show window:

```
Set currPres = SlideShowWindows(1).Presentation
```

Opening a Presentation

To open a presentation file, use the `Open` method of the `Presentations` collection. The `Open` method has several arguments you can use to fine-tune your presentation openings, but only one of these is mandatory. Here's the simplified syntax showing the one required argument (for the rest of the arguments, look up the `Open` method in the VBA Help system):

```
Presentations.Open(FileName)
```

    FileName   The full name of the presentation file, including the drive and folder that contain the file.

For example, to open a presentation named `Proposal.pptx` in the current's user's `Documents` folder, you would use the following statement:

```
Presentations.Open Environ("UserProfile") & "\Documents\Proposal.pptx"
```

> **NOTE** The string expression `Environ("UserProfile")` & `"\Documents\"` returns the current user's `Documents` folder in Windows Vista. If you're using Windows XP, use the following string expression, instead:
> ```
>     Environ("UserProfile") & "\My Documents\
> ```

Creating a New Presentation

If you need to create a new presentation, use the `Presentations` collection's `Add` method:

```
Presentations.Add(WithWindow)
```

    WithWindow   A Boolean value that determines whether or not the presentation is created in a visible window. Use `True` for a visible window (this is the default); use `False` to hide the window.

`Presentation` **Object Properties**

Here's a list of a few common properties associated with `Presentation` objects:

- *Presentation*.`FullName`—Returns the full pathname of the specified *Presentation*. The full pathname includes the presentation's path (the drive and folder in which the file resides) and the filename.

- *Presentation*.Name—Returns the filename of the *Presentation*.
- *Presentation*.Path—Returns the path of the *Presentation* file.

A new, unsaved presentation's Path property returns an empty string (" ").

- *Presentation*.Saved—Determines whether changes have been made to the specified *Presentation* since it was last saved.
- *Presentation*.SlideMaster—Returns a Master object that represents the slide master for the specified *Presentation*.
- *Presentation*.Slides—Returns a Slides object that represents the collection of Slide objects contained in the specified *Presentation*.
- *Presentation*.SlideShowSettings—Returns a SlideShowSettings object that represents the slide show setup options for the specified *Presentation*.

Presentation **Object Methods**

A Presentation object has methods that let you save the presentation, close it, print it, and more. Here are the methods you'll use most often:

- *Presentation*.ApplyTemplate—Applies a design template to the specified *Presentation*. This method uses the following syntax:

  Presentation.ApplyTemplate(FileName)

Presentation	The Presentation object to which you want to apply the template.
FileName	The full name of the template (.potx, .potm, or .pot) file.

  For example, the following statement applies the Classic Photo Album template to the active presentation:

  ```
  ActivePresentation.ApplyTemplate _
      Environ("ProgramFiles") & "\Microsoft Office\Templates\1033\
  ➥ClassicPhotoAlbum.potx"
  ```

- *Presentation*.Close—Closes the specified *Presentation*. If the file has unsaved changes, PowerPoint asks the user whether he or she wants to save those changes.
- *Presentation*.PrintOut—Prints the specified *Presentation*, using the following syntax:

  Presentation.PrintOut([From][, To][, PrintToFile][, Copies][, Collate])

Presentation	The Presentation object you want to print.
From	The page number from which to start printing.
To	The page number of the last page to print.

9

PrintToFile	The name of a file to which you want the presentation printed.
Copies	The number of copies to print. The default value is 1.
Collate	If this argument is `True` and `Copies` is greater than 1, VBA collates the copies.

> **NOTE** By default, the `PrintOut` method prints only the presentation's slides. If you want to print other presentation elements such as handouts, notes pages, or the outline, you need to set the `Presentation` object's `PrintOptions.OutputType` property to the appropriate constant, such as `ppPrintOutputFourSlideHandouts`, `ppPrintOutputNotesPages`, or `ppPrintOutputOutline`. See the VBA Help system for the complete list of constants.

- *Presentation*.`Save`—Saves the specified *Presentation*. If the presentation is new, use the `SaveAs` method instead.

- *Presentation*.`SaveAs`—Saves the specified *Presentation* to a different file. Here's the syntax for the `SaveAs` method:

  `Presentation.SaveAs(FileName[, FileFormat][, EmbedTrueTypeFonts])`

Presentation	The `Presentation` object you want to save to a different file.
FileName	The full name of the new presentation file, including the drive and folder where you want the file to reside.
FileFormat	The PowerPoint format to use for the new file. Use one of the predefined `ppSaveAs` constants (such as `ppSaveAsPresentation` or `ppSaveAsHTML`).
EmbedTrueTypeFonts	If `True`, PowerPoint embeds the presentation's TrueType fonts in the new file.

The Juggling Application

Throughout this chapter, I'll put the PowerPoint objects, methods, and properties that we talk about to good use in an application that builds an entire presentation from scratch. (It's unlikely in practice that you'll ever need to use VBA to build a presentation. However, this code at least shows you how it's done, which should help you use VBA with PowerPoint, whatever your needs.) This presentation consists of a series of slides that provide instructions on how to juggle.

The code for the application consists of six procedures:

- `Main`—This procedure ties the entire application together by calling each of the other procedures in the module.

- CreateJugglingPresentation—This procedure creates a new Presentation object and saves it.

- CreateJugglingSlides—This procedure adds the slides to the presentation and then formats them.

- SetUpFirstSlide—This procedure adds and formats text for the presentation title slide.

- SetUpJugglingSlides—This procedure adds and formats a title, picture, and instruction text for each of the four pages that explain how to juggle.

- RunJugglingSlideShow—This procedure asks the user whether he or she wants to run the slide show, and then runs it if Yes is chosen.

9

To get started, Listing 9.1 shows the Main procedure.

Listing 9.1   This Procedure Ties Everything Together by Calling Each of the Code Listings Individually

```
' Global variable
Dim pres As Presentation

Sub Main()
    '
    ' Create the presentation file
    '
    CreateJugglingPresentation
    '
    ' Add the slides
    '
    AddJugglingSlides
    '
    ' Set up the title slide
    '
    SetUpStartSlide
    '
    ' Set up the Juggling slides
    '
    SetUpJugglingSlides
    '
    ' Save it and then run it
    '
    pres.Save
    RunJugglingSlideShow
End Sub
```

First, the pres variable is declared as a Presentation object. Notice that this variable is defined at the top of the module, *before* any of the procedures. When you define a variable like this, it means that it can be used in all the procedures in the module. Then Main begins by calling the CreateJugglingPresentation procedure, shown in Listing 9.2. From there, the other procedures (discussed later in this chapter) are called and the presentation is saved.

Listing 9.2   This Procedure Creates a New Presentation and Then Saves It

```
Sub CreateJugglingPresentation()
    Dim p As Presentation
    '
    ' If the old one is still open, close it without saving
    '
    For Each p In Presentations
        If p.Name = "Juggling" Then
            p.Saved = True
            p.Close
        End If
    Next p
    '
    ' Create a new Presentation object and store it in pres
    '
    Set pres = Presentations.Add
    pres.SaveAs FileName:="Juggling.pptx"
End Sub
```

A `For Each...Next` loop runs through each open presentation and checks the `Name` property. If it equals `Juggling.pptx`, you know the file is already open. If it's open (say, from running the application previously), the procedure closes it without saving it. The `pres` variable is `Set` and then the presentation is saved by the `SaveAs` method.

> **NOTE**
> The presentation and code used in this chapter's sample application can be found on my website at the following address:
>
> http://www.mcfedries.com/Office2007VBA/Chapter09.pptm

Working with PowerPoint Slide Objects

PowerPoint presentations consist of a series of slides. In PowerPoint VBA, a slide is a `Slide` object that contains a number of properties and methods that you can wield in your code. These include options for setting the slide's layout, specifying the transition effect, and copying and deleting slides. The next few sections discuss these and other slide techniques.

Specifying a Slide

To work with a slide, you need to specify a `Slide` object. For a single slide, the easiest way to do this is to use the `Slides` object. `Slides` is the collection of all the slides in a particular presentation. To specify a slide, either use the slide's index number (where 1 represents the first slide in the presentation, 2 the second slide, and so on), or enclose the slide name in quotation marks. For example, if Slide1 is the first slide, the following two statements would be equivalent:

```
ActivePresentation.Slides(1)
ActivePresentation.Slides("Slide1")
```

If you need to work with multiple slides (say, to apply a particular layout to all the slides), use the `Range` method of the `Slides` object:

```
Presentation.Slides.Range(Index)
```

`Presentation`	The `Presentation` object that contains the slides.
`Index`	An array that specifies the slides.

For the `Index` argument, use VBA's `Array` function with multiple instances of slide index numbers or slide names. For example, the following statement specifies the slides named Slide1 and Slide2:

```
ActivePresentation.Slides.Range(Array("Slide1","Slide2"))
```

> **TIP**
> To work with every slide in the presentation, use the `Range` method without an argument, as in this example:
>
> ```
> ActivePresentation.Slides.Range
> ```
>
> You can also use the `Presentation` object's `SlideMaster` property to work with the slide master. This changes the default settings for every slide in the presentation.

Creating a New Slide

After you've created a presentation, you need to populate it with slides. To insert a new `Slide` object into a presentation, use the `Add` method of the `Slides` collection:

```
Presentation.Slides.Add(Index, Layout)
```

`Presentation`	The `Presentation` object in which you want to add the slide.
`Index`	The index number of the new slide within the `Slides` object. Use `1` to make this the first slide; use `Slides.Count + 1` to make this the last slide.
`Layout`	A constant that specifies the layout of the new slide. PowerPoint defines more than two dozen constants, including `ppLayoutText` (for a text-only slide), `ppLayoutChart` (for a chart slide), and `ppLayoutBlank` (for a blank slide). Look up the `Add` method in the VBA Help system to see the full list of constants.

The following statements add an organization chart slide to the end of the active presentation:

```
With ActivePresentation.Slides
    .Add Index:=.Count + 1, Layout:=ppLayoutOrgchart
End With
```

Inserting Slides from a File

Rather than create slides from scratch, you might prefer to pilfer one or more slides from an existing presentation. The `InsertFromFile` method lets you do this. It uses the following syntax:

```
Presentation.Slides.InsertFromFile(FileName, Index[, SlideStart][, SlideEnd])
```

Presentation	The `Presentation` object in which you want to add the slides.
FileName	The name of the file (including the drive and folder) that contains the slides you want to insert.
Index	The index number of an existing slide in *Presentation*. The slides from *FileName* are inserted after this slide.
SlideStart	The index number of the first slide in *FileName* that you want to insert.
SlideEnd	The index number of the last slide in *FileName* that you want to insert.

For example, the following procedure fragment inserts the first five slides from `Budget.pptx` at the end of the active presentation:

```
With ActivePresentation.Slides
    .InsertFromFile _
        FileName:="G:\Presentations\Budget.pptx", _
        Index:=.Count, _
        SlideStart:=1, _
        SlideEnd:=5
End With
```

`Slide` **Object Properties**

To let you change the look and feel of your slides, PowerPoint VBA offers a number of `Slide` object properties. These properties control the slide's layout, background, color scheme, name, and more. This section runs through a few of the more useful `Slide` object properties.

> **NOTE**
> If you specify multiple slides using the `Range` method described earlier, PowerPoint returns a `SlideRange` object that references the slides. This object has the same properties and methods as a `Slide` object, so you can work with multiple slides the same way that you work with a single slide.

- `Slide`.Background—Returns or sets the background of the specified `Slide`. Note that this property actually returns a `ShapeRange` object. (See "Dealing with `Shape` Objects" later in this chapter.)

You normally use this property with the slide master to set the background for all the slides in the presentation. For example, the following statements store the slide master background in a variable and then use the Shape object's Fill property to change the background pattern for all the slides in the active presentation:

```
Set slideBack = ActivePresentation.SlideMaster.Background
slideBack.Fill.PresetGradient _
    Style:=msoGradientHorizontal, _
    Variant:=1, _
    PresetGradientType:=msoGradientFire
```

If you just want to change the background for a single slide, you must first set the slide's FollowMasterBackground property to False, like so:

```
With ActivePresentation.Slides(1)
    .FollowMasterBackground = False
    .Background.Fill.PresetGradient _
        Style:=msoGradientHorizontal, _
        Variant:=1, _
        PresetGradientType:=msoGradientFire
End With
```

- *Slide*.FollowMasterBackground—As mentioned earlier, this property returns or sets whether or not the specified *Slide* uses the same Background property as the slide master. Set this property to False to set a unique background for an individual slide.

- *Slide*.Layout—Returns or sets the layout for the specified *Slide*. Again, see the VBA Help system for the full list of layout constants.

- *Slide*.Master—Returns the slide master for the specified *Slide*. The following two statements are equivalent:
```
ActivePresentation.SlideMaster
ActivePresentation.Slides(1).Master
```

- *Slide*.Name—Returns or sets the name of the specified *Slide*.

- *Slide*.Shapes—Returns a Shapes collection that represents all the Shape objects on the specified *Slide*.

- *Slide*.SlideShowTransition—Returns a SlideShowTransition object that represents the transition special effects used for the specified *Slide* during a slide show.

The Juggling Application: Creating the Slides

Listing 9.3 shows the AddJugglingSlides procedure, which adds four slides to the Juggling presentation (represented, remember, by the pres variable) and then uses the SlideMaster object to set the default background for the slides.

Listing 9.3   A Procedure That Adds the Slides to the Juggling Presentation and Formats Them

```
Sub AddJugglingSlides()
    Dim i As Integer

    With pres
```

continues

9

Listing 9.3 Continued

```
     With .Slides
         '
         ' Add the opening slide
         '
         .Add(Index:=1, Layout:=ppLayoutTitle).Name = "Opener"
         '
         ' Now add the slides for each step
         '
         For i = 1 To 4
             .Add(Index:=i + 1, Layout:=ppLayoutTitle).Name = _
                               "Juggling" & i
         Next i
     End With
     '
     ' Set the background for all the slides
     '
     .SlideMaster.Background.Fill.PresetGradient _
         Style:=msoGradientHorizontal, _
         Variant:=1, _
         PresetGradientType:=msoGradientNightfall
     End With
 End Sub
```

Slide **Object Methods**

PowerPoint VBA defines a few Slide object methods that let you cut, copy, paste, dupli-
cate, export, select, and delete slides. I don't expect you'll use these methods very often, so I
won't discuss them in detail here. All are straightforward, however, so you should be able to
figure them out from the VBA Help system.

Dealing with Shape **Objects**

PowerPoint slides are really just a collection of objects: titles, text boxes, pictures, labels,
lines, curves, and so on. In PowerPoint VBA, each of these items is a Shape object.
Therefore, to get full slide control in your VBA procedures, you must know how to add,
edit, format, and otherwise manipulate these objects. That's the goal of this section.

Specifying a Shape

You have to specify a Shape object before you can work with it. The techniques you use for
this are similar to those I outlined earlier for Slide objects.

For a single shape, use the Shapes object, which is the collection of all Shape objects on a
particular slide. To specify a shape, either use the shape's index number (where 1 represents
the first shape added to the slide, 2 is the second shape, and so on), or enclose the shape
name in quotation marks. For example, if Rectangle 1 is the first shape, the following two
statements would be equivalent:

```
ActivePresentation.Shapes(1)
ActivePresentation.Shapes("Rectangle 1")
```

If you need to work with multiple shapes, use the `Range` method of the `Shapes` object:

```
Slide.Shapes.Range(Index)
```

> Slide   The `Slide` object that contains the shapes.
>
> Index   An array that specifies the shapes.

As with multiple slides, use VBA's `Array` function for the `Index` argument, like so:

```
Presentations(1).Slides(1).Shapes.Range(Array("Oval 1","TextBox 2"))
```

> **TIP**   To work with every shape in the slide, use the `Range` method without an argument:
> ```
> Presentations(1).Slides(1).Shapes.Range
> ```

Adding Shapes to a Slide

The `Slides` object has fourteen different methods you can use to insert shapes into a slide. Many of these methods use similar arguments, so before listing the methods, let's take a quick tour of the common arguments:

> BeginX   For connectors and lines, the distance (in points) from the shape's starting point to the left edge of the slide window.
>
> BeginY   For connectors and lines, the distance (in points) from the shape's starting point to the top edge of the slide window.
>
> EndX   For connectors and lines, the distance (in points) from the shape's ending point to the left edge of the slide window.
>
> EndY   For connectors and lines, the distance (in points) from the shape's ending point to the top edge of the slide window.
>
> FileName   The path and name of the file used to create the shape (such as a picture or an OLE object).
>
> Height   The height of the shape (in points).
>
> Left   The distance (in points) of the left edge of the shape from the left edge of the slide window.
>
> Orientation   The orientation of text within a label or text box. For horizontal text use the constant `msoTextOrientationHorizontal`; for vertical text use the constant `msoTextOrientationVerticalFarEast`.

> *SafeArrayOfPoints*   For curves and polylines, this is an array of coordinate pairs that specify the vertices and control points for the object.
>
> *Top*   The distance (in points) of the top edge of the shape from the top edge of the slide window.
>
> *Width*   The width of the shape (in points).

Here's a list of the Shapes object methods and arguments that you can use to create shapes:

- *Slide*.Shapes.AddComment—Adds a comment to the specified *Slide*, using the following syntax:

  Slide.Shapes.AddComment(*Left, Top, Width, Height*)

- *Slide*.Shapes.AddConnector—Adds a connector to the specified *Slide*, using the following syntax:

  Slide.Shapes.AddConnector(*Type, BeginX, BeginY, EndX, EndY*)

  Type   A constant that specifies the connector type:

Type	Connector
msoConnectorCurve	A curved connector
msoConnectorElbow	A connector with an elbow
msoConnectorStraight	A straight connector

> **NOTE** The AddConnector method returns a Shape object that represents the new connector. You use this object's ConnectorFormat property to set up the beginning and ending points of the connector. In other words, you use the ConnectorFormat.BeginConnect and ConnectorFormat.EndConnect methods to specify the shapes attached to the connector.

- *Slide*.Shapes.AddCurve—Adds a curved line to the specified *Slide*, using the following syntax:

  Slide.Shapes.AddCurve(*SafeArrayOfPoints*)

- *Slide*.Shapes.AddLabel—Adds a label to the specified *Slide*, using the following syntax:

  Slide.Shapes.AddLabel(*Orientation, Left, Top, Width, Height*)

> **NOTE** I'll show you how to add text to a label and text box when we look at Shape object properties later in this chapter (see "Some Shape Object Properties").

- *Slide*.Shapes.AddLine—Adds a straight line to the specified *Slide*, using the following syntax:

  Slide.Shapes.AddLine(*BeginX, BeginY, EndX, EndY*)

- `Slide.Shapes.AddMediaObject`—Adds a multimedia file to the specified `Slide`, using the following syntax:

  `Slide.Shapes.AddMediaObject(FileName, Left, Top, Width, Height)`

- `Slide.Shapes.AddPicture`—Adds a graphic to the specified `Slide`, using the following syntax:

  `Slide.Shapes.AddPicture(FileName, LinkToFile, SaveWithDocument, Left,`
  `↪Top, Width, Height)`

  Here's a summary of the extra arguments used in this method:

`LinkToFile`	Set this argument to `True` to set up a link to the original file. If this argument is `False`, an independent copy of the picture is stored in the slide.
`SaveWithDocument`	Set this argument to `True` to save the picture with the presentation. Note that this argument must be `True` if `LinkToFile` is `False`.

- `Slide.Shapes.AddPolyline`—Adds an open polyline or a closed polygon to the specified `Slide`, using the following syntax:

  `Slide.Shapes.AddPolyline(SafeArrayOfPoints)`

- `Slide.Shapes.AddShape`—Adds an AutoShape to the specified `Slide`, using the following syntax:

  `Slide.Shapes.AddShape(Type, Left, Top, Width, Height)`

  Here, the `Type` argument is a constant that specifies the AutoShape you want to add. PowerPoint VBA defines dozens of these constants. To see the full list, look up the `AutoShapeType` property in the VBA Help system.

- `Slide.Shapes.AddTextbox`—Adds a text box to the specified `Slide`, using the following syntax:

  `Slide.Shapes.AddTextbox(Left, Top, Width, Height)`

- `Slide.Shapes.AddTextEffect`—Adds a WordArt text effect to the specified `Slide`, using the following syntax:

  `Slide.Shapes.AddTextEffect(PresetTextEffect, Text, FontName,`
  `↪FontSize, FontBold, FontItalic, Left, Top)`

  Here's a summary of the extra arguments used in this method:

`PresetTextEffect`	A constant that specifies one of WordArt's preset text effects. Look up this method in the VBA Help system to see the few dozen constants that are available.
`Text`	The WordArt text.
`FontName`	The font applied to `Text`.
`FontSize`	The font size applied to `Text`.
`FontBold`	Set to `True` to apply bold to `Text`.
`FontItalic`	Set to `True` to apply italics to `Text`.

- *Slide*.Shapes.AddTitle—Adds a title to the specified *Slide*. This method takes no arguments. However, be aware that the AddTitle method raises an error if the slide already has a title. To check in advance, use the HasTitle property, as shown in the following example:

```
With ActivePresentation.Slides(1).Shapes
    If Not .HasTitle Then
        .AddTitle.TextFrame.TextRange.Text = "New Title"
    End If
End With
```

Some Shape **Object Properties**

PowerPoint VBA comes equipped with more than three dozen Shape object properties that control characteristics such as the dimensions and position of a shape, whether or not a shape displays a shadow, and the shape name. Let's take a quick look at a few of these properties:

- *Shape*.AnimationSettings—This property returns an AnimationSettings object that represents the animation effects applied to the specified *Shape*. AnimationSettings contains various properties that apply special effects to the shape. Here's a sampler (see the VBA Help system for the complete list, as well as the numerous constants that work with these properties):

  - AdvanceMode—A constant that determines how the animation advances. There are two choices: automatically (in other words, after a preset amount of time; use ppAdvanceOnTime), or when the user clicks the slide (use ppAdvanceOnClick). For the latter, you can specify the amount of time by using the AdvanceTime property.

  - AfterEffect—A constant that determines how the shape appears after the animation is complete.

  - Animate—A Boolean value that turns the shape's animation on (True) or off (False).

  - AnimateTextInReverse—When this Boolean value is True, PowerPoint builds the text animation in reverse order. For example, if the shape is a series of bullet points and this property is True, the animation displays the bullet points from last to first.

  - EntryEffect—A constant that determines the special effect applied initially to the shape's animation. For example, you can make the shape fade in by using the ppEffectFade constant.

  - TextLevelEffect—A constant that determines the paragraph level that gets animated.

  - TextUnitEffect—A constant that determines how PowerPoint animates text: by paragraph, by word, or by letter.

- *Shape*.AutoShapeType—For an AutoShape object, this property returns or sets the shape type for the specified *Shape*.

- *Shape*.Fill—This property returns a FillFormat object that represents the fill formatting for the specified *Shape*. The FillFormat object defines numerous methods you can wield to apply a fill to a shape:

  - Background—Sets the fill to match the slide's background.

  - OneColorGradient—Sets the fill to a one-color gradient.

  - Patterned—Sets the fill to a pattern.

  - PresetGradient—A constant that sets the fill to one of PowerPoint's preset gradients.

  - PresetTextured—A constant that sets the fill to one of PowerPoint's preset textures.

  - Solid—Sets the fill to a solid color. After running this method, use the Fill.ForeColor property to set the fill color.

> **NOTE**
> PowerPoint's color properties (such as ForeColor) return a ColorFormat object. This object represents either the color of a one-color object, or the background or foreground color of an object with a pattern or gradient. To set a color, use the ColorFormat object's RGB property and VBA's RGB function to set a red-green-blue value, as in this example:
>
> ```
> Shapes(1).Fill.Solid.ForeColor.RGB = RGB(255,0,0)
> ```

  - TwoColorGradient—Sets the fill to a two-color gradient.

  - UserPicture—Sets the fill to a graphics file that you specify.

  - UserTexture—Sets the fill to a specified graphics image that gets tiled to cover the entire shape.

- *Shape*.HasTextFrame—A Boolean value that tells you whether the specified *Shape* has a text frame (True) or not (False). See the TextFrame property, discussed later.

- *Shape*.Height—Returns or sets the height, in points, for the specified *Shape*.

- *Shape*.Left—Returns or sets the distance, in points, between the left edge of the bounding box of the specified *Shape* and the left edge of the presentation window.

- *Shape*.Name—This property returns or sets the name for the specified *Shape*.

- *Shape*.Shadow—This property returns a ShadowFormat object that represents the shadow for the specified *Shape*. The ShadowFormat object contains various properties that control the look of the shadow. For example, Shadow.ForeColor controls the shadow color, and Shadow.Visible is a Boolean value that turns the shadow on (True) or off (False).

- *Shape*.TextEffectFormat—For a WordArt object, this property returns a TextEffectFormat object that represents the text effects of the specified *Shape*.

- *Shape*.TextFrame—This property returns a TextFrame object for the specified *Shape*. A text frame is an area within a shape that can hold text. The frame's text, as a whole, is represented by the TextRange object, and the actual text is given by the Text property of the TextRange object. This rather convoluted state of affairs means that you need to use the following property to a refer to a shape's text:

   Shape.TextFrame.TextRange.Text

   For example, the following statements add to the active presentation a new slide that contains only a title, and then they set the title text to 2008 Budget Proposal:

   ```
   With ActivePresentation.Slides
       With .Add(1, ppLayoutTitleOnly).Shapes(1)
           .TextFrame.TextRange.Text = "2008 Budget Proposal"
       End With
   End With
   ```

- Also note that the TextFrame object has a number of other properties that control the text margins, orientation, word wrap, and more.

- *Shape*.Top—Returns or sets the distance, in points, between the top edge of the bounding box of the specified *Shape* and the top edge of the presentation window.

- *Shape*.Visible—A Boolean value that makes the specified *Shape* either visible (True) or invisible (False).

- *Shape*.Width—Returns or sets the width, in points, for the specified *Shape*.

The Juggling Application: Creating the Title Slide

To put some of these properties through their paces, Listing 9.4 shows the Juggling application's SetUpStartPage procedure.

Listing 9.4   A Procedure That Sets Up the Text and Animation Settings for the First Slide of the Juggling Presentation

```
Sub SetUpStartSlide()
    Dim shapeTitle As Shape
    Dim shapeSubTitle As Shape

    With pres.Slides("Opener")
        Set shapeTitle = .Shapes(1)      ' The title
        Set shapeSubTitle = .Shapes(2)   ' The subtitle
        '
        ' Add the title text
        '
        With shapeTitle.TextFrame.TextRange
            .Text = "Juggling"
            With .Font
                .Name = "Arial"
                .Size = 44
                .Bold = True
                .Color.RGB = RGB(255, 255, 255)
            End With
        End With
```

```
           '
           ' Set the title animation
           '
           With shapeTitle.AnimationSettings
               .Animate = True
               .AdvanceMode = ppAdvanceOnTime
               .AdvanceTime = 0
               .TextUnitEffect = ppAnimateByCharacter
               .EntryEffect = ppEffectFlyFromLeft
           End With
           '
           ' Add the subtitle text
           '
           With shapeSubTitle.TextFrame.TextRange
               .Text = "A Step-By-Step Course"
               With .Font
                   .Name = "Arial"
                   .Size = 36
                   .Bold = True
                   .Color.RGB = RGB(255, 255, 255)
               End With
           End With
           '
           ' Set the subtitle animation
           '
           With shapeSubTitle.AnimationSettings
               .Animate = True
               .AdvanceMode = ppAdvanceOnTime
               .AdvanceTime = 0
               .TextUnitEffect = ppAnimateByWord
               .EntryEffect = ppEffectFlyFromBottom
           End With
       End With
   End Sub
```

The first slide is named Opener, and this is the object used through most of the procedure. The shapeTitle variable is Set to the slide's title—Shapes(1)—and the shapeSubTitle variable is Set to the subtitle text box—Shapes(2).

From there, the title's TextFrame property is used to add and format the title text. Then its AnimationSettings property is used to animate the text. A similar sequence of code adds text, formatting, and animation to the subtitle.

Some Shape Object Methods

The Shape object comes with a number of methods that let you perform standard actions such as cutting, copying, pasting, and deleting. Here's a list of some other useful methods:

- Shape.Apply—This method applies to the specified Shape the formatting that was captured from another shape using the PickUp method (described later).

- Shape.Duplicate—This method makes a copy of the specified Shape in the same slide. The new shape is added to the Shapes object immediately after the specified Shape. Note, too, that this method returns a Shape object that refers to the new shape.

- *Shape*.Flip—This method flips the specified *Shape* around its horizontal or vertical axis. Here's the syntax:

  ```
  Shape.Flip(FlipCmd)
  ```

Shape	The Shape object you want to flip.
FlipCmd	A constant that determines how the shape is flipped. Use either msoFlipHorizontal or msoFlipVertical.

- *Shape*.IncrementLeft—Moves the specified *Shape* horizontally, using the following syntax:

  ```
  Shape.IncrementLeft(Increment)
  ```

Shape	The Shape object you want to move.
Increment	The distance, in points, that you want the shape moved. Use a positive number to move the shape to the right; use a negative number to move the shape to the left.

- *Shape*.IncrementRotation—Rotates the specified *Shape* around its z-axis, using the following syntax:

  ```
  Shape.IncrementRotation(Increment)
  ```

Shape	The Shape object you want to move.
Increment	The number of degrees you want the shape rotated. Use a positive number to rotate the shape clockwise; use a negative number to rotate the shape counter-clockwise.

- *Shape*.IncrementTop—Moves the specified *Shape* vertically, using the following syntax:

  ```
  Shape.IncrementTop(Increment)
  ```

Shape	The Shape object you want to move.
Increment	The distance, in points, that you want the shape moved. Use a positive number to move the shape down; use a negative number to move the shape up.

- *Shape*.PickUp—Copies the formatting of the specified *Shape*. Use the Apply method (discussed earlier) to apply the copied formatting to a different object.

- *Shape*.Select—This method selects the specified *Shape* using the following syntax:

  ```
  Shape.Select(Replace)
  ```

Shape	The Shape object you want to select.
Replace	A Boolean value that either adds the shape to the current selection (False) or replaces the current selection (True). True is the default.

The Juggling Application: Creating the Instructions

To continue the Juggling application, the `SetUpJugglingSlides` procedure, shown in Listing 9.5, is run. This procedure serves to set up the title, picture, and instruction text for each of the four instruction slides.

Listing 9.5 A Procedure That Sets Up the Titles, Pictures, and Text Instructions for Each of the Juggling Slides

```
Sub SetUpJugglingSlides()
    Dim thisPres As Presentation
    Dim slideTitle As Shape
    Dim slidePicture As Shape
    Dim slideText As Shape
    Dim strImagePath As String
    Dim i As Integer

    For i = 1 To 4
        With pres.Slides("Juggling" & i)
            '
            ' Get the path of the picture for this slide
            ' Assume it's in the same folder as Chapter09.pptm
            '
            Set thisPres = Presentations("Chapter09.pptm")
            strImagePath = thisPres.Path & "\Juggling" & i & ".jpg"
            '
            ' Adjust the layout and then set the Shape variables
            '
            .Layout = ppLayoutObjectOverText
            Set slideTitle = .Shapes(1)
            Set slidePicture = .Shapes(2)
            Set slideText = .Shapes(3)
            '
            ' Add the title text
            '
            With slideTitle.TextFrame.TextRange
                Select Case i
                    Case 1
                        .Text = "Step 1: The Home Position"
                    Case 2
                        .Text = "Step 2: The First Throw"
                    Case 3
                        .Text = "Step 3: The Second Throw"
                    Case 4
                        .Text = "Step 4: The Third Throw"
                End Select
                With .Font
                    .Name = "Arial"
                    .Size = 44
                    .Bold = True
                    .Color.RGB = RGB(255, 255, 255)
                End With
            End With
            '
            ' Set up the picture
```

continues

9

Listing 9.5 Continued

```
        '
        With slidePicture
            '
            ' Add the picture
            '
            .Fill.UserPicture strImagePath
            .Width = 542
            .Left = 90
            '
            ' Configure the picture animation and shadow
            '
            With .AnimationSettings
                .Animate = True
                .AdvanceMode = ppAdvanceOnTime
                .AdvanceTime = 0
                .EntryEffect = ppEffectFade
            End With
            With .Shadow
                .ForeColor.RGB = RGB(0, 0, 0)
                .OffsetX = 10
                .OffsetY = 10
                .Visible = True
            End With
        End With
        '
        ' Add the instruction text
        '
        With slideText.TextFrame.TextRange
            Select Case i
            Case 1
            .Text = "Place two balls in your dominant hand, " & _
                "one in front of the other." & Chr(13) & _
                "Hold the third ball in your other hand." & _
                Chr(13) & _
                "Let your arms dangle naturally and bring " & _
                "your forearms parallel to the ground (as " & _
                "though you were holding a tray.)" & Chr(13) & _
                "Relax your shoulders, arms, and hands."
            Case 2
            .Text = "Of the two balls in your dominant hand, " & _
                "toss the front one toward your other hand " & _
                "in a smooth arc." & Chr(13) & _
                "Make sure the ball doesn't spin too much." & _
                Chr(13) & _
                "Make sure the ball goes no higher than " & _
                "about eye level."
            Case 3
            .Text = "As soon as the first ball reaches the top of " & _
                "its arc, toss the ball in your other hand." & _
                Chr(13) & _
                "Throw the ball toward your dominant hand, " & _
                "making sure it flies UNDER the first ball." & _
                Chr(13) & _
                "Again, try not to spin the ball and make " & _
                "sure it goes no higher than eye level."
```

```
                    Case 4
                    .Text = "Now for the tricky part (!). Soon " & _
                        "after you release the second ball, the " & _
                        "first ball will approach your hand. Go " & _
                        "ahead and catch the first ball." & Chr(13) & _
                        "When the second ball reaches its apex, " & _
                        "throw the third ball (the remaining ball " & _
                        "in your dominant hand) under it." & Chr(13) & _
                        "At this point, it just becomes a game of " & _
                        "catch-and-throw-under, catch-and-throw-" & _
                        "under. Have fun!"
                End Select
                With .Font
                    .Name = "Times New Roman"
                    .Size = 24
                    .Bold = False
                    .Color.RGB = RGB(255, 255, 255)
                End With
            End With
        End With
    Next i

End Sub
```

A For...Next loop runs through each of the four instructional slides. (Recall that earlier the CreateJugglingSlides procedure gave these slides the names Juggle1 through Juggle4.) Here's a summary of the various chores that are run within this loop:

- The first task is to load the pictures that illustrate each step. These pictures are named Juggle1.jpg through Juggle4.jpg, and the code assumes they're in the same folder as the Chaptr09.pptm file. (The images are also in the file itself.) To get them into the Juggling presentation, the code first stores the path of the current slide's image file in the strImagePath variable.

- The slide's Layout property is set to ppLayoutObjectOverText and the three variables that represent the three shapes on each slide are Set.

- Next, the title text is added. Here, a Select Case structure is used to add a different title to each slide, and then the text is formatted.

- You add the image to the slide by setting the slidePicture object's Fill.UserPicture property to the strImagePath value, and then the Width and Left properties adjust the size and position of the image.

- The picture is animated, and a shadow is added.

- The last chunk of code uses another Select Case to add the appropriate instructions for each slide, and then the instruction text is formatted.

Operating a Slide Show

With your presentation created and saved, the slides added and set up, and shapes inserted and formatted, your file is just about ready to roll. All that remains is to add a few slide show settings and transition effects. This section shows you how to do that, as well as how to run your slide show when it's complete.

Slide Show Transitions

Each Slide object has a SlideShowTransition property that determines how the slide advances during a slide show. This property is actually a SlideShowTransitions object, and you set up the transition effect by modifying this object's properties. Here's a list of the key properties:

- Slide.SlideShowTransition.AdvanceOnClick—For the specified Slide, this property returns or sets whether or not the slide advances when it's clicked. Set this property to True to advance the slide by clicking it.

- Slide.SlideShowTransition.AdvanceOnTime—For the specified Slide, this property returns or sets whether or not the slide advances after a period of time has elapsed (as set by the AdvanceTime property). Set this property to True to advance the slide after a period of time.

- Slide.SlideShowTransition.AdvanceTime—This property returns or sets the amount of time, in seconds, after which the specified Slide advances, assuming the AdvanceOnTime property is set to True.

> **NOTE** To allow a slide to advance based on time, you also need to set the SlideShowSettings object's AdvanceMode property to ppSlideShowUseSlideTimings. This object is a property of the Presentation object, and I'll discuss it in detail in the section "Slide Show Settings."

- Slide.SlideShowTransition.EntryEffect—A constant that determines the special effect used in the transition for the specified Slide. Look up this property in the VBA Help system to see the dozens of available constants.

- Slide.SlideShowTransition.Hidden—This property returns or sets whether or not the specified Slide is hidden during the slide show. Use True to hide the slide or False to make the slide visible.

- Slide.SlideShowTransition.Speed—This property returns or sets the speed of the transition for the specified Slide. Use one of the following constants:
  - ppTransitionSpeedSlow
  - ppTransitionSpeedMedium
  - ppTransitionSpeedSlow
  - ppTransitionSpeedMixed

Slide Show Settings

The `Presentation` object has a `SlideShowSettings` property that controls various global settings for the slide show. This property is actually a `SlideShowSettings` object and the settings are the properties of this object. Here's a rundown of the settings you'll utilize most often:

- `Presentation.SlideShowSettings.AdvanceMode`—Returns or sets how the slides advance for the specified `Presentation`. Use `ppSlideShowManualAdvance` to advance slides manually (by clicking) or `ppSlideShowUseSlideTimings` to advance slides based on the `AdvanceTime` property for each slide. You can also use the `ppSlideShowRehearseNewTimings` constant to run the slide show in Rehearsal mode (which lets you set the timings by advancing the slides manually).

- `Presentation.SlideShowSettings.EndingSlide`—Returns or sets the index number of the last slide that is displayed in the slide show for the specified `Presentation`.

- `Presentation.SlideShowSettings.LoopUntilStopped`—Returns or sets whether or not the slide show for the specified `Presentation` plays continuously. Set this property to `True` to play the slide show in a continuous loop until the user presses Esc; set this property to `False` to play the slide show just once.

- `Presentation.SlideShowSettings.ShowType`—Returns or sets the slide show type for the specified `Presentation`. Use `ppShowTypeSpeaker` (for the standard, full-screen slide show), `ppShowTypeWindow` (to run the slide show in a window), or `ppShowTypeKiosk` (to run the slide show in kiosk mode—full screen with a continuous loop).

- `Presentation.SlideShowSettings.ShowWithAnimation`—Returns or sets whether or not the slide show for the specified `Presentation` uses the animation settings applied to each slide's shapes. Set this property to `True` to enable animation; use `False` to disable animation.

- `Presentation.SlideShowSettings.ShowWithNarration`—Returns or sets whether or not the slide show for the specified `Presentation` uses narration. Set this property to `True` to enable narration; use `False` to disable narration.

- `Presentation.SlideShowSettings.StartingSlide`—Returns or sets the index number of the first slide that is displayed in the slide show for the specified `Presentation`.

Running the Slide Show

At long last you're ready to display the presentation's slide show for all to see. To do so, simply invoke the `Run` method of the `SlideShowSettings` object:

```
Presentation.SlideShowSettings.Run
```

For example, Listing 9.6 shows the last of the Juggling application's procedures. In this case, the procedure presents a dialog box that asks the user whether he or she wants to run the slide show. If Yes is clicked, some transition effects are applied to the instruction slides and then the `Run` method is invoked.

> **Listing 9.6   This Procedure Asks the User Whether He or She Wants to Run the Presentation's Slide Show**

```
Sub RunJugglingSlideShow
    If MsgBox("Start the slide show?", vbYesNo, "Juggling") _
                = vbYes Then
        With pres
            .Slides("Juggling1").SlideShowTransition.EntryEffect =
            ➥ppEffectBlindsHorizontal
            .Slides("Juggling2").SlideShowTransition.EntryEffect =
            ➥pEffectCheckerboardAcross
            .Slides("Juggling3").SlideShowTransition.EntryEffect =
            ➥ppEffectBoxIn
            .Slides("Juggling4").SlideShowTransition.EntryEffect =
            ➥ppEffectStripsLeftDown
            .SlideShowSettings.Run
        End With
    End If
End Sub
```

From Here

- For a general discussion of VBA objects, **see** Chapter 5, "Working with Objects," **p. 71**.

- To learn how to work with For Each...Next, For..Next, and Select Case, **see** Chapter 6, "Controlling Your VBA Code," **p. 91**.

Programming Access Databases

In the past few chapters you've learned about the objects, properties, and methods associated with Word, Excel, and PowerPoint. You've seen that it's possible to manipulate these objects to automate routine tasks and gain an unprecedented amount of control over these programs.

In this chapter, you'll see that using VBA with Access is quite a bit different because you won't learn anything about Access objects. Yes, Access does have an `Application` object and there's a whole hierarchy of objects for things such as forms and reports. However, it's a rare that a VBA programmer ever has to manipulate Access with these objects. Instead, what Access programmers really want to get their hands on is the *data* contained in Access tables and queries.

The secret to doing this is that you use an entirely different object hierarchy altogether to access database info. It's called *ActiveX Data Objects (ADO)* and it's the link between your Access VBA programs and the databases, tables, and queries with which you want to work. The amazing thing about all this is that you can use ADO to work with Access databases from *other* Office applications. For example, you could use ADO programming to grab data from an Access table and insert it in an Excel range. This chapter takes you through the basics of using ADO to connect to and work with Access databases.

10

IN THIS CHAPTER

Getting Ready: Two Steps Before You Begin

When programming Word, Excel, and PowerPoint, you just create or open a module in the Visual Basic Editor and start typing away. Database programming is different because there's a bit of prep work you need to do before you start "slinging code," as programming types like to say. The next two sections explain the details.

Step One: Create a Reference

This may sound strange, but the ability to program a database with ADO is *not* built into Access VBA by default! As I mentioned at the top of the chapter, Access VBA is set up to program forms and reports (among other things); it just can't work with the data that's in those forms and reports, not to mention the tables where the data actually resides. It's weird, I know. So why did Microsoft set things up this way? In simplest terms, there are actually several different ways to program data, and Microsoft quite rightly didn't want to foist a particular method on VBA programmers. (Dedicated database coders are *very* particular about how they access their data; not only that, but Microsoft has developed several new ways to program databases in recent years, so there are compatibility issues to worry about: A program written using a old method doesn't work with any of the new methods.)

> **NOTE**
> ADO isn't part of Access 2007 by default, but another database object model is: *Data Access Objects* (*DAO*). Microsoft says that DAO-based macros run faster than ADO scripts with Access databases. So why teach you ADO? Mostly because ADO is simpler, cleaner, and works well with other database types, such as SQL Server. So if you expand your database programming, you'll be better off knowing ADO than DAO.

So the first thing you need to do is tell Access which method of database programming you want to use. Technically, you're choosing the database *object model*. If you have no idea which one to choose, don't worry about it: As a beginning database programmer, your best bet by far is to choose the most recent object model, which is the Microsoft ActiveX Data Objects 2.8 Library, a mouthful that I'll usually just shorten to ADO in the rest of this chapter. Follow these steps:

1. In the Visual Basic Editor, highlight your project in the Project Explorer. (Access allows only one project—that is, one database—to be open at a time, so this step isn't technically necessary.)
2. Select Tools, References to display the References dialog box.
3. In the Available References list, activate the check box beside the Microsoft ActiveX Data Objects 2.8 Library item, as shown in Figure 10.1. (Note that there's also a Microsoft ActiveX Data Objects 6.0 Library. Microsoft claims this library is "functionally equivalent" to the 2.8 library, so it doesn't matter which one you choose.)
4. Click OK.

Figure 10.1
Use the References dialog box to activate the Microsoft ActiveX Data Objects 2.7 Library check box.

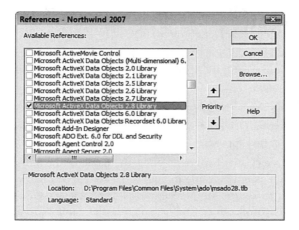

Note that you although you have to do this only once for a given Access database, you must repeat these steps for each subsequent Access database that you use.

> **TIP** The interesting thing about database programming is that you can do it from programs other than Access! For example, you could create a VBA program in Excel that works with data in a separate Access database. The secret to this powerful idea is the References dialog box and the Microsoft ActiveX Data Objects 2.8 Library. By following the steps in this section in, say, Excel (for Step 1, you'd highlight the Excel VBA project you want to work with), you can use all the database programming techniques that you'll learn in the rest of this chapter.

Step Two: Create a Data Source

Another strange thing about database programming is that you always have to set up a *connection*, which is a kind of behind-the-scenes communications link that your code uses to request and change the data. There are two ways to set up a connection.

The first way is to declare a variable as a `Connection` type and then use the `CurrentProject` object's `Connection` property to return the connection:

```
Dim conn As Connection
Set conn = CurrentProject.Connection
```

Alternatively, you need to create a *data source* that specifies the database, and then (as you'll see in the next section) you use your program code to connect to that data source. The good news is that you have to do this only once for each database. Here are the steps to follow:

1. If the database for which you are creating a data source is open in Access, close it.

2. Open the Windows Control Panel and launch the ODBC Data Sources icon. If you see just the Control Panel categories, you need to perform some extra steps:

- **Windows XP**—Click Switch to Classic View, double-click Administrative Tools and then double-click Data Sources (ODBC).
- **Windows Vista**—Click Classic View, double-click Administrative Tools, double-click Data Sources (ODBC), and then enter your User Account Control credentials, if prompted.

3. In the System DSN tab, click A<u>d</u>d. The Create New Data Source dialog box appears.
4. Click Microsoft Access Driver (`*.mdb`, `*.accdb`) and click Finish. The ODBC Microsoft Access Setup dialog box appears.
5. Use the Data Source <u>N</u>ame text box to enter the name of the new data source. Note that this is the name you'll be using in your VBA code. For the code listings in this chapter, I'm going to use the sample `Northwind 2007.accdb` database that you can download from Microsoft Office Online, so enter the name **Northwind**.

> **NOTE** To download the Northwind 2007 sample database, run Access, select Office, <u>N</u>ew, click Sample, click Northwind 2007, and then click <u>C</u>reate.

6. Enter an optional <u>D</u>escription.
7. Click <u>S</u>elect, use the Select Database dialog box to click the Access database file you want to use, and click OK. Figure 10.2 shows the completed dialog box.
8. Click OK to return to the ODBC Data Source Administrator.
9. Click OK.

Figure 10.2
Use the ODBC Microsoft Access Setup dialog box to define the data source.

Working with Database Records: Opening a Recordset

With all those preliminaries out of the way, you can finally get down to the business of database programming. For the purposes of this chapter, database programming consists of manipulating a *recordset*, which represents either the records in a table from an Access database or the records that result from a query. In ADO, you use the `Recordset` object to do all this.

The first thing your procedures will always do is open a recordset. You do that by setting up a connection to a data source, which then gives you access to whatever database was specified when you created the data source. From there you specify the table you want to use, or you set up a query. As you'll see, ADO handily enables you to do all this with a single statement.

Before all that, however, you must declare a variable as a `Recordset` type, as in this example:

```
Sub RecordsetOpenTable()
    Dim rs As ADODB.Recordset
End Sub
```

With that done, you then `Set` the variable equal to a new `Recordset` object:

```
Set rs = CreateObject("ADODB.Recordset")
```

Because ADO isn't "built in" to Access (or any other program), you must create its objects explicitly by using VBA's `CreateObject` method.

Opening a Recordset Using a Table

Now you're ready to open the `Recordset` object by invoking its `Open` method. Here's a simplified version of the syntax:

```
Recordset.Open [Source][, Connection]
```

`Recordset`	The `Recordset` object you want to open.
`Source`	The source of the recordset, which can be a table name or an SQL `SELECT` statement (which I'll explain a bit later).
`Connection`	The connection to use, which for our purposes is just the name of the data source that contains the data with which you want to work.

The easiest way to open a `Recordset` object is to open a table that already exists within the data source. For example, the following statement opens the table named Employees in the Northwind data source:

```
rs.Open "Employees", "Northwind"
```

> **CAUTION**
>
> Before you attempt to run any code against the Northwind 2007 database (or whatever database you're using), first make sure that database is closed. If it's open, VBA generates an error message.

Listing 10.1 shows a complete procedure demonstrating how to declare, open, and close a `Recordset` object.

10

Listing 10.1   Using a Table to Open a Recordset **Object**

```
Sub RecordsetOpenTable()
    Dim rs As ADODB.Recordset
    '
    ' Create the Recordset object
    '
    Set rs = CreateObject("ADODB.Recordset")
    '
    ' Open it
    '
    rs.Open "Employees", "Northwind"
    MsgBox "The " & rs.Source & " table is now open!"
    '
    ' Close it
    '
    rs.Close
    Set rs = Nothing
End Sub
```

> **NOTE**
> The code used in this chapter's examples can be found on my website at the following address:
> http://www.mcfedries.com/Office2007VBA/Chaptr10.xlsm

This example doesn't do much, although it shows you how to fully handle a Recordset object. The first few statements declare the Recordset object, create it, and then open it. In this case, the code opens the Employees table, using the Northwind data source, and then displays a message that the table is open. (Notice that the Source property returns the name of the table.) We're not ready to do anything with the recordset just yet, so the last two statements close the Recordset and Set the variable to the keyword Nothing, which is a useful housekeeping chore that saves memory.

Opening a Recordset: the Full Open Method Syntax

Specifying a table is probably the way you'll open most of your recordsets, but there are other ways to do it. To use them, you need to know the full syntax of the Open method:

Recordset.Open [*Source*][, *Connection*][, *CursorType*][, *LockType*][, *Options*]

Recordset	The Recordset object you want to open.
Source	The source of the recordset, which can be a table name or a SQL SELECT statement.
Connection	The connection to use, which for our purposes is just the name of the data source that contains the data you want to work with.

CursorType	A constant that specifies how the recordset is opened:

adOpenForwardOnly—This is a read-only, forward-scrolling cursor. Use this option for faster performance if you're making just a single pass through the records. This is the default.

adOpenDynamic—This is a dynamic cursor that enables you to insert and update records, and to see changes made by other users.

adOpenKeyset—This is a keyset cursor that enables you to insert and update records, and to see all changes made by other users, except record inserts.

adOpenStatic—This is a static copy of the records. You can insert and update records, but you can't see changes made by other users.

LockEdit	A constant that specifies the locking characteristics of the new recordset:

adLockReadOnly—Prevents users from making changes to the records. This is the default.

adLockPessimistic—In a multiuser environment, the current record is locked as soon as you make changes to it.

adLockOptimistic—In a multiuser environment, the current recordset isn't locked until you run the Update method.

adLockOptimisticBatch—Implements batch optimistic updating (batch mode). You use this when you want to change multiple records and then update them all at once.

Options	A constant that specifies how the provider should interpret the *Source* value. See the VBA Help system for the various adCmd and adAsync constants that are available.

It's worth noting that you can also open a recordset after first setting the following Recordset object properties:

- *Recordset*.Source—A table name or SQL SELECT statement that sets or returns the source of the specified *Recordset* object.
- *Recordset*.ActiveConnection—The connection to use for the specified *Recordset* object.
- *Recordset*.CursorType—The cursor to use with the specified *Recordset* object.
- *Recordset*.LockType—A constant that specifies the locking characteristics of the specified *Recordset* object.

10

After setting these properties, you then run the Open method without specifying any parameters, as shown in Listing 10.2.

Listing 10.2   Using Properties to Open a Recordset **Object**

```
Sub RecordsetOpenProperties()
    Dim rs As ADODB.Recordset
    '
    ' Create the Recordset object
    '
    Set rs = CreateObject("ADODB.Recordset")
    '
    ' Open it
    '
    With rs
        .Source = "Employees"
        .ActiveConnection = "Northwind"
        .Open
        MsgBox "The " & .Source & " table is now open!"
    End With
    '
    ' Close it
    '
    rs.Close
    Set rs = Nothing
End Sub
```

This procedure does the same thing as the one shown earlier in Listing 10.1. This time, however, the Recordset object's Source and ActiveConnection properties are set before the Open method is run.

Opening a Recordset Using a SELECT String

Rather than opening an entire table, you may prefer to open only a subset of a table. The easiest way to do that is to create a Structured Query Language (SQL) statement. This is the language that Access uses when you create a query. SQL is a complex bit of business, but you need only concern yourself with a small portion of it, called the SELECT statement. The SELECT statement is used to create a recordset based on the table, fields, criteria, and other clauses specified in the statement. Here's a simplified syntax of the SELECT statement:

```
SELECT [DISTINCT] field_names
    FROM table_name
    WHERE criteria
    ORDER BY field_names [DESC];
```

SELECT	The SELECT statement always begins with the SELECT keyword.
DISTINCT	This optional keyword specifies that you want only unique records (that is, no duplicates).
field_names	If you want only certain fields to appear in the recordset, enter their names here, separated by commas. If you want all the fields, use *, instead.

FROM *table_name*	This is the name of table that contains the data.
WHERE *criteria*	This filters the data to give you only those records that match the specified *criteria*.
ORDER BY *field_names* [DESC]	This sorts the results in ascending order based on the data in the fields specified by *field_names* (separated by commas, if you have more than one). Use the optional DESC keyword to sort the records in descending order.

For example, the following SELECT statement takes all the fields from the Customers table, restricts the data to those records where the State/Province field equals "CA," and sorts the results, using the data in the Company field:

```
SELECT * FROM Customers WHERE [State/Province]='CA' ORDER BY Company;
```

As another example, the following SELECT statement takes just the Product Name and Standard Cost fields from the Products table and restricts the data to those records where the Standard Cost field is less than 20:

```
SELECT [Product Name], [Standard Cost] FROM Products
WHERE [Standard Cost] < 20;
```

> **TIP**
>
> If you're new to SELECT statements, there's an easy way to avoid errors: Use Access to create a temporary Select query in Access. When the resulting data is what you want, select the Design tab, pull down the View menu, and then choose the SQL View command to display the underlying SELECT statement. You can then copy this statement to your VBA code and delete the query. (One caution: change any double quotation marks (") to single quotes (') to avoid errors when using the SELECT statement within a VBA string variable.)

To use a SELECT statement in your VBA database code, either enter the SELECT string directly into the Recordset object's Open method as the *Source* value, or store it in a String variable and put the variable in the Open method, as shown in Listing 10.3.

Listing 10.3   Opening a Recordset **Object Using a** SELECT **Statement**

```
Sub RecordsetOpenSELECT()
    Dim rs As ADODB.Recordset
    Dim strSELECT As String
    '
    ' Create the Recordset object
    '
    Set rs = CreateObject("ADODB.Recordset")
    '
    ' Open it
    '
    strSELECT = "SELECT * FROM Customers " & _
```

continues

10

Listing 10.3   Continued

```
                "WHERE [State/Province]='CA' " & _
                "ORDER BY Company;"
    rs.Open strSELECT, "Northwind", adOpenKeyset
    MsgBox "The " & rs.Source & " table is now open!"
    '
    ' Close it
    '
    rs.Close
    Set rs = Nothing
End Sub
```

Working with a Recordset

The examples you've seen so far haven't done very much with the Recordset objects they've opened. To do something useful with the records you need to wield the Recordset object's properties and methods. You learn the most useful of these properties and methods in the next few sections.

Getting at the Recordset Data

In most cases, the point of opening a recordset is to get your hands on the data that's in a certain record. More specifically, you'll most often want to get whatever data is in a certain *field* within a record. You do that by invoking the Recordset object's Fields property:

Recordset.Fields(*FieldName*)

Recordset	The Recordset object with which you want to work.
FieldName	A string or String variable containing the name of the field that contains the data you want.

For example, if you're working with Northwind's Customers table, the following statement stores the data from the current record's First Name and Last Name fields in a variable named currentContact:

```
currentContact = rs.Fields("First Name") & " " & rs.Fields("Last Name")
```

Note, however, that Fields is the default property for a Recordset object, so you can save some typing by leaving out the .Fields part. In other words, the following two values are equivalent:

```
rs.Fields("First Name")
rs("First Name")
```

Listing 10.4 shows another example.

Listing 10.4   Getting Recordset Data

```
Sub RecordsetData()
    Dim rs As ADODB.Recordset
    Dim strSELECT As String
    '
    ' Create the Recordset object
    '
    Set rs = CreateObject("ADODB.Recordset")
    '
    ' Open it
    '
    strSELECT = "SELECT * FROM Customers " & _
                "WHERE [State/Province]='CA' " & _
                "ORDER BY Company;"
    rs.Open strSELECT, "Northwind", adOpenKeyset
    '
    ' Display the contact name and company name from the first record
    '
    MsgBox rs.("First Name") & " " & rs.("Last Name") & _
           ", " & rs("Company")
    '
    ' Close it
    '
    rs.Close
    Set rs = Nothing
End Sub
```

In this procedure, a recordset is opened with a SELECT statement that restricts the customers to just those where the State/Province field equals "CA." Then a MsgBox function displays the data from the First Name, Last Name, and Company fields for the first record.

> **CAUTION**
>
> When using a SELECT statement with a WHERE clause, there's always the possibility that the resulting recordset may contain no records. In that case, if your code attempts to access the data in the "current" record, an error results. To avoid this, open the recordset using either the adOpenKeyset or adOpenStatic cursor types and then check the Recordset object's RecordCount property. If this is greater than 0, it means the recordset has at least one record and so it's safe to proceed. Here's a snippet that modifies part of Listing 10.4 to check for at least one record before displaying the data:
>
> ```
> rs.Open strSELECT, "Northwind", adOpenKeyset
> If rs.RecordCount > 0 Then
>     MsgBox rs("ContactName") & ", " & rs("CompanyName")
> End If
> ```

Navigating Records

As I mentioned in the previous section, the Fields property returns the data from a field in the current record. When you first open a recordset, the current record is the first record. To get to another record, you need to navigate to it. There are a number of ways to do this, but the following four methods are the ones you'll probably use most often:

- *Recordset*.MoveFirst—Moves to the first record in the specified *Recordset* object.
- *Recordset*.MoveLast—Moves to the last record in the specified *Recordset* object.
- *Recordset*.MoveNext—Moves to the next record in the specified *Recordset* object.
- *Recordset*.MovePrevious—Moves to the previous record in the specified *Recordset*.

> **CAUTION** _____
>
> Note that the MoveLast and MovePrevious methods don't work if you use the
> adOpenForwardOnly cursor to open the recordset.

With these methods you're changing a value that points to the current record. This is all straightforward except in two situations:

- You're on the first record and you run the MovePrevious method.
- You're on the last record and you run the MoveNext method.

VBA lets you do these things, but in a sense they enable you to move "outside" the record-set. If you try to access the data, you get an error message that begins Either BOF or EOF is True. Here, BOF means *beginning of file* and EOF means *end of file*. These are properties of the Recordset object:

- *Recordset*.BOF—Returns True if the cursor is before the first record in the specified *Recordset* object.
- *Recordset*.EOF—Returns True if the cursor is after the first record in the specified *Recordset* object.

To avoid the error, you should use test properties in your code. For example, the following snippet runs the MoveNext method and then checks the EOF property. If it's True, then the cursor is moved to the last record:

```
rs.MoveNext
If rs.EOF Then
    rs.MoveLast
End If
```

Another way to move is to use the Recordset object's Move method, which moves the cursor a set number of records from the current record:

Recordset.Move *NumRecords*[, *Start*]

Recordset	The Recordset object with which you want to work.
NumRecords	The number of records you want to move. Use a positive number to move toward the end of the recordset; use a negative number to move toward the beginning of the recordset.
Start	Use this optional parameter to specify a starting record from which to perform the move.

The *Start* parameter should be the name of a `Variant` variable that contains a *bookmark*, which is a saved location in a recordset. You set and read bookmarks with the `Recordset` object's `Bookmark` property. Listing 10.5 provides an example.

Listing 10.5 Using a Bookmark to Navigate a Recordset

```
Sub RecordsetBookmarkNavigation()
    Dim rs As ADODB.Recordset
    Dim strSELECT As String
    Dim savedRecord As Variant

    ' Create the Recordset object

    Set rs = CreateObject("ADODB.Recordset")

    ' Open it

    strSELECT = "SELECT * FROM Products " & _
                "WHERE [Standard Cost] < 20 " & _
                "ORDER BY [Product Name];"
    rs.Open strSELECT, "Northwind", adOpenKeyset

    ' Move, save the current record as a Bookmark, and display the data

    rs.Move 3
    savedRecord = rs.Bookmark
    MsgBox rs("Product Name") & " - " & rs("Standard Cost")

    ' Move the current record

    rs.Move -2
    MsgBox rs("Product Name") & " - " & rs("Standard Cost")

    ' Move relative to the Bookmark

    rs.Move 5, savedRecord
    MsgBox rs("Product Name") & " - " & rs("Standard Cost")

    ' Move to the bookmark

    rs.Bookmark = savedRecord
    MsgBox rs("Product Name") & " - " & rs("Standard Cost")

    ' Close it

    rs.Close
    Set rs = Nothing
End Sub
```

After the recordset is opened, the `Move` method is used to move forward three records, and then the `Bookmark` property is used to save the current record to the `savedRecord` variable. The code moves back two records and then moves forward five records from the bookmark. Finally the cursor is returned to the saved record by setting the value of the `Bookmark` property to `savedRecord`. Note that the following two statements do the same thing:

```
rs.Bookmark = savedRecord
rs.Move 0, savedRecord
```

Finding a Record

Another way to navigate a recordset is to search for a specific record, using one or more criteria. ADO gives you two methods to use—Find and Seek. Find searches some or all of the recordset directly using criteria, but Seek can only search using an index defined on the recordset. However, you need to learn how to use only the Find method because it's simpler than Seek and works well on all but the largest recordsets.

Here's the syntax for the Find method:

```
Recordset.Find Criteria[, SkipRows][, SearchDirection][, Start]
```

Recordset	The Recordset object with which you want to work.
Criteria	An expression that specifies the criteria you want to use to find the record.
SkipRows	An optional value that specifies the number of rows from the current record (or the record specified by the Start parameter) where the search should begin. The default value is 0.
SearchDirection	An optional constant that specifies which direction the search should take. Use adSearchForward (the default value) to search forward through the records; use adSearchBackward to search backward.
Start	An optional bookmark that specifies the starting record from which to perform the search.

When you run this method, one of two things will happen:

- **A record is found that matches the criteria**—In this case, the cursor is moved to that record.
- **No record is found that matches the criteria**—If the SearchDirection parameter is adSearchForward, the search stops at the end of the recordset (the EOF property returns True); if the SearchDirection parameter is adSearchBackward, the search stops at the beginning of the recordset (the BOF property returns True).

This tells you that you can determine whether or not the search was successful by testing the EOF or BOF property (depending on the search direction) after running the Find method. Listing 10.6 gives an example.

Listing 10.6 Using the Find Method

```
Sub SearchRecordsWithFind()
    Dim rs As ADODB.Recordset
    Dim strCriteria As String
```

```
'
' Create the Recordset object
'
Set rs = CreateObject("ADODB.Recordset")
'
' Open it
'
With rs
    .Source = "Employees"
    .ActiveConnection = "Northwind"
    .CursorType = adOpenKeyset
    .Open
End With
'
' Run the Find method
'
strCriteria = "City='Seattle'"
rs.Find strCriteria
'
' Loop to find other records that meet the criteria
'
Do While Not rs.EOF
    '
    ' Display the data
    '
    MsgBox rs("First Name") & " " & rs("Last Name")
    '
    ' Search again, but skip a row
    '
    rs.Find strCriteria, 1
Loop
'
' Close the recordset
'
rs.Close
Set rs = Nothing
End Sub
```

After opening the Employees table as the recordset, this code uses the strCriteria variable to hold the criteria string "City='Seattle'". Then the Find method locates the first record that meets this criteria. A Do While...Loop is set up to loop as long as rs.EOF is False. Inside the loop, the employee's name is displayed and then the Find method is run again, although with the *SkipRows* parameter set to 1 to avoid finding the same record over and over again.

Editing a Record

After you've navigated to or found the record you want, you may want to do more than just display the data or store the data in a variable or two. Instead, you may want to edit the data by making changes to one or more fields. Editing the current record is a two-step process:

1. Change the data in one or more fields. Changing the data is straightforward because you treat each field just like a variable:

```
rs("Title") = "Account Manager"
rs("UnitPrice") = 19.95
```

2. Update the record to write the new data to the table. You do this by running the Recordset object's Update method.

Listing 10.7 puts these steps to work.

Listing 10.7   Editing Recordset Data

```
Sub EditingARecord()
    Dim rs As ADODB.Recordset
    Dim strCriteria As String
    '
    ' Create the Recordset object
    '
    Set rs = CreateObject("ADODB.Recordset")
    '
    ' Open it
    '
    With rs
        .Source = "Employees"
        .ActiveConnection = "Northwind"
        .CursorType = adOpenKeyset
        .LockType = adLockPessimistic
        .Open
    End With
    '
    ' Run the Find method
    '
    strCriteria = "[Job Title]='Sales Representative'"
    rs.Find strCriteria
    '
    ' Loop to find other records that meet the criteria
    '
    Do While Not rs.EOF
        '
        ' Display the data
        '
        rs("Job Title") = "Account Manager"
        rs.Update
        MsgBox rs("First Name") &" ." & rs("Last Name") & ", " & rs("Job Title")
        '
        ' Search again, but skip a row
        '
        rs.Find strCriteria, 1
    Loop
    '
    ' Close the recordset
    '
    rs.Close
    Set rs = Nothing
End Sub
```

After opening the Employees table, the `Find` method is used to locate the first record where the `Job Title` field equals "Sales Representative." A `Do While...Loop` checks the `EOF` property. Inside the loop, the `Job Title` field is changed to "Account Manager" and the `Update` method finalizes the changes for the current record. The `Find` method is run again to continue the process.

Adding a New Record

If you have new information to insert into a table, ADO enables you to add a new record and populate its fields with the new data. This is accomplished with the `Recordset` object's `AddNew` method.

There are two ways to use `AddNew`. In the simplest case, you follow a three-step procedure:

1. Run the `AddNew` method.
2. Add the data to the new record's fields.
3. Call the `Update` method to write the new record and data to the table.

> **CAUTION**
>
> To successfully add a new record to a table, you need to open the recordset with the `LockType` parameter or property set to either `adLockOptimistic` or `adLockPessimistic`.

Listing 10.8 takes you through an example.

Listing 10.8 Adding a New Record

```
Sub AddingARecord()
    Dim rs As ADODB.Recordset
    '
    ' Create the Recordset object
    '
    Set rs = CreateObject("ADODB.Recordset")
    '
    ' Open it
    '
    With rs
        .Source = "Customers"
        .ActiveConnection = "Northwind"
        .CursorType = adOpenKeyset
        .LockType = adLockOptimistic
        .Open
    End With
    '
    ' Create the new record
    '
    rs.AddNew
    '
    ' Enter the data for the new record
    '
```

continues

Listing 10.8   Continued

```
    rs("Company") = "Ayrshire Haggis"
    rs("First Name") = "Angus"
    rs("Last Name") = "Dunlop"
    rs("E-mail Address") = "adunlop@ayrshirehaggis.co.uk"
    rs("Job Title") = "Owner"
    rs("Address") = "123 Cathcart St."
    rs("City") = "Ayr"
    rs("State/Province") = "Ayrshire"
    rs("ZIP/Postal Code") = "KA18 4PN"
    rs("Country/Region") = "Scotland"
    rs("Business Phone") = "01290 555555"
    rs("Fax Number") = "01290 666666"
    '
    ' Write the new record to the table
    '
    rs.Update
    '
    ' Close the recordset
    '
    rs.Close
    Set rs = Nothing
End Sub
```

This code opens the Customers table (notice that LockType is set to adLockOptimistic). Then the AddNew method is run and the various fields in the new record are populated with data. Finally, the Update method writes the new record to the table.

The second way to use the AddNew method combines the first two steps into a single statement:

Recordset.AddNew [*FieldList*][, *Values*]

Recordset	The Recordset object with which you want to work.
FieldList	A field name or an array of field names.
Values	A single value or an array of values for the fields in the new record.

Here's a statement that creates a new record and populates a single field:

```
rs.AddNew "Company", "Ayrshire Haggis"
```

Here's another that uses the Array function to populate an entire record in a single statement:

```
rs.AddNew Array("Company", "First Name", "Last Name", _
        "E-mail Address", "Job Title", "Address", _
        "City", "State/Province", "ZIP/Postal Code", _
        "Country/Region", "Business Phone", "Fax Number"), _
    Array("Ayrshire Haggis", "Angus", "Dunlop", _
        "adunlop@ayrshirehaggis.co.uk", "Owner", "123 Cathcart St.", _
        "Ayr", "Ayrshire", "KA18 4PN", _
        "Scotland", "01290 555555", "01290 666666")
```

Deleting a Record

If a record is obsolete or simply no longer needed for some reason, you should delete it from the table to reduce clutter and keep the table up to date. This is handled easily by the Recordset object's Delete method, which marks the current record for deletion. You then run the Update method to confirm the deletion.

> **TIP** If you run the Delete method and then decide against the deletion, you can back out of it by running the CancelUpdate method before running the Update method.

Listing 10.9 puts the Delete method through its paces.

Listing 10.9 Deleting a Record

```
Sub DeletingARecord()
    Dim rs As ADODB.Recordset
    Dim strCriteria As String
    '
    ' Create the Recordset object
    '
    Set rs = CreateObject("ADODB.Recordset")
    '
    ' Open it
    '
    With rs
        .Source = "Customers"
        .ActiveConnection = "Northwind"
        .CursorType = adOpenKeyset
        .LockType = adLockOptimistic
        .Open
    End With
    '
    ' Run the Find method
    '
    strCriteria = "Company='Ayrshire Haggis'"
    rs.Find strCriteria
    '
    ' Loop to find other records that meet the criteria
    '
    If Not rs.EOF Then
        rs.Delete
        rs.Update
        MsgBox "The customer with " & strCriteria & " has been deleted."
    Else
        MsgBox "The customer with " & strCriteria & " was not found!"
    End If
    '
    ' Close the recordset
    '
    rs.Close
    Set rs = Nothing
End Sub
```

10

After opening the recordset (again, notice that you need to set LockType to either adLockOptimistic or adLockPessimistic), the Find method is used to locate the record to be deleted. If the record was found (that is, the recordset's EOF property is False), the code runs the Delete method, followed by the Update method. A message tells the user that the record has been deleted.

Retrieving Data into Excel

As I mentioned near the top of the chapter, you normally use ADO from a program other than Access (or in Access when the database you want to work with isn't the current database). Most people work with table data in Excel because the row-and-column layout of a worksheet fits well with the record-and-field layout of a table.

To get data from a table into an Excel worksheet, you have three choices:

- Retrieving an individual field value.
- Retrieving one or more entire records.
- Retrieving an entire recordset.

Retrieving an Individual Field Value

For individual field values, move to the record you want to work with and then assign the value of the field to the worksheet cell. For example, the following statement returns the value of the current record's Country field and stores it in cell A1 of the active worksheet:

```
ActiveSheet.[A1] = rs("Country")
```

Retrieving One or More Entire Rows

To get full records, use the Recordset object's GetRows method:

```
Recordset.GetRows [Rows][, Start][, Fields]
```

Recordset	The Recordset object with which you want to work.
Rows	The number of records you want to retrieve, starting from the current record. If you want to retrieve the rest of the records (that is, all the records from the current records to the end of the recordset) use the constant value adGetRowsRest.
Start	Use this optional parameter to specify a bookmark as the starting point from which to retrieve the records.
Fields	Use this optional parameter to specify the fields that are retrieved. Use a single field name or an array of field names.

The GetRows method returns the records in a two-dimensional array, where the first subscript is a number that represents the field (the first field is 0) and the second subscript represents the record number (where the first record is 0). Listing 10.10 shows an example.

Listing 10.10   Retrieving Entire Records into Excel

```
Sub RetrievingEntireRecords()
    Dim rs As ADODB.Recordset
    Dim strCriteria As String
    Dim recordArray As Variant
    '
    ' Create the Recordset object
    '
    Set rs = CreateObject("ADODB.Recordset")
    '
    ' Open it
    '
    With rs
        .Source = "Customers"
        .ActiveConnection = "Northwind"
        .CursorType = adOpenKeyset
        .Open
    End With
    '
    ' Head for Database Records worksheet
    '
    Worksheets("Database Records").Activate
    With Worksheets("Database Records").[a1]
        '
        ' Clear the sheet
        '
        .CurrentRegion.Clear
        '
        ' Read the data using GetRows
        '
        recordArray = rs.GetRows(50)
        '
        ' Run through the array and write the data to the worksheet
        '
        For i = 0 To UBound(recordArray, 2)
            For j = 0 To UBound(recordArray, 1)
                .Offset(i + 1, j) = recordArray(j, i)
            Next j
        Next i
        '
        ' Enter the field names in the first row and format the cells
        '
        For j = 0 To rs.Fields.Count - 1
            .Offset(0, j) = rs.Fields(j).Name
            .Offset(0, j).Font.Bold = True
            .Offset(0, j).EntireColumn.AutoFit
        Next j
    End With
    '
    ' Close the recordset
    '
    rs.Close
    Set rs = Nothing
End Sub
```

10

After opening the Customers table, this procedure performs a few Excel VBA chores, including activating the "Database Records" worksheet and clearing the sheet to remove any existing data. Then GetRows is used to retrieve the first 50 rows of the table. A For...Next loop runs through the two-dimensional array writing the data in the worksheet's rows and columns. Then another For...Next loop writes the column names on the top row and formats the cells for easier reading.

Retrieving an Entire Recordset

If you need to retrieve an entire recordset into a worksheet, one way to do it would be to run GetRows(adGetRowsRest) from the first record and then use the technique in Listing 10.10 to write the data to the worksheet. However, Excel offers you an easier method—the Range object's CopyFromRecordset method:

```
Range.CopyFromRecordset(Data[, MaxRows][, MaxColumns])
```

Range	A *Range* object that specifies the upper-left corner of the destination range.
Data	The recordset containing the data you want to retrieve.
MaxRows	The maximum number of records to retrieve. If you omit this optional parameter, Excel copies every record.
MaxColumns	The maximum number of fields to retrieve. If you omit this optional parameter, Excel copies every field.

Here are a few notes to bear in mind when working with CopyFromRecordset:

- Excel begins the copying from the current record. If you want to retrieve every record, make sure you run the MoveFirst method to move to the first record.
- When the CopyFromRecordset method is done, the Recordset object's EOF property is True.
- CopyFromRecordset fails if the Recordset object has a field that contains binary data (that is, if it's an OLE object field).

Listing 10.11 shows the RetrieveProducts procedure that uses the CopyFromRecordset method.

Listing 10.11   Retrieving an Entire Recordset

```
Sub RetrieveProducts()
    Dim rs As ADODB.Recordset
    Dim fld As Field
    Dim strSELECT As String, i As Integer
    '
    ' Create the Recordset object
    '
    Set rs = CreateObject("ADODB.Recordset")
    '
    ' Open it
```

```
'
With rs
    .Source = "Products"
    .ActiveConnection = "Northwind"
    .CursorType = adOpenKeyset
    .Open
End With
'
' The strSELECT variable will hold the SQL SELECT statement
' that filters the Recordset to remove binary fields
'
strSELECT = "SELECT "
'
' Run through the recordset fields
'
For Each fld In rs.Fields
    '
    ' Check for binary fields
    '
    If fld.Type <> adBinary And fld.Type <> adLongVarBinary Then
        '
        ' If it's not an OLE Object field,
        ' add it to the SELECT statement
        '
        strSELECT = strSELECT & "[" & fld.Name & "],"
    End If
Next fld
'
' Remove the trailing comma
'
strSELECT = Left(strSELECT, Len(strSELECT) - 1)
'
' Add the FROM clause
'
strSELECT = strSELECT & " FROM Products"
'
' Open the filtered recordset
'
With rs
    .Close
    .Source = strSELECT
    .ActiveConnection = "Northwind"
    .CursorType = adOpenKeyset
    .Open
End With
'
' Activate the Database Records worksheet
'
Worksheets("Database Records").Activate
With Worksheets("Database Records").[a1]
    '
    ' Clear the sheet
    '
    .CurrentRegion.Clear
    '
    ' Get the entire recordset
    '
```

10

continues

Listing 10.11 Continued

```
        .Offset(1).CopyFromRecordset rs
        '
        ' Enter the field names and format the cells
        '
        For i = 0 To rs.Fields.Count - 1
            .Offset(0, i) = rs.Fields(i).Name
            .Offset(0, i).Font.Bold = True
            .Offset(0, i).EntireColumn.AutoFit
        Next i
    End With
    '
    ' Close and release the objects
    '
    rs.Close
    Set rs = Nothing
    Set fld = Nothing
End Sub
```

The RetrieveProducts procedure opens the Products table as the Recordset object. You want to make sure that you don't try to copy any OLE Object fields, so the procedure constructs a SQL SELECT statement that excludes any fields that contain binary data (OLE objects). The strSELECT variable holds the SELECT statement, so it's initialized to SELECT followed by a space. Then a For...Next loop runs through each field in rs and looks for OLE Object fields (where the Type property is adBinary or adLongVarBinary). If a field isn't an OLE Object type, its name (surrounded by square brackets—[and]— and followed by a comma separator) is appended to the SELECT statement.

Next, the trailing comma is removed and the FROM clause is concatenated to the SELECT statement. A new recordset is opened based on strSELECT, and then the CopyFromRecordset method retrieves the records.

From Here

- I used the MsgBox function a few times in this chapter. **See** "Getting Input Using MsgBox," **p. 45**.

- For information on working with Excel's objects, **see** Chapter 8, "Programming Excel," **p. 139**.

Programming Outlook Email

Not many people know it, but Microsoft Outlook also incorporates VBA, so you can create Outlook-based VBA macros and applications. Outlook itself is a big program, so you can imagine that the Outlook object model is huge, with dozens of objects and untold numbers of properties, methods, and events. Space limitations prevent me from examining this model in detail, so this chapter takes you through just those objects related to Outlook's email features.

Getting Started

Although Outlook has an `Application` object at the top of its hierarchy, your Outlook programming will rarely need to use it. Instead, your programs will always begin with the `NameSpace` object. This oddly named item acts as a top-level object for a *data source*, which, as its name implies, is a kind of container for data. The `NameSpace` object enables you to log in to the source, access the data, and then log out. In Outlook's case, the only supported data source is something called *MAPI—Mail Application Programming Interface*—which represents the data in an Outlook personal folders store (a `.pst` file).

After you've started Outlook, you've already logged in, so your code can simply refer to the current session as the namespace. To do that, you use the default Outlook object, which is called `ThisOutlookSession`. Use this object's `Session` property to get the `NameSpace` object:

```
Dim ns As NameSpace
Set ns = ThisOutlookSession.Session
```

Working with Outlook Folders

The NameSpace object stores all the Outlook folders, which means you can use it to return a reference to a folder and then work with that folder. Note that in the Outlook object model, folders are MAPIFolder objects.

Referencing Default Folders

One way to return a MAPIFolder object is to use the GetDefaultFolder method, which returns the default folder for a given type in the current profile. Here's the syntax:

NameSpace.GetDefaultFolder(*FolderType*)

NameSpace	The NameSpace object.
FolderType	A constant that specifies the type of folder. Here are the defined constants you'll use most often: olFolderCalendar, olFolderContacts, olFolderDeletedItems, olFolderInbox, olFolderJournal, olFolderJunk, olFolderNotes, olFolderOutbox, olRssFeeds, olFolderSentMail, and olFolderTasks.

For example, if you wanted to work with the Inbox folder, your procedure would start with the following statements:

```
Dim ns As NameSpace
Dim ib As MAPIFolder
Set ns = ThisOutlookSession.Session
Set ib = ns.GetDefaultFolder(olFolderInbox)
```

Using the Folders Property

Alternatively, you can use the NameSpace object's Folders property to return a Folders object that represents all the MAPIFolder objects in the PST file. To reference a specific folder, use Folders(*Index*), where *Index* is one of the following:

- An integer value with the first folder being 1, the second folder being 2, and so on.
- The name of the folder in quotation marks.

The NameSpace object has only one folder—known as the *root*—which is usually called "Personal Folders." Therefore, the following statements are equivalent (assume ns is a NameSpace object):

```
ns.Folders(1)
ns.Folders("Personal Folders")
```

All the other mail folders are subfolders of this root. To get at them, you tack on another Folders property in the same way. For example, the first subfolder in the root is usually Deleted Items, so the following are equivalent:

```
ns.Folders(1).Folders(1)
ns.Folders("Personal Folders").Folders("Deleted Items")
```

To help give you a feel for how these folders work, Listing 11.1 shows a procedure that runs through the first- and second-level folders in the namespace. Before you run this code, however, display the Visual Basic Editor's Immediate window by activating the <u>V</u>iew, <u>I</u>mmediate Window command (or by pressing Ctrl+G).

➔ For more information about the Immediate window, **see** "Using the Immediate Window," **p. 348**.

Listing 11.1   A Procedure That Lists the First- and Second-Level Folders in the Outlook Namespace

```
Sub ListFolders()
    Dim ns As NameSpace
    Dim folder As MAPIFolder
    Dim subfolder As MAPIFolder
    '
    ' Set up the namespace
    '
    Set ns = ThisOutlookSession.Session
    '
    ' Run through the first-level folders
    '
    For Each folder In ns.Folders
        Debug.Print folder.Name
        '
        ' Run through the second-level folders, if any
        '
        If folder.Folders.Count > 1 Then
            For Each subfolder In folder.Folders
                Debug.Print "    " & subfolder.Name
            Next 'subfolder
        End If
    Next 'folder
    Set ns = Nothing
End Sub
```

> **NOTE**
>
> For the Outlook procedures in this chapter, I've put everything into a text file named `Chapter11.txt`, which you'll find on my website:
>
> http://www.mcfedries.com/Office2007VBA/Chapter11.txt
>
> To use the code, create a module in Outlook's Visual Basic Editor, copy the code from `Chapter11.txt`, and then paste it into the module.

After establishing the namespace session, the For Each...Next loop runs through the folders. The Debug.Print command is used to display the name of each folder (as given by the Name property) in the Immediate window, as shown in Figure 11.1. If the folder has subfolders, another For Each...Next loop runs through the subfolders in the same manner.

Figure 11.1
When you run the
ListFolders
procedure, the
names of the email
folders and subfold-
ers are printed in the
Immediate window.

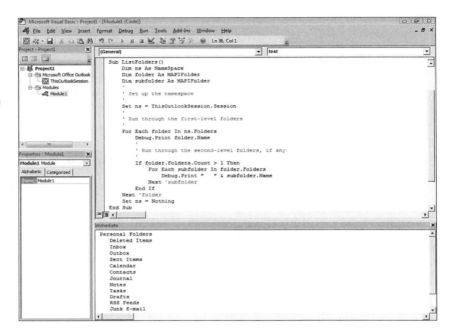

Prompting the User for a Folder

Another way to get a folder is to use the NameSpace object's PickFolder method:

NameSpace.PickFolder

> *NameSpace*   The NameSpace object.

This method displays the Select Folder dialog box so that the user can choose a folder. The
return value depends on the button the user clicks:

- If the user clicks OK, the return value is a MAPIFolder object corresponding to the
  folder highlighted by the user.
- If the user clicks Cancel, the return value is Nothing.

Listing 11.2 shows an example that invokes PickFolder and then tests the result.

Listing 11.2   A Procedure to Test the PickFolder **Method**

```
Sub PickFolderTest()
    Dim ns As NameSpace
    Dim folder As MAPIFolder
    '
    ' Set up the namespace
    '
    Set ns = ThisOutlookSession.Session
    '
    ' Display the Select Folder dialog box
```

```
    '
    Set folder = ns.PickFolder
    '
    ' Test the return value
    '
    If Not folder Is Nothing Then
        MsgBox "You picked " & folder.Name
    End If
End Sub
```

Notice that the code uses the following test for the dialog box result:

```
If Not folder Is Nothing Then
```

If this returns `True` (that is, if the value of the folder variable is not equal to `Nothing`), then the name of the folder is displayed.

Some MAPIFolder **Methods**

Although you probably won't use them very often, the `MAPIFolder` object does come with a few methods:

- *MAPIFolder*.CopyTo—Copies the specified *MAPIFolder* to another folder:

  ```
  MAPIFolder.CopyTo(DestinationFolder)
  ```

MAPIFolder	The `MAPIFolder` object you want to copy.
DestinationFolder	The `MAPIFolder` object to which you want the folder copied.

- *MAPIFolder*.Delete—Deletes the specified *MAPIFolder*.

- *MAPIFolder*.MoveTo—Moves the specified *MAPIFolder* to another folder:

  ```
  MAPIFolder.MoveTo(DestinationFolder)
  ```

MAPIFolder	The `MAPIFolder` object you want to move.
DestinationFolder	The `MAPIFolder` object to which you want the folder moved.

Handling Incoming and Outgoing Messages

Much of the VBA work you'll do in Outlook will be in response to either incoming or outgoing messages. For example, you may want your code to examine incoming messages to look for a certain subject line or priority, and then process the message accordingly. Similarly, you might want to configure outgoing messages so that Outlook asks you whether to store a message in Sent Items.

11

Incoming: Handling the ItemAdd Event

To handle incoming messages, you need to set up the Inbox folder as a programmable object, which enables you to write code that examines every incoming message and then performs some action on each message.

To begin, open Outlook's VBA Editor, open the default project (Project1), and then open the Microsoft Office Outlook Objects branch. Double-click ThisOutlookSession to open the module window you'll use to enter the code. At the top of the module, add the following statements to declare two global variables:

```
Dim ns As NameSpace
Private WithEvents inboxItems As Items
```

Listing 11.3 shows two event handlers that you also need to add to the module. (An *event handler* is procedure that runs when a particular event fires. For example, Outlook's Application object has a Startup event that fires each time you launch Outlook.)

Listing 11.3   Event Handlers for Outlook's Startup and Quit Events

```
Private Sub Application_Startup()
    '
    ' Set up the namespace
    '
    Set ns = ThisOutlookSession.Session
    '
    ' Get the Inbox Items object
    '
    Set inboxItems = ns.GetDefaultFolder(olFolderInbox).Items
End Sub

Private Sub Application_Quit()
    '
    ' Clear the objects to save memory
    '
    Set inboxItems = Nothing
    Set ns = Nothing
End Sub
```

The Application_Startup event handler runs automatically each time you start Outlook. The procedure initializes two variables: ns, which stores the NameSpace object that enables you to work with Outlook folders and items, and inboxItems, which stores the Item objects (messages) in the Inbox folder. The Application_Quit event handler runs when you shut down Outlook, and it sets the inboxItems and ns objects to Nothing to save memory.

To work with messages as they come in, you need another event handler, this time to run when the ItemAdd event fires. Listing 11.4 shows a skeleton of this event handler.

Listing 11.4   A Skeleton Event Handler for the `ItemAdd` **Event**

```
Private Sub inboxItems_ItemAdd(ByVal Item As Object)
    '
    ' Code to process the new message goes here
    '
End Sub
```

This code is the event handler for the Inbox folder's `ItemAdd` event, which runs automatically each time a new message is added to the Inbox. The procedure is passed the `Item` object, which represents the message added to the Inbox. You'll see specific examples of this event handler a bit later.

Outgoing: Handling the `ItemSend` Event

To process outgoing mail, you need to add code to handle another `Application` object event: `ItemSend`. As with the `ItemAdd` event that I discussed in the previous section, you set up the event handler by using the `ThisOutlookSession` object, which is part of the default Outlook VBA project. In the Visual Basic Editor, click `ThisOutlookSession` and then click Application in the Object list. Outlook adds the following stub to the module:

```
Private Sub Application_ItemSend(ByVal Item As Object, Cancel As Boolean)

End Sub
```

In the procedure's arguments, `Item` represents the message you're sending and `Cancel` is a `Boolean` variable that you set to `True` if you don't want Outlook to send the message.

For example, as you may know, Outlook is set up by default to always save a copy of each outgoing message in the Sent Items folder. However, there may be times when you don't want a copy of an outgoing message stored in Sent Items. For example, you may not want to save forwarded messages or messages that contain large attachments. Listing 11.5 shows an event handler for `ItemSend` that prompts you to choose whether Outlook should save the outgoing message in Sent Items.

 You can toggle the saving of outgoing messages in the Sent Items folder by choosing Tools, Options, clicking E-mail Options in the Preferences tab, and then clicking the Save Copies of Messages in Sent Items Folder check box.

11

Listing 11.5   An Event Handler for `ItemSend` **That Prompts You to Save a Copy of an Outgoing Message in the Sent Items Folder**

```
Private Sub Application_ItemSend(ByVal Item As Object, Cancel As Boolean)
    Dim nResult As Integer
    '
    ' Display the prompt
    '
```

continues

Listing 11.5 Continued

```
    nResult = MsgBox("Save this message in Sent Items?", vbSystemModal +
➥vbYesNoCancel)
    '
    ' Check the result
    '
    If nResult = vbCancel Then
        Cancel = True
    End If

    If nResult = vbNo Then
        '
        ' If the user clicked No, don't save the message in Sent Items
        '
        Item.DeleteAfterSubmit = True
    End If
End Sub
```

A Yes/No/Cancel `MsgBox` function asks whether you want the message saved in Sent Items, and the response is stored in the `nResult` variable. If you click the Cancel button, the procedure sets `Cancel` to `True`, which means Outlook doesn't send the message. (The message stays onscreen.) If you click the No button, instead, the procedure sets the message's `DeleteAfterSubmit` property to `True`, which means Outlook doesn't store a copy in Sent Items.

Working with Email Messages

After you have your `NameSpace` session and have referenced the `MAPIFolder` object you want to work with, you'll probably want to do something with the messages in that folder: display them, move them, respond to them, and so on. To access the messages, you use the `MAPIFolder` object's `Items` collection, which contains all the messages in the folder. Each of these messages is a `MailItem` object, and it's to this object that you'll turn your attention for most of the rest of this chapter.

`MailItem` **Object Properties**

The `MailItem` object boasts dozens of properties that cover everything from the message recipients to the assigned sensitivity. Here's a list of the most useful `MailItem` properties:

- *`MailItem`*`.BCC`—Returns the display names (separated by semicolons) of the addresses listed as blind courtesy (or carbon) copy recipients for the specified *`MailItem`*.

- *`MailItem`*`.Body`—Returns or sets the body text for the specified *`MailItem`*.

- *`MailItem`*`.BodyFormat`—Returns or sets the format of the body text for the specified *`MailItem`*. Possible values are the following constants: `olFormatHTML`, `olFormatPlain`, `olFormatRichText`, and `olFormatUnspecified`.

- *MailItem*.CC—Returns the display names (separated by semicolons) of the addresses listed as courtesy (or carbon) copy recipients for the specified *MailItem*.

- *MailItem*.FlagRequest—Returns or sets a string that specifies the action to take for a flagged *MailItem*.

- *MailItem*.HTMLBody—Returns or sets the HTML body text for the specified *MailItem*.

- *MailItem*.Importance—Returns or sets the importance level for the specified *MailItem*. This property can be one of the following constants: olImportanceHigh, olImportanceLow, or olImportanceNormal.

- *MailItem*.ReadReceiptRequested—Returns True if the sender has requested a read receipt for the specified *MailItem*; returns False otherwise.

- *MailItem*.ReceivedTime—Returns or sets the date and time that the specified *MailItem* was received.

- *MailItem*.Recipients—Returns a Recipients object—the collection of recipients—for the specified *MailItem*. See "Specifying the Message Recipients," later in this chapter.

- *MailItem*.SenderName—Returns the display name of the sender of the specified *MailItem*.

- *MailItem*.SenderEmailAddress—Returns the email address of the sender of the specified *MailItem*.

- *MailItem*.Sensitivity—Returns or sets the sensitivity level of the specified *MailItem*. This property can be one of the following constants—olConfidential, olNormal, olPersonal, or olPrivate.

- *MailItem*.SentOn—Returns the date and time that the specified *MailItem* was sent.

- *MailItem*.Size—Returns the size of the specified *MailItem* in bytes.

- *MailItem*.Subject—Returns or sets the subject line of the specified *MailItem*.

- *MailItem*.To—Returns the display names (separated by semicolons) of the addresses listed in the To line of the specified *MailItem*. To learn how to add recipients, see "Specifying the Message Recipients," later in this chapter.

- *MailItem*.UnRead—Returns True if the specified *MailItem* has not been read; returns False otherwise. You can also set this property.

MailItem **Object Methods**

With the methods available to the MailItem object, you can send messages, as well as reply to and forward messages. See "Sending a Message," later in this chapter, to learn how to use these methods that send messages. Otherwise, you can also open messages, move them to another folder, delete them, and more. Here's a summary of some of these more useful MailItem object methods:

11

- *MailItem*.Close—Closes the window in which the specified *MailItem* object is displayed (see the Display method, later in this list). This method uses the following syntax:

  MailItem.Close(SaveMode)

MailItem	The MailItem object you want to close.
SaveMode	A constant that determines how the window is closed:

olDiscard	Closes the window without saving changes.
olPromptForSave	Prompts the user to save changes.
olSave	Saves changes automatically.

- *MailItem*.Copy—Creates a copy of the specified *MailItem* object. This method returns a MailItem object that represents the copy.

- *MailItem*.Delete—Deletes the specified *MailItem* object (that is, sends the message to the Deleted Items folder).

- *MailItem*.Display—Displays the specified *MailItem* object in a new window, using the following syntax:

  MailItem.Display([Modal])

MailItem	The MailItem object with which you want to work.
Modal	(optional) Use True to display the message in a *modal* window, which means the user can't switch back to Outlook until he or she closes the window; use False for a nonmodal window (this is the default).

For example, if you have a procedure that runs through all the messages in the Inbox folder (such as the NewMail event handler shown earlier in Listing 11.3), you could include code that looks for messages with expired flags. If it finds such a message, it can run the Display method and then alert you. Here's a code snippet that does this:

```
If msg.FlagDueBy < Date Then
    msg.Display
    MsgBox "The displayed message has an expired flag!"
End If
```

- *MailItem*.Move—Moves the specified *MailItem* object to a different folder, using the following syntax:

  MailItem.Move(DestinationFolder)

MailItem	The MailItem object with which you want to work.
DestinationFolder	The MAPIFolder object to which you want to move the message.

For example, suppose you have a folder named Confidential and you want all incoming messages where the sensitivity is set to Confidential moved to that folder. In your `NewMail` event handler, you'd include the following code:

```
If Item.Sensitivity = olConfidential Then
    Item.Move ns.Folders(1).Folders("Confidential")
End If
```

Example: Creating Advanced Rules for Incoming Messages

Outlook's E-mail Rules feature (choose Tools, Rules and Alerts) is a powerful tool for processing incoming messages, but it has some unfortunate limitations. Here are two examples:

- Suppose you create a rule where you specify both an address in the "from people or distribution list" condition and a word in the "with specific words in the body" condition. Outlook applies this rule only to a message that satisfies *both* conditions. However, what if you want to apply the rule to messages that satisfy *either* condition?

- Suppose you create a rule where you enter two words in the "with specific words in the subject" condition. Outlook applies this rule to any message that contains *either* word. However, what if you want to apply the rule only to messages that contain *both* words in the subject?

To work around these limitations, you need to add code to the `ItemAdd` event handler that examines every incoming message (see Listing 11.4, earlier) and then applies your own rules. Listing 11.6 shows a procedure that implements a couple of custom rules for handling incoming messages.

Listing 11.6   An Event Handler for the `ItemAdd` Event That Implements Custom Rules

```
Private Sub inboxItems_ItemAdd(ByVal Item As Object)
    Dim topFolder As MAPIFolder
    Dim ruleFolder As MAPIFolder
    '
    ' Store the Personal Folders folder
    '
    Set topFolder = ns.Folders("Personal Folders")
    '
    ' Custom Rule #1
    ' Move messages from "president@whitehouse.gov"
    ' OR with "politics" in the body
    '
    If Item.SenderEmailAddress = "president@whitehouse.gov" _
        Or InStr(Item.Body, "politics") <> 0 Then
        Set ruleFolder = topFolder.Folders("Politics")
        Item.Move ruleFolder
    End If
    '
    ' Custom Rule #2
    ' Flag messages with "Conference" AND "2007" in the subject
    '
    If InStr(Item.Subject, "Conference") <> 0 _
```

11

continues

Listing 11.6   Continued

```
        And InStr(Item.Subject, "2007") <> 0 Then
          Item.FlagStatus = olFlagMarked
          Item.FlagRequest = "Review"
          Item.FlagIcon = olBlueFlagIcon
          Item.FlagDueBy = Now() + 7
          Item.Save
      End If
  End Sub
```

The procedure begins by storing the `Folder` object for Personal Folders in the `topFolder` variable. Now the code implements two custom rules:

- Custom Rule #1—This is an example of a rule that looks for messages that satisfy one condition *or* another. In this case, the `If` test checks to see whether the `Item` object's `SenderEmailAddress` property equals "president@whitehouse.gov" or the `Item` object's `Body` property (the message body) contains the word "politics." If either condition is true, the message is moved to the "Politics" folder.

- Custom Rule #2—This is an example of a rule that uses two criteria in a single condition and looks for messages that satisfy *both* criteria. In this case, the `If` test checks to see whether the `Item` object's `Subject` property includes the word "Conference" and the word "2007." If both criteria are true, the code applies a blue "Review" flag to the message and sets the flag to expire seven days from today.

Example: Canning Spam

Outlook 2007 comes with an excellent junk mail filter that catches most spam and herds it into the Junk E-mail folder. Unfortunately, spammers are becoming increasingly sophisticated at crafting messages that thwart the junk mail filter. One common technique is to put the body of the message in an image attached to the message. Most of these spams use GIF images. Outlook's email rules enable you to look for messages with attachments, but you can't specify, say, an image type. So if you want to handle these spam messages, you need to use VBA. Listing 11.7 shows a procedure that uses the `ItemAdd` event to look for messages with specific attachments.

→ For more details on dealing with message attachments, **see** "Working with Attachments," **p. 229**.

Listing 11.7   An Event Handler for the `ItemAdd` Event That Moves Junk Email

```
Private Sub inboxItems_ItemAdd(ByVal Item As Object)
    Dim att As Attachment
    '
    ' Does the message have attachments?
    '
    If Item.Attachments.Count > 0 Then
        '
        ' If so, loop through them
        '
        For Each att In Item.Attachments
```

```
      '
      ' Is it a .gif image?
      '
      If InStr(att.FileName, ".gif") <> 0 Then
          '
          ' If so, move it to the Junk E-mail folder
          '
          Debug.Print "Moving message """ & Item.Subject & """"
          Item.Move ns.GetDefaultFolder(olFolderJunk)
      End If
   Next 'att
  End If
End Sub
```

This code examines the message's `Attachments` property, which is the collection of files attached to the message. If the `Count` is greater than 0, it means the message has at least one attachment, so the code then uses a `For Each...Next` loop to run through them. For each attachment, the code examines the `FileName` property to see whether it contains the string `.gif`. If it does, the `Move` method moves the message to the Junk E-mail folder.

Sending a Message

In addition to enabling you to simply read messages, Outlook VBA also enables you to send messages. As you'll see over the next few sections, Outlook VBA gives you a number of ways to go about this.

Creating a New Message

To send a new message (that is, one that isn't a reply or forward), you first need to create a new `MailItem` object. You do this by invoking the `Application` object's `CreateItem` method and specifying the `olMailItem` constant as the type of item you want to create.

For example, the following statements declare a `MailItem` object and then create it:

```
Dim mi as MailItem
Set mi = Application.CreateItem(olMailItem)
```

Creating a Reply or Forward

Alternatively, you can create a `MailItem` object by reply to or forwarding an existing message. You have three choices:

- *MailItem*.`Forward`—Forwards the specified *MailItem* object. This method returns a new `MailItem` object that represents the message to be forwarded.

- *MailItem*.`Reply`—Replies to the sender of the specified *MailItem* object. This method returns a new *MailItem* object that represents the reply to be sent.

- *MailItem*.`ReplyAll`—Replies to the sender and to all the other recipients of the specified *MailItem* object. This method returns a new *MailItem* object that represents the reply to be sent.

Specifying the Message Recipients

Now that your `MailItem` object has been created, you may also need to add one or more recipients. The collection of recipients for a `MailItem` object is contained in the `Recipients` object. To add a recipient, you use the `Recipients` object's `Add` method:

`MailItem.Recipients.Add(Name)`

> `MailItem`   The `MailItem` object to which you want to add the recipient.
>
> `Name`   The recipient's email address. If the recipient is in the Contacts list, you can use just his or her display name.

You can run the `Add` method as many times as you like for the same `MailItem`. Outlook separates each new recipient with a semicolon (;).

Each recipient in a message is a `Recipient` object and has the following properties (among others):

- `Recipient.Address`—Returns or sets the email address of the specified `Recipient`.
- `Recipient.Name`—Returns or sets the display name of the specified `Recipient`.
- `Recipient.Type`—Determines the address line to which the specified `Recipient` will be added (To, Cc, or Bcc). Use `olTo` for the To line, `olCC` for the Cc line, or `olBCC` for the Bcc line. For example, assuming that `msg` is an object variable that represents a `MailItem`, the following statements add two recipients—one on the To line and one on the Cc line:
```
msg.Recipients.Add("Millicent Peeved").Type = olTo
msg.Recipients.Add("bob@weave.com").Type = olCC
```

> **NOTE** If you add a recipient and then later decide to remove that person, use the `Recipient.Delete` method, which deletes the specified `Recipient`.

Sending the Message

With the recipients determined, you can also tweak other `MailItem` properties such as `Subject`, `Body`, and `Importance` (see "`MailItem` Object Properties," earlier in this chapter). With that done, you can then send the message by running the `Send` method:

`MailItem.Send`

> `MailItem`   The `MailItem` object you want to send.

Listing 11.8 shows a procedure that creates a new `MailItem` object, sets up the recipient, subject, and body, and then sends the message.

Listing 11.8   A Procedure That Sends an Email Message

```
Sub SendAMessage()
    Dim ns As NameSpace
    Dim msg As MailItem
    '
    ' Set up the namespace
    '
    Set ns = ThisOutlookSession.Session
    '
    ' Create the new MailItem
    '
    Set msg = Application.CreateItem(olMailItem)
    '
    ' Specify the recipient, subject, and body
    ' and then send the message
    '
    With msg
        '
        ' Adjust the following address!
        '
        .Recipients.Add "blah@yadda.com"
        .Subject = "Just Testing"
        .Body = "This is only a test"
        .Send
    End With
End Sub
```

Example: Supplementing a Reminder with an Email Message

If you set up an appointment or task with a reminder, or if you set up a message or contact with a flag that has a due date, Outlook displays a Reminder window that tells you the item is due. That's a useful visual cue, unless you're out of the office or away from your desk, in which case the reminder becomes far less helpful.

If you have email access when you're away, one way to work around this problem is to have Outlook send you an email message when it processes the reminder. The procedure in Listing 11.9 shows you how to set this up.

Listing 11.9   A Procedure to Send an Email Message When Outlook Processes a Reminder

```
Private Sub Application_Reminder(ByVal Item As Object)
    Dim msg As MailItem
    '
    ' Create a new message
    '
    Set msg = Application.CreateItem(olMailItem)
    '
    ' Set up the message with your address and the reminder subject
    '
    msg.To = "youraddress@wherever.com"
    msg.Subject = Item.Subject
    msg.Body = "Reminder!" & vbCrLf & vbCrLf
```

continues

Listing 11.9   Continued

```
    '
    ' Set up the message body using properties
    ' appropriate to the different reminder types
    '
    Select Case Item.Class
        Case olAppointment
            msg.Body = "Appointment Reminder!" & vbCrLf & vbCrLf & _
            "Start: " & Item.Start & vbCrLf & _
            "End: " & Item.End & vbCrLf & _
            "Location: " & Item.Location & vbCrLf & _
            "Appointment Details: " & vbCrLf & Item.Body
      Case olContact
            msg.Body = "Contact Reminder!" & vbCrLf & vbCrLf & _
            "Contact: " & Item.FullName & vbCrLf & _
            "Company: " & Item.CompanyName & vbCrLf & _
            "Phone: " & Item.BusinessTelephoneNumber & vbCrLf & _
            "E-mail: " & Item.Email1Address & vbCrLf & _
            "Contact Details: " & vbCrLf & Item.Body
      Case olMail
            msg.Body = "Message Reminder!" & vbCrLf & vbCrLf & _
            "Sender: " & Item.SenderName & vbCrLf & _
            "E-mail: " & Item.SenderEmailAddress & vbCrLf & _
            "Due: " & Item.FlagDueBy & vbCrLf & _
            "Flag: " & Item.FlagRequest & vbCrLf & _
            "Message Body: " & vbCrLf & Item.Body
      Case olTask
            msg.Body = "Task Reminder!" & vbCrLf & vbCrLf & _
            "Due: " & Item.DueDate & vbCrLf & _
            "Status: " & Item.Status & vbCrLf & _
            "Task Details: " & vbCrLf & Item.Body
    End Select
    '
    ' Send the message
    '
    msg.Send
    '
    ' Release the msg object
    '
    Set msg = Nothing
End Sub
```

The `Application_Reminder` procedure is an event handler that runs whenever Outlook processes a reminder, and the `Item` variable that's passed to the procedure represents the underlying Outlook item: an appointment, contact, message, or task. You should paste this procedure into the `ThisOutlookSession` module in Visual Basic Editor.

The procedure declares a `MailItem` (message) variable named `msg`, uses it to store a new message, and then sets up the message's `To`, `Subject`, and initial `Body` properties. Then a `Select Case` statement processes the four possible `Item` classes: `olAppointment`, `olContact`, `olMail`, and `olTask`. In each case, the message body is extended to include data from the item. Finally, the message is sent, using the `Send` method, and the `msg` variable is released.

NOTE If you want to send the email to multiple recipients, one option is to use the `MailItem` object's `Cc` or `Bcc` properties. If you prefer to place multiple addresses in the message's To field, use the `Recipients.Add` method as often as needed, like so:

```
msg.Recipients.Add "another@domain.com"
```

Working with Attachments

As you saw earlier (see Listing 11.7), if you want to work with files attached to a message, use the `MailItem` object's `Attachments` property. This returns the collection of `Attachment` objects for the message. For each `Attachment` object, you can manipulate the following properties and methods:

- *Attachment*`.DisplayName`—Returns the name below the icon for the specified *Attachment*.
- *Attachment*`.Filename`—Returns the filename of the specified *Attachment*.
- *Attachment*`.Delete`—Deletes the specified *Attachment*.
- *Attachment*`.SaveAs`—Saves the specified *Attachment* to disk:

  Attachment`.SaveAs(`*Path*`)`

Attachment	The `Attachment` object you want to save.
Path	The path and filename to which you want to save the file.

Example: Removing Attachments from a Forwarded Message

Listing 11.10 shows a procedure that creates a forwarded message and removes all the attachments before sending it.

Listing 11.10 A Procedure That Creates a Forwarded Message and Deletes Any Existing Attachments Before Sending the Message

```
Sub ForwardAndDeleteAttachments()
    Dim insp As Inspector
    Dim msg As MailItem
    Dim att As Attachment
    '
    ' Return the open message window
    '
    Set insp = Application.ActiveInspector
    '
    ' Make sure we got one
    '
    If insp Is Nothing Then Exit Sub
    '
    ' Create the forwarded message
    '
```

11

continues

Listing 11.10 Continued

```
    Set msg = insp.CurrentItem.Forward
    With msg
        '
        ' Delete all the attachments
        '
        For Each att in .Attachments
            att.Delete
        Next 'att
        '
        ' Display it
        '
        .Display
    End With
End Sub
```

This code is a bit different from what you've seen so far. In particular, the code makes use of Outlook's `Inspector` object, which represents a window in which an item is displayed. For example, if you double-click a message to open it, the window containing that message is an `Inspector` object. If that window currently has the focus, then you can reference it by using the `ActiveInspector` object, which is what this procedure does. In other words, for this procedure to work, you must first open the message that you're going to forward. (Just in case you run this procedure without first opening the message, the code checks to see whether the `insp` object is `Nothing`; if it is, the procedure exits.)

Given an `Inspector` object, the `CurrentItem` property returns whatever object is open in the window, and the code uses the `Forward` method to create a new `MailItem` object. The procedure then runs through all the attachments and deletes them. Finally, the forwarded message is displayed so you can pick your recipients and send it.

Attaching a File to a Message

To add an attachment to an outgoing message, use the `Attachments` object's `Add` method:

MailItem.Attachments.Add(*Source*[, *Type*][, *Position*][, *DisplayName*])

MailItem	The `MailItem` object to which you want to add the attachments.
Source	The path and filename for the attachment.
Type	(optional) A constant that specifies what kind of attachment you want to send:

`olByValue`	Sends the attachment as is (this is the default).
`olByReference`	Sends the attachment as a link to the original file.
`olEmbeddedItem`	Sends the attachment as a link to an Outlook item.

Position	(optional) The position of the attachment within the message body. Use 1 to place the attachment at the beginning of the message; use any value *n* to position the attachment before the *n*th character in the message.
DisplayName	(optional) The name that appears below the attachment icon if *Type* is olByValue.

You can run the Add method as many times as you like for the same MailItem.

Programming Outlook from Other Applications

If you want to interact with Outlook from another application, there are a few things you need to do differently. I'll use this section to explain what you need to do.

Setting Up a Reference to Outlook

In the other application's Visual Basic Editor, follow these steps to set up a reference to Outlook:

1. In the Project Explorer, select the project you'll be using for the Outlook programming.

2. Choose Tools, References to display the References dialog box.

3. In the Available References list, activate the check box beside the Microsoft Outlook 12.0 Object Library item, as shown in Figure 11.2.

Figure 11.2
Use the References dialog box to activate the Microsoft Outlook 12.0 Object Library check box.

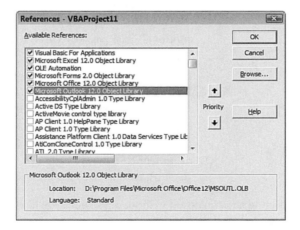

4. Click OK.

Remember that this reference works only for the project you selected. If you want to program Outlook from another project (either in the same application or in a different application), you have to repeat these steps.

Getting the NameSpace **Object**

When you work with Outlook from another application, you need to start right at the top of the object hierarchy, at the Application object. You use this object to return information about the current Outlook session and to gain access to the rest of the Outlook hierarchy. To establish a connection with this object, you use the CreateObject function. For example, the following statements establish a connection to Outlook:

```
Dim ol As Outlook.Application
Set ol = CreateObject("Outlook.Application")
```

Now you need to get a NameSpace object so you can log on and off, return information about the current user, and more. To return a NameSpace object, you use the GetNameSpace method with the "MAPI" argument:

```
Dim ol As Outlook.Application
Dim ns As NameSpace
Set ol = CreateObject("Outlook.Application")
Set ns = ol.GetNameSpace("MAPI")
```

Logging On to an Outlook Session

After you have the NameSpace object, you can log on to establish a MAPI session by invoking the Logon method:

```
NameSpace.Logon([Profile][, Password][, ShowDialog][, NewSession])
```

NameSpace	The NameSpace object.
Profile	(optional) The name of the Outlook profile to use in the MAPI session. If you omit this value, VBA logs on to the default profile.
Password	(optional) The password used with the profile.
ShowDialog	(optional) A Boolean value that determines whether or not Outlook displays the Logon dialog box. Use False to bypass the dialog box (this is the default); use True to display the dialog box.
NewSession	(optional) A Boolean value that determines whether or not Outlook creates a new MAPI session. Set this argument to True to start a new session (this is the default); use False to log on to the current session.

In most cases, you'll use the Logon method without any arguments (assuming that the current NameSpace is represented by a variable named ns):

```
ns.Logon
```

If you have multiple profiles set up, however, then you need to specify which one you want to use. For example, the following statement logs on to an Outlook session, using the "Personal E-Mail" profile:

```
ns.Logon "Personal E-Mail"
```

> **NOTE** To add, edit, or delete profiles, open the Windows Control Panel and launch the Mail icon.

Logging Off an Outlook Session

When you've completed your labors in an Outlook session, you can log off by running the
NameSpace object's Logoff method:

NameSpace.Logoff

    NameSpace   The NameSpace object.

Listing 11.11 shows a procedure that logs on to a MAPI session, runs through the items in
the default Inbox folder, and records the SenderName, SenderEmailAddress, Subject, Size,
ReceivedTime, and the first 100 characters of the Body onto a worksheet.

Listing 11.11   A Procedure That Reads Inbox Data into a Worksheet

```
Sub ReadInboxData()
    Dim ol As Outlook.Application
    Dim ns As NameSpace
    Dim folder As MAPIFolder
    Dim ws As Worksheet
    Dim i As Integer
    '
    ' Establish a connection and log on
    '
    Set ol = CreateObject("Outlook.Application")
    Set ns = ol.GetNamespace("MAPI")
    ns.Logon
    '
    ' Get the default Inbox folder
    '
    Set folder = ns.GetDefaultFolder(olFolderInbox)
    '
    ' Set the Receive Mail worksheet
    '
    Set ws = Worksheets("Receive Mail")
    '
    ' Run through each item in the Inbox
    '
    For i = 1 To folder.Items.Count
        With folder.Items(i)
            '
            ' Record the sender, subject, size,
            ' received time, and some of the body
            '
            ws.[A1].Offset(i, 0) = .SenderName
            ws.[A1].Offset(i, 1) = .SenderEmailAddress
            ws.[A1].Offset(i, 2) = .Subject
            ws.[A1].Offset(i, 3) = .Size
            ws.[A1].Offset(i, 4) = .ReceivedTime
```

continues

Listing 11.11 Continued

```
            ws.[A1].Offset(i, 5) = Left(.Body, 100)
        End With
    Next 'i
    '
    ' Log off the session
    '
    ns.Logoff
    Set ol = Nothing
End Sub
```

> **NOTE**
> You'll find Listing 11.11 in the file named Chapter11.xlsm on my website:
> http://www.mcfedries.com/Office2007VBA/Chapter11.xlsm

When you run this code for the first time, Outlook will likely display a dialog box like the one shown in Figure 11.3. This is a security feature that prevents viruses and Trojan horse malware from surreptitiously sending emails through your Outlook account. In this case, you know the operation is safe, so click Allow.

Figure 11.3
When Use the References dialog box to activate the Microsoft Outlook 12.0 Object Library check box.

From Here

■ For the details on Excel's VBA techniques, **see** Chapter 8, "Programming Excel," **p. 139**.

■ For another example of working with data remotely, **see** Chapter 10, "Programming Access Databases," **p. 189**.

■ To learn more about the Immediate window, see "Using the Immediate Window," **p. 348**.

Getting the Most out of VBA

III

Creating Custom VBA Dialog Boxes

12

VBA procedures are only as useful as they are convenient. There isn't much point in creating a procedure that saves you (or your users) a few keystrokes if you (or they) have to expend a lot of time and energy hunting down a routine. Shortcut keys are true time-savers, but some applications (such as Excel) have only a limited supply to dole out (and our brains can memorize only so many Ctrl+*key* combinations).

Instead, you need to give some thought to the type of user interface you want to create for your VBA application. The interface includes not only the design of the documents, but also two other factors that let the user interact with the model: dialog boxes and Ribbon commands. Although you certainly can give the user access to the application's built-in dialogs and Ribbon interface, you'll find that you often need to create your own interface elements from scratch. This chapter starts you off by showing you how to use VBA's Microsoft Forms feature to create custom dialog boxes and input forms. Chapter 13, "Customizing the Office 2007 Ribbon," shows you how to add custom commands to the Ribbon.

The InputBox function you learn about in Chapter 3, "Understanding Program Variables," works fine if you need just a single item of information, but what if you need four or five? Or, what if you want the user to choose from a list of items? In some cases, you can use the application's built-in dialog boxes (which I discussed in Chapter 5, "Working with Objects"), but these might not have the exact controls you need, or they might have controls to which you don't want the user to have access.

→ For the InputBox function details, **see** "Getting Input Using InputBox," **p. 50**.

→ To learn how to use the built-in dialog boxes, **see** "Accessing an Application's Built-In Dialog Boxes," **p. 83**.

The solution to this problem is to build your own dialog boxes. Using custom dialog boxes you can add as many controls as you need (including list boxes, option buttons, and check boxes), and your procedures will have complete access to all the results. Best of all, the Visual Basic Editor makes constructing even the most sophisticated dialog boxes as easy as clicking and dragging the mouse pointer. The next few sections show you how to create dialog boxes and integrate them into your applications.

> **NOTE**
> In VBA, dialog boxes are called user forms or just forms, for short. (A VBA form is a close cousin to the form objects that are used for data entry in Microsoft Access.) Because the term "form" is used in the Visual Basic Editor, I'll use that term throughout the rest of this chapter. Just remember, however, that a form is nothing but a dialog box that you create yourself.

Adding a Form to Your Project

Forms are separate objects that you add to your VBA projects. To do this, open the Visual Basic Editor and either choose Insert, UserForm or drop down the Insert toolbar button (the second from the left) and click UserForm. As you can see in Figure 12.1, VBA performs the following tasks in response to this command:

- It adds a Forms branch to the project tree in the Project Explorer.
- It creates a new UserForm object and adds it to the Forms branch.
- It displays the form in the work area.
- It displays the Toolbox.

Figure 12.1
Selecting Insert, UserForm adds a new form to the project.

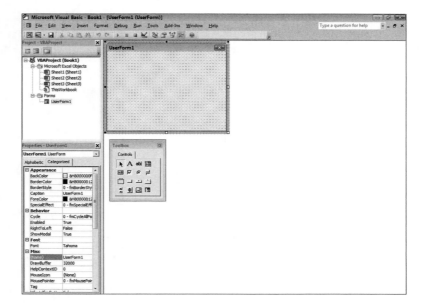

Changing the Form's Design-Time Properties

Forms (and all the control objects you can add to a form) have an extensive list of properties that you can manipulate by entering or selecting values in the Properties window. (Recall that you display the Properties window by activating <u>V</u>iew, Properties <u>W</u>indow or by pressing F4.)

For a form, there are more than three dozen properties arranged into seven categories (in the Properties window, activate the Categorized tab to see the properties arranged by category, as shown in Figure 12.1), as described in the next few sections.

> **NOTE**
> In addition to modifying form properties at design time (that is, before you run the form), you can also modify many of the properties at runtime by including the appropriate statements in your VBA procedures. I talk about this in greater detail later in this chapter (see the section "Using a Form in a Procedure").

The Appearance Category

The properties in the Appearance category control the look of the form:

- `BackColor`—Sets the color of the form's background. For this and all the color properties, you select a color by first clicking the drop-down arrow to display a color menu. In this menu, you can either choose a predefined color from the System tab or a built-in color from the Palette tab.

- `BorderColor`—Sets the color of the form's border. Note that for this property to have any effect, you have to assign a border to the form by using the `BorderStyle` property.

- `BorderStyle`—Choose `fmBorderStylSingle` to apply a border around the form. Use `fmBorderStyleNone` for no border.

- `Caption`—Specifies the text that's displayed in the form's title bar.

- `ForeColor`—Sets the default color of text used in the form's controls.

- `SpecialEffect`—Controls how the form appears relative to the form window (for example, raised or sunken).

> **NOTE**
> If you're running Windows Vista's Aero color scheme, the transparency effects will apply to your VBA forms, as well.

The Behavior Category

The properties in the Behavior category control aspects of how the user interacts with the form:

- `Cycle`—Determines what happens when the user presses Tab while the focus is on the last control in the form. If this property is set to `fmCycleAllForms` and the form has

12

multiple pages (see "Tab Strips and MultiPage Controls," later in this chapter), focus is set to the first control on the next page. If this property is set to `fmCycleCurrentForm`, focus is set to the first control on the current page.

- `Enabled`—Set this property to `True` to enable the form or `False` to disable it. The latter prevents the user from manipulating the form or any of its controls.

> **TIP**
>
> Why would you want to disable a form? This is handy if you want to display the form for a certain amount of time and then close it automatically. To set this up, first create a procedure that closes the form:
>
> ```
> Public Sub CloseForm()
>     Unload UserForm1
> End Sub
> ```
>
> Next, in the form's initialize event, add the `OnTime` method and set it up to run the `CloseForm` procedure a specified number of seconds or minutes after the form loads. For example, the following code runs `CloseForm` 30 seconds from when the form loads:
>
> ```
> Private Sub UserForm_Initialize()
>     Application.OnTime Now + TimeValue("00:00:30"), "Close Form"
> End Sub
> ```

- `RightToLeft`—When `True`, this property changes the tab order of the form so that pressing Tab moves the highlight among the controls from right to left (instead of the usual left to right).

- `ShowModal`—Set this property to `True` to display the form as modal, which means the user won't be able to interact with the underlying application until he or she closes the form.

The Font Category

The `Font` property determines the default font used throughout the form. When you activate this property, click the ellipsis (…) button to display the Font dialog box, from which you can select the font, style, size, and effects.

The Misc Category

As its name implies, the Misc category contains a collection of eight properties that don't fit anywhere else, although almost all these properties are obscure and can be safely ignored. The one exception is the `Name` property, which you use to give a name to your form. (You'll use this name to refer to the form in your VBA code, so use only alphanumeric characters in the name.)

Although you might be tempted to stick with the default form name supplied by VBA (such as UserForm1), your code will be easier to read if you give the form a more descriptive name. Indeed, this advice applies not only to forms, but to *all* controls. Note that it's conventional to precede the form name with the frm prefix (for example, frmBudget).

The Picture Category

In the Picture category, use the Picture property to set a background image for the form. (Again, click the ellipsis button to select a picture file from a dialog box.) The other properties determine how the picture is displayed:

- PictureAlignment—Specifies where on the form the picture is displayed. You can align it in the center of the form, the top left, top right, bottom left, or bottom right.
- PictureSizeMode—Specifies how the picture is displayed relative to the form:
  - fmPictureSizeModeClip—Crops any part of the picture that's larger than the form.
  - fmPictureSizeModeStretch—Stretches or shrinks the picture so that it fits the entire form
  - fmPictureSizeModeZoom—Enlarges or reduces the picture until it hits the vertical or horizontal edge of the form.
- PictureTiling—For small images, set this property to True to fill the background with multiple copies of the image.

The Position Category

The properties in the Position category specify the dimensions of the form (Height and Width), and the position of the form within the application window. For the latter, you can either use the StartUpPosition property to center the form relative to the application window (CenterOwner) or to the screen (CenterScreen), or you can choose Manual and specify the Left and Top properties. (The latter two properties set the form's position in points from the application window's left and top edges, respectively.)

The Scrolling Category

The properties in the Scrolling category determine whether the form displays scroll bars and, if it does, what format the scroll bars have:

- KeepScrollBarsVisible—Determines which of the form's scroll bars remain visible even if they aren't needed.
- ScrollBars—Determines which scrollbars are displayed on the form. That is, VBA only displays a scrollbar if it's necessary.

12

- ScrollHeight—Specifies the total height of the form's scrollable region. For example, if the form's Height property is set to 200 and you set the ScrollHeight property to 400, you double the total vertical area available in the form.

- ScrollLeft—If ScrollWidth is greater than the width of the form, use the ScrollLeft property to set the initial position of the horizontal scroll bar's scroll box. For example, if the ScrollWidth is 200, setting ScrollLeft to 100 starts the horizontal scroll bar at the halfway position.

- ScrollTop—If ScrollHeight is greater than the height of the form, use the ScrollTop property to set the initial position of the vertical scroll bar's scroll box.

- ScrollWidth—Specifies the total width of the form's scrollable region.

Working with Controls

Now that your form is set up with the design-time properties you need, you can get down to the brass tacks of form design. In other words, you can start adding controls to the form, adjusting those controls to get the layout you want, and setting the design-time properties of each control. I discuss the unique characteristics of each type of control later in this chapter (see the section "Types of Form Controls"). For now, though, I'll run through a few techniques that you can apply to any control.

Inserting Controls on a Form

The new form object is an empty shell that doesn't become a useful member of society until you populate it with controls. As with the form-building tools in Word and Access, the idea is that you use this shell to "draw" the controls you need. Later, you can either link the controls directly to other objects (such as Excel worksheet cells) or create procedures to handle the selections.

The Toolbox contains buttons for all the controls you can add to a form. Here are the basic steps to follow to add any control to the form:

1. Click the button you want to use.

2. Move the mouse pointer into the form and position it where you want the top-left corner of the control to appear.

3. Click and drag the mouse pointer. VBA displays a gray border indicating the outline of the control.

4. When the control is the size and shape you want, release the mouse button. VBA creates the control and gives it a default name (such as CheckBox*n*, where *n* signifies that this is the *n*th check box you've created on this form).

If you want to add multiple instances of the same type of control, double-click the appropriate Toolbox button. The button will remain pressed, and you can draw as many instances of the control as you need. When you're finished, click an empty part of the Toolbox to reset the control.

Selecting Controls

Before you can work with a control, you must select it. For a single control, you select it by clicking it. If you prefer to work with multiple controls, the Visual Basic Editor gives you a number of techniques:

- Hold down the Ctrl key and click each control.
- You also can "lasso" multiple controls by clicking and dragging the mouse. Move the mouse pointer to an empty part of the form, hold down the left button, and then click and drag. The VBE displays a box with a dashed outline, and any control that falls within this box (in whole or in part) will be selected.
- To select every control, make sure the form is active and then select Edit, Select All. (For faster service, you can also either press Ctrl+A or right-click an empty part of the form and choose Select All from the shortcut menu.)
- To exclude a control from the selection, hold down the Ctrl key and click inside the control.

After you've selected multiple controls, you can set properties for all the controls at once. Note, however, that the Properties window shows only those properties that are common to all the controls. (See "Common Control Properties" later in this chapter.) Not only that, but if you size, move, copy, or delete one of the selected controls (as described in the next few sections), your action applies to all the controls.

Each control is surrounded by an invisible rectangular *frame*. When you select a control, the VBE displays a gray outline that represents the control's frame and this outline is studded with white *selection handles* at the frame's corners and midpoints, as shown in Figure 12.2.

Figure 12.2
A selected control displays a frame and various selection handles.

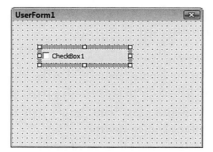

Sizing Controls

You can resize any control to change its shape or dimensions. The following procedure outlines the steps to work through:

1. Select the object you want to size.

2. Position the mouse pointer over the selection handle you want to move. The pointer changes to a two-headed arrow. To change the size horizontally or vertically, use the appropriate handle on the middle of a side. To change the size in both directions at once, use the appropriate corner handle.

3. Click and drag the handle to the position you want.

4. Release the mouse button. The Visual Basic Editor redraws the object and adjusts the frame size.

> **NOTE** To size the form itself, click an empty part of the form and then click and drag the selection handles that appear around the form.

Moving Controls

You can move any control to a different part of the form by following these steps:

1. Select the control you want to move.

2. Position the mouse pointer inside the control. (You can also position the pointer over the control's frame, although you need to make sure the pointer isn't over a selection handle. In this case, the pointer changes to a four-headed arrow.)

3. Click and drag the control to the position you want. As you drag the object, a dashed outline shows you the new position.

4. Release the mouse button. The VBE redraws the control in the new position.

Copying Controls

If you've formatted a control and then decide that you need a similar control, don't bother building the new control from scratch. Instead, follow the steps outlined next to make as many copies of the existing control as you need:

1. Select the control you want to copy.

2. Hold down the Ctrl key, position the mouse pointer inside the control, and press the left mouse button. The pointer changes to an arrow with a plus sign.

3. Click and drag the pointer to the position you want. As you drag the mouse, a dashed outline shows you the position of the copied control.

4. Release the mouse button. The VBE copies the control to the new position.

You also can use the Clipboard to copy controls. In this case, you click the control, choose Edit, Copy, and then choose Edit, Paste. The Visual Basic Editor adds a copy of the control to the form that you can then move to the appropriate position.

> **TIP** You also can right-click the control and click Copy from the control's shortcut menu. To paste the control, right-click an empty part of the form, and then click Paste. Alternatively, use Ctrl+C to copy a selected control and Ctrl+V to paste it.

Deleting Controls

To delete a control, select it and then choose Edit, Delete. The Visual Basic Editor deletes the control.

> **TIP** To delete a control quickly, select it and press the Delete key. Alternatively, you can right-click the control and click Delete in the shortcut menu.

Grouping Controls

The Visual Basic Editor lets you create control *groups*. A group is a collection of controls you can format, size, and move—similar to the way you format, size, and move a single control. To group two or more controls, select them and use any of the following techniques:

- Choose the Format, Group command.
- Right-click inside any one of the selected controls and click Group from the shortcut menu.
- Click the UserForm toolbar's Group button.

> **NOTE** The UserForm toolbar contains many useful one-click shortcuts for working with forms. To display this toolbar, either choose View, Toolbars, UserForm, or right-click the Standard toolbar and click UserForm in the shortcut menu.

The Visual Basic Editor treats a group as a single control with its own frame. To select an entire group, you need to select just one control from the group.

To ungroup controls, select the group and use one of these methods:

- Choose Format, Ungroup.
- Right-click inside any one of the selected controls and click Ungroup from the shortcut menu.
- Click the UserForm toolbar's Ungroup button.

Setting Control Properties

A form control is an object with its own set of properties. A check box, for example, is a `CheckBox` object, and it has properties that control the name of the check box, whether it is initially checked, what its accelerator key is, and more.

You can manipulate control properties during program execution (in other words, at run-time), either before you display the form or while the form is displayed. (For example, you might want to disable a control in response to a user's action.) However, you can also set some control properties in the Visual Basic Editor (in other words, at design time) by using the Properties window. To display a particular control's properties in the Properties window, you have two choices:

- Click the control in the form.
- Select the control from the drop-down list near the top of the Properties window.

Common Control Properties

Later in this chapter I'll run through each of the default controls and explain their unique features. However, a few properties are common to many of the controls. Most of these properties perform the same function as those I outlined for a form earlier in this chapter. These properties include the following: `BackColor`, `ForeColor`, `SpecialEffect`, `Enabled`, `Font`, `Picture`, `PicturePosition`, `Height`, `Width`, `Left`, and `Top`. (Note that the latter two are relative to the left and top edges of the form.)

Here's a list of a few other properties that are common to some or all of the default controls:

- `Accelerator`—This property determines the control's accelerator key. (In other words, the user can select this control by holding down Alt and pressing the specified key.) The letter you enter into this property appears underlined in the control's caption.

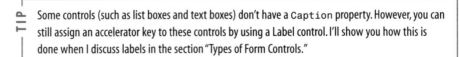

> **TIP** Some controls (such as list boxes and text boxes) don't have a `Caption` property. However, you can still assign an accelerator key to these controls by using a Label control. I'll show you how this is done when I discuss labels in the section "Types of Form Controls."

- `AutoSize`—If this property is set to `True`, the control resizes automatically to fit its text (as given by the `Caption` property).
- `BackStyle`—Determines whether the control's background is opaque (use `fmBackStyleOpaque`) or transparent (use `fmBackStyleTransparent`).
- `ControlSource`—In the Visual Basic Editor for Excel, this property specifies which cell will be used to hold the control's data. You can enter either a cell reference or a range name.

CAUTION

The value of a cell linked to a control changes whenever the value of the control changes, even when the user clicks Cancel to exit the form. It's usually better (and safer) to assign a control's value to a variable and then, if appropriate, place the value in the cell by using code in your VBA procedure.

- `Caption`—Sets the control's text, which is usually just the name of the feature represented by the control.
- `ControlTipText`—Sets the "control tip" that pops up when the user lets the mouse pointer linger over the control for a second or two.
- `Locked`—Set this property to `True` to prevent the user from editing the current value of the control.
- `TabIndex`—Determines where the control appears in the tab order (in other words, the order in which VBA navigates through the controls when the user presses the Tab key). See the next section, "Setting the Tab Order."
- `TabStop`—Determines whether the user can navigate to the control by pressing Tab. If this property is set to `False`, the user can't select the control by using the Tab key.
- `Visible`—Determines whether the user can see the control (`True`) or not (`False`). For example, you might want to hide a control until the user selects a particular option.

Setting the Tab Order

As you know, you can navigate a form by pressing the Tab key. The order in which the controls are selected is called the *tab order*. VBA sets the tab order according to the order you create the controls on the form. You'll often find that this order isn't what you want to end up with, so the Visual Basic Editor lets you control the tab order yourself. The following procedure shows you how it's done:

1. Select <u>V</u>iew, T<u>a</u>b Order. (You can also right-click an empty part of the form and click T<u>a</u>b Order in the shortcut menu.) The Visual Basic Editor displays the Tab Order dialog box, shown in Figure 12.3.

Figure 12.3
Use the Tab Order dialog box to set the order in which the user navigates the form when pressing the Tab key.

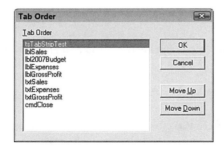

12

2. In the Tab Order list, click the control with which you want to work.

3. Click Move Up to move the item up in the tab order, or click Move Down to move the control down.

4. Repeat steps 2 and 3 for other controls you want to move.

5. Click OK.

Handling Form Events

An *event-driven* language is one in which code can respond to specific events, such as a user clicking a command button or selecting an item from a list. The procedure can then take appropriate action, whether it's validating the user's input or asking for confirmation of the requested action. A form responds to more than 20 separate events, including activating and deactivating the form, displaying the form, clicking the form, and resizing the form.

For each event associated with an object, VBA has set up mini procedures called *event handlers*. These procedures are really just Sub and End Sub statements. You process the event by filling in your own VBA code between these statements. Here are the steps to follow:

1. Click the object for which you want to define an event handler.

2. Either select View, Code or double-click the object. (You can also press F7 or right-click the object and then click select View Code in the shortcut menu.) VBA displays the code module for the object, as shown in Figure 12.4.

Figure 12.4
For each event, VBA defines a mini procedure. You define the procedure by entering code into this stub.

3. Use the procedure drop-down list (the one on the right) to select the event with which you want to work.

4. Enter the rest of the procedure code between the Sub and End Sub statements.

Types of Form Controls

The default Toolbox offers 14 different controls for your custom forms. The next few sections introduce you to each type of control and show you the various options and properties associated with each object.

Command Buttons

Most forms include command buttons to let the user accept the form data (an OK button), cancel the form (a Cancel button), or carry out some other command at a click of the mouse.

To create a command button, use the CommandButton tool in the Toolbox. A command button is a `CommandButton` object that includes many of the common control properties mentioned earlier, as well as the following design-time properties (among others):

- `Cancel`—If this property is set to `True`, the button is selected when the user presses Esc. Note that you can have only one cancel button on a form.
- `Caption`—Returns or sets the text that appears on the button face.
- `Default`—If this property is set to `True`, the button is selected when the user presses Enter. Also, the button is displayed with a thin black border. You can have only one default button on a form.

Labels

You use labels to add text to the form. To create labels, use the Label button in the Toolbox to draw the label object, and then edit the `Caption` property. Although labels are mostly used to display text, you can also use them to name controls that don't have their own captions—such as text boxes, list boxes, scroll bars, and spinners.

It's even possible to define an accelerator key for the label and have that key select another control. For example, suppose you want to use a label to describe a text box, but you also want to define an accelerator key that the user can press to select the text box. The trick is that you must first create a label and set its `Accelerator` property. You then create the text box immediately after. Because the text box follows the label in the tab order, the label's accelerator key selects the text box.

> **TIP**
>
> To assign a label and accelerator key to an existing control, add the label and then adjust the tab order so that the label comes immediately before the control in the tab order.

Text Boxes

Text boxes are versatile controls that let the user enter text, numbers, and, in Excel, cell references and formulas. To create a text box, use the TextBox button in the Toolbox. Here are a few useful properties of the `TextBox` object:

- `EnterFieldBehavior`—Determines what happens when the user tabs into the text box. If you select 0 (`fmEnterFieldBehaviorSelectAll`), the text within the field is selected. If you select 1 (`fmEnterFieldBehaviorRecallSelect`), only the text that the user selected the last time he was in the field is selected; the first time the user enters the field, the cursor is placed at the end of the text.

- **EnterKeyBehavior**—When set to `True`, this property lets the user start a new line within the text box by pressing Enter. (Note that this is applicable only if you set `MultiLine` to `True`, as described in a moment.) When this property is `False`, pressing Enter moves the user to the next field.

- **MaxLength**—This property determines the maximum number of characters that the user can enter.

- **MultiLine**—Set this property to `True` to let the user enter multiple lines of text. If you've set `EnterKeyBehavior` to `False`, the user can start a new line of text by pressing Ctrl+Enter.

- **PasswordChar**—If this property is set to `True`, the text box displays the user's entry as asterisks (which is useful if you're using the text box to get a password or other sensitive data).

- **Text**—Returns or sets the text inside the text box.

- **WordWrap**—When this property is `True`, the text box wraps to a new line when the user's typing reaches the right edge of the text box.

Frames

You use frames to create groups of two or more controls. There are three situations in which frames come in handy:

- **To organize a set of controls into a logical grouping**—Let's say your form contains controls for setting program options and obtaining user information. You could help the user make sense of the form by creating two frames: one to hold all the controls for the program options, and one to hold the controls for the user information.

- **To move a set of controls as a unit**—When you draw controls inside a frame, these controls are considered to be part of the frame object. Therefore, when you move the frame, the controls move right along with it. This can make it easier to rearrange multiple controls on a form.

- **To organize option buttons**—If you enter multiple option buttons inside a frame (see the next section), VBA treats them as a group and therefore allows the user to activate only one of the options.

To create a frame, click the Frame button in the Toolbox and then click and drag a box inside the form. Note that you use the Frame object's `Caption` property to change the caption that appears at the top of the box.

Option Buttons

Option buttons are controls that usually appear in groups of two or more; the user can select only one of the options. To create an option button, use the OptionButton tool. You can determine whether an option button starts off activated or deactivated by setting the `Value` property: If it's `True`, the option is activated; if it's `False`, the option is deactivated.

For option buttons to work effectively, you need to group them so that the user can select only one of the options at a time. VBA gives you three ways to do this:

- Create a frame and then draw the option buttons inside the frame. For example, Figure 12.5 shows an example form with three option buttons inside a frame.

Figure 12.5
One way to group option buttons and ensure that the user can select only one option at a time is to draw them all inside a single frame.

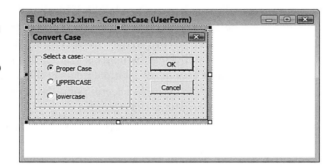

- Use the same `GroupName` property for the options you want to group.
- If you don't draw the option buttons inside a frame or use the `GroupName` property, VBA treats all the option buttons in a form as one group.

> **TIP**
> If you already have one or more "unframed" option buttons on your form, you can still insert them into a frame. Just select the buttons, cut them to the Clipboard, select the frame, and paste. VBA then adds the buttons to the frame.

Check Boxes

Check boxes let you include options that the user can toggle on or off. To create a check box, click the CheckBox button in the Toolbox.

As with option buttons, you can control whether a check box is initially activated (checked). Set its `Value` property to `True` to activate the check box, or to `False` to deactivate it.

Toggle Buttons

A toggle button is a cross between a check box and a command button: Click it once, and the button stays pressed; click it again, and the button returns to the unpressed state. You create toggle buttons by using the ToggleButton tool in the Toolbox.

You control whether a toggle button is initially activated (pressed) by setting its `Value` property to `True` to press the button or to `False` to "unpress" the button.

List Boxes

VBA offers two different list objects you can use to present the user with a list of choices: a `ListBox` and a `ComboBox`.

The `ListBox` **Object**

The `ListBox` object is a simple list of items from which the user selects an item or items. Use the ListBox button to create a list box. Here are some `ListBox` object properties to note:

- `ColumnCount`—The number of columns in the list box.
- `ColumnHeads`—If this property is `True`, the list columns are displayed with headings.
- `MultiSelect`—Set this property to `fmMultiSelectSingle` to enable the user to select only one item in the list; if you set this property to `fmMultiSelectMulti`, the user may select multiple items in the list by clicking the items; if you set this property to `fmMultiSelectExtended`, the user may select multiple items in the list by holding down Ctrl and clicking the items. (For the multiple selection options, note that clicking or Ctrl+clicking are toggles that select and deselect items.)
- `RowSource`—Determines the items that appear in the list. In Excel, enter a range or a range name.
- `Text`—Sets or returns the selected item. For example, if the list box contains a list of months and you want August to be selected at startup, then you'd include the following code in the form's `Initialize` event:

```
ListBox1.Text = "August"
```

The `ComboBox` **Object**

The `ComboBox` object is a control that combines a text box with a list box. The user either enters an item in the text box or clicks the drop-down arrow to display the list box and then selects an item from the list. Use the ComboBox button to create this control.

Because the `ComboBox` is actually two separate controls, the available properties are an amalgam of those discussed earlier for a text box and a list box. You can also work with the following properties that are unique to a `ComboBox` object:

- `ListRows`—Determines the number of items that appear when the user drops the list down.
- `MatchRequired`—If this property is `True`, the user can enter only values from the list. If it's `False`, the user can enter new values.
- `Style`—Determines the type of `ComboBox`. Use 0 (`fmStyleDropDownCombo`) for a list that includes a text box; use 2 (`fmStyleDropDownList`) for a list only.

List Box Techniques

How do you specify the contents of a list if the `RowSource` property isn't applicable (that is, if you're not working in Excel or if the data you want in the list isn't part of an Excel range)? In this case, you must build the list at runtime. You can use the `AddItem` method, described later in this section, or you can set the `List` property. For the latter, you must specify an array of values. For example, the following statements use a form's `Initialize` event to populate a list box with the days of the week:

```
Private Sub UserForm_Initialize()
    ListBox1.List() = Array("Monday", "Tuesday", "Wednesday",
➥"Thursday"," "Friday", "Saturday", "Sunday")
End Sub
```

List boxes also have a few useful methods for controlling from your VBA code the items that appear in a list box:

- `AddItem`—Adds an item to the specified list box. Here's the syntax:

  `object.AddItem(text,index)`

`object`	The name of the `ListBox` object to which you want to add the item.
`text`	The item's text.
`index`	The new item's position in the list. If you omit this argument, VBA adds the item to the end of the list.

- `Clear`—Removes all the items from the specified list box.
- `RemoveItem`—Removes an item from the specified list box using the following syntax:

  `object.RemoveItem(index)`

`object`	The `ListBox` object from which you want to remove the item.
`index`	The index number of the item you want to remove.

Scrollbars

Scrollbars are normally used to navigate windows, but by themselves you can use them to enter values between a predefined maximum and minimum. Use the ScrollBar button to create either a vertical or horizontal scrollbar. Here's a rundown of the `ScrollBar` object properties you'll use most often in your VBA code:

- `LargeChange`—Returns or sets the amount that the scrollbar value changes when the user clicks between the scroll box and one of the scroll arrows.
- `Max`—Returns or sets the maximum value of the scrollbar.
- `Min`—Returns or sets the minimum value of the scrollbar.
- `SmallChange`—Returns or sets the amount that the scrollbar value changes when the user clicks one of the scroll arrows.
- `Value`—Returns or sets the current value of the scrollbar.

Spin Buttons

A spin button is similar to a scrollbar in that the user can click the button's arrows to increment or decrement a value. To create a spin button, use the SpinButton tool in the Toolbox. The properties for a `SpinButton` object are the same as those for a `ScrollBar` (except that there is no `LargeChange` property).

12

Most spin buttons have a text box control beside them to give the user the choice of entering the number directly or selecting the number by using the spin button arrows. You have to use VBA code to make sure that the values in the text box and the spinner stay in sync. (In other words, if you increment the spinner, the value shown in the text box increments as well, and vice versa.)

To do this, you have to add event handler code for both controls. For example, suppose you have a text box named TextBox1 and a spin button named SpinButton1. Listing 12.1 shows the basic event handler code that keeps the values of these two controls synchronized.

Listing 12.1   Event Handler Code That Keeps a Text Box and a Spin Button in Sync

```
Private Sub TextBox1_Change()
    SpinButton1.Value = TextBox1.Value
End Sub

Private Sub SpinButton1_Change()
    TextBox1.Value = SpinButton1.Value
End Sub
```

> **NOTE**
> I use Excel as the underlying application for the procedures in this chapter. To get the code for these procedures, see my website:
>
> http://www.mcfedries.com/Office2007VBA/Chapter12.xlsm
>
> For Listing 12.1, see the code for the form named TestForm.

Tab Strips and MultiPage Controls

I mentioned earlier that you can use frames to group related controls visually and help the user make sense of the form. However, there are two situations in which a frame falls down on the job.

The first situation is when you need the form to show multiple sets of the same (or similar) data. For example, suppose you have a form that shows values for sales and expense categories. You might want the form to be capable of showing separate data for various company divisions. One solution would be to create separate frames for each division and populate each frame with the same controls, but this is clearly inefficient. A second solution would be to use a list or a set of option buttons. This will work, but it might not be obvious to the user how he is supposed to display different sets of data, and these extra controls just serve to clutter the frame. A better solution is to create a tabbed form where each tab represents a different set of data.

The second situation is when you have a lot of controls. In this case, even the judicious use of frames won't be enough to keep your form from becoming difficult to navigate and understand. In situations where you have a large number of controls, you're better off creating a tabbed form that spreads the controls over several tabs.

In both of these situations, the tabbed form solution acts much like the tabbed dialog boxes you work with in Windows, Office, and other modern programs. To create tabs in your forms, VBA offers two controls: `TabStrip` and `MultiPage`.

The `TabStrip` Control

The `TabStrip` is an ideal way to give the user an intuitive method of displaying multiple sets of data. The basic idea behind the `TabStrip` control is that as the user navigates from tab to tab, the visible controls remain the same, and only the data displayed inside each control changes. The advantage here is that you need to create only a single set of controls on the form, and you use code to adjust the contents of these controls.

You create a `TabStrip` by clicking the `TabStrip` button in the Toolbox and then clicking and dragging the mouse until the strip is the size and shape you want. Here are a few points to keep in mind:

- The best way to set up a `TabStrip` is to add it as the first control on the form and then add the other controls inside the `TabStrip`.

- If you already have controls defined on the form, draw the `TabStrip` over the controls and then use the Send to Back command on the UserForm toolbar (or press Ctrl+K) to send the `TabStrip` to the bottom of the Z-order.

- You can also display a series of buttons instead of tabs. To use this format, select the `TabStrip` and change the `Style` property to `fmTabStyleButtons` (or 1).

Figure 12.6 shows a form that contains a `TabStrip` control and an Excel worksheet that shows budget data for three different divisions. The goal here is to use the `TabStrip` to display budget data for each division as the user selects the tabs.

Figure 12.6
Using the form's TabStrip to display budget data from the three divisions in the Excel worksheet.

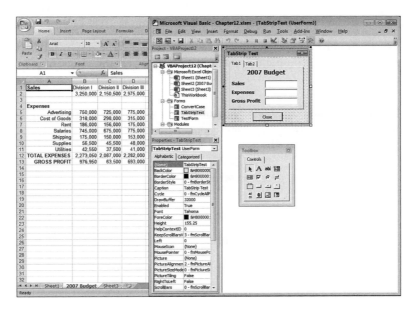

12

The first order of business is to use code to change the tab captions, add a third tab, and enter the initial data. Listing 12.2 shows an `Initialize` event procedure that does just that.

Listing 12.2   An `Initialize` Event Procedure That Sets Up a `TabStrip`

```
Private Sub UserForm_Initialize()
    '
    ' Rename the existing tabs
    '
    With TabStrip1
        .Tabs(0).Caption = "Division I"
        .Tabs(1).Caption = "Division II"
        '
        ' Add a new tab
        '
        .Tabs.Add "Division III"
    End With
    '
    ' Enter the intial data for Division I
    '
    With Worksheets("2007 Budget")
        txtSales = .[B2]
        txtExpenses = .[B12]
        txtGrossProfit = .[B13]
    End With
End Sub
```

The code first uses the `Tabs` collection to change the captions of the two existing tabs. The `Tabs` collection represents all the tabs in a `TabStrip`, and you refer to individual tabs by using an index number (where the first tab is 0, the second is 1, and so on). Then the `Tabs` collection's `Add` method is used to add a third tab titled Division III to the `TabStrip`. Finally, the three text boxes within the `TabStrip` (named `txtSales`, `txtExpenses`, and `txtGrossProfit`) are set to their respective values for Division I in the 2004 Budget worksheet.

Now you must set up a handler for when the user clicks a tab. This fires a `Change` event for the `TabStrip`, so you use this event handler to adjust the values of the text boxes, as shown in Listing 12.3.

Listing 12.3   A `Change` Event Procedure That Modifies the Controls Within a Tab Strip Whenever the User Selects a Different Tab

```
Private Sub TabStrip1_Change()
        With Worksheets("2007 Budget")
            Select Case TabStrip1.Value
                Case 0
                    '
                    ' Enter the data for Division I
                    '
                    txtSales = .[B2]
                    txtExpenses = .[B12]
                    txtGrossProfit = .[B13]
                Case 1
                    '
```

```
            ' Enter the data for Division II
            '
            txtSales = .[C2]
            txtExpenses = .[C12]
            txtGrossProfit = .[C13]
            Case 2
            '
            ' Enter the data for Division III
            '
            txtSales = .[D2]
            txtExpenses = .[D12]
            txtGrossProfit = .[D13]
        End Select
    End With
End Sub
```

Here, a `Select Case` checks the `Value` property of the `TabStrip` (where the first tab has the value 0, the second tab has the value 1, and so on). Figure 12.7 shows the form in action. (See "Displaying the Form" later in this chapter to learn how to run a form.)

Figure 12.7
Clicking each tab displays the data for the appropriate division.

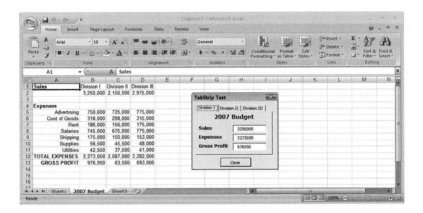

The MultiPage Control

The `MultiPage` control is similar to a `TabStrip` in that it displays a series of tabs along the top of the form. The major difference, however, is that each tab represents a separate form (called a *page*). Therefore, you use a `MultiPage` control whenever you want to display a different set of controls each time the user clicks a tab.

You add a `MultiPage` control to your form by clicking the MultiPage button in the Toolbox and then clicking and dragging the mouse until the control is the size and shape you want.

It's important to remember that each page in the control is a separate object (a `Page` object). So each time you select a page, the values that appear in the Properties window apply only to the selected page. For example, the `Caption` property determines the text that appears in the page's tab. Also, you set up a page by selecting it and then drawing controls inside the page. (If you have controls on the form already, you can put them inside a page by cutting them to the Clipboard, selecting the page, and pasting the controls.)

Working with a `MultiPage` control in code is very similar to working with a `TabStrip`:

- The `Pages` collection represents all the pages inside a `MultiPage` control. You refer to individual pages by their index numbers.
- Use the `Pages.Add` method to add more pages to the control.
- When the user selects a different tab, the `MultiPage` control's `Change` event fires.

Using a Form in a Procedure

After you've created your form, the next step is to incorporate your handiwork into some VBA code. This involves three separate techniques:

- Displaying the form
- Handling events while the form is displayed
- Processing the form results

Displaying the Form

Each `UserForm` object has a `Show` method that you use to display the form to the user. For example, to display a form named UserForm1, you would use the following statement:

```
UserForm1.Show
```

Alternatively, you may want to load the form into memory but keep it hidden from the user. For example, you may need to perform some behind-the-scenes manipulation of the form before showing it to the user. You can do this by executing the `Load` statement:

```
Load Form
```

      Form   The name of the form you want to load.

This statement brings the form object into memory and fires the form's `Initialize` event. From there, you can display the form to the user at any time by running the form's `Show` method as discussed earlier.

> **TIP**   Before getting to the code stage, you might want to try out your form to make sure it looks okay. To do this, activate the form and then select <u>R</u>un, Run Sub/UserForm, or press F5, or click the Run Sub/UserForm button on the toolbar.

Unloading the Form

After the user has filled out the form, you'll probably want to include on the form a command button to put whatever values the user entered into effect. Alternatively, the user could click some sort of Cancel button to dismiss the form without affecting anything.

However, just clicking a command button doesn't get rid of the form—even if you've set up a command button with the `Default` or `Cancel` property set to `True`. Instead, you have to add the following statement to the event handler for the command button:

```
Unload Me
```

The `Unload` command tells VBA to dismiss the form. Note that the `Me` keyword refers to the form in which the event handler resides. For example, the following event handler processes a click on a command button named `cmdCancel`:

```
Private Sub cmdCancel_Click()
    Dim result as Integer
    result = MsgBox("Are you sure you want to Cancel?", _
                    vbYesNo + vbQuestion)
    If result = vbYes Then Unload Me
End Sub
```

You should note, however, that simply unloading a form doesn't remove the form object from memory. To ensure proper cleanup (technically, to ensure that the form object class fires its internal `Terminate` event), `Set` the form object to `Nothing`. For example, the following two lines `Show` the `TabStripTest` form and then `Set` it to `Nothing` to ensure termination:

```
TabStripTest.Show
Set TabStripTest = Nothing
```

Processing the Form Results

When the user clicks OK or Cancel (or any other control that includes the `Unload Me` statement in its `Click` event handler), you usually need to examine the form results and process them in some way.

Obviously, how you proceed depends on whether the user has clicked OK or Cancel because this almost always determines whether the other form selections should be accepted or ignored.

- If OK is clicked, the `Click` event handler for that button can process the results. In other words, it can read the `Value` property for each control (for example, by storing them in variables for later use in the program).

- If Cancel is clicked, the code can move on without processing the results. (As shown earlier, you can include code to ask the user whether he's sure he wants to cancel.)

Table 12.1 lists all the controls that have a `Value` property and provides a description of what kind of data gets returned.

12

Table 12.1 Value Properties for Some Form Controls

Object	What It Returns
CheckBox	True if the check box is activated; False if it's deactivated; Null otherwise.
ComboBox	The position of the selected item in the list (where 1 is the first item).
ListBox	The position of the selected item in the list (where 1 is the first item).
MultiPage	An integer that represents the active page (where 0 is the first page).
OptionButton	True if the option is activated; False if it's deactivated; Null otherwise.
ScrollBar	A number between the scrollbar's minimum and maximum values.
SpinButton	A number between the spinner's minimum and maximum values.
TabStrip	An integer that represents the active tab (where 0 is the first tab).
TextBox	The value entered in the box
ToggleButton	True if the button is pressed; False otherwise.

TIP

If you've set up your list box to accept multiple selections, simply checking the Value property won't work. Instead, you need to run through all the items in the list and check each item to see whether its Selected property is True. If a list item is selected, then you use the corresponding item in the List array to return the value of the selected item. The following code demonstrates this technique by using the form's Terminate event (fired when the form is closed) to store the selected list values in a worksheet:

```
Private Sub UserForm_Terminate()
    Dim nItem As Integer
    Dim nSelected As Integer
    nSelected = 0
    For nItem = 0 To ListBox1.ListCount - 1
        If ListBox1.Selected(nItem) Then
            ActiveSheet.Range("A1").Offset(nSelected, 0) =
➥ListBox1.List(nItem)
            nSelected = nSelected + 1
        End If
    Next 'i
End Sub
```

For example, Figure 12.8 shows the Convert Case form created in the Visual Basic Editor. The idea behind this form is to convert the selected cells to proper case, uppercase, or lowercase, depending on the option chosen.

Figure 12.8
A custom form that lets the user change the case of the selected worksheet cells.

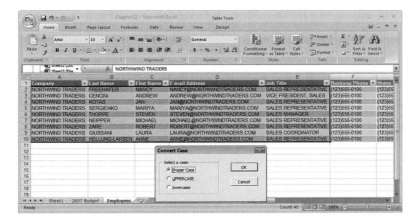

To load this form, I created a macro named `ConvertCase` that contains the two statements shown earlier:

```
ConvertCase.Show
Set ConvertCase = Nothing
```

Here, `ConvertCase` is the name of the form shown in Figure 12.8. The three option buttons are named `optProper`, `optUpper`, and `optLower`; the OK button is named `cmdOK`. Listing 12.4 shows the event handler that runs when the user clicks OK.

Listing 12.4   A Procedure That Processes the `ConvertCase` Custom Form

```
Private Sub cmdOK_Click()
    Dim c As Range
    For Each c In Selection
        If optProper.Value = True Then
            c.Value = StrConv(c, vbProperCase)
        ElseIf optUpper.Value = True Then
            c.Value = StrConv(c, vbUpperCase)
        ElseIf optLower.Value = True Then
            c.Value = StrConv(c, vbLowerCase)
        End If
    Next 'c
    Unload Me
End Sub
```

12

The procedure runs through the selected cells, checking to see which option button was chosen, and then converts the text by using VBA's StrConv function:

StrConv(*String, Conversion*)

String	The string you want to convert.
Conversion	A constant that specifies the case you want:

Conversion	Resulting Case
vbProperCase	Proper Case
vbUpperCase	UPPERCASE
vbLowerCase	lowercase

From Here

- Handling form results often means using loops and control structures (such as If...Then...Else and Select Case). To learn about these VBA statements, **see** Chapter 6, "Controlling Your VBA Code," **p. 91**.

- The MsgBox function provides simple form capabilities in a single statement. For the details on this function, **see** "Getting Input Using MsgBox," **p. 45**.

- You can also use the InputBox function as a basic form; **see** "Getting Input Using InputBox," **p. 50**.

- To learn how to use the built-in dialog boxes available in VBA applications, **see** "Accessing an Application's Built-In Dialog Boxes," **p. 83**.

- To complete your look at VBA user-interface design, **see** Chapter 13, "Customizing the Office 2007 Ribbon," **p. 263**.

12

Customizing the Office 2007 Ribbon

13

In Chapter 1, "Creating and Running Recorded Macros," and Chapter 2, "Writing Your Own Macros," I showed you a number of methods for running your VBA macros. However, all these methods assume that you know which task each macro performs. If you're constructing procedures for others to wield, they might not be so familiar with what each macro name represents. Not only that, but you might not want novice users scrolling through a long list of procedures in the Macro dialog box or, even worse, having to access the Visual Basic Editor.

To help you avoid these problems, this chapter presents some techniques for making your macros more accessible. To wit, I'll show you how to enable your users to use familiar tools—namely, the Office 2007 Ribbon and its tabs, groups, and various buttons—to run your macros.

Understanding Ribbon Extensibility

If you've used previous versions of Office to customize menus and toolbars, you'll no doubt be disappointed to learn that all your hard-won customization knowledge must now be discarded. Most unfortunately, Microsoft offers no direct method for customizing the Ribbon and its various tabs, groups, and buttons. Note that this does *not* mean that the Ribbon isn't customizable. It certainly is, but it's just that now the process is much more involved and requires quite a few more steps.

→ If you just want a quick way to run some of your own macros, the Office 2007 programs enable you to add macros to the Quick Access toolbar; **see** "Creating a Quick Access Toolbar Button for a Recorded Macro," **p. 11**.

I just told you that the Ribbon is customizable, but to be accurate I should really say that the Ribbon is *extensible*. This makes sense (at least a little bit) when you understand that the Office 2007 applications are built around the Office Open XML Formats, where XML stands for eXtensible Markup Language. It's this use of XML throughout Office 2007 that enables you to extend the Ribbon with your own custom interface elements, including tabs, groups within tabs, and buttons within groups.

This book is, by design, short on theory and long of practicality. However, before getting to the nuts and bolts of extending the Ribbon, you need to understand just a bit of background about the Office XML file formats, not least because they are quite unlike any file format you've probably seen.

The first thing you need to know about the Office XML formats is that a given file (such as a Word .docx document or an Excel .xlsx workbook) isn't really a single file at all. Instead, it's a *container*—or *package*—that contains multiple folders and files. In fact, this package is actually a file that uses the standard zip (compressed) file format. When, say, a Word document uses the .docx extension, it appears to be just a single file that works just like any other Word document. However, if you rename the file with a .zip extension, it automagically converts to a valid zip container format. And if you open that container, you see the folders and files that it contains. For example, I took this chapter's example file— Chapter13.docm—added the .zip extension, and then opened it, as shown in Figure 13.1.

> **NOTE** As you'll see, much of the work you perform in this chapter involves changing the extensions of Office files to .zip and back again. To do this, you must configure Windows to display file extensions. Click Start, Control Panel, and then open the Folder Options icon. (In Vista's Control Panel, you might have to first click Appearance and Personalization.) Click the View tab and then click to deactivate the Hide Extensions For Known File Types check box. Click OK.

Figure 13.1
Rename an Office 2007 file with the .zip extension and it becomes a zip package that contains other folders and files.

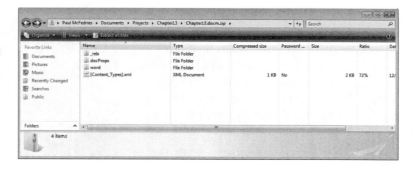

Each of the files in the container is called a *part*, and the parts are grouped roughly into three categories:

- Built-in elements that are shared by all Office applications, including document properties, comments, hyperlinks, and objects such as charts, SmartArt, and shapes.

- Built-in elements that are specific to each Office application, such as Word headers and footers, Excel worksheets, and PowerPoint slides.

- User-defined content, including the document text and VBA elements added to the document project, including macros and user forms.

All this is tied together by a special XML file named `.rels` in the container's `_rels` folder. This document consists of several `<Relationship>` elements, each of which has the following general form:

```
<Relationship Id="ID" Type="relationshipType" Target="targetPart" />
```

ID	A string that names the relationship. This name must be unique within the `.rels` file.
relationshipType	The address of the XML schema that specifies the type of relationship.
targetPart	The path and file name within the package that points to the part governed by the relationship.

In a Word document, for example, the document text part is in the `word/document.xml` file within the container and the schema for this part is located here:

```
http://schemas.openxmlformats.org/officeDocument/2006/relationships/
➥officeDocument
```

Here then is the complete `<Relationship>` element for this part:

```
<Relationship Id="rId1"
            Type="http://schemas.openxmlformats.org/
            ➥officeDocument/2006/relationships/officeDocument"
            Target="word/document.xml" />
```

The key point for the purposes of this chapter is that, just as with any zip file, you can add files to an Office XML container. In particular, you can add an XML file that specifies your custom Ribbon configuration. The next time you load that Office document, the program parses your custom XML document and extends the Ribbon accordingly. The next section takes you through an example.

Extending the Ribbon: An Example

The rest of this chapter takes you through the specifics of extending the Ribbon with custom tabs, groups, and controls such as buttons, menus, and galleries. Before we get to that, let's run through a specific example that shows you the process of adding to an Office document some custom XML content that extends the Ribbon content. The next few sections take you through the details.

Step 1: Create a Macro-Enabled Office Document or Template

Because you'll be associating your custom Ribbon controls with macros, you need to begin with a macro-enabled file. You have several choices:

13

- If you only want the custom Ribbon interface available for a specific document, create a macro-enabled document (.docm, .xlsm, or .pptm).
- If you want the custom Ribbon interface available only for any document based on a particular template, create a macro-enabled template (.dotm, .xltm, or .potm).
- If you want the custom Ribbon interface available for any open document in Word, modify the Normal template.
- If you want the custom Ribbon interface available for any open document in Excel or PowerPoint, you need to create an Add-in file (.xlam or .ppam).

> **NOTE** If you want to work with an add-in file, remember that you have to first create the file and then load it. To create the add-in, start a new document or open an existing document (such as one that has macros you want to include in the add-in). Choose Office, Save As to open the Save As dialog box, click Save as Type to choose the add-in type (Excel Add-In or PowerPoint Add-In), and then click Save. Note that you might want to store the file in the AddIns folder:
>
>   %UserProfile%\appdata\Roaming\Microsoft\AddIns
>
> To load the add-in in Excel, choose Office, Excel Options and the click Add-Ins. Use the Manage list to click Excel Add-ins, and then click Go to open the Add-Ins dialog box. If you didn't save the add-in in the AddIns folder, click Browse, click the add-in, and then click OK. The procedure for loading PowerPoint add-ins is similar.

> **TIP** When you go to save the file, bear in mind that Ribbon customization requires multiple files (as you'll soon see). In my experience, the best way to keep your Ribbon customizations organized is to create a separate folder for each document or template that you want to customize with Ribbon extensions. That way, you can store all the files you need in the same folder, and it will be easy to keep everything straight.

You can now add your macros to the document or template. Here's the general form to use:

```
Sub ProcedureName(ByVal control As iRibbonControl)
    [Statements]
End Sub
```

ProcedureName	A unique macro name.
control	An iRibbonControl object that represents the Ribbon control that was clicked to trigger the macro. You'll see later that you sometimes use this object to work with the control (for example, to determine which item in a menu was clicked).
Statements	The VBA code you want the macro to run.

Here's an example:

```
Sub MyButton(ByVal control As iRibbonControl)
    MsgBox "Hello Ribbon World!"
End Sub
```

In the language of custom Office 2007 interfaces, the macro that runs when you click an interface element is known as a *callback*.

When you're finished, save and close the document.

Step 2: Create a Text File and Add the Custom XML Markup

You're now ready to create the custom XML markup for the Ribbon tabs, groups, and controls you want to display. In the same folder that you're using to store the macro-enabled document or template, create a text document named (for example) `MyRibbon.xml`. Open the file in Notepad or some other text editor and then begin the XML markup as follows:

> **NOTE** If you're working with Word's Normal template, you can open its folder by pressing Windows Logo+R, entering the following path in the Run dialog box, and then clicking OK:
>
> `%UserProfile%\appdata\Roaming\Microsoft\Templates`

> **NOTE** The XML and VBA code for this chapter's examples is available on my website at www.mcfedries.com/Office2007VBA/.

```
<customUI xmlns="http://schemas.microsoft.com/office/2006/01/customui">
    <ribbon>
        <tabs>
        </tabs>
    </ribbon>
</customUI>
```

Now add a tab (see "Creating a New Tab," later in this chapter, for the details):

```
<customUI xmlns="http://schemas.microsoft.com/office/2006/01/customui">
    <ribbon>
        <tabs>
            <tab id="CustomTab" label="My Tab">
            </tab>
        </tabs>
    </ribbon>
</customUI>
```

Now add a group (see "Creating a New Group," later in this chapter):

```
<customUI xmlns="http://schemas.microsoft.com/office/2006/01/customui">
    <ribbon>
        <tabs>
            <tab id="CustomTab" label="My Tab">
                <group id="CustomGroup" label="My Group" >
```

13

```
            </group>
          </tab>
        </tabs>
      </ribbon>
</customUI>
```

Finally, add the markup for a button (see "Creating Custom Controls," later in this chapter):

```
<customUI xmlns="http://schemas.microsoft.com/office/2006/01/customui">
    <ribbon>
        <tabs>
            <tab id="CustomTab" label="My Tab">
                <group id="CustomGroup" label="My Group" >
                    <button id="CustomButton1"
                            imageMso="HappyFace"
                            label="Hello World!"
                            size="large"
                            onAction="Module1.MyButton" />
                </group>
            </tab>
        </tabs>
    </ribbon>
</customUI>
```

Note, in particular, that the button's `onAction` parameter references the callback macro added to the document earlier (`Module1.MyButton`).

Step 3: Copy the Custom XML Markup File to the Document Package

You're now ready to take the custom XML markup file that you created in step 2 and add it to the document package. Begin by renaming the document or template so that you add `.zip` to the end of the filename. When Windows asks you to confirm the extension change, click Yes. You can now click and drag the custom XML file and then drop it on the zip container to add it to the document package.

At this point, the custom XML is in the package, but the Office application doesn't know what to do with it. You now need to define a relationship that points the Office application to the new XML part. Open the zip container and then open the _rels folder. You need to get the .rels file out of the container so that you can edit it, and then return it when you're finished. Here's one method that takes advantage of the fact that you have the document package in its own folder:

1. Right-click the .rels file and then click Copy.
2. Return to the folder that contains the document package.
3. Right-click the folder and then click Paste.
4. Right-click the copy of the .rels file and then click Edit to open it in Notepad.
5. Make your edits (as described after these steps), save the file, and then exit Notepad.
6. Right-click the copy of the .rels file and then click Copy.
7. Open the zip container and then open the _rels folder.

8. Right-click the folder and then click Paste.

9. When Windows asks you to confirm, click Copy and Replace (in Vista) or Yes (in XP).

When you have the `.rels` file open for editing, you need to add a new `<Relationship>` element that points to your custom XML file in the container. Insert this element between the `<Relationships>` and `</Relationships>` elements, but not within any existing `<Relationship>` elements. Here's the general format:

```
<Relationship
Id="ID"
Type="http://schemas.microsoft.com/office/2006/relationships/ui/extensibility"
Target="CustomXMLFile"/>
```

ID	A string identifier that's unique in the `.rels` file.
CustomXMLFile	The name of the file that contains the custom XML markup.

Here's an example:

```
<Relationship
Id="MyRibbonID"
Type="http://schemas.microsoft.com/office/2006/relationships/ui/extensibility"
Target="MyRibbon.xml"/>
```

Step 4: Rename and Open the Document

Your customization work is done, so close the container and then rename the file to remove the `.zip` extension. The next time you open the document, the application parses the custom XML file and displays the new Ribbon elements.

Figure 13.2 shows Word with the new tab, group, and button specified by the custom XML file used as an example in step 2 ("Create a Text File and Add the Custom XML Markup"). Clicking the button runs the associated macro, which displays the dialog box.

Figure 13.2
Microsoft Word 2007 with the Ribbon extended to display a new tab and group, as well as a button associated with a macro.

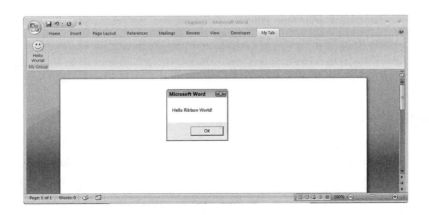

13

> **TIP**
>
> The process of creating callbacks, generating custom XML, and adding new interface parts to document packages is so time consuming and finicky that I predict there will be a booming market in Ribbon interface editors. As I write this, there is one editor available via the OpenXML Developer site: the Microsoft Office 2007 Custom UI Editor. With this nice little utility, you open the macro-enabled Office document or template, and then use the Custom UI tab (essentially a large edit box) to add your custom XML code. A Validate button on the toolbar lets you know whether your code is well formed. When you save the file, the editor adds the XML to the document package and updates the `.rels` file. It even comes with a Generate Callbacks button that adds the stub procedures for the callback macros to your document. You can download the editor here:
>
> http://openxmldeveloper.org/articles/customuieditor.aspx

> **CAUTION**
>
> If you do use the Custom UI Editor discussed in the preceding Tip, never open a document in the Editor and in its Office application at the same time. A bug in the Custom UI Editor (possibly resolved by the time you read this, but you never know) causes the editor to strip out some or all of the document's existing macros.

More Complexity Means More Power

As I mentioned earlier, and as you saw in the preceding steps, extending the Office 2007 Ribbon is a far more involved (some would say *convoluted*) process than the relatively simple and straightforward menu and toolbar customizations in earlier versions of Office. Fortunately, as you'll soon see, there is an upside to the more difficult Ribbon procedure. That added complexity also gives you added power. Your previous Office customizations were restricted to mere buttons that ran macros. With Office 2007, you can extend the Ribbon not only with buttons, but also with check boxes, drop-down lists, menus, dialog box launchers, and even galleries. In short, you can create a much richer interface for your Office applications.

The rest of this chapter takes you through the specifics of what is known as *RibbonX*, the XML code that you use to extend the Ribbon with custom tabs, groups, and controls.

Hiding the Built-In Ribbon

Most of the time, your RibbonX customizations will augment the Office program's built-in Ribbon interface by adding one or more custom tabs or by adding new groups and controls to existing tabs. Occasionally, however, your VBA application might require that you hide the built-in Ribbon and display only your custom interface. You'll see in the next few sections that you can hide individual tabs (as well as groups and controls within a tab), but you don't have to hide all the program's tabs individually to hide the built-in Ribbon. Instead, in your custom XML markup you modify the `<ribbon>` element to include the `startFromScratch` attribute:

```
<ribbon startFromScratch = "true¦false">
```

If you set this attribute to `true`, the Office application hides the built-in Ribbon and displays just your custom interface. Here's some bare-bones XML that does that:

```
<customUI xmlns="http://schemas.microsoft.com/office/2006/01/customui">
    <ribbon startFromScratch="true">
    </ribbon>
</customUI>
```

Figure 13.3 shows the result when you load the document in Word. As you can see, the Ribbon is completely hidden and the Office menu includes only the New, Open, and Save commands, as well as the Word Options and Exit Word buttons.

Figure 13.3
Word 2007 with the
built-in Ribbon hidden.

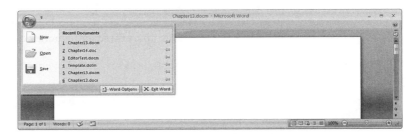

Creating Custom Tabs

The Ribbon in each Office application is divided into several tabs, and those tabs contain the groups and controls that expose the application's functionality. With RibbonX, you can create your own custom tabs or you can customize any of the application's existing tabs. Either way, your markup must appear between the `<tabs>` and `</tabs>` elements, so your tab-based RibbonX markup always begins like this:

```
<customUI xmlns="http://schemas.microsoft.com/office/2006/01/customui">
    <ribbon>
        <tabs>
        </tabs>
    </ribbon>
</customUI>
```

Creating a New Tab

If you're building an interface for a number of macros and user forms, you can make it easy for the user to find the custom tools by placing them within a new tab in the Ribbon. This gives you plenty of room to add whatever groups and controls you need to build your interface.

13

In RibbonX, you create a tab by using the `<tab>` element. Here's the basic syntax:

```
<tab id="ID" label="Label" InsertAfterMso="AfterID"
➥InsertBeforeMso="BeforeID" keytip="KeyTip">
</tab>
```

ID	A unique string identifier for the tab.
Label	The text that appears on the tab.
AfterID	The string identifier of the built-in tab after which you want your tab inserted. See the next section to learn about built-in tab identifiers.
BeforeID	The string identifier of the built-in tab before which you want your tab inserted.
KeyTip	The character or characters that appear when the user presses Alt. The user can then press the character or characters to choose the tab via the keyboard. Enter up to three alphanumeric characters.

Place your `<tab>` elements between the `<tabs>` and `</tabs>` elements in your XML markup file. Here's an example:

```
<customUI xmlns="http://schemas.microsoft.com/office/2006/01/customui">
    <ribbon>
        <tabs>
            <tab id="CustomTab" label="My Tab" keytip="Z">
            </tab>
        </tabs>
    </ribbon>
</customUI>
```

Figure 13.4 shows Word with the new tab added to the Ribbon. When you press Alt, as shown in Figure 13.4, the keytip Z appears over the new tab.

Figure 13.4
The Word 2007 Ribbon with a new tab added.

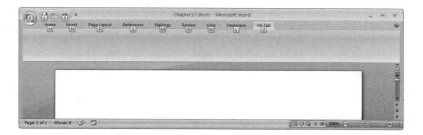

Customizing an Existing Tab

If you have just a few macros that require an interface, building a new tab is probably overkill. Instead, you can add controls for those macros to one of the application's built-in tabs. To work with a built-in tab, you again use the `<tab>` element, but the syntax is slightly different. Here's a simplified version:

```
<tab idMso="ID" visible="true¦false" />
```

> *ID*   The unique string identifier for the built-in tab.

The value of the `idMso` attribute takes one of the following forms:

- `TabName`—This is the most common form and it's used for most regular built-in tabs. Here, *Name* is the name that appears on the tab, with spaces and punctuation marks (such as dashes) removed. For example, the `isMso` value for Word's Insert tab is `TabInsert`, and the value for PowerPoint's Slide Show tab is `TabSlideShow`.

- `TabContextName`—This is the form used for contextual tabs (the tabs that appear only when you select certain objects, such as pictures or tables). Here, *Context* is the overall name of the contextual tabs and *Name* is the name of the specific contextual tab. For example, when you click a picture object, you see the Picture Tools tab and the Format tab. So the `isMso` value for the Format tab is `TabPictureToolsFormat`.

- `TabNameApplication`—This is the form used for tabs that are common to multiple applications. Here, *Name* is the name of the tab and *Application* is the name of the application. So the `isMso` value for Word's Page Layout tab is `TabPageLayoutWord`, whereas the value for Excel's Page Layout tab is `TabPageLayoutExcel`.

> **CAUTION**
>
> Unfortunately, there are lots of exceptions to the various tab naming conventions. For example, even though the View tab is common to Word, Excel, and PowerPoint, its `idMso` value is `TabView` in all the programs. The only way to be sure of the correct `idMso` values is to download Microsoft's Lists of Control IDs, a collection of Excel worksheets that provide the `idMso` values for every interface element. Go to the following site and search for "lists of control ids":
>
> http://www.microsoft.com/downloads/

You'll work with built-in tabs in more detail later in this chapter when you learn how to add groups and controls to existing tabs. For now, you can use the `visible` attribute to hide built-in tabs that you don't want the user to see. For example, the following XML code hides the Developer tab:

```
<tab idMso="TabDeveloper" visible="false" />
```

Creating Custom Groups

Within each tab on the Ribbon, related controls are organized into several groups, which makes it easier for the user to find a specific control. In your VBA application, you can use RibbonX to create your own custom groups on a new or built-in tab. You can also modify any of the built-in groups.

Your group-based markup must appear in the custom XML file between a `<tab>` and `</tab>` container.

Creating a New Group

If you have a lot of controls to add to a custom tab, you should probably organize them into groups to keep things organized. Even if you think your VBA application doesn't need multiple groups, note that you must create at least one group in your custom tab.

In RibbonX, you create a group by using the <group> element. Here's the basic syntax:

```
<group id="ID" label="Label" InsertAfterMso="AfterID"
➥InsertBeforeMso="BeforeID">
</tab>
```

ID	A unique string identifier for the group.
Label	The text that appears below the group.
AfterID	The string identifier of the built-in group after which you want your group inserted. See the next section to learn about built-in group identifiers.
BeforeID	The string identifier of the built-in group before which you want your group inserted.

In your XML markup, place your <group> element between the <tab> and </tab> elements that represent the tab in which you want the group to appear. This can be either a custom tab or a built-in tab. Here's an example:

```
<customUI xmlns="http://schemas.microsoft.com/office/2006/01/customui">
    <ribbon>
        <tabs>
            <tab id="CustomTab" label="My Tab" keytip="AZ>
                <group id="CustomGroup" label="My Group" >
                </group>
            </tab>
        </tabs>
    </ribbon>
</customUI>
```

Figure 13.5 shows Word with the new group added to My Tab.

Figure 13.5
A custom group added to the custom tab named My Tab.

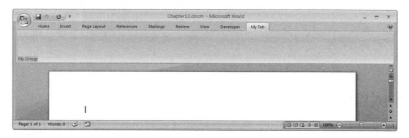

Customizing an Existing Group

If you have one or two macros that you want to add to the Ribbon and those macros are related to the controls in a built-in group, you can add controls for those macros to the group. To work with a built-in group, you use the `<group>` element with the following (simplified) syntax:

```
<group idMso="ID" visible="true¦false"/>
```

     `ID`   The unique string identifier for the built-in group.

The value of the `idMso` attribute takes one of the following forms:

- `GroupName`—This is the most common form and it's used for most regular built-in groups. Here, `Name` is the name that appears under the group, with spaces removed. For example, the `isMso` value for Word's Font group (Home tab) is `GroupFont`, and the value for Excel's Function Library group (Formulas tab) is `GroupFunctionLibrary`.

- `GroupTabName`—This form combines the `Tab` in which the group appears and the `Name` of the group. For example, the `idMso` value for Word's Text group on the Insert tab is `GroupInsertText`.

- `GroupNameApplication`—This is the form used for groups that are common to multiple applications. Here, `Name` is the name of the group and `Application` is the name of the application. So the `isMso` value for Word's Themes group (Page Layout tab) is `GroupThemesWord`, whereas the value for Excel's Themes group is `GroupThemesExcel`.

CAUTION

Again, the group names aren't fully consistent across the Office 2007 applications, so check the Lists of Control IDs collection mentioned in the previous Caution.

You'll work with built-in tabs in more detail later in this chapter when you learn how to add controls to existing tabs. For now, you can use the `visible` attribute to hide built-in groups that you don't want the user to see. For example, the following XML code hides the Macros group (View tab):

```
<tab idMso="TabView">
    <group idMso="GroupMacros" visible="false" />
</tab>
```

Creating Custom Controls

With your custom tab added to the Ribbon and populated with at least one custom group, you're ready to bring your RibbonX extensions into the realm of the practical by adding controls that actually perform actions. The rest of this chapter takes you through the three most common control types supported by the Ribbon interface: buttons, menus, and split buttons. You'll learn the RibbonX XML code required to add and configure each control, as well as the VBA code needed to make a control perform an action.

13

Common Control Attributes

Before getting to the specific control types, let's take a second to run through the a few attributes that are common to all or more of the controls:

`id`	A unique string identifier for a custom control.
`idMso`	A unique string identifier for a built-in control.

> **TIP**
> To get the name of a built-in control, you can use the Lists of Controls Ids worksheets that I mentioned earlier. Alternatively, right-click the Quick Access toolbar and then click Customize Quick Access Toolbar. Use the Choose Commands From list to display the category of the command that corresponds to the control you want to work with and then hover the mouse pointer over the command. In the banner text that pops up, the command name appears in parentheses.

`label`	The text that appears on the control.
`imageMso`	A string that represents the name of an icon associated with a built-in control. This icon appears with your control.

> **TIP**
> The `imageMso` attribute refers to the icons you see with all the controls on all the Office 2007 application Ribbons and commands. Office 2007 has hundreds of these icons, and you can use any of them in your custom interface. The only problem is finding out the name of a particular icon so that you can use it as the `imageMso` value. There is no easy way to determine this, but the following link takes you to an Excel workbook that contains several galleries that display all the Office 2007 icons:
>
> http://www.sunflowerhead.com/msimages/Office2007IconsGallery.zip
>
> Pull down a gallery and hover the mouse pointer over an icon to see the icon's name.

`size`	The relative size that you want to use for the control. Use either `normal` or `large`.
`InsertAfterMso`	The string identifier of the built-in control after which you want your control inserted.
`InsertBeforeMsoID`	The string identifier of the built-in control before which you want your control inserted.
`onAction`	A string that specifies the macro to run when the control is clicked. Use the form *Module.Macro*, where *Module* is the name of the module that holds the procedure and *Macro* is the name of the procedure.

enabled	Set to `false` to disable the control; set to `true` to enable the control.
visible	Set to `false` to hide the control; set to `true` to display the control.
screentip	The title of the SuperTip banner that appears when the user hovers the mouse pointer over the control. If SuperTips are turned off, the user sees just this text.
supertip	The text that appears in the SuperTip banner when the user hovers the mouse pointer over the control. Use this text to explain what the control does.
keytip	The character or characters that appear when the user presses Alt. The user can then press the character or characters to choose the control via the keyboard. Enter up to three alphanumeric characters.

Creating a Button

The most basic control and the control you'll use most often is the button which, when clicked, runs a macro that you specify:

```
<button id="value"
        label="value"
        imageMso="value"
        size="normal¦large"
        InsertAfterMso="value"
        InsertBeforeMso="value"
        onAction="value"
        enabled="true¦false"
        visible="true¦false"
        screentip="value"
        supertip="value"
        keytip="value" />
```

Here's an example:

```
<button id="CustomButton1"
        imageMso="HappyFace"
        label="Hello World!"
        size="large"
        onAction="Module1.MyButton"
        screentip="Hello World"
        supertip="Displays the canonical Hello World! message."
        keytip="M" />
```

Figure 13.6 shows the button in the custom tab. I've hovered the mouse pointer over the button so that you can see the control's associated SuperTip banner.

13

Figure 13.6
A custom button added to the Ribbon.

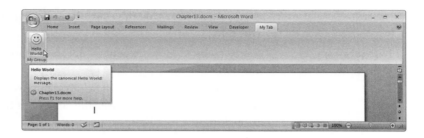

Creating a Menu

If you have a small collection of related macros, you can save space in your custom interface by bundling the buttons for all those macros into a menu. You create the menu control by using the <menu> element:

```
<menu id="value"
      label="value"
      imageMso="value"
      itemSize="normal¦large"
      InsertAfterMso="value"
      InsertBeforeMso="value"
      onAction="value"
      enabled="true¦false"
      visible="true¦false"
      screentip="value"
      supertip="value"
      keytip="value">
```

Note that you use itemSize instead of size, and that this attribute affects every item in the menu.

You populate the menu by adding two or more <button> elements between <menu> and </menu>. Here's an example:

```
<menu id="menu1" label="Close Document">
    <button id="btnSaveChanges"
            label="Save Changes"
            imageMso="FileSave"
            onAction="Module1.btnSaveChanges_OnAction" />
    <button id="btnDoNotSaveChanges"
            label="Don't Save Changes"
            imageMso="SaveAndClose"
            onAction="Module1.btnDoNotSaveChanges_OnAction" />
    <button id="btnPromptToSaveChanges"
            label="Prompt to Save Changes"
            imageMso="WorkflowPending"
            onAction="Module1.btnPromptToSaveChanges_OnAction" />
</menu>
```

Figure 13.7 shows the resulting menu.

Figure 13.7
A custom menu added to the Ribbon.

TIP If you do even mildly extensive customizations with RibbonX, your new interface will consist of a fair number of controls, many of which will have several associated callback macros. In other words, you can easily end up with *dozens* of interface elements to maintain. To help you keep everything straight, it's best to use certain naming conventions. For control names, use prefixes that indicate the control type: btn (for a button), sb (split button), chk (check box), tb (toggle button), lst (drop-down list), gal (gallery), cb (combo box), ed (edit box), and dl (dialog launcher). For callback macros, use the following format:

```
control_attribute
```

Here, replace *control* with the name of the control, and replace *attribute* with the attribute that calls the macro. For example, for the onAction callback macro for a button named btnSaveChanges, you'd use the following name:

```
btnSaveChanges_OnAction
```

In the preceding example, each menu button calls a different procedure. Here are the associated procedures:

```
Sub SaveChanges_OnAction(ByVal control As IRibbonControl)
    ActiveDocument.Close wdSaveChanges
End Sub

Sub DoNotSaveChanges_OnAction(ByVal control As IRibbonControl)
    ActiveDocument.Close wdDoNotSaveChanges
End Sub

Sub btnPromptToSaveChanges_OnAction(ByVal control As IRibbonControl)
    ActiveDocument.Close wdPromptToSaveChanges
End Sub
```

In such a case, it probably makes more sense to use a single callback macro that determines which button was clicked and proceeds accordingly. To determine the button that was clicked, you use the control object's ID property, which returns the id attribute of the button that was clicked.

First, you need to adjust the RibbonX code so that each <button> uses the same onAction value:

```
<menu id="mnuCloseDocument2" label="Close Document">
    <button id="btnSaveChanges2"
```

13

```
            label="Save Changes"
            imageMso="FileSave"
            onAction="Module1.mnuCloseDocument2_OnAction" />
    <button id="btnDoNotSaveChanges2"
            label="Don't Save Changes"
            imageMso="SaveAndClose"
            onAction="Module1.mnuCloseDocument2_OnAction" />
    <button id="btnPromptToSaveChanges2"
            label="Prompt to Save Changes"
            imageMso="WorkflowPending"
            onAction="Module1.mnuCloseDocument2_OnAction" />
</menu>
```

Here's a callback procedure that uses Select Case to check the ID property and then proceeds accordingly:

```
Sub mnuCloseDocument2_OnAction(ByVal control As IRibbonControl)
    Select Case control.ID
        Case "btnSaveChanges2"
            ActiveDocument.Close wdSaveChanges
        Case "btnDoNotSaveChanges2"
            ActiveDocument.Close wdDoNotSaveChanges
        Case "btnPromptToSaveChanges2"
            ActiveDocument.Close wdPromptToSaveChanges
    End Select
End Sub
```

Creating a Split Button

A split button is a control that has a regular button control on the top half and a menu control on the bottom half. The idea here is that the button control represents the default choice, and if you want some other choice, you pull down the menu to select it. You create the split button control by using the <splitButton> element:

```
<splitButton id="value"
             label="value"
             imageMso="value"
             size="normal¦large"
             InsertAfterMso="value"
             InsertBeforeMso="value"
             onAction="value"
             enabled="true¦false"
             visible="true¦false"
             screentip="value"
             supertip="value"
             keytip="value"
             showLabel="true¦false" />
```

The only unique attribute here is showLabel. When you set this attribute to true (this is the default value), the button control's label appears; if you set it to false, instead, the label doesn't appear.

You populate the split button by adding a <button> element and then a <menu> element between <splitButton> and </splitButton>. Here's an example:

```
<splitButton id="splitButton1" size="large">
```

```
<button id="btnRecentDocuments"
    label="Recent Documents"
    imageMso="InkEraseMode"
    onAction="Module1.btnClearRecentDocuments_OnAction" />
<menu id="splitButton3" itemSize="large">
    <button id="btnClearRecentDocuments"
        label="Clear Recent Documents"
        imageMso="InkEraseMode"
        oAction="Module1.btnClearRecentDocuments_OnAction" />
     <button id="btnChangeNumberOfRecentDocuments"
        label="Change Number of Recent Docs"
        imageMso="ReadingViewShowPrintedPage"
        onAction="Module1.btnChangeNumberOfRecentDocuments_OnAction" />
    <button id="btnDisableRecentDocuments"
        label="Disable Recent Documents"
        imageMso="DeclineInvitation"
        onAction="Module1.btnDisableRecentDocuments_OnAction" />
</menu>
</splitButton>
```

Figure 3.8 shows the split button created by this code.

> **NOTE** Notice in Figure 3.8 that a separator bar appears between some of the controls in my custom tab. You add a separator bar by using the `<separator>` element:
>
> ```
> <separator id="value"
>                 InsertAfterMso="value"
>                 InsertBeforeMso="value"
>                 visible="true¦false" />
> ```

Figure 13.8
A split button menu
added to the Ribbon.

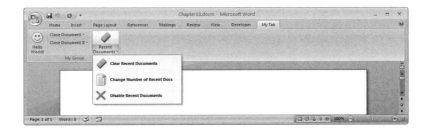

Creating a Check Box

If you have a macro that toggles some setting on or off, then a button or menu element isn't a great choice as a front-end for the macro because these elements have no way of showing the current state of the setting. A much better choice would be a check box: When it's checked, the setting is activated; when it's unchecked, the setting is deactivated.

You create the check box control by using the `<checkBox>` element:

```
<checkBox id="value"
        label="value"
        InsertAfterMso="value"
```

```
InsertBeforeMso="value"
onAction="value"
enabled="true¦false"
visible="true¦false"
screentip="value"
supertip="value"
keytip="value">
```

For example, the following XML code creates a check box that, when clicked, runs a macro named `chkToggleProofingErrors_OnAction`:

```
<checkbox id="chkToggleProofingErrors"
          label="Show Proofing Errors"
          onAction="Module1.chkToggleProofingErrors_OnAction" />
```

Figure 13.9 shows the resulting check box.

Figure 13.9
A check box added to the Ribbon.

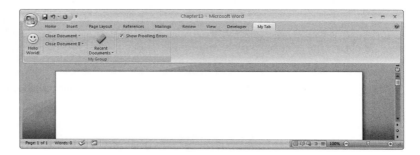

Here's the `chkToggleProofingErrors_OnAction` macro:

```
Sub chkToggleProofingErrors_OnAction(ByVal control As IRibbonControl,
➡pressed As Boolean)
    With ActiveDocument
        .ShowSpellingErrors = pressed
        .ShowGrammaticalErrors = pressed
    End With
    Application.ScreenRefresh
End Sub
```

Notice that the `Sub` statement includes not only the `IRibbonControl` object, but also a `Boolean` variable named `pressed`. This variable passes to the macro the current state of the check box control: `pressed` is `True` when the check box is activated, and it's `False` when the check box is deactivated. In this case, you use the `pressed` value to toggle the active document's `ShowSpellingErrors` and `ShowGrammaticalErrors` properties on and off.

Creating a Toggle Button

A toggle button control is very similar to a check box in that it switches between one of two states: pressed and not pressed. Therefore, as with a check box, you can use it to run a macro that toggles some setting on and off. You create a toggle button by using the `<toggleButton>` element:

```
<toggleButton id="value"
              label="value"
              imageMso="value"
              size="normal¦large"
              InsertAfterMso="value"
              InsertBeforeMso="value"
              onAction="value"
              enabled="true¦false"
              visible="true¦false"
              screentip="value"
              supertip="value"
              keytip="value" />
```

For example, the following XML code creates a toggle button that, when clicked, runs a macro named `ToggleDeveloperTab`:

Here's an example:

```
<toggleButton id="tbToggleDeveloperTab"
              imageMso="VisualBasic"
              label="Show Developer Tab"
              size="large"
              onAction="Module1.tbToggleDeveloperTab_OnAction" />
```

Figure 13.10 shows the resulting toggle button.

Figure 13.10
A toggle button added to the Ribbon.

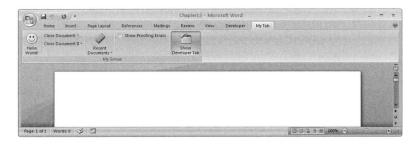

Here's the `tbToggleDeveloperTab_OnAction` macro:

```
Sub tbToggleDeveloperTab_OnAction(ByVal control As IRibbonControl,
➥pressed As Boolean)
    Options.ShowDevTools = pressed
End Sub
```

→ When your toggle button (or check box) alters an application setting, the control's initial state should reflect the current value of the setting. To learn how to do this, **see** "Initializing Controls," **p. 290**.

As with the `<checkBox>` element, the `Sub` statement for the `<toggleButton>` element includes a `Boolean` variable named `pressed` that passes the current state of the toggle button. In Figure 13.10, you can see that the toggle button is activated, so `pressed` is `True`, which then becomes the `ShowDevTools` property value (which means the Developer tab appears in Figure 13.10).

13

Creating a Drop-Down List

Check boxes and toggle buttons are fine when your macro toggles a setting on or off or chooses between two states. However, you'll often need to provide more choices than that. For example, in Chapter 7 you saw the `InsertHyperlinks` function that inserts a hyperlink for each instance of a specified style, which you passed to the function as a string. As a front-end for this function, you might want to give the user a choice of styles from which the hyperlinks are created.

→ To get the details on the `InsertHyperlinks` function, **see** "Programming the `Paragraph` Object," **p. 136.**

In a case such as this where you have more than two choices, you can place those items in a drop-down list. To set this up in RibbonX, you begin with the `<dropdown>` element:

```
<dropDown id="value"
          label="value"
          imageMso="value"
          size="normal¦large"
          InsertAfterMso="value"
          InsertBeforeMso="value"
          onAction="value"
          enabled="true¦false"
          visible="true¦false"
          screentip="value"
          supertip="value"
          keytip="value"
          showItemImage="true¦false"
          showItemLabel="true¦false"
          showImage="true¦false"
          showLabel="true¦false">
```

Here, the `showImage` attribute determines whether the image specified by the `imageMso` attribute is displayed, and the `showLabel` attribute determines whether the text specified by the `label` attribute is displayed.

Here's an example:

```
<dropDown id="lstInsertHyperlinksFor"
          label="Insert Hyperlinks For"
          onAction="Module1.lstInsertHyperlinksFor_OnAction">
</dropDown>
```

The `<dropdown>` element creates just an empty drop-down list. To populate the list, you create multiple `<item>` elements:

```
<item id="value"
      label="value"
      imageMso="value"
      screentip="value"
      supertip="value" />
```

In the `<dropdown>` element, you can use the `showItemImage` attribute to determine whether the `<item>` elements' images are displayed. You can also use the `showItemLabel` attribute to determine whether the `<item>` elements' labels are displayed.

You insert the `<item>` elements between the `<dropdown>` and `</dropdown>` elements, as in this example:

```
<dropDown id="lstInsertHyperlinksFor"
          label="Insert Hyperlinks For"
          onAction="Module1.lstInsertHyperlinksFor_OnAction">
    <item id="heading1" label="Heading 1"/>
    <item id="heading2" label="Heading 2"/>
    <item id="heading3" label="Heading 3"/>
</dropDown>
```

Figure 13.11 shows the resulting drop-down list.

→ By default, no list item is selected when your custom drop-down code first executes; to learn how to select an item at startup, **see** "Initializing Controls," **p. 290**.

Figure 13.11
A drop-down list added
to the Ribbon.

Here's the `lstInsertHyperlinksFor_OnAction` macro:

```
Sub lstInsertHyperlinksFor_OnAction(control As IRibbonControl, id As String,
➥index As Integer)
    Select Case id
        Case "heading1"
            InsertHyperlinks "Heading 1"
        Case "heading2"
            InsertHyperlinks "Heading 2"
        Case "heading3"
            InsertHyperlinks "Heading 3"
    End Select
End Sub
```

Notice that the `Sub` statement includes not only the usual `IRibbonControl` object, but also a `String` variable named `id` and an `Integer` variable named `index`. The `id` variable returns the value of the `id` attribute of the `<item>` object that was clicked in the drop-down list; the `index` variable returns the index of the clicked `<item>` object within the list, where the first item in the list has index 0, the second item has index 1, and so on. The procedure uses `Select Case` to process the `id` value, and then calls the `InsertHyperlinks` function with the corresponding style string.

Creating a Gallery

The more choices you have to offer, the less attractive becomes the drop-down list control because the list just gets too long to navigate efficiently. A better solution for a large number of options is a gallery control, which displays multiple items in the number of rows and columns you specify. To create a gallery in RibbonX, begin with the `<gallery>` element:

13

```
<gallery id="value"
        label="value"
        imageMso="value"
        size="normal¦large"
        InsertAfterMso="value"
        InsertBeforeMso="value"
        onAction="value"
        enabled="true¦false"
        visible="true¦false"
        screentip="value"
        supertip="value"
        keytip="value"
        showItemImage="true¦false"
        showItemLabel="true¦false"
        showImage="true¦false"
        showLabel="true¦false">
        rows="value"
        columns="value">
```

Here's an example:

```
<gallery id="galInsertHyperlinksFor"
        columns="3"
        size="large"
        label="Insert Hyperlinks For"
        imageMso="HyperlinkInsert"
        onAction="Module1.galInsertHyperlinksFor_OnAction">
</gallery>
```

The <gallery> element creates an empty drop-down list. To populate the list, you create multiple <item> elements, followed by one or more <button> elements, if needed. The basic idea is that the <item> elements provide the user with several predefined choices, whereas the <button> elements run code that enable the user to make other choices, change the configuration, and so on. You use the <gallery> element's rows and columns attributes to specify the configuration of the items within the gallery.

You insert the <item> and <button> elements between the <gallery> and </gallery> elements, with the <item> elements first, as shown in this example:

```
<gallery id="gallery1"
        columns="3"
        size="large"
        label="Insert Hyperlinks For"
        imageMso="HyperlinkInsert"
        onAction="Module1.galInsertHyperlinksFor_OnAction">
    <item id="galleryheading1" imageMso="_1" label="Heading 1" />
    <item id="galleryheading2" imageMso="_2" label="Heading 2" />
    <item id="galleryheading3" imageMso="_3" label="Heading 3" />
    <item id="galleryheading4" imageMso="_4" label="Heading 4" />
    <item id="galleryheading5" imageMso="_5" label="Heading 5" />
    <item id="galleryheading6" imageMso="_6" label="Heading 6" />
    <item id="galleryheading7" imageMso="_7" label="Heading 7" />
    <item id="galleryheading8" imageMso="_8" label="Heading 8" />
    <item id="galleryheading9" imageMso="_9" label="Heading 9" />
    <button id="btnChooseAnotherStyle"
            label="Choose Another Style..."
            imageMso="StylesPane"
```

```
                    onAction="Module1.btnChooseAnotherStyle_OnAction" />
</gallery>
```

Figure 13.12 shows the resulting gallery.

Figure 13.12
A gallery added to the
Ribbon.

Here are the `lstInsertHyperlinksFor_OnAction` and `btnChooseAnotherStyle_OnAction`
macros:

```
Sub galInsertHyperlinksFor_OnAction(control As IRibbonControl, id As String,
➥index As Integer)
    Select Case id
        Case "galleryheading1"
            InsertHyperlinks "Heading 1"
        Case "galleryheading2"
            InsertHyperlinks "Heading 2"
        Case "galleryheading3"
            InsertHyperlinks "Heading 3"
        Case "galleryheading4"
            InsertHyperlinks "Heading 4"
        Case "galleryheading5"
            InsertHyperlinks "Heading 5"
        Case "galleryheading6"
            InsertHyperlinks "Heading 6"
        Case "galleryheading7"
            InsertHyperlinks "Heading 7"
        Case "galleryheading8"
            InsertHyperlinks "Heading 8"
        Case "galleryheading9"
            InsertHyperlinks "Heading 9"
    End Select
End Sub

Sub btnChooseAnotherStyle_OnAction(ByVal control As IRibbonControl)
    Dim strStyle As String
    strStyle = InputBox("Type the style you want to use:")
    If strStyle <> "" Then InsertHyperlinks (strStyle)
End Sub
```

As with the `<dropDown>` element, the `Sub` statement for a `<gallery>` element includes a
`String` variable named `id` and an `Integer` variable named `index`. The `id` variable returns
the value of the `id` attribute of the `<item>` object that was clicked in the gallery; the `index`
variable returns the index of the clicked `<item>` object within the gallery, where the first
item in the gallery has index 0, the second item has index 1, and so on.

Creating a Combo Box

If you want to provide the user with the choice of either selecting an item from a list or typing a value, you need to create a combo box control. To set this up in RibbonX, you begin with the `<comboBox>` element:

```
<comboBox id="value"
          label="value"
          imageMso="value"
          size="normal¦large"
          InsertAfterMso="value"
          InsertBeforeMso="value"
          enabled="true¦false"
          visible="true¦false"
          screentip="value"
          supertip="value"
          keytip="value"
          showItemImage="true¦false"
          showImage="true¦false"
          showLabel="true¦false">
          onChange="value"
          sizeString="value"
          maxLength="value">
```

The first thing to notice here is that instead of the `onAction` attribute, the `<comboBox>` element uses the `onChange` attribute. This specifies a macro to run whenever the value of the combo box changes (when either a new value is entered in the edit box or a new value is selected in the list).

The other new attributes here are `sizeString`, a string of characters that determines the width of the edit box (for example, mmmmmmmmmm), and `maxLength`, which specifies the maximum number of characters that the user can enter into the edit box.

Here's an example:

```
<comboBox id="cbWindows"
          label="Windows"
          onChange="Module1.cbWindows_OnAction"
          sizeString="mmmmmmmmmm"
          maxLength="20">
```

The `<comboBox>` element creates an empty drop-down list. As with the drop-down control, you populate the list with multiple `<item>` elements.

See "Working with Ribbon Commands at Runtime," later in this chapter, for an example of a combo box control.

> **NOTE** If you want to use just a text box in your custom Ribbon, RibbonX offers the `<editBox>` element. This control uses most of the same attributes as `<comboBox>`, including `onChange`, `sizeString`, `maxLength`, and `getText` (discussed later in this chapter).

Creating a Dialog Launcher

You've probably seen the small button that appears in the lower-right corner of some Ribbon groups. In Word's Home tab, for example, the button appears in the Clipboard, Font, Paragraph, and Styles groups. In each case, clicking the button opens a dialog box. In the Font group, for example, clicking the button opens the Font dialog box.

This button is called a *dialog box launcher*, and you can add them to your custom Ribbon groups. Your custom dialog box launchers can open any of the application's built-in dialog boxes or a custom dialog box that you've built in the Visual Basic Editor.

→ To learn how to open built-in dialog boxes, **see** "Accessing an Application's Built-In Dialog Boxes," **p. 83**.

→ To learn how to open custom dialog boxes, **see** "Displaying the Form," **p. 258**.

You begin with an empty `<dialogBoxLauncher>` element:

```
<dialogBoxLauncher>
</dialogBoxLauncher>
```

Between these elements, you add a single `<button>` element:

```
<dialogBoxLauncher>
    <button id="dlLaunchInsertHyperlinkDialog"
            onAction="Module1.dlLaunchInsertHyperlinkDialog_OnAction" />
</dialogBoxLauncher>
```

In Figure 13.13, I've created a new custom group for the Insert Hyperlinks For gallery (see the previous section), and the dialog box launcher appears in the lower-right corner of the group.

Dialog box launcher

Figure 13.13
A dialog box launcher added to a custom group.

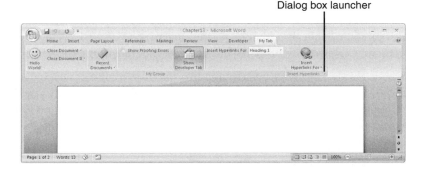

Here's the code for the `LaunchInsertHyperlinkDialog` macro:

```
Sub dlLaunchInsertHyperlinkDialog_OnAction(ByVal control As IRibbonControl)
    Dialogs(wdDialogInsertHyperlink).Show
End Sub
```

Working with Ribbon Commands at Runtime

The controls you've seen so far are all ideally suited to running macros: You click a button or select a menu item, and the associated callback macro executes. That may be all you're really looking for as far as customizing the Ribbon goes. If so, you can cheerfully skip the rest of this chapter. However, if you also want to set up the Ribbon to produce certain "states" that your macros can use, then you need to delve further into the RibbonX control toolkit.

What do I mean by "state"? I mean a set of conditions that your macros can examine and to which they react accordingly. In practice, this means handling the following three tasks in your code:

- **Initializing controls**—This means using code to set up your controls when your VBA application first loads. This might mean setting the state of a check box or toggle button, enabling or disabling a button, or populating a gallery element.
- **Resetting controls**—This means re-initializing your controls.
- **Getting control values**—This means using code to return the current state of some other control. With a check box control, for example, your macro can do one thing if the check box is activated, and it can do something else if it's deactivated.
- **Changing control values**—This means using code to modify the current state of a control. For example, your code might change the state of a toggle button or change the selected item in a drop-down list.

The next three sections take you through each task in more detail.

Initializing Controls

Your custom RibbonX code might need to set your controls to a particular value or state when your VBA application first loads. For example, earlier in this chapter you saw toggle button code that turned the Developer tab on and off. However, regardless of the current state of the Developer tab, VBA always shows a toggle in its unpressed state at startup. In this case, the application should get the current state of the Developer tab via the Options.ShowDevTools property, and then set the state of the toggle button to match.

You do this by specifying an attribute that points to a callback macro, and that macro returns a value that determines the initial state of the control. The attribute that determines whether a <toggleButton> element is initially pressed or unpressed is getPressed. Here's the <toggleButton> element from earlier in this chapter with the getPressed attribute added:

```
<toggleButton id="tbToggleDeveloperTab"
              imageMso="VisualBasic"
              label="Show Developer Tab"
              size="large"
              getPressed="Module1.tbToggleDeveloperTab_GetPressed"
              onAction="Module1.tbToggleDeveloperTab_OnAction" />
```

When the document first loads, the program runs the macro specified by getPressed, which in this case is tbToggleDeveloperTab_GetPressed:

```
Sub tbToggleDeveloperTab_GetPressed(ByVal control As IRibbonControl, ByRef
➥returnVal)
    returnVal = Options.ShowDevTools
End Sub
```

The `returnVal` variable (which can have any name you like) returns to the toggle button control the value given by `Options.ShowDevTools`, and this determines whether the toggle button appears pressed.

You can also initialize other attributes such as `enabled`, `visible`, `size`, `label`, and more. In each case, you do this by specifying callback attributes that point to callback macros, and those macro return values that determine the initial state of the control. Here are some common callback attributes:

getEnabled	Initializes the control's `enabled` attribute.
getImageMso	Initializes the control's `imageMso` attribute.
getKeyTip	Initializes the control's `keyTip` attribute.
getLabel	Initializes the control's `label` attribute.
getPressed	Initializes the state of a check box (checked or unchecked) or toggle button (pressed or unpressed).
getScreentip	Initializes the control's `screentip` attribute.
getSelectedItemID	Initializes a drop-down list by specifying the `id` of the item that should be selected at first. Use either this attribute or `getSelectedItemIndex`, but not both.
getSelectedItemIndex	Initializes a drop-down list by specifying the `index` of the item that should be selected at first. Use either this attribute or `getSelectedItemID`, but not both.
getShowLabel	Initializes the control's `showLabel` attribute.
getSize	Initializes the control's `size` attribute.
getSupertip	Initializes the control's `supertip` attribute.
getVisible	Initializes the control's `visible` attribute.

With a drop-down list, Office doesn't show a selected item by default at startup, which can be disconcerting. The `getSelectedItemID` and `getSelectedItemIndex` attributes are very handy for making sure that a drop-down list displays an item at startup. In most cases, you'll want the first item in the list selected, and you can accomplish this most easily by using `getSelectedItemIndex`:

```
getSelectedItemIndex="lstInsertHyperlinksFor_GetSelectedItemIndex"
```

Here's the callback macro:

```
Sub lstInsertHyperlinksFor_GetSelectedItemIndex(ByVal control As
➥IRibbonControl, ByRef returnVal)
    returnVal = 0
End Sub
```

This works fine for drop-down lists where you've defined static <menu> items in your custom XML code. However, it's often useful to populate a drop-down list on the fly when you first load the document. You can do this by including three attributes in the `<dropDown>` element:

`getItemCount`	Returns the number of items you want to add to the list.
`getItemID`	Returns the `id` value of each item you want to add to the list.
`getItemLabel`	Returns the `label` value of each item you want to add to the list.

In each case, you specify a callback macro that returns the list data.

You can also use the `attributes` to populate the list portion of a `<comboBox>` element at startup. To place an initial value in the edit box, you use the `getText` attribute to specify a callback macro that returns a string value that appears in the edit box.

To demonstrate how these callbacks work, let's run through an example that populates a combo box control with a list of the application's open windows.

Here's the XML:

```
<comboBox id="cbWindows"
        label="Windows"
        sizeString="mmmmmmmmmmmm"
        getItemCount="Module1.cbWindows_GetItemCount"
        getItemID="Module1.cbWindows_GetItemID"
        getItemLabel="Module1.cbWindows_GetItemLabel"
        getText="Module1.cbWindows_GetText" />
```

Here's the `getItemCount` attribute's callback macro:

```
Sub cbWindows_GetItemCount(ByVal control As IRibbonControl, ByRef returnVal)
    returnVal = Windows.Count
End Sub
```

This procedure just returns the value of the `Windows` collection's `Count` property. When RibbonX knows the count, it then proceeds to call the `getItemID` and `getItemLabel` callback macros that number of times. For example, if three documents are open, RibbonX calls the `getItemID` macro three times and then it calls the `getItemLabel` macro three times. Each time, the macros return the ID and label, respectively, of the next item in the list.

To see how this is done, here's the code for the `getItemID` attribute's callback macro:

```
Sub cbWindows_GetItemID(ByVal control As IRibbonControl, index As Integer,
➥ByRef returnVal)
    returnVal = "cbWindowsItem" & index
End Sub
```

Notice that the `Sub` statement includes an extra argument named `index`. The list items are stored internally as an array, so `index` is the subscript of the next item in the array. The first time RibbonX calls this procedure, the value of `index` is 0, the second time `index` is 1, and so on. So, in the callback macro, you can create unique `id` values by appending the current index value to some string. In this case, the item IDs are `cbWindowsItem0`, `cbWindowsItem1`, and so on.

Finally, here's the code for the `getItemLabel` attribute's callback macro:

```
Sub cbWindows_GetItemLabel(ByVal control As IRibbonControl,
➥index As Integer, ByRef returnVal)
    returnVal = Windows(index + 1)
End Sub
```

Again, the `Sub` statement includes the `index` value. In this case, however, use that value to return the corresponding member of the `Windows` collection—`Windows(1)`, `Windows(2)`, and so on. Each of these returns the name of the window, so those are the names that appear in the drop-down list.

> **NOTE** You can use the same procedure to populate a gallery control at startup. The `<gallery>` element also supports the `getItemCount`, `getItemID`, and `getItemLabel` attributes.

With a `<comboBox>` element, you can also specify the initial edit box value with the `getText` attribute. Here's an example callback macro:

```
Sub cbWindows_GetItemCount(ByVal control As IRibbonControl, ByRef returnVal)
    returnVal = "Select a window..."
End Sub
```

In this example, you don't actually want the user to type a value, so the edit box is initially populated with the `Select a window...` instruction, as shown in Figure 13.14.

Figure 13.14
A combo box with its list and edit box initialized at startup.

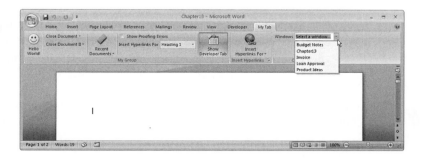

Resetting Controls

The attribute callback macros run when RibbonX initializes your custom interface. What happens, however, if a change of state in your program also requires a change of state in a custom Ribbon control? For example, in the previous section, you saw an example where I populated a combo box control with a list of the open windows. What happens if you open another document or close an existing document? RibbonX offers no way of recognizing events of any kind, so it has no way of knowing that the collection of open windows has changed. What you need is to implement some mechanism that enables you to repopulate the list.

To do this, you have to let VBA know that your Ribbon interface exists. This requires three things. First, you need to add a module-level variable declared with the `IRibbonUI` type:

```
Private myRibbon As IRibbonUI
```

Second, you include the following procedure to initialize the `myRibbon` object:

```
Sub Ribbon_OnLoad(ByVal ribbon As Office.IRibbonUI)
    Set myRibbon = ribbon)
End Sub
```

Finally, you add the `onLoad` attribute to the `<customUI>` element and set it equal to the name of your initialization procedure:

```
<customUI xmlns="http://schemas.microsoft.com/office/2006/01/customui"
➥onLoad="Ribbon customization_OnLoad">
```

The significance of these three steps is that your code can now work with an `IRibbonUI` object, which has no properties but does come with two important methods:

```
ribbon.Invalidate()
ribbon.InvalidateControl(ControlID)
```

ribbon	An `IRibbonUI` object.
ControlID	A string value that specifies the ID of a Ribbon control in your custom XML.

You use these methods to reinitialize some or all of your custom interface. If you run `InvalidateControl`, RibbonX reinitializes the specified control; if you run `Invalidate`, instead, RibbonX reinitializes every one of your custom controls.

> **CAUTION**
>
> If you have many controls, or if you have controls with lengthy initialization callbacks, running the `Invalidate` method could take a while. Therefore, it's almost always best to use `InvalidateControl`, instead, so that you reinitialize only a specific control.

To see how this works, let's add a button to the same group as the combo box from the previous section:

```
<button id="btnRefreshList"
        label="Refresh List"
        imageMso="Refresh"
        onAction="Module1.btnRefreshList_OnAction" />
```

Figure 13.15 shows the button added to the Close Windows group.

Figure 13.15
The Refresh button updates the Windows list.

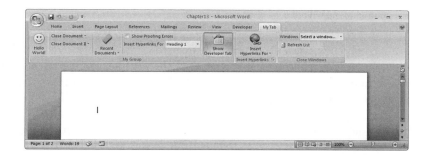

Here's the `btnRefreshList_OnAction` macro:

```
Sub btnRefreshList_OnAction(ByVal control As IRibbonControl)
    myRibbon.InvalidateControl "combobox1"
End Sub
```

This procedure invalidates the `btnRefreshList` control. This tells RibbonX to run through all of that control's callback macros, which in this case serves to repopulate the list with the current set of open windows, as well as reset the edit box text.

Getting and Changing Control Values

To round out your RibbonX interface, you'll want at least some of the controls to interact with each other. For example, when you activate a particular check box, you might want this to also disable a certain button. Similarly, if the user selects or enters a value in a combo box, you might want to use that value in a procedure.

The bad news is that when it comes to determining the current state or value of a control, you're on your own. That is, RibbonX does *not* offer any properties or methods by which you can work with custom Ribbon controls directly. The good news is that it's not difficult to provide your code with limited access to the current state or value of a control.

The trick to all this is to establish module-level variables that hold the state or value of your controls. For a check box or toggle button, use a `Boolean` variable that you set to `True` when the control is checked or pressed, and that you set to `False` when the control is unchecked or unpressed. You initialize this variable in the `getPressed` callback macro, and you update the variable in the `onAction` callback macro. Here's some code that declares a module-level `Boolean` variable named `booDeveloperTools`, and then shows a toggle button's `getPressed` and `onAction` callback macros, both of which change the value of `booDeveloperTools`:

```
Private booDeveloperTools As Boolean
Sub tbToggleDeveloperTools_GetPressed(ByVal control As IRibbonControl,
➥ByRef returnVal)
    returnVal = Options.ShowDevTools
    booDeveloperTools = returnVal
End Sub

Sub tbToggleDeveloperTools_OnAction(ByVal control As IRibbonControl,
➥pressed As Boolean)
    Options.ShowDevTools = pressed
```

13

```
    booDeveloperTools = pressed
End Sub
```

For a combo box, use a `String` variable that stores the value entered or selected by the user. Use the `getText` callback macro to initialize the variable, and use the `onChange` callback macro to update the variable. In the combo box example, you can declare a module-level named `strSelectedWindow` and update the callback macros as follows:

```
Private strSelectedWindow As String
Sub cbWindows_GetText(ByVal control As IRibbonControl, ByRef returnVal)
    returnVal = "Select a window..."
    strSelectedWindow = ""
End Sub

Sub cbWindows_OnChange(ByVal control As IRibbonControl, text As String)
    strSelectedWindow = text
End Sub
```

Notice that in this case `strSelectedWindow` is initially set to the null string because at first no window is selected.

Because these new variables are module-level, you can them use them in any other procedure in the module. For example, suppose you want to take the currently selected window in the combo box and close it. One way to accomplish this would be to add a new button to the Ribbon, and you want to set up that button so that it closes the selected window. Here's the XML for the new button:

```
<button id="btnCloseWindow"
        label="Close Window"
        imageMso="FileClose"
        onAction="Module1.btnCloseWindow_OnAction" />
```

Figure 13.16 shows the button added to the Close Windows group.

Figure 13.16
The Close Window button closes the currently selected window.

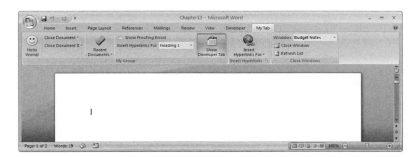

Here's the `btnCloseWindow_OnAction` macro:

```
Sub btnCloseWindow_OnAction(ByVal control As IRibbonControl)
    If strSelectedWindow <> "" Then
        Windows(strSelectedWindow).Close
        myRibbon.InvalidateControl "combobox1"
    End If
End Sub
```

The code makes sure that `strSelectedWindow` isn't the null string, and then runs the `Close` method on the window name stored in `strSelectedWindow`. Because closing an open window puts the window list out of date, the code also runs `InvalidateControl` on the combo box to reset it.

The `btnCloseWindow_OnAction` code checks `strSelectedWindow` to make sure it's not null. However, a properly constructed interface would disable the Close Window button while not window is selected. To handle this, you must first add a `getEnabled` attribute to the Close Window button:

```
<button id="btnCloseWindow"
        label="Close Window"
        imageMso="FileClose"
        getEnabled="Module1.btnCloseWindow_GetEnabled"
        onAction="Module1.btnCloseWindow_OnAction" />
```

Here's the callback macro:

```
Sub btnCloseWindow_GetEnabled(ByVal control As IRibbonControl, ByRef returnVal)
    If strSelectedWindow = "" Then
        returnVal = False
    Else
        returnVal = True
    End If
End Sub
```

If `strSelectedWindow` is the null string, the macro returns `False` and the button is disabled; otherwise it returns `True` and the button is enabled.

The `enabled` state of the button also needs to be checked when the combo box changes and when we refresh the list. Here are the corresponding macros updated to run the `InvalidateControl` method on the `btnCloseWindow` element:

```
Sub cbWindows_OnChange(ByVal control As IRibbonControl, text As String)
    strSelectedWindow = text
    myRibbon.InvalidateControl "btnCloseWindow"
End Sub

Sub btnRefreshList_OnAction(ByVal control As IRibbonControl)
    myRibbon.InvalidateControl "cbWindows"
    myRibbon.InvalidateControl "btnCloseWindow"
End Sub
```

From Here

- If you just want a quick way to run some of your own macros, the Office 2007 programs enable you to add macros to the Quick Access toolbar; **see** "Creating a Quick Access Toolbar Button for a Recorded Macro," **p. 11**.

- To learn how to open built-in dialog boxes, **see** "Accessing an Application's Built-In Dialog Boxes," **p. 83**.

- For the details on using VBA with Word, see Chapter 7, "Programming Word," **p. 115**.

13

- To get the details on the `InsertHyperlinks` function, **see** "Programming the `Paragraph` Object," **p. 136**.
- To learn how to open custom dialog boxes, **see** "Displaying the Form," **p. 258**.

VBA Tips and Techniques

14

Although I've labeled this a "Tips and Techniques" chapter, it's more like a hodgepodge of miscellaneous VBA ideas and methods that simply didn't fit anywhere else in the book. Although you can write powerful and useful VBA applications without using any of the techniques I've outlined in this chapter (with the possible exception of the section "Tips for Faster Procedures"), they're indispensable when you *do* need them. For example, if you want to run your own VBA projects without having to enable the macros every time, you need to digitally sign each project. Similarly, any time you need to store user choices or program parameters, the Registry is the ideal place to do so. And although accessing the file system via VBA sounds hopelessly arcane, you'll be pleasantly surprised at just how often this crucial skill comes in handy. This chapter covers all these techniques and much more.

Working with Modules

You've seen so far that modules are where most of the VBA action takes place. True, you've also seen that much VBA work happens within user form windows and the Properties window, but modules are really the heart of VBA. Given that, it will help to have a few module manipulation techniques under your belt. To that end, the next four sections show you how to rename, export, import, and remove modules.

Renaming a Module

When you insert a new module, VBA gives it an uninspiring name such as Module1. That's fine if you'll just be using the one module in your project, but if you'll be working with multiple modules, you should consider giving meaningful names to each module to help differentiate them.

To rename a module, follow these steps:

1. Select the module in the Project Explorer.
2. In the Properties window, use the (Name) property to rename the module. Make sure the name you use begins with a letter, contains no spaces or punctuation marks (underscores are acceptable, however), and is no longer than 31 characters.

Exporting a Module

The procedures and functions in a module are usually specific to the application in which the project was created. For example, procedures in a Word-based module usually reference Word-specific objects such as bookmarks and paragraphs. However, you might have generic procedures and functions that can be used in different contexts. How, then, can you share code between applications?

One way to do it would be to use the Clipboard to copy data from one module and paste it in a module in a different application. Another way is to *export* the module to a BAS (.bas) file. In the next section, I'll show you how to import BAS files into your VBA projects.

The BAS (Basic) file format is the one used by Visual Basic modules (which means you could use your VBA code in a Visual Basic project), but it's really just a simple text file. Here are the steps to follow to export a module:

1. In the Project Explorer, click the module you want to export.
2. Choose File, Export File, or press Ctrl+E. The Visual Basic Editor displays the Export File dialog box.
3. Select a location and type a filename for the BAS file.
4. Click Save. The Visual Basic Editor creates the new BAS file.

Importing a Module

If you exported a module to a BAS file, you can import that file as a module in another application's VBA project. Also, if you've used Visual Basic before, you can leverage your existing code by importing Visual Basic modules into your project. Here are the steps to follow:

1. If you have multiple projects open, use the Project Explorer to click any object in the project you want to use to store the imported file.
2. Choose File, Import File, or press Ctrl+M to display the Import File dialog box.
3. Click the BAS file that you want to import.
4. Click Open. The Visual Basic Editor adds a new module for the BAS file.

14

Removing a Module

If you no longer need a module, you should remove it from your project to reduce the clutter in the Project Explorer. Use the following technique:

1. Click the module in the Project Explorer.
2. Choose File, Remove *Module*, where *Module* is the name of the module.
3. The Visual Basic Editor asks if you want to export the module before removing it:
   - If you want to export the module first, click Yes and use the Export File dialog box to export the module to a BAS file.
   - Otherwise, click No to remove the module.

Configuring Macro Security Settings

With macro viruses becoming an increasing threat, working with VBA projects can be difficult. This is true even if you just want to run your own VBA projects, because Office 2007 disables macros in documents that aren't in a trusted location. You have three ways to work around this problem:

- Store your macro-enabled documents in a trusted location. Office allows those documents' macros to run, while disabling macros in every other document.
- Enable all macros in all documents. This ensures that you can run your own macros, but it also leaves you open to viruses in third-party documents.
- Create a personal security certificate and use it to digitally sign your VBA projects.

For the last of these options, see the next section to learn how to create a personal security certificate. For the first two options, the next two sections show you how to configure the Office 2007 macro security settings.

Setting Up a Trusted Location

The easiest way to ensure that you can run your own VBA projects without also leaving yourself open to malware in third-party documents is to set up one or more trusted locations and use them to store your macro-enabled documents. Office comes with several predefined trusted locations for documents such as templates and add-ins, but none of them are easy to find. A better idea is to set up a location such as your user profile's Documents (or My Documents in Windows XP) folder or one of its subfolders. Here are the steps to follow to set up a folder as a trusted location:

1. In an Office application, choose Office *Application* Options, where *Application* is the name of the program you're working with.
2. Click Trust Center.

14

3. Click Trust Center Settings to open the Trust Center dialog box.

4. Click Trusted Locations.

5. Click Add New Location to open the Microsoft Office Trusted Location dialog box.

6. Use the Path text box to type the folder path, or click Browse to use the Browse dialog box to select the folder.

7. If you want the folder's subfolders to also be trusted locations, click to activate the Subfolders of This Location Are Also Trusted check box.

8. Click OK.

9. Repeat steps 5 through 8 to add more trusted locations.

10. Click OK to return to the Options dialog box.

11. Click OK.

12. Repeat steps 1 through 11 for any other Office applications that you use to create VBA projects.

> ┌─ **CAUTION** ───
> │ After you set up a folder as a trusted location, keep it secure by using it to store only macro-enabled
> │ documents that you know are safe. In most cases, you should use the trusted location to store only
> │ your own VBA projects and macro-enabled documents that you've scanned with anti-virus software.
> └───

With your trusted locations in place, you should now ensure that each Office application is set up to disable all macros except those in documents that reside in trusted locations. The next section tells you how to do this.

Setting the Macro Security Level

By default, the Office 2007 applications disable document macros unless they're in a document from a trusted location. When you open a macro-enabled document outside of a trusted location, you see the Security Warning message bar, which tells you that `Macros have been disabled`. Clicking the Options button displays the Microsoft Office Security Options dialog box, shown in Figure 14.1. If you want to use the document's macros, you click the Enable This Content option and then click OK.

Message bar

Figure 14.1
By default, the Office
2007 applications disable
macros from untrusted
locations.

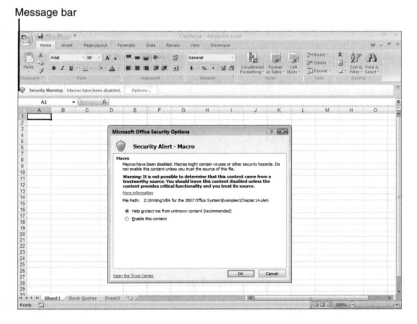

This default behavior is reasonable and should ensure that you minimize the chances of unleashing a VBA virus on your system. However, you might want to change the default macro security level in three situations:

- You never enable macros from untrusted locations, so you can configure Office to not display the Security Warning pane.

- You digitally sign your own macros (as described in the next section), so you can configure Office to only enable macros from digitally signed VBA projects.

- The only macro-enabled documents you use are those you create yourself or those that you have scanned with an anti-virus program, so you can configure Office to allow all macros.

If any of these situations applies to you, follow these steps to change the macro security level:

1. In an Office application, choose Office *Application* Options, where *Application* is the name of the program you're working with.

2. Click Trust Center.

3. Click Trust Center Settings to open the Trust Center dialog box.

4. Click Macro Settings.

14

5. Click to activate one of the following options:

- **Disable All Macros Without Notification**—Click this option to prevent the Office application from showing the Security Warning pane when you open a macro-enabled document.

- **Disable All Macros With Notification**—This is the default setting.

- **Disable All Macros Except Digitally Signed Macros**—Click this option to enable only VBA projects that have a valid digital signature.

- **Enable All Macros**—Click this option to enable code in any document that contains macros.

6. Click OK to return to the Options dialog box.

7. Click OK.

8. Repeat steps 1 through 7 for any other Office applications that you use to create VBA projects.

Digitally Signing a VBA Project

The macro virus situation is even worse if you want to distribute your VBA applications, because many people are loath to accept files that have macros. Even if your reputation is such that people won't worry about files that come from you, how can they be sure that the code they have really was created by you? The Visual Basic Editor enables you to use a certificate to digitally sign your projects. A certificate is your iron-clad guarantee that you created a project. You get a certificate from a certified signing authority, such as VeriSign (www.verisign.com) or Thawte (www.thawte.com).

> **TIP**
> To see more code signing options, you can also run a web search for "code signing vba." You can also check out the list of companies that are members of Microsoft's Root Certificate Program, found at the following URL:
>
> http://msdn.microsoft.com/library/en-us/dnsecure/html/rootcertprog.asp

What if you just want to sign your own projects? In that case, you don't need a third-party certificate. Instead, Office 2007 comes with a tool that enables you "self-certify"—create a personal digital certificate that you can apply to your own projects. Follow these steps:

1. Choose Start, All Programs, Microsoft Office, Microsoft Office Tools, Digital Certificate for VBA Projects. The Create Digital Certificate dialog box appears.

2. Use the Your Certificate's Name text box to type your name (or whatever name you want to use), and then click OK.

3. When you see the SelfCert success dialog box, click OK.

When you have your certificate installed, follow these steps to digitally sign a project:

1. In the Visual Basic Editor, use the Project pane to click any object in the project you want to sign.
2. Choose Tools, Digital Signature. The Digital Signature dialog box appears.
3. Click Choose to display the Select Certificate dialog box, shown in Figure 14.2.

Figure 14.2
Use the Select Certificate dialog box to choose your certificate.

4. Click the certificate and then click OK. You're returned to the Digital Signature dialog box.
5. Click OK.

Saving Application Settings in the Registry

In a VBA procedure, you use variables to store values you need to use while you're running the procedure. When the procedure finishes, the values of those variables are wiped from memory. What do you do if you have values that you want to preserve from one VBA session to another? You could store the values somewhere in the document, but this isn't a great idea because those values could be easily changed or even deleted.

A better idea is to use the Registry. Windows uses the Registry to store thousands of settings related to software, hardware, and user options. Not only that, but most applications make use of the Registry as a place to store setup options, customization values selected by the user, and much more. VBA doesn't enable you to access the Registry as a whole. Instead, it provides you with a special key in which you can add, read, change, and delete your own keys, settings, and values. VBA also provides a number of statements that enable you to perform these Registry tasks, and the next few sections show you how to use these statements.

14

Storing Settings in the Registry

To store a setting in the Registry, use the SaveSetting statement:

```
SaveSetting appname, section, key, setting
```

appname	The name you want to use to identify your application in the Registry.
section	The section in which to store the value. This will be a subkey of the appname key.
key	The name of the key setting that you want to store.
setting	The value to which key is being set.

When you run this statement, VBA creates a new key in the Registry, as follows:

```
\HKEY_CURRENT_USER\Software\VB and VBA Program Settings\appname\section\
```

The key setting is added to this subkey, and its value is set to setting. For example, consider the following statement:

```
SaveSetting "VBA for the 2007 Office System", "Chapter 14", "Test", "OK"
```

Figure 14.3 shows how the new setting appears in the Registry Editor.

Figure 14.3
Use the
SaveSetting
statement to store
application settings
in the Registry.

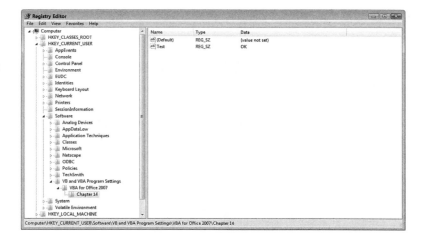

Reading Settings from the Registry

After you've stored a value in the Registry, you can read that value by using the GetSetting statement:

```
GetSetting(appname, section, key[, default])
```

appname	The name you're using to identify your application in the Registry.
section	The section in which the value is stored.
key	The name of the key setting that you want to retrieve.
default	(Optional) The value to be returned if key doesn't exist or isn't set.

To retrieve the value stored using the `SaveSetting` example shown earlier, you would use a statement similar to the following:

```
str = GetSetting("VBA for Office 2007", "Chapter 14", "Test")
```

Deleting Settings from the Registry

If you no longer need to track a particular key setting, use the `DeleteSetting` statement to remove the setting from the Registry:

```
DeleteSetting appname, section[, key]
```

appname	The name you're using to identify your application in the Registry.
section	The section in which the key value is stored.
key	(Optional) The name of the key setting that you want to delete. If you omit *key*, VBA deletes the entire `appname\section` subkey.

To delete the `Test` key setting used in the earlier examples, you would use the following statement:

```
DeleteSetting "VBA for Office 2007", "Chapter 14", "Test"
```

Tracking File Usage

Let's work through a concrete example of these Registry statements. Suppose you'd like to track the number of times a particular document has been opened, as well as the last date and time the file was opened. Listing 14.1 shows an event handler for the `Open` event in the `Chaptr14.xlsm` workbook. This procedure creates the following subkey:

> **NOTE** The VBA code for this chapter's examples is available on my website at www.mcfedries.com/Office2007VBA/.

```
\HKEY_CURRENT_USER\Software\VB and VBA Program Settings\VBA for Office 2007\
➥Chapter 14\
```

Within this subkey, three settings are stored:

- `NumberOfAccesses`—Holds the number of times that the file has been opened.
- `LastAccessDate`—Holds the date that the file was last opened.
- `LastAccessTime`—Holds the time that the file was last opened.

This procedure performs the following chores:

- It first uses `GetSetting` to return the `NumberOfAccess` value, with a default of 0.
- If the returned value is 0, this means that the setting doesn't exist, so this must be the first time the user has opened the file. In this case, a welcome message is displayed, and the `numAccesses` variable is set to 1.

14

- Otherwise, the `LastAccessDate` and `LastAccessTime` settings are retrieved, and a different welcome message—showing the Registry settings—is displayed.

- Three `SaveSettings` statements update the Registry values.

Note, too, that you can run the `RemoveChapter14Settings` procedure to clear the Registry entries.

Listing 14.1   The Event Handler for the Chaptr14.xlsm Workbook's Open **Event**

```
Private Sub Workbook_Open()
    Dim numAccesses As Integer
    Dim lastAccessDate As Date
    Dim lastAccessTime As Date
    Dim msg As String
    '
    ' Get the number of accesses from the Registry
    '
    numAccesses = GetSetting("VBA for Office 2007", "Chapter 14", _
                "NumberOfAccesses", 0)
    If numAccesses = 0 Then
        '
        ' This is the first time this file has been opened
        '
        MsgBox "Welcome to the Chapter 14 code listings!" _
                & vbCrLf & vbCrLf & _
                "This is the first time you have opened this file." _
                & vbCrLf & _
                "The Registry settings will now be created."
        numAccesses = 1
    Else
        '
        ' File has been opened more than once. Get the last date and time.
        '
        lastAccessDate = CDate(GetSetting("VBA for Office 2007", "Chapter 14",
        ➥"LastAccessDate"))
        lastAccessTime = CDate(GetSetting("VBA for Office 2007", "Chapter 14",
        ➥"LastAccessTime"))
        msg = "Welcome to the Chapter 14 code listings!" & _
                vbCrLf & vbCrLf & _
                "You have opened this file " & numAccesses & " times." & _
                vbCrLf & _
                "You last opened this file on " & lastAccessDate & " at " &
                ➥lastAccessTime
        MsgBox msg, vbOKOnly + vbInformation, "VBA for Office 2007"
    End If
    '
    ' Update the settings
    '
    SaveSetting "VBA for Office 2007", "Chapter 14", "NumberOfAccesses", _
                numAccesses + 1
    SaveSetting "VBA for Office 2007", "Chapter 14", "LastAccessDate", Date
    SaveSetting "VBA for Office 2007", "Chapter 14", "LastAccessTime", Time
```

```
End Sub
Sub RemoveChapter14Setting()
    DeleteSetting "VBA for Office 2007", "Chapter 14"
End Sub
```

Reading All the Section Settings

Rather than just reading one setting at a time, VBA lets you retrieve every setting in a given section by using the GetAllSettings statement:

GetAllSettings(*appname, section*)

       appname   The name you're using to identify your application in the Registry.

       section   The section in which the values are stored.

In this case, VBA returns a two-dimensional array of values in which the first index is the name of the key setting and the second index is the current value of the setting. Listing 14.2 shows a procedure that returns all the Chapter 14 subkey settings created in the preceding section.

Listing 14.2   Using GetAllSettings **to Return Every Setting in the** Chapter 14 **Subkey and Then Print the Setting Names and Values**

```
Sub GetAllChapter14Settings()
    Dim ch14Settings As Variant
    Dim i As Integer
    '
    ' Get the settings
    '
    ch14Settings = GetAllSettings("VBA for Office 2007", "Chapter 14")
    '
    ' Run through the key settings, displaying the name and value
    '
    For i = 0 To UBound(ch14Settings, 1)
        Debug.Print ch14Settings(i, 0); ": "; ch14Settings(i, 1)
    Next 'i
End Sub
```

Accessing the File System Through VBA

If your applications need to work with the file system, VBA boasts quite a few features that make it easy. These features include a number of statements that return information about files and folders, as well as a number of functions with which you can manipulate files and folders. There are also powerful functions that give you direct access to files. This section examines all VBA's file-related statements and functions.

14

Returning File and Folder Information

If you need information about the file system—whether it's the name of the current directory, whether or not a particular file exists, or a file's date and time stamp—VBA has a function that can do the job. The next few sections look at five VBA functions that return file system data: CurDir, Dir, FileDateTime, FileLen, and GetAttr.

The CurDir Function

If you need to know the name of the active folder on a specific drive, use either the CurDir or the CurDir$ function:

```
CurDir(drive)
CurDir$(drive)
```

> drive   The disk drive with which you want to work. If you omit *drive*, VBA uses the current drive.

The CurDir function returns the path as a Variant, and the CurDir$ function returns the path as a String. For example, the following statements display the current folder on drive D and the letter of the current drive:

```
MsgBox "Current folder on drive D is " & CurDir$("D")
MsgBox "The current drive is " & Left(CurDir$, 1)
```

To change the current drive and folder, see the descriptions of the ChDrive and ChDir statements later in this chapter.

The Dir Function

To return the name of a file or folder, use the Dir function:

```
Dir(Pathname, Attributes)
```

> Pathname   A String value that gives the file or folder specification. Note that you can use the standard wildcard characters—? for single characters and * for multiple characters.

> Attributes   One or more constants that specify the file attributes:

Constant	Attribute
vbNormal (or 0)	Normal
vbReadOnly (or 1)	Read-Only
vbHidden (or 2)	Hidden
vbSystem (or 4)	System
vbVolume (or 8)	Volume label
vbDirectory (or 16)	Folder

If Dir is unsuccessful—that is, if no such file or folder exists—it returns the null string (""). This is a handy way to check for the existence of a file. Listing 14.3 shows an example.

Listing 14.3   A Procedure That Checks for the Existence of a File Before Opening It

```
Sub OpenToDoList()
    Dim strFile As String
    strFile = Environ("UserProfile") & "\Documents\To-Do List.txt"
    If Dir(strFile) <> "" Then
        Shell "Notepad " & strFile, vbNormalFocus
    End If
End Sub
```

This procedure builds the file path by using the Environ function to return the value of the %UserProfile% environment variable, to which \Documents\To-Do List.txt is added. The Dir function then checks to see whether this file exists and, if so, it uses the Shell function to load the file into Notepad.

If Dir is successful, it returns the first file or folder name that matches the *Pathname* file specification. To return the next file or folder name that matches the specification, you call Dir again, but this time without any arguments. Listing 14.4 shows a procedure that utilizes this technique to store the names of all the files from the user profile's Documents folder in a worksheet. After a bit of preparation, the procedure runs Dir to return the first file. Then a Do While loop runs Dir until there are no more filenames to return. Along the way, the filenames are stored in a worksheet. Then, when all is said and done, the filenames are sorted. At this point, you could use the sorted list to populate a list box or some other control.

Listing 14.4   A Procedure That Reads All the Filenames from the User Profile's Documents **Folder, Stores Them in Sheet1, and Sorts Them by Name**

```
Sub GetFilenames()
    Dim i As Integer
    i = 0
    '
    ' Start at cell A1
    '
    With Worksheets("Sheet1").[A1]
        '
        ' Clear the current values, if any
        '
        .CurrentRegion.Clear
        '
        ' Get the initial file and store it in A1
        '
        .Value = UCase(Dir(Environ("UserProfile") & "\Documents\", vbNormal))
        '
        ' Get the rest of the files and store them in Column A
        '
        Do While .Offset(i, 0) <> ""
            i = i + 1
            .Offset(i, 0) = UCase(Dir)
        Loop
        '
        ' Sort the filenames
        '
```

continues

14

Listing 14.4   Continued

```
        .Sort Key1:=Worksheets("Sheet1").Columns("A")
    End With
End Sub
```

The FileDateTime Function

If you need to know when a file was last modified, use the FileDateTime function:

FileDateTime(*Pathanme*)

> *Pathname*   A string that specifies the file with which you want to work (including, optionally, the drive and folder where the file resides).

If successful, FileDateTime returns a Variant date expression that holds the date and time stamp for the specified file.

The FileLen Function

If you need to know the size of a file (to see whether it will fit on a disk, for example), use the FileLen function:

FileLen(*Pathanme*)

> *Pathname*   A string that specifies the file with which you want to work (including, optionally, the drive and folder where the file resides).

The FileLen function returns a Long value that tells you the number of bytes in the specified file. (On the odd chance that the file is already open, FileLen returns the size of the file when it was last saved.)

To help you try this function, Listing 14.5 presents the GetFolderUsage procedure, which calculates the total disk space used by the files in a folder. This procedure prompts you for a folder name and then uses the Dir function to return the filenames in that folder. For each filename, the FileLen function returns the number of bytes, and a running total is kept in the totalBytes variable.

```
Sub GetFolderUsage()
    Dim folder As String
    Dim filename As String
    Dim totalBytes As Long
    '
    ' Get the folder name
    '
    folder = InputBox("Enter the folder name:", "Bytes Used in Folder")
    '
    ' Did the user click Cancel?
```

14

```
    If folder <> "" Then
        '
        ' Make sure there's a backslash at the end
        '
        If Right(folder, 1) <> "\" Then
            folder = folder & "\"
        End If
        '
        ' Get the first filename
        '
        filename = Dir(folder, vbNormal)
        totalBytes = 0
        '
        ' Loop through the rest of the files
        '
        Do While filename <> ""
            '
            ' Update the total number of bytes
            '
            totalBytes = totalBytes + FileLen(folder & filename)
            '
            ' Get the next filename
            '
            filename = Dir
        Loop
        '
        ' Display the total
        '
        MsgBox "The folder " & folder & " uses " & totalBytes & " bytes" & _
               " or " & totalBytes / 1048576 & " MB."
    End If
End Sub
```

The GetAttr Function

As you may know, each file and folder has a set of attributes that indicate its status on the system (such as read-only or hidden). You can test for these attributes by using the GetAttr function:

GetAttr(*Pathanme*)

    Pathname   A string that specifies the file or folder with which you want to work.

The return value is an integer that represents the sum of one or more of the following constants:

Constant	Value	Attribute
vbReadOnly	1	Read-only (the object can't be modified)
vbHidden	2	Hidden (the object isn't visible in the normal Explorer view)
vbSystem	4	System (the object is a system file)
vbDirectory	16	Directory (the object is a folder)
vbArchive	32	Archive (the object has been modified since it was last backed up)

14

To test for any of these attributes, you use the And operator to compare the result of the GetAttr function with the appropriate constant (this is known in the trade as a *bitwise comparison*). For example, if the following statement returns a nonzero value, the object given by path is read-only:

```
GetAttr(path) And vbReadOnly
```

In Listing 14.6, the GetAttributes procedure prompts you for a filename (using Excel's GetOpenFilename method), uses GetAttr to return the file's attributes, and performs several bitwise comparisons to determine all the file's attributes.

Listing 14.6   A Procedure That Prompts for a Filename and then Returns the Attributes of the Selected File

```
Sub GetAttributes()
    Dim pathname As String
    Dim attr As Integer
    Dim msg As String
    '
    ' Get the filename
    '
    pathname = Application.GetOpenFilename("All Files (*.*), *.*")
    '
    ' Did the user click Cancel?
    '
    If pathname <> "" Then
        '
        ' Get the file's attributes
        '
        attr = GetAttr(pathname)
        msg = "Attributes for " & pathname & ":" & vbCrLf
        '
        ' Determine the file's attributes and display them
        '
        If attr And vbReadOnly Then msg = msg & vbCrLf & "Read-Only"
        If attr And vbHidden Then msg = msg & vbCrLf & "Hidden"
        If attr And vbSystem Then msg = msg & vbCrLf & "System"
        If attr And vbDirectory Then msg = msg & vbCrLf & "Directory"
        If attr And vbArchive Then msg = msg & vbCrLf & "Archive"
        MsgBox msg
    End If
End Sub
```

Manipulating Files and Folders

In addition to just finding out file system information, VBA also lets you manipulate various aspects of the file system, including changing the current drive and folder, creating new folders, and deleting and renaming files and folders. The next few sections take you through each of VBA's file system manipulation statements.

The ChDir **Statement**

Each Office application maintains a *default folder* setting, which is the folder that appears initially when you display a folder-based dialog box, such as Open or Save As. To change an application's default folder, use the ChDir statement:

```
ChDir Path
```

      Path   A string that specifies the new default folder.

If the *Path* parameter doesn't include a drive designator, VBA changes the folder on whatever drive is current. If *Path* does include a drive, VBA changes the default folder on that drive, but it doesn't change the current drive. For example, if the current drive is C and you run ChDir D:\, the default folder is changed on drive D, but drive C remains the current drive. If you want the folder on D to appear in Open or Save As by default, you must also change the default drive, as explained in the next section.

The ChDrive **Statement**

To change the default drive, use the ChDrive statement:

```
ChDrive Drive
```

      Drive   A string that specifies the letter of the new default drive.

For example, the following statement changes the default drive to D:

```
ChDrive "D"
```

The FileCopy **Statement**

If you need to copy a disk file from one location to another, use VBA's FileCopy statement:

```
FileCopy(Source, Destination)
```

      Source   A String value that specifies the name of the file you want to copy (including, optionally, the drive and folder in which the file resides).

      Destination   A String value that specifies the name of the destination file (including, optionally, the drive and folder).

The following statements set the *Source* variable to a filename, set the *Destination* variable to a filename on a network drive, and use FileCopy to copy the file:

```
source = Environ("User Profile") & "\Documents\Letter.doc"
destination = "\\Server\pub\users\paul\Letter.doc"
FileCopy source, destination
```

The Kill **Statement**

When you need to delete files from the system, use the aptly (if perhaps a bit violently) named Kill statement:

14

```
Kill Pathname
```

> Pathname   A String value that specifies the name of the file you want to delete (including, optionally, the drive and folder in which the file resides).

You can use the ? and * wildcard characters in the Pathname argument to delete multiple files. Note that the Kill statement generates an error if the specified file is open or doesn't exist. To avoid the latter error, first use the Dir function to see whether the file exists:

```
If Dir("C:\Garbage.txt") <> "" Then
    Kill "C:\Garbage.txt"
End If
```

The MkDir Statement

If your application requires a new folder in which to store files, you can use the MkDir statement to create the folder:

```
MkDir Path
```

> Path   A string that specifies the new folder. If you don't include the drive letter, VBA creates the folder on the current drive.

The following statement creates a new Backup folder on drive E:

```
MkDir "E:\Backup"
```

The Name Statement

You can rename a file or folder by running the Name statement:

```
Name oldpathname As newpathname
```

> oldpathname   A String value that specifies the pathname of the folder or file you want to rename. (Wildcards are not supported.)
>
> newpathname   A String value that specifies the new name of the folder or file. If you change the path but not the name of the file, VBA moves the file to the new location.

The Name statement generates an error if the specified file is open or doesn't exist.

The RmDir Statement

To let you delete a folder you no longer need, VBA offers the RmDir statement:

```
RmDir Path
```

> Path   A string that specifies the folder you want to delete. If you don't include the drive letter, VBA deletes the folder from the current drive.

Note that RmDir raises an error if the folder you specify still contains files. Your code should check to see whether a folder contains files and, if it does, it should first use Kill to delete the files and then use RmDir to delete the folder. Listing 14.7 shows a procedure that does exactly that. After getting the name of the folder to delete, the procedure uses Dir to loop through the folder's files. (You might want to modify this code to check for subfolders as well.) If the folder contains files, the total is reported to the user, who then has the option of canceling the deletion. If the user elects to proceed, `Kill` is used to delete each file, and then `RmDir` deletes the folder.

Listing 14.7   This Procedure Deletes a Folder, First Deleting Any Files the Folder Contains

```
Sub DeleteFolder()
    Dim folder As String
    Dim filename As String
    Dim totalFiles As Integer
    '
    ' Get the folder name
    '
    folder = InputBox("Enter the name of the folder to delete:")
    '
    ' Did the user click Cancel?
    '
    If folder <> "" Then
        '
        ' Make sure there's a backslash at the end
        '
        If Right(folder, 1) <> "\" Then
            folder = folder & "\"
        End If
        '
        ' Get the first filename
        '
        filename = Dir(folder, vbDirectory)
        '
        ' Bail out if the folder doesn't exist
        '
        If filename = "" Then
            MsgBox "Folder doesn't exist!"
            Exit Sub
        End If
        '
        ' Loop through the rest to get the file total
        '
        totalFiles = 0
        Do While filename <> ""
            '
            ' Get the next filename
            '
            filename = Dir
            '
            ' Ignore the parent (..) and the last Dir
            '
            If filename <> ".." And filename <> "" Then
                '
                ' Update the total number of files
                '
                totalFiles = totalFiles + 1
            End If
```

continues

Listing 14.7   Continued

```
        Loop
        '
        ' Check the total
        '
        If totalFiles > 0 Then
            '
            ' If there are files, let the user know
            '
            If MsgBox("The folder " & folder & _
                    " contains " & totalFiles & _
                    IIf(totalFiles > 1, " files.", "file.") & _
                    vbCrLf & _
                    "Are you sure you want to delete it?", _
                    vbOKCancel + vbQuestion) = vbCancel Then
                Exit Sub
            End If
            '
            ' Get the first filename
            '
            filename = Dir(folder, vbNormal)
            '
            ' Loop through and Kill the rest of the files
            '
            Do While filename <> ""
                Kill folder & filename
                '
                ' Get the next filename
                '
                filename = Dir
            Loop
        End If
        '
        ' Delete the folder
        '
        RmDir folder
    End If
End Sub
```

The SetAttr **Statement**

Earlier you saw how to use the GetAttr function to return the attributes of a file or folder. However, you can also set these attributes by invoking the SetAttr statement:

```
SetAttr Pathanme, Attributes
```

> Pathname   A string that specifies the file or folder with which you want to work.
>
> Attributes   One or more constants that specify the attributes you want to set.

The constants recognized by VBA are the same as those outlined earlier for the GetAttr function (except that you can set the Directory attribute): vbReadOnly, vbHidden, vbSystem, and vbArchive. Note that this statement produces an error if you attempt to set the attributes of an open file.

Tips for Faster Procedures

Short procedures usually are over in the blink of an eye. However, the longer your procedures get, and the more they interact with application objects, the more time they take to complete their tasks. For these more complex routines, you need to start thinking not only about *what* the procedure does, but *how* it does it. The more efficient you can make your code, the faster the procedure will execute. This section gives you a few tips for writing efficient code that runs quickly.

Turn Off Screen Updating

One of the biggest drags on procedure performance is the constant screen updating that occurs. If your procedure uses many statements that format text, enter formulas, or cut and copy data, the procedure will spend most of its time updating the screen to show the results of these operations. This not only slows everything down, but it also looks unprofessional. It's much nicer when the procedure performs all its chores behind the scenes and then presents the user with the finished product at the end of the procedure.

You can do this with the `Application` object's `ScreenUpdating` property. Set `ScreenUpdating` to `False` to turn off intermediate screen updates that you don't want the user to see, and set it back to `True` to resume updating.

Hide Your Documents

If your procedure does a lot of switching between documents, you can speed things up by hiding the documents while you work with them. To do this, set the document's `Visible` property to `False`. You can work with hidden documents normally, and when your procedure is done, you can set `Visible` to `True` to display the results to the user.

 As soon as you've hidden an active document, VBA deactivates it. Therefore, if your procedures reference the active document, you need to activate the document (using the `Activate` method) right after hiding it.

Don't Select Data Unless You Have To

Two of VBA's slowest methods are `Activate` and `Select`, so you should use them sparingly. In the majority of cases, you can indirectly work with ranges, worksheets, text, and other data. In Excel, for example, you can work with a `Range` object by referencing it as an argument in the `Range` method (or in any other VBA statement that returns a `Range` object) and the `Worksheets` collection.

In Excel, Don't Recalculate Until You Have To

As you know, manual calculation mode prevents Excel from recalculating a worksheet until you say so. This saves you time when you're using sheets with complicated models—models in which you don't necessarily want to see a recalculation every time you change a variable.

14

You can get the same benefits in your procedures by using the `Application` object's `Calculation` property. Place Excel in manual calculation mode (as described earlier in this chapter) and then, when you need to update your formula results, use the `Calculate` method.

Optimize Your Loops

One of the cornerstones of efficient programming is loop optimization. Because a procedure might run the code inside a loop hundreds or even thousands of times, a minor improvement in loop efficiency can result in considerably reduced execution times.

When analyzing your loops, make sure that you're particularly ruthless about applying the preceding tips. One `Select` method is slow; a thousand will drive you crazy. Also, make sure that you define any counter used in your loops as `Integer` variables, which use the least memory of the numeric types.

Also, weed out from your loops any statements that return the same value each time. For example, consider the following procedure fragment:

```
For i = 1 To 50000
    Application.StatusBar = "Value: " & Worksheets("Sheet1").[A1].Value
Next 'i
```

The idea of this somewhat useless code is to loop 50,000 times, each time displaying in the status bar the contents of cell A1 in the Sheet1 worksheet. The value in cell A1 never changes, but it takes time for Excel to get the value, slowing the loop considerably. A better approach would be the following:

```
currCell = Worksheets("Sheet1").[A1].Value
For i = 1 To 50000
    Application.StatusBar = "Value: " & currCell
Next I
```

Transferring the unchanging `currCell` calculation outside the loop and assigning it to a variable means that the procedure has to call the function only once.

To test the difference, Listing 14.8 shows the `TimingTest` procedure. This procedure uses the `Timer` function (which returns the number of seconds since midnight) to time two `For...Next` loops. The first loop is unoptimized, and the second is optimized. On my system, the unoptimized loop takes about nine seconds, and the optimized loop takes only three seconds—a third of the time.

Listing 14.8   A Procedure That Tests the Difference Between an Optimized and an Unoptimized Loop

```
Sub TimingTest()
    Dim i As Long, currCell As Variant
    Dim start1 As Long, finish1 As Long
    Dim start2 As Long, finish2 As Long
    '
    ' Start timing the unoptimized loop
```

```
        '
        start1 = Timer
        For i = 1 To 50000
            Application.StatusBar = "The value is " & Worksheets("Sheet1").[A1].
➥Value
        Next i
        finish1 = Timer
        '
        ' Start timing the optimized loop
        '
        start2 = Timer
        currCell = Worksheets("Sheet1").[A1].Value
        For i = 1 To 50000
            Application.StatusBar = "The value is " & currCell
        Next i
        finish2 = Timer
        MsgBox "The first loop took " & finish1 - start1 & " seconds." & _
                vbCrLf & _
                "The second loop took " & finish2 - start2 & " seconds."
        Application.StatusBar = False
End Sub
```

From Here

- For the basics of the Visual Basic Editor, **see** "Touring the Visual Basic Editor," **p. 17.**

- For the details on arrays, **see** "Using Array Variables," **p. 40.**

- To learn how to use the And operator, **see** "Working with Logical Expressions," **p. 66.**

- For information on the Do...Loop, **see** "Using Do...Loop Structures," **p. 105.**

14

Trapping Program Errors

15

In Chapter 6, "Controlling Your VBA Code," I showed you how to use `If...Then` and other control structures to add "intelligence" to your VBA programs. You'll notice, however, that whenever people write about coding programs for decision-making and other "smart" things, they always put words such as "intelligence" and "smart" in quotation marks (as I'm doing now). Why? Well, the cynics in the crowd (and those who've suffered through a few too many BSODs—blue screens of death) would say it's because using the words *intelligence* and *program* in the same sentence borders on the oxymoronic. However, the more common reason is the obvious fact that these techniques don't make your procedures truly intelligent; they just make them seem that way to the user.

In the end, programs are really pretty dumb. After all, they can only do what you, the programmer, tell them to do. For example, if you tell a program to copy a file to a nonexistent disk, the dim brute just doesn't have the smarts to pull back from the abyss.

In Chapter 16, "Debugging VBA Procedures," I'll show you quite a few techniques that will prove invaluable for stomping on program bugs, so you'll be more likely to ship problem-free applications. However, a pervasive paranoia about potential program problems should be your alliterative frame of mind whenever you create an application. In other words, *always* assume that something, somewhere, at some time can and will go wrong (think of this as a kind of "Murphy's Law of Coding"). After all, you might have tested your code thoroughly on *your* system, but you never know what strange combination of hardware and software it's likely to find out in the cold, cruel world. Similarly, you don't have all that much control over how a user interacts with your program. For example, the user might supply an invalid argument for a function or forget to insert a memory card for a backup operation.

Given this heightened (enlightened?) state of paranoia, you must code your applications to allow for potential errors, no matter how obscure. A properly designed program doesn't leave the user out in the cold if an error rears its ugly head. Instead, you need to install code that *traps* the error and fixes the problem (if possible), alerts the user to the error so that he or she can fix it (such as by inserting a card in a memory drive), or reports a meaningful explanation of what went wrong so that the user can give you feedback. To that end, this chapter takes you through VBA's error-trapping techniques.

A Basic Error-Trapping Strategy

For many programmers, adding error-trapping code to procedures can usually be found near the bottoms of their to-do lists (probably just before adding comments!). Error-trapping code isn't even remotely glamorous, and the optimistic (some would say foolhardy) programmer assumes it will never be needed.

That's a shame, because setting up a bare-bones error trap takes very little time. Even a more sophisticated trap can be reused in other procedures, so you really have only a one-time expenditure of energy. To help you get started down this crucial path toward good program hygiene, this section presents a basic strategy for writing and implementing error-trapping code. This strategy will unfold in four parts:

- Setting the error trap
- Coding the error handler
- Resuming program execution
- Disabling the error trap

Setting the Trap

In the simplest error-trapping case, VBA offers what I call the "never mind" statement:

```
On Error Resume Next
```

When inserted within a procedure, this statement tells VBA to bypass any line in the procedure that generates an error and to resume execution with the line that immediately follows the offending statement. No error message is displayed, so the user remains blissfully unaware that anything untoward has occurred. There are three things to note about implementing this statement:

- The trap applies to any executable statement that occurs *after* the On Error Resume Next statement.
- The trap also applies to any executable statement within each procedure that is called by the procedure containing the On Error Resume Next statement.
- The trap is disabled when the procedure ends.

Because the On Error Resume Next statement does nothing to resolve whatever caused the error, and because skipping the offending statement might cause further errors, this error trap is used only rarely.

To set a true error trap, use the `On Error GoTo` statement instead:

```
On Error GoTo line
```

Here, `line` is a line label, which is a statement that's used to mark a spot within a procedure (line labels aren't executable). The idea is that if an error occurs, the procedure containing the `On Error GoTo` statement will branch immediately to the first statement after the line label. This statement should be the beginning of the *error handler* code that processes the error in some way (see the next section). Here's the general structure that sets up a procedure to trap and handle an error:

```
Sub Whatever()
    On Error GoTo ErrorHandler
    [regular procedure statements go here]
    '
    ' If no error occurs, bypass the error handler
    '
    Exit Sub
    '
    ' If an error occurs, the code will branch here
    '
ErrorHandler:
    [error handler code goes here]
End Sub
```

Here are some notes about this structure:

- To ensure that all statements are protected, place the `On Error GoTo` statement at the top of the procedure.
- The last statement before the error handler line label should be `Exit Sub` (or `Exit Function` if you're working with a `Function` procedure). This ensures that the procedure bypasses the error handler if no error occurs.
- The line label is a string—without spaces or periods—followed by a colon (:) at the end to tell VBA that it's just a label and should not be executed.

Coding the Error Handler

The `On Error GoTo` statement serves as the mechanism by which errors are trapped, but the nitty-gritty of the trap is the error handler. The handler is a group of statements designed to process the error, either by displaying a message to the user or by resolving whatever problem raised the error.

The simplest error handler just displays a message that tells the user that a problem occurred. Listings 15.1 and 15.2 provide an example. Listing 15.1 uses a couple of `InputBox` functions to get two numbers from the user: a dividend and a divisor. With these values in hand, the procedure calls the `Divide` function, as shown in Listing 15.2.

> **NOTE** You'll find the example code used in this chapter on my website at www.mcfedries.com/Office2007VBA.

Listing 15.1 `GetNumbers` **Procedure Prompts the User for a Dividend and a Divisor**

```
Sub GetNumbers()
    Dim done As Boolean
    Dim divisor As Variant
    Dim dividend As Variant
    '
    ' Prompt user for dividend and divisor.
    '
    done = False
    Do While Not done
        dividend = InputBox("Enter the dividend:", "Divider")
        divisor = InputBox("Enter the divisor:", "Divider")
        done = Divide(dividend, divisor)
    Loop
End Sub
```

The purpose of the `Divide` function, shown in Listing 15.2, is to divide the `dividend` argument by the `divisor` argument. To trap a "division by zero" error, an `On Error GoTo` statement tells VBA to branch to the `DivByZeroHandler` label. (Actually, this statement will trap *any* error, not just a division by zero error.) The division is performed, and, if all goes well, a `MsgBox` displays the result. However, if the `divisor` value is `0`, an error occurs and the code branches to the `DivByZeroHandler` label. This error handler displays a message and asks the user whether he wants to try again. The function's return value is set according to the user's choice.

Listing 15.2 `Divide` **Function Divides the Dividend by the Divisor and Traps "Division by Zero" Errors**

```
Function Divide(dividend, divisor) As Boolean
    Dim msg As String
    Dim result As Single
    '
    ' Set the trap
    '
    On Error GoTo DivByZeroHandler
    '
    ' Perform the division
    '
    result = dividend / divisor
    '
    ' If it went okay, display the result
    '
    msg = dividend & _
          " divided by " & _
          divisor & _
          " equals " & _
          result
    MsgBox msg
    '
    ' Set the return value and bypass the error handler
    '
    Divide = True
```

```
    Exit Function
    '
    ' Code branches here if an error occurs
    '
DivByZeroHandler:
    '
    ' Display the error message
    '
    result = MsgBox("You entered 0 as the divisor! Try again?", _
                    vbYesNo + vbQuestion, _
                    "Divider")
    '
    ' Return the user's choice
    '
    If result = vbYes Then
        Divide = False
    Else
        Divide = True
    End If
End Function
```

In this example, setting up the error handler was no problem because the potential error—division by zero—was a fairly obvious one. (Also note that in a production application you'd confirm a nonzero divisor as soon as the user entered the value rather than wait for the division to occur.) In practice, however, your error handlers will require a more sophisticated approach that tests for multiple error types. For this you need to know about error numbers. I'll discuss those later in this chapter, in the section "`Err` Object Properties."

Resuming Program Execution

In Listing 15.2, the error message displayed to the user asks whether he or she wants to input the values again, and an `If...Then` tests the response and sets the function's return value accordingly. This example is a bit contrived because your errors won't necessarily occur inside a `Function` procedure or loop. However, you'll often still need to give the user a choice of continuing with the program or bailing out. To do this, you can add one or more `Resume` statements to your error handlers. VBA defines three varieties of `Resume` statement:

- `Resume`—Tells VBA to resume program execution at the same statement that caused the error.

- `Resume Next`—Tells VBA to resume program execution at the first executable statement after the statement that caused the error.

- `Resume line`—Tells VBA to resume program execution at the label specified by *line*.

Listing 15.3 shows an example. The `BackUpToDrive` procedure is designed to get a drive letter from the user and then save the active workbook to that drive. If a problem occurs (such as having no disk in the drive), the routine displays an error message and gives the user the option of trying again or quitting.

Listing 15.3   Procedure That Backs Up the Active Workbook to a Drive Specified by the User and Traps Any Errors (such as Having No Disk in the Drive)

```
Sub BackUpToDrive()
    Dim backupDrive As String
    Dim backupName As String
    Dim msg As String
    Dim done As Boolean
    Dim result As Integer
    '
    ' Define the location of the error handler
    '
    On Error GoTo ErrorHandler
    '
    ' Initialize some variables and then loop
    '
    Application.DisplayAlerts = False
    done = False
    backupDrive = "A:"
    While Not done
        '
        ' Get the drive to use for the backup
        '
        backupDrive = InputBox( _
            Prompt:="Enter the drive letter for the backup:", _
            Title:="Backup", _
            Default:=backupDrive)
        '
        ' Did the user click OK?
        '
        If backupDrive <> "" Then
            '
            ' Make sure the backup drive contains a colon (:)
            '
            If InStr(backupDrive, ":") = 0 Then
                backupDrive = Left(backupDrive, 1) & ":"
            End If
            '
            ' First, save the file
            '
            ActiveWorkbook.Save
            '
            ' Assume the backup will be successful,
            ' so set done to True to exit the loop
            '
            done = True
            '
            ' Concatenate drive letter and workbook name
            '
            backupName = backupDrive & ActiveWorkbook.Name
            '
            ' Make a copy on the specified drive
            '
            ActiveWorkbook.SaveCopyAs FileName:=backupName
```

```
            Else
                  Exit Sub
            End If
      Wend
      '
      ' Bypass the error handler
      '
      Exit Sub
      '
      ' Code branches here if an error occurs
      '
ErrorHandler:
      msg = "An error has occurred!" & vbCrLf & vbCrLf & _
            "Select Abort to bail out, Retry to re-enter the drive" & _
            vbCrLf & "letter, or Ignore to attempt the backup again."
      result = MsgBox(msg, vbExclamation + vbAbortRetryIgnore)
      Select Case result
            Case vbAbort
                  done = True
            Case vbRetry
                  done = False
                  Resume Next
            Case vbIgnore
                  Resume
      End Select
End Sub
```

The bulk of the procedure asks the user for a drive letter, saves the workbook, concatenates the drive letter and workbook name, and saves a copy of the workbook on the specified drive.

The error routine is set up with the following statement at the top of the procedure:

```
On Error GoTo ErrorHandler
```

If an error occurs, the procedure jumps to the ErrorHandler label. The error handler's MsgBox function gives the user three choices (see Figure 15.1), which get processed by the subsequent Select Case structure:

- **Abort**—Selecting this option (Case vbAbort) bails out of the While...Wend loop by setting the done variable to True.

- **Retry**—A user who selects this option (Case vbRetry) wants to reenter the drive letter. The done variable is set to False, and then the Resume Next statement is run. If the error occurs during the SaveCopyAs method, the next statement is Wend, so the procedure just loops back (because we set done to False) and runs the InputBox function again.

- **Ignore**—A user who selects this option (Case vbIgnore) wants to attempt the backup again. For example, if the user forgot to insert a disk in the drive, or if the drive door wasn't closed, the user would fix the problem and then select this option. In this case, the error handler runs the Resume statement to retry the SaveCopyAs method (or whatever).

Figure 15.1
If an error occurs,
the error handler
displays this dialog
box.

Disabling the Trap

Under normal circumstances, an error trap set by the On Error GoTo statement is disabled automatically when the procedure containing the statement is finished executing. However, there might be times when you want to disable an error trap before the end of a procedure. For example, when you're testing a procedure, you might want to enable the trap for only part of the code and let VBA generate its normal runtime errors for the rest of the procedure.

To disable an error trap at any time during a procedure, even within an error handler, use the following statement:

```
On Error GoTo 0
```

Working with the Err Object

The problem with the error traps set so far is a lack of information. For example, the Divide function (in Listing 15.2) assumes that any error that occurs is a result of an attempted division by zero. However, there are two other runtime error possibilities:

- **Overflow**—This error is raised if *both* the dividend and divisor are 0.
- **Type mismatch**—This error is raised if either value is nonnumeric.

You're likely to want your error handler to treat these errors differently. For example, a division by 0 error requires only that the divisor be reentered, but an overflow error requires that both the dividend and the divisor be reentered.

To handle different errors, VBA provides the Err object, which holds information about any runtime errors that occur. You can use the properties of this object to get specific error numbers and descriptions, and you can use the methods of this object to control errors programmatically.

Err **Object Properties**

The Err object has a number of properties, but the following three are the ones you'll use most often:

- Err.Description—Returns the error description.
- Err.Number—Returns the error number.
- Err.Source—Returns the name of the project in which the error occurred.

For example, Listing 15.4 shows a procedure that attempts to divide two numbers. The Err object is used in two places within the error handler:

■ The error message displayed to the user contains both Err.Number and Err.Description.

■ A Select Case structure examines Err.Number to allow the handler to perform different actions, depending on the error.

Listing 15.4 Procedure That Divides Two Numbers and Traps Three Specific Errors: Division by Zero, Overflow, and Type Mismatch

```
Sub DivideNumbers()
    '
    ' Set the trap
    '
    On Error GoTo DivByZeroHandler
    '
    ' Declare variables
    '
    Dim divisor As Variant
    Dim dividend As Variant
    Dim result As Single
    Dim msg As String
    '
    ' Prompt user for the dividend
    '
GetDividendAndDivisor:
    dividend = InputBox("Enter the dividend:", "Divider")
    If dividend = "" Then Exit Sub
    '
    ' Prompt user for the divisor
    '
GetDivisorOnly:
    divisor = InputBox("Enter the divisor:", "Divider")
    If divisor = "" Then Exit Sub
    '
    ' Perform the division
    '
    result = dividend / divisor
    '
    ' If it went okay, display the result
    '
    msg = dividend & _
          " divided by " & _
          divisor & _
          " equals " & _
          result
    MsgBox msg
    '
    ' Bypass the error handler
    '
    Exit Sub
    '
    ' Code branches here if an error occurs
```

continues

15

15

Listing 15.4   Continued

```
    '
DivByZeroHandler:
    '
    ' Display the error message
    '
    msg = "An error occurred!" & vbCrLf & vbCrLf & _
          "Error number:  " & Err.Number & vbCrLf & _
          "Error message: " & Err.Description
    MsgBox msg, vbOKOnly + vbCritical
    '
    ' Check the error number
    '
    Select Case Err.Number
        '
        ' Division by zero
        '
        Case 11
            Resume GetDivisorOnly
        '
        ' Overflow
        '
        Case 6
            Resume GetDividendAndDivisor
        '
        ' Type mismatch
        '
        Case 13
            If Not IsNumeric(dividend) Then
                Resume GetDividendAndDivisor
            Else
                Resume GetDivisorOnly
            End If
        '
        ' Anything else, just quit
        '
        Case Else
            Exit Sub
    End Select
End Sub
```

Err **Object Methods**

The Err object also comes equipped with a couple of methods you can use:

- Err.Clear—This method resets all of the Err object's properties. (In other words, numeric properties are set to 0, and string properties are set to the null string.) Note that this method is invoked automatically whenever your code runs any of the following statements:
    - Exit Function
    - Exit Property
    - Exit Sub

- On Error GoTo 0
- On Error GoTo *line*
- On Error Resume Next
- Resume
- Resume *line*
- Resume Next

- `Err.Raise`—This method generates a runtime error. You normally use this method during debugging to create an error on purpose and thus check to see that your error handler is operating correctly. In this case, you need only use the following simplified syntax:

  `Err.Raise Number`

  Number   The number of the error you want to raise.

(This method also has a few other parameters that let you define your own errors for use in, say, a custom class object. See the VBA Help file for details.)

Trappable VBA Errors

VBA has dozens of trappable errors. They're all described in Table 15.1.

Table 15.1   VBA's Trappable Errors

Number	Description	Number	Description
3	Return without `GoSub`	28	Out of stack space
5	Invalid procedure call	35	Sub, Function, or Property not defined
6	Overflow	47	Too many DLL application clients
7	Out of memory	48	Error in loading DLL
9	Subscript out of range	49	Bad DLL calling convention
10	This array is fixed or temporarily locked	51	Internal error
11	Division by zero	52	Bad filename or number
13	Type mismatch	53	File not found
14	Out of string space	54	Bad file mode
16	Expression too complex	55	File already open
17	Can't perform requested operation	57	Device I/O error
18	User interrupt occurred	58	File already exists
20	Resume without error	59	Bad record length

continues

15

Table 15.1   Continued

Number	Description	Number	Description
61	Disk full	336	ActiveX component not correctly registered
62	Input past end of file		
63	Bad record number	337	ActiveX component not found
67	Too many files	338	ActiveX component did not run correctly
68	Device unavailable		
70	Permission denied	360	Object already loaded
71	Disk not ready	361	Can't load or unload this object
74	Can't rename with different drive	363	ActiveX control specified not found
75	Path/file access error	364	Object was unloaded
76	Path not found	365	Unable to unload within this context
91	Object variable or `With` block variable not set	368	The specified file is out of date. This program requires a later version.
92	`For` loop not initialized	371	The specified object can't be used as an owner form for `Show`
93	Invalid pattern string		
94	Invalid use of `Null`	380	Invalid property value
97	Can't call `Friend` procedure on an object that is not an instance of the defining class	381	Invalid property-array index
		382	`Property Set` can't be executed at runtime
98	A property or method call cannot include a reference to a private object, either as an argument or a as return value	383	`Property Set` can't be used with a read-only property
		385	Need property-array index
		387	`Property Set` not permitted
298	System DLL could not be loaded	393	`Property Get` can't be executed at runtime
320	Can't use character device names in specified filenames	394	`Property Get` can't be executed on write-only property
321	Invalid file format	400	Form already displayed; can't show modally
322	Can't create necessary temporary file		
325	Invalid format in resource file	402	Code must close topmost modal form first
327	Data value named not found	419	Permission to use object denied
328	Illegal parameter; can't write arrays	422	Property not found
335	Could not access system registry	423	Property or method not found

Number	Description	Number	Description
424	Object required	459	This component doesn't support events
425	Invalid object use	460	Invalid Clipboard format
429	ActiveX component can't create object or return reference to this object	461	Specified format doesn't match format of data
430	Class doesn't support Automation	462	The remote server machine does not exist or is unavailable
432	Filename or class name not found during Automation operation	463	Class not registered on local machine
438	Object doesn't support this property or method	480	Can't create AutoRedraw image
440	Automation error	481	Invalid picture
442	Connection to type library or object library for remote process has been lost	482	Printer error
		483	Printer driver doesn't support the specified property
443	Automation object doesn't have a default value	484	Problem getting printer information from the system. Make sure the printer is set up correctly.
445	Object doesn't support this action		
446	Object doesn't support named arguments	485	Invalid picture type
447	Object doesn't support current locale setting	486	Can't print form image to this type of printer
448	Named argument not found	520	Can't empty Clipboard
449	Argument not optional, or invalid property assignment	521	Can't open Clipboard
		735	Can't save file to TEMP directory
450	Wrong number of arguments, or invalid property assignment	744	Search text not found
		746	Replacements too long
451	Object not a collection	31001	Out of memory
452	Invalid ordinal	31004	No object
453	Specified DLL function not found	31018	Class is not set
454	Code resource not found	31027	Unable to activate object
455	Code resource lock error	31032	Unable to create embedded object
457	This key is already associated with an element of this collection	31036	Error saving to file
		31037	Error loading from file
458	Variable uses a type not supported in Visual Basic		

15

From Here

- An important part of trapping errors is letting the user know what's happening and, possibly, giving him or her some kind of clue how to fix the problem. **See** "Storing User Input in a Variable," **p. 45**.

- You can eliminate many trappable errors by making sure your code is as bug-free as possible. **See** Chapter 16, "Debugging VBA Procedures," **p. 337**.

Debugging VBA Procedures

It's usually easy to get short `Sub` and `Function` procedures up and running. However, as your code grows larger and more complex, errors inevitably creep in. Many of these errors—programmers call them *bugs*—are simple syntax problems you can fix easily, but others will be more subtle and harder to find. For the latter—whether the errors are incorrect values being returned by functions or problems with a procedure's overall logic—you'll need to be able to look "inside" your code to scope out what's wrong. The good news is that VBA gives you several reasonably sophisticated *debugging* tools that can remove some of the burden of program problem solving. This chapter looks at these tools and shows you how to use them to help recover from most programming errors.

16

NOTE

There's a popular and appealing tale of how the word *bug* came about. Apparently, an early computer pioneer named Grace Hopper was working on a machine called the Mark II in 1947. While investigating a glitch, she found a moth among the vacuum tubes, so from then on glitches were called bugs. Appealing, yes, but true? Not quite. In fact, engineers had already been referring to mechanical defects as "bugs" for at least 60 years before Ms. Hopper's discovery. As proof, the Oxford English Dictionary offers the following quotation from an 1889 edition of the Pall Mall Gazette:

"Mr. Edison, I was informed, had been up the two previous nights discovering 'a bug' in his phonograph—an expression for solving a difficulty, and implying that some imaginary insect has secreted itself inside and is causing all the trouble."

A Basic Strategy for Debugging

Debugging, like most computer skills, involves no great secrets. In fact, all debugging is usually a matter of taking a good, hard, dispassionate look at your code. Although there are no set-in-stone techniques for solving programming problems, you *can* formulate a basic strategy that will get you started.

When a problem occurs, the first thing you need to determine is what kind of error you're dealing with. There are four basic types: syntax errors, compile errors, runtime errors, and logic errors.

Syntax Errors

These errors arise from misspelled or missing keywords and incorrect punctuation. VBA catches most (but not all) of these errors when you enter your statements. Note, too, that the VBA Editor uses a red font to display any statements that contain syntax errors.

Syntax errors are flagged right away by VBA, which means that you just have to read the error message and then clean up the offending statement. Unfortunately, not all of VBA's error messages are helpful. For example, one common syntax error is to forget to include a closing quotation mark in a string. When this happens, VBA reports the following unhelpful message:

```
Expected: list separator or )
```

Compile Errors

When you try to run a procedure, VBA takes a quick look at the code to make sure things look right. If it sees a problem (such as an If...Then statement without a corresponding End If), it highlights the statement where the problem has occurred and displays an error message.

Fixing compile errors is also usually straightforward. Read the error message and see where VBA has highlighted the code. Doing so almost always gives you enough information to fix the problem.

Runtime Errors

These errors occur during the execution of a procedure. They generally mean that VBA has stumbled upon a statement that it can't figure out. It might be a formula attempting to divide by zero or a property or method that is used with the wrong object.

Runtime errors produce a dialog box such as the one shown in Figure 16.1. These error messages usually are a little vaguer than the ones you see for syntax and compile errors. It often helps to see the statement where the offense has occurred. You can do this by clicking the Debug button. This activates the module and places the insertion point on the line where the error has occurred. If you still can't see the problem, you need to rerun the procedure and pause at or near the point in which the error occurs. This lets you examine the state of the program when it tries to execute the statement. These techniques are explained later in this chapter.

Figure 16.1
A typical runtime error message.

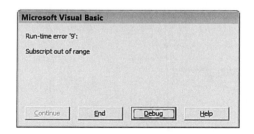

Logic Errors

If your code zigs instead of zags, the cause is usually a flaw in the logic of your procedure. It might be a loop that never ends or a Select Case that doesn't select anything.

Logic errors are the toughest to pin down because you don't get any error messages to give you clues about what went wrong and where. To help, VBA lets you trace through a procedure one statement at a time. This allows you to watch the flow of the procedure and see whether the code does what you want it to do. You can also keep an eye on the values of individual variables and properties to make sure they're behaving as expected. Again, you'll learn how to trace a procedure later in this chapter (see "Stepping Through a Procedure").

Pausing a Procedure

Pausing a procedure in midstream lets you see certain elements such as the current values of variables and properties. It also lets you execute program code one statement at a time so you can monitor a procedure's flow.

When you pause a procedure, VBA enters *break mode*, which means it displays the code window, highlights the current statement (the one that VBA will execute next) in yellow, and displays a yellow arrow in the margin indicator bar that points to the current statement. See the done = False statement in Figure 16.2.

Figure 16.2
A VBA procedure in break mode.

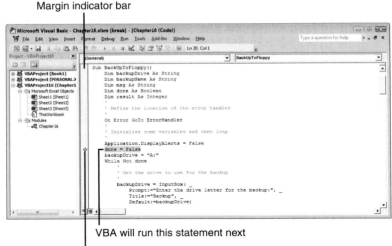

Margin indicator bar

VBA will run this statement next

Break mode indicator

Entering Break Mode

VBA gives you five ways to enter break mode:

- From a runtime error dialog box.
- By pressing F8 at the beginning of a procedure.
- By pressing Esc or Ctrl+Break while a procedure is running.
- By setting a breakpoint.
- By using a Stop statement.

Entering Break Mode from an Error Dialog Box

When a runtime error occurs, the dialog box that appears only tells you the error number and the error description (see Figure 16.1, shown earlier). It doesn't tell you where the error occurred. Instead of scouring your code for possible bugs, you should click the Debug button to enter break mode. This will take you directly to the line that caused the error so that you can investigate the problem immediately.

Entering Break Mode at the Beginning of a Procedure

If you're not sure where to look for the cause of an error, you can start the procedure in break mode. Place the insertion point anywhere inside the procedure and then choose Debug, Step Into (or press F8). VBA enters break mode and highlights the Sub statement.

> **TIP**
> Many of the menu commands that I discuss in this chapter have button equivalents on the Debug toolbar. If you don't see this toolbar onscreen, activate the View, Toolbars, Debug command.

Entering Break Mode by Pressing the Esc Key

If your procedure isn't producing an error but appears to be behaving strangely, you can enter break mode by pressing Esc (or by choosing Run, Break) while the procedure is running. VBA pauses on whatever statement it was about to execute.

Alternatively, you can press Ctrl+Break to display the dialog box shown in Figure 16.3. Click Debug to put VBA into break mode.

Figure 16.3
This dialog box appears if you press Ctrl+Break while a procedure is running.

16

Setting a Breakpoint

If you know approximately where an error or logic flaw is occurring, you can enter break mode at a specific statement in the procedure. This is called a *breakpoint*.

To set breakpoints, follow these steps:

1. Open the module containing the procedure you want to run.
2. Place the insertion point anywhere inside the statement where you want to enter break mode. VBA will run every line of code up to, but not including, this statement.
3. Choose Debug, Toggle Breakpoint. (Alternatively, press F9 or click beside the statement in the margin indicator bar.) As shown in Figure 16.4, VBA highlights the entire line in red and adds a breakpoint indicator in the margin indicator bar.
4. Repeat steps 2 and 3 to set breakpoints for any other statements where you want the procedure to enter break mode (you can set as many as you need).

Figure 16.4
When you set a breakpoint, VBA highlights the entire line in red.

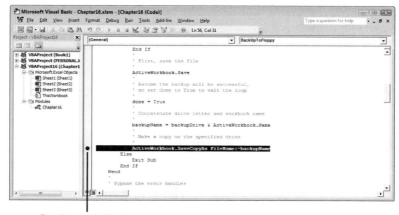

Breakpoint indicator

> **NOTE** The command that sets a breakpoint is a toggle, so you can remove a breakpoint by placing the insertion point on the same line and running the command again. To remove all the breakpoints in the module, select <u>D</u>ebug, <u>C</u>lear All Breakpoints or press Ctrl+Shift+F9.

Entering Break Mode by Using a Stop Statement

When developing your projects, you'll often test the robustness of a procedure by sending it various test values or by trying it out under different conditions. In many cases, you'll want to enter break mode to make sure things look okay. You could set breakpoints at specific statements, but you lose them if you close the file. For something a little more permanent, you can include a Stop statement in a procedure. VBA automatically enters break mode whenever it encounters a Stop statement.

Figure 16.5 shows the BackUpToFloppy procedure with a Stop statement inserted just before the statement that runs the SaveCopyAs method.

Figure 16.5
You can insert Stop statements to enter break mode at specific procedure locations.

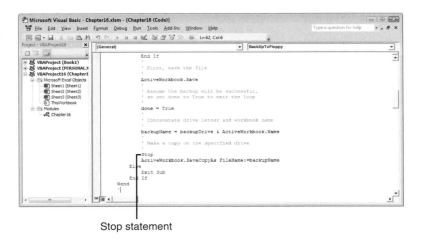

Stop statement

Exiting Break Mode

To exit break mode, you can use either of the following methods:

- Resume normal program execution by choosing <u>R</u>un, <u>C</u>ontinue (or by pressing F5).
- End the procedure by selecting <u>R</u>un, <u>R</u>eset.

Stepping Through a Procedure

One of the most common (and most useful) debugging techniques is to step through the code one statement at a time. This lets you get a feel for the program flow to make sure that things such as loops and procedure calls are executing properly. You can use three techniques:

- Stepping into a procedure
- Stepping over a procedure
- Stepping to a cursor position

Stepping into a Procedure

Stepping into a procedure means you execute one line at a time (in break mode), starting at the beginning of the procedure. If you haven't started a procedure yet, you step into it using the technique described in the section "Entering Break Mode at the Beginning of a Procedure."

Alternatively, you might prefer to run your code until it's about to call a particular procedure, and then step into that procedure. To do this, set a breakpoint on the statement that calls the procedure. As soon as your code hits that breakpoint, step into the procedure by choosing the Debug, Step Into command (or by pressing F8).

When you're inside the procedure, repeat the Step Into command to execute the procedure code one line at a time. Keep stepping through until the procedure ends or until you're ready to exit break mode and resume normal execution.

Stepping Over a Procedure

Some statements call other procedures. If you're not interested in stepping through a called procedure, you can step over it. This means that VBA executes the procedure normally and then resumes break mode at the next statement *after* the procedure call. To step over a procedure, first either step into the procedure until you come to the procedure call you want to step over, or set a breakpoint on the procedure call and run the project. When you're in break mode, you can step over the procedure by choosing Debug, Step Over (or by pressing Shift+F8).

Stepping Out of a Procedure

It's very common (and very frustrating) to accidentally step into a procedure that you wanted to step over. If the procedure is short, you can just step through it until you're back in the original procedure. If it's long, however, you don't want to waste time going through every statement. Instead, invoke the Step Out feature by choosing Debug, Step Out (or by pressing Ctrl+Shift+F8).

VBA executes the rest of the procedure and then reenters break mode at the first line after the procedure call.

Stepping to the Cursor

Instead of stepping over an entire procedure, you might need to step over a few statements. To do this, enter break mode, place the insertion point inside the line where you want to reenter break mode, and then choose Debug, Run To Cursor (or press Ctrl+F8).

Monitoring Procedure Values

Many runtime and logic errors are the result of (or, in some cases, can result in) variables or properties assuming unexpected values. If your procedure uses or changes these elements in several places, you need to enter break mode and monitor the values of these elements to see where things go awry. The Visual Basic Editor offers a number of methods for monitoring values, and I discuss them in the next few sections.

Using the Locals Window

Most of the values you'll want to monitor will be variables. Although watch expressions (discussed in the next section) are best if you want to keep an eye on only one or two variables, the Visual Basic Editor gives you an easy method to use if you want to monitor *all* the variables in any procedure. This method makes use of a special Visual Basic Editor window called the Locals window. You can display this window by activating the View, Locals Window command.

When your procedure enters break mode, the Locals window displays a line for each declared variable in the current procedure. As you can see in Figure 16.6, each line shows the variable name, its current value, and its type.

Figure 16.6
Use the Locals window to keep track of the current value of all your variables.

Adding a Watch Expression

In addition to variable values, VBA also lets you monitor the results of any expression or the current value of an object property. To do this, you need to set up a *watch expression* that defines what you want to monitor. These watch expressions appear in the Watch window, which you can display by activating the View, Watch Window command.

To add a watch expression, follow these steps:

1. If the expression exists inside the procedure (for example, an object property), specify the expression as follows:
   - For single-word expressions, place the insertion point anywhere inside the word.
   - For more complex expressions, select the entire expression.

2. Choose <u>D</u>ebug, <u>A</u>dd Watch to display the Add Watch dialog box, shown in Figure 16.7. (Note that in the vast majority of cases you can skip the following steps 3 through 5 and head right to step 6.)

Figure 16.7
Use the Add Watch dialog box to add watch expressions.

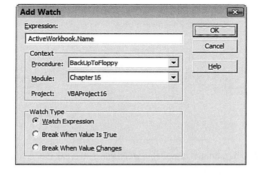

3. If the expression you want to monitor isn't already shown in the <u>E</u>xpression text box, enter the expression. You can enter a variable name, a property, a user-defined function name, or any other valid VBA expression.

4. Use the Context group to specify the context of the variable (that is, where the variable is used). You enter the <u>P</u>rocedure and the <u>M</u>odule.

5. Use the Watch Type group to specify how VBA watches the expression:
   - **<u>W</u>atch Expression**—Displays the expression in the Watch window when you enter break mode.
   - **Break When Value Is <u>T</u>rue**—Tells VBA to automatically enter break mode when the expression value becomes true (or nonzero).
   - **Break When Value <u>C</u>hanges**—Automatically enters break mode whenever the value of the expression changes.

6. Click OK.

After you've added a watch expression, you monitor it by entering break mode and examining the expression in the Watch window, as shown in Figure 16.8.

Figure 16.8
The Watch window with a few watch expressions.

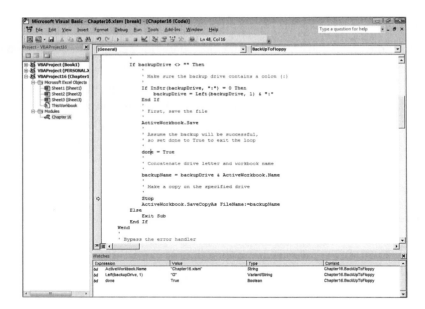

> **TIP**
>
> The Debug, Add Watch command is available when you're in break mode, so you can add more watch expressions if necessary.

Editing a Watch Expression

You can make changes to a watch expression while in break mode. Follow these steps:

1. In the Watch window, click the watch expression you want to edit.
2. Choose Debug, Edit Watch (or press Ctrl+W; you can also double-click the watch expression). The Visual Basic Editor displays the Edit Watch dialog box.
3. Make your changes to the watch expression.
4. Click OK to return to the Debug window.

Deleting a Watch Expression

To delete a watch expression you no longer need to monitor, follow these steps:

1. In the Watch window, click the watch expression you want to delete.
2. Choose Debug, Edit Watch (or press Ctrl+W; you can also double-click the watch expression). The Visual Basic Editor displays the Edit Watch dialog box.
3. Click the Delete button (or click the expression in the Watch window and press the Delete key). VBA deletes the expression and returns you to the Debug window.

Displaying Data Values Quickly

Many variables, properties, and expressions are set once, and they don't change for the rest of the procedure. To avoid cluttering the Watch window with these expressions, VBA offers a couple of methods for quickly displaying an expression's current value: data tips and Quick Watch.

The data tips feature is one of the handiest of VBA's debugging tools. When you're in break mode, simply move the mouse pointer over the variable or property whose value you want to know. After a brief pause, VBA displays a banner showing the current value of the expression, as shown in Figure 16.9.

16

Figure 16.9
VBA displays a data tip banner when you hover the mouse pointer over an expression in break mode.

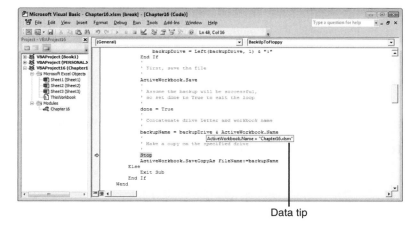

Data tip

The Quick Watch feature displays a dialog box that shows the expression, its current context, and its current value. To try this, follow these steps:

1. Enter break mode.
2. Either place the insertion point inside the expression you want to display or select the expression.
3. Choose Debug, Quick Watch (or press Shift+F9). The Visual Basic Editor displays a Quick Watch dialog box like the one shown in Figure 16.10.

Figure 16.10
Use the Quick Watch dialog box to quickly display the value of an expression.

If you want to add the expression to the Watch window, click the Add button. To return to break mode without adding the expression, click Cancel.

Using the Immediate Window

The Watch window tells you the current value of an expression, but you'll often need more information than this. You also might want to plug in different values for an expression while in break mode. You can perform these tasks with VBA's Immediate window, which you display by activating the View, Immediate Window command.

Printing Data in the Immediate Window

You can use the Print method of the special Debug object to print text and expression values in the Immediate window. There are two ways to do this:

- By running the Print method from the procedure
- By entering the Print method directly into the Immediate window

The Print method uses the following syntax:

```
Debug.Print OutputList
```

> OutputList   An expression or list of expressions to print in the Immediate window. If you omit OutputList, a blank line is printed.

Here are a few notes to keep in mind when using this method:

- Use Spc(n) in OutputList to print n space characters.
- Use Tab(n) in OutputList to print n tab characters.
- Separate multiple expressions with either a space or a semicolon.

Running the Print Method from a Procedure

If you know that a variable or expression changes at a certain place in your code, enter a Debug.Print statement at that spot. When you enter break mode, the OutputList expressions appear in the Immediate window. For example, Figure 16.11 shows a procedure in break mode. The information displayed in the Immediate window was generated by the following statement:

```
Debug.Print "The backup filename is "; backupName
```

Figure 16.11
Use `Debug.Print` in your code to display information in the Immediate window.

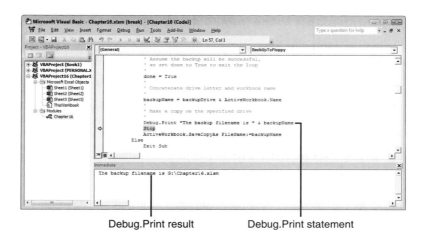

Debug.Print result   Debug.Print statement

Running the `Print` Method in the Immediate Window

You can also use the `Print` method directly in the Immediate window to display information. Note that when you're in break mode you don't need to specify the `Debug` object.

Figure 16.12 shows a couple of examples. In the first line, I typed **print backupdrive** and pressed Enter. The Visual Basic Editor responded with `G:\`. In the second example, I typed **? backupname** (? is the short form of the Print method), and VBA responded with `G:\:Chapter16.xlsm`.

Figure 16.12
You can enter `Print` statements directly in the Immediate window. Note the use of the question mark (?) as a short form of the `Print` method.

Executing Statements in the Immediate Window

Perhaps the most effective use of the Immediate window, however, is to execute statements. There are many uses for this feature while you're in break mode:

- To try some experimental statements to see their effect on the procedure.
- To change the value of a variable or property. For example, if you see that a variable with a value of zero is about to be used as a divisor, you could change that variable to a nonzero value to avoid crashing the procedure.
- To run other procedures or user-defined functions to see whether they operate properly under the current conditions.

You enter statements in the Immediate window just as you do in the module itself. For example, entering the following statement in the Immediate window changes the value of the backupName variable:

```
backupName = "H:\Chapter16.xls"
```

> **TIP**
> You can execute multiple statements in the Immediate window by separating each statement with a colon. For example, you can test a For...Next loop by entering a statement similar to the following:
>
> ```
> For i=1 To 10:Print i^2:Next
> ```

Debugging Tips

Debugging your procedures can be a frustrating job, even during the best of times. Here are a few tips to keep in mind when tracking down programming problems.

Indent Your Code for Readability

VBA code is immeasurably more readable when you indent your control structures. Readable code is that much easier to trace and decipher, so your debugging efforts have one less hurdle to negotiate. Indenting code is a simple matter of pressing Tab an appropriate number of times at the beginning of a statement.

It helps if VBA's automatic indentation feature is enabled. To check this, choose Tools, Options to display the Options dialog box and, in the Editor tab, activate the Auto Indent check box.

> **NOTE**
> By default, VBA moves the insertion point four spaces to the right when you press the Tab key. You can change this default by typing a new value in the Tab Width text box in the Editor tab of the Options dialog box.

Turn on Syntax Checking

VBA's automatic syntax checking is a real time-saver. To make sure this option is turned on, activate the Auto Syntax Chec*k* check box in the Editor tab of the Options dialog box.

Require Variable Declarations

To avoid errors caused by using variables improperly, you should always declare your procedure variables. To make VBA display an error if you don't declare a variable, add the following statement to the top of the module:

```
Option Explicit
```

> **TIP** To have VBA include the `Option Explicit` statement in every new module, activate the *R*equire Variable Declaration check box in the Editor tab of the Options dialog box.

Break Down Complex Procedures

Don't try to solve all your problems at once. If you have a large procedure that isn't working right, test it in small chunks to try to narrow down the problem. To test a piece of a procedure, add an `Exit Sub` statement after the last line of the code you want to test.

Enter VBA Keywords in Lowercase

If you always enter keywords in lowercase letters, you can easily detect a problem when you see that VBA doesn't change the word to its normal case when you move the cursor off the line.

Comment Out Problem Statements

If a particular statement is giving you problems, you can temporarily deactivate it by placing an apostrophe at the beginning of the line. This tells VBA to treat the line as a comment.

Don't forget that VBA has a handy Comment Block feature that will comment out multiple statements at once. To use this feature, select the statements you want to work with and then click the Comment Block button on the Edit toolbar.

Break Up Long Statements

One of the most complicated aspects of procedure debugging is making sense out of long statements (especially formulas). The Immediate window can help (you can use it to print parts of the statement), but it's usually best to keep your statements as short as possible. After you get things working properly, you can often recombine statements for more efficient code.

Use Excel's Range Names Whenever Possible

In Excel, procedures are much easier to read and debug if you use range names in place of cell references. Not only is a name such as Expenses!Summary more comprehensible than Expenses!A1:F10, it's safer, too. If you add rows or columns to the Summary range, the name's reference changes as well. With cell addresses, you have to adjust the references yourself.

Take Advantage of User-Defined Constants

If your procedure uses constant values in several different statements, you can give yourself one less debugging chore by creating a user-defined constant for the value (see Chapter 3, "Understanding Program Variables"). This gives you three important advantages:

- It ensures that you don't enter the wrong value in a statement.
- It's easier to change the value because you have to change only the constant declaration.
- It makes your procedures easier to understand.

From Here

- You can avoid many design-time errors by using the Visual Basic Editor's IntelliSense features; **see** "Taking Advantage of IntelliSense," **p. 27**.
- To learn how to trap any errors that occur while your programs are running, **see** Chapter 15, "Trapping Program Errors," **p. 323**.

Appendixes

IV

VBA Statements

Throughout this book, I've introduced you to various VBA statements. (It's worth mentioning here that a *statement* is any VBA keyword or construct that isn't a function, object, property, or method.) These statements appeared on an "as-needed" basis whenever I wanted to explain a particular VBA topic (such as If...Then...Else and the other control structures you saw in Chapter 6, "Controlling Your VBA Code"). Although I covered many VBA statements in this book, I bypassed quite a few in the interests of brevity and simplicity.

In an effort to put some finishing touches on our VBA coverage, this appendix presents a brief, but complete, look at every VBA statement. I give you the name of the statement, the arguments it uses (if any; note, too, that required arguments are shown in **bold type**), and a short description. For those statements that I didn't cover in this book, you can get full explanations and examples from the Statements section of the VBA Help file.

Table A.1   VBA Statements

Statement	Description
AppActivate *title, wait*	Activates the running application with the title or task ID given by title.
Beep	Beeps the computer's internal speaker.
Call *name, argumentlist*	Calls the *name* procedure. (Because you can call a procedure just by using its name, the Call statement is rarely used in VBA programming.)
ChDir *path*	Changes the current directory (folder) to *path*.
ChDrive *drive*	Changes the current drive to *drive*.
Close *filenumberlist*	Closes one or more I/O files opened with the Open statement.
Const *CONSTNAME*	Declares a constant variable named *CONSTNAME*.
Date = *date*	Changes the system date to *date*.
Declare *name*	Declares a procedure from a dynamic link library (DLL).
DefBool *letterrange*	A module-level statement that sets the default data type to Boolean for all variables that begin with the letters in *letterrange* (for example, DefBool A-F).
DefByte *letterrange*	Sets the default data type to Byte for all variables that begin with the letters in *letterrange*.
DefCur *letterrange*	Sets the default data type to Currency for all variables that begin with the letters in *letterrange*.
DefDate *letterrange*	Sets the default data type to Date for all variables that begin with the letters in *letterrange*.
DefDbl *letterrange*	Sets the default data type to Double for all variables that begin with the letters in *letterrange*.
DefInt *letterrange*	Sets the default data type to Integer for all variables that begin with the letters in *letterrange*.
DefLng *letterrange*	Sets the default data type to Long for all variables that begin with the letters in *letterrange*.
DefObj *letterrange*	Sets the default data type to Object for all variables that begin with the letters in *letterrange*.
DefSng *letterrange*	Sets the default data type to Single for all variables that begin with the letters in *letterrange*.
DefStr *letterrange*	Sets the default data type to String for all variables that begin with the letters in *letterrange*.
DefVar *letterrange*	Sets the default data type to Variant for all variables that begin with the letters in *letterrange*.

A

Statement	Description
DeleteSetting *appname,section,key*	Deletes a *section* or *key* from the Registry.
Dim *varname*	Declares a variable named *varname*.
Do...Loop	Loops through one or more statements while a logical condition is True.
End *keyword*	Ends a procedure, function, or control structure.
Enum *name*	Module-level statement that declares an enumeration variable.
Erase *arraylist*	Frees the memory allocated to a dynamic array or reinitializes a fixed-size array.
Error *errornumber*	Simulates an error by setting Err to *errornumber*.
Event *procedurename*(arglist)	Class module-level statement that declares a user-defined event.
Exit *keyword*	Exits a procedure, function, or control structure.
FileCopy *source, destination*	Copies the *source* file to *destination*.
For Each...Next	Loops through each member of a collection.
For...Next	Loops through one or more statements until a counter hits a specified value.
Function	Declares a user-defined function procedure.
Get #*filenumber, varname*	Reads an I/O file opened by the Open statement into a variable.
GoSub...Return	Branches to and returns from a subroutine within a procedure. (However, creating separate procedures makes your code more readable.)
GoTo *line*	Sends the code to the line label given by *line*.
If...Then...Else	Runs one of two sections of code based on the result of a logical test.
Implements *InterfaceName, Class*	Specifies the name of an interface or a class to be implemented in a class module.
Input #*filenumber, varlist*	Reads data from an I/O file into variables.
Kill *pathname*	Deletes the file *pathname* from a disk.
Let *varname = expression*	Sets the variable *varname* equal to *expression*. Let is optional and is almost never used.
Line Input #*filenumber, var*	Reads a line from an I/O file and stores it in *var*.
Load	Loads a user form into memory without displaying it.
Lock #*filenumber*, recordrange	Controls access to an I/O file.

A

continues

Table A.1 Continued

Statement	Description
LSet *stringvar* = *string*	Left-aligns a string within a String variable.
LSet *var1* = *var2*	Copies a variable of one user-defined type into another variable of a different user-defined type.
MkDir *path*	Creates the directory (folder) named *path*.
Name *oldpathname* As *newpathname*	Renames a file or directory (folder).
On Error	Sets up an error-handling routine.
On...GoSub, On...GoTo	Branches to a line based on the result of an expression.
Open *pathname*, etc.	Opens an input/output (I/O) file.
Option Base 0¦1	Determines (at the module level) the default lower bound for arrays.
Option Compare Text¦Binary	Determines (at the module level) the default mode for string comparisons.
Option Explicit	Forces you to declare all variables used in a module. Enter this statement at the module level.
Option Private	Indicates that the module is private and can't be accessed by other procedures outside the module. Enter this statement at the module level.
Print *#filenumber*	Writes data to an I/O file.
Private *varname*	Declares the *varname* variable to be a private variable that can be used only in the module in which it's declared. Enter this statement at the module level.
Property Get	Declares a property procedure.
Property Let	Assigns a value to a property in a property procedure.
Property Set	Sets a reference to an object in a property procedure.
Public *varname*	Makes the *varname* variable available to all procedures in a module.
Put *#filenumber*, *varname*	Writes data from the variable *varname* to an I/O file.
RaiseEvent *eventname*, *arguments*	Fires the event given by *eventname*.
Randomize *number*	Initializes the random-number generator. Omit *number* to get a different random number each time.
ReDim *varname*	Reallocates memory in a dynamic array.
Rem *comment*	Tells VBA that the following text is a comment. The apostrophe (') is more widely used.

Statement	Description
Reset	Closes all I/O files that were opened with Open.
Resume	After an error, resumes program execution at the line that caused the error.
RmDir *path*	Deletes a directory (folder).
RSet *stringvar* = *string*	Right-aligns a string within a String variable.
SaveSetting *appname*, etc.	Creates or saves a setting in the Windows Registry.
Seek #*filenumber*, *position*	Sets the current position in an I/O file.
Select Case	Executes one of several groups of statements based on the value of an expression.
SendKeys *string,* wait	Sends the keystrokes given by *string* to the active application.
Set *objectvar* = *object*	Assigns an *object* to an Object variable named *objectvar*.
SetAttr *pathname, attr*	Assigns the attributes given by *attr* (for example, vbReadOnly) to the file given by *pathname*.
Static *varname*	Declares *varname* to be a variable that will retain its value as long as the code is running.
Stop	Places VBA in Pause mode.
Sub	Declares a procedure.
Time = *time*	Sets the system time to *time*.
Type *varname*	Declares a user-defined data type. (Used at the module level only.)
Unload	Removes a user form from memory.
Unlock #*filenumber*, recordrange	Removes access controls on an I/O file.
While...Wend	Loops through a block of code while a condition is True.
Width #*filenumber, width*	Assigns an output line width to an I/O file.
With...End With	Executes a block of statements on a specified object.
Write #*filenumber*	Writes data to an I/O file.

A

VBA Functions

Although I discussed quite a few VBA functions in this book, my coverage was by no means exhaustive. VBA boasts more than 160 built-in functions that cover data conversion, dates and times, math, strings, and much more. This appendix presents a categorical list of VBA functions and the arguments they use (required arguments are shown in **bold type**). You can get full explanations and examples for all the functions in the Functions section of the VBA Help file.

Table B.1   Conversion Functions

Function	What It Returns
CBool(*expression*)	An *expression* converted to a Boolean value.
CByte(*expression*)	An *expression* converted to a Byte value.
CCur(*expression*)	An *expression* converted to a Currency value.
CDate(*expression*)	An *expression* converted to a Date value.
CDbl(*expression*)	An *expression* converted to a Double value.
CDec(*expression*)	An *expression* converted to a Decimal value.
CInt(*expression*)	An *expression* converted to an Integer value.
CLng(*expression*)	An *expression* converted to a Long value.
CSng(*expression*)	An *expression* converted to a Single value.
CStr(*expression*)	An *expression* converted to a String value.
CVar(*expression*)	An *expression* converted to a Variant value.
CVDate(*expression*)	An *expression* converted to a Date value. (Provided for backward compatibility. Use CDate instead.)
CVErr(*errornumber*)	A Variant of subtype Error that contains *errornumber*.

Table B.2   Date and Time Functions

Function	What It Returns
Date	The current system date as a Variant.
Date$()	The current system date as a String.
DateAdd(*interval, number, date*)	A Date value derived by adding *number* time *intervals* (months, quarters, and so on) to *date*.
DateDiff(*interval, date1, date2,...*)	The number of time *intervals* between *date1* and *date2*.
DatePart(*interval, date,...*)	The *interval* given by *date*.
DateSerial(*year, month, day*)	A Date value for the specified *year*, *month*, and *day*.
DateValue(*date*)	A Date value for the *date* string.
Day(*date*)	The day of the month given by *date*.
Hour(*time*)	The hour component of *time*.
Minute(*time*)	The minute component of *time*.
Month(*date*)	The month component of *date*.
MonthName(*month,abbreviate*)	The name of the month associated with the specified *month* number.

Function	What It Returns
Now	The current system date and time.
Second(*time*)	The second component of *time*.
Time	The current system time as a Variant.
Time$	The current system time as a String.
Timer	The number of seconds since midnight.
TimeSerial(*hour, minute, second*)	A Date value for the specified *hour*, *minute*, and *second*.
TimeValue(*time*)	A Date value for the *time* string.
Weekday(*date*)	The day of the week, as a number, given by *date*.
WeekdayName(*weekday*,*abbreviate*)	The name of the weekday associated with the specified *weekday* number.
Year(*date*)	The year component of *date*.

Table B.3   Error Functions

Function	What It Returns
Error(*errornumber*)	The error message, as a Variant, that corresponds to the *errornumber*.
Error$(*errornumber*)	The error message, as a String, that corresponds to the *errornumber*.

Table B.4   File and Directory Functions

Function	What It Returns
CurDir(*drive*)	The current directory as a Variant.
CurDir$(*drive*)	The current directory as a String.
Dir(*pathname, attributes*)	The name, as a Variant, of the file or directory (folder) specified by *pathname* and satisfying the optional *attributes* (for example, vbHidden). Returns Null if the file or directory doesn't exist.
Dir$(*pathname, attributes*)	The name, as a String, of the file or directory (folder) specified by *pathname* and satisfying the optional *attributes* (for example, vbHidden). Returns Null if the file or directory doesn't exist.
EOF(*filenumber*)	True if the end of file specified by *filenumber* has been reached; False otherwise.

continues

Table B.4 Continued

Function	What It Returns
FileAttr(*filenumber*, *returnType*)	The file mode (if *returnType* is 1) or the file handle (if *returnType* is 2) of the file given by *filenumber*.
FileDateTime(*pathname*)	The Date that the file given by *pathname* was created or last modified.
FileLen(*pathname*)	The length, in bytes, of the file given by *pathname*.
FreeFile(*rangenumber*)	The next available file number available to the Open statement.
GetAttr(*pathname*)	An integer representing the attributes of the file given by *pathname*.
Loc(*filenumber*)	The current read/write position in an open I/O file.
LOF(*filenumber*)	The size, in bytes, of an open I/O file.
Seek(*filenumber*)	The current read/write position, as a Variant, in an open I/O file.
Shell(*pathname*, *windowstyle*)	The task ID of the executed program given by *pathname*.

Table B.5 Financial Functions

Function	What It Returns
DDB(*cost, salvage, life, period*, *factor*)	The depreciation of an asset over a specified period, using the double-declining balance method.
FV(*rate, nper, pmt*, *pv, type*)	The future value of an investment or loan.
IPmt(*rate, per, nper, pv*, *fv, type*)	The interest payment for a specified period of a loan.
IRR(*values*, *guess*)	The internal rate of return for a series of cash flows.
MIRR(*values, finance_rate, reinvest_rate*)	The modified internal rate of return for a series of periodic cash flows.
NPer(*rate, pmt, pv*, *fv, type*)	The number of periods for an investment or loan.
NPV(*rate, value1*, *value2...*)	The net present value of an investment based on a series of cash flows and a discount rate.
Pmt(*rate, nper, pv*, *fv, type*)	The periodic payment for a loan or investment.

Function	What It Returns
PPmt(*rate, per, nper, pv*, fv, type)	The principal payment for a specified period of a loan.
PV(*rate, nper, pmt*, fv, type)	The present value of an investment.
Rate(*nper, pmt, pv*, fv, type, guess)	The periodic interest rate for a loan or investment.
SLN(*cost, salvage, life*)	The straight-line depreciation of an asset over one period.
SYD(*cost, salvage, life, period*)	The sum-of-years digits depreciation of an asset over a specified period.

Table B.6   Math Functions

Function	What It Returns
Abs(*number*)	The absolute value of *number*.
Atn(*number*)	The arctangent of *number*.
Cos(*number*)	The cosine of *number*.
Exp(*number*)	*e* (the base of the natural logarithm) raised to the power of *number*.
Fix(*number*)	The integer portion of *number*. If *number* is negative, Fix returns the first negative integer greater than or equal to *number*.
Hex(*number*)	The hexadecimal value, as a Variant, of *number*.
Hex$(*number*)	The hexadecimal value, as a String, of *number*.
Int(*number*)	The integer portion of *number*. If *number* is negative, Int returns the first negative integer less than or equal to *number*.
Log(*number*)	The natural logarithm of *number*.
Oct(*number*)	The octal value, as a Variant, of *number*.
Oct$(*number*)	The octal value, as a String, of *number*.
Rnd(*number*)	A random number.
Round(*expression*, numberdecimalplaces)	The numeric *expression* rounded to a specified number of decimal places.
Sgn(*number*)	The sign of *number*.
Sin(*number*)	The sine of *number*.

B

continues

Table B.6   Continued

Function	What It Returns
Sqr(***number***)	The square root of ***number***.
Tan(***number***)	The tangent of ***number***.

Table B.7   Miscellaneous Functions

Function	What It Returns
Array(***arglist***)	A Variant array containing the values in ***arglist***.
CallByName(***object***,***procname***, etc.)	The value of the ***procname*** property of the specified ***object***. Also can run the object's ***procname*** method.
Choose(***index***, ***choice1***, etc.)	A value from a list of choices.
CreateObject(***class***)	An Automation object of type ***class***.
DoEvents	Yields execution to the operating system so that it can process pending events from other applications (such as keystrokes and mouse clicks).
Environ(***envstring¦number***)	A String value that represents the operating system environment variable given by *envstring* or *number*.
Format(***expression***, *format*)	The ***expression***, as a Variant, according to the string *format*.
Format$(***expression***, *format*)	The ***expression***, as a String, according to the string *format*.
FormatCurrency(***Expression***, etc.)	***Expression*** formatted as a currency value.
FormatDateTime(***Date***, *NamedFormat*)	***Date*** formatted as a date or time value.
FormatNumber(***Expression***, etc.)	***Expression*** formatted as a numeric value.
FormatPercent(***Expression***, etc.)	***Expression*** formatted as a percentage value.
GetAllSettings(***appname***, ***section***)	All the settings in the specified ***section*** of the Registry.
GetObject(*pathname*, *class*)	The Automation object given by *pathname* and *class*.
GetSetting(***appname***, etc.)	A setting from the Registry.
IIf(***expr***, ***truepart***, ***falsepart***)	The ***truepart*** value if ***expr*** is True; returns ***falsepart*** otherwise.
Input(***number***, ***#filenumber***)	***number*** characters, as a Variant, from the I/O file given by ***filenumber***.

Function	What It Returns
`Input$(`*number, #filenumber*`)`	*number* characters, as a `String`, from the I/O file given by *filenumber*.
`InputB(`*number, #filenumber*`)`	*number* bytes, as a `Variant`, from the I/O file given by *filenumber*.
`InputB$(`*number, #filenumber*`)`	*number* bytes, as a `String`, from the I/O file given by *filenumber*.
`InputBox(`*prompt, etc.*`)`	Prompts the user for information.
`IsArray(`*varname*`)`	`True` if *varname* is an array.
`IsDate(`*expression*`)`	`True` if *expression* can be converted into a date.
`IsEmpty(`*expression*`)`	`True` if *expression* is empty.
`IsError(`*expression*`)`	`True` if *expression* is an error.
`IsMissing(`*argname*`)`	`True` if the argument specified by *argname* was not passed to the procedure.
`IsNull(`*expression*`)`	`True` if *expression* is the null string (" ").
`IsNumeric(`*expression*`)`	`True` if *expression* is a number.
`IsObject(`*expression*`)`	`True` if *expression* is an object.
`LBound(`*arrayname, dimension*`)`	The lowest possible subscript for the array given by *arrayname*.
`MsgBox(`*prompt, etc.*`)`	The button a user selects from the `MsgBox` dialog box.
`Partition(`*number, start, stop,...*`)`	A `String` that indicates where *number* occurs within a series of ranges.
`QBColor(`*color*`)`	The RGB color code that corresponds to *color* (a number between 1 and 15).
`RGB(`*red, green, blue*`)`	The color that corresponds to the *red*, *green*, and *blue* components.
`Switch(`*expr1, value1, etc.*`)`	Evaluates the expressions (*expr1* and so on) and returns the associated value (*value1* and so on) for the first expression that evaluates to `True`.
`Tab(`*n*`)`	Positions output for the `Print #` statement or the `Print` method.
`TypeName(`*varname*`)`	A string that indicates the data type of the *varname* variable.
`UBound(`*arrayname, dimension*`)`	The highest possible subscript for the array given by *arrayname*.
`VarType(`*varname*`)`	A constant that indicates the data type of the *varname* variable.

B

Table B.8   String Functions

Function	What It Returns
Asc(*string*)	The ANSI character code of the first letter in *string*.
AscB(*string*)	The byte corresponding to the first letter in *string*.
AscW(*string*)	The Unicode character code of the first letter in *string*.
Chr(*charcode*)	The character, as a Variant, that corresponds to the ANSI code given by *charcode*.
Chr$(*charcode*)	The character, as a String, that corresponds to the ANSI code given by *charcode*.
ChrB(*charcode*)	The byte that corresponds to the ANSI code given by *charcode*.
ChrW(*charcode*)	The Unicode character that corresponds to the ANSI code given by *charcode*.
Filter(*sourcearray*,*match*, *etc.*)	Given an array of strings (*sourcearray*), returns a subset of strings (that is, another array) that match a criteria (*match*).
InStr(*start*, *string1*, *string2*)	The character position of the first occurrence of *string2* in *string1*, beginning at *start*.
InStrB(*start*, *string1*, *string2*)	The byte position of the first occurrence of *string2* in *string1*, starting at *start*.
InStrRev(*stringcheck*,*stringmatch*,*start*)	The character position (working from the end of the string) of the first occurrence of *stringmatch* in *stringcheck*, beginning at *start*.
Join(*sourcearray*, *delimiter*)	A string consisting of the concatenated values in a string array (*sourcearray*), separated by *delimiter*.
LCase(*string*)	*string* converted to lowercase as a Variant.
LCase$(*string*)	*string* converted to lowercase as a String.
Left(*string, length*)	The leftmost *length* characters from *string* as a Variant.
Left$(*string, length*)	The leftmost *length* characters from *string* as a String.

Function	What It Returns
LeftB(*string*)	The leftmost *length* bytes from *string* as a Variant.
LeftB$(*string*)	The leftmost *length* bytes from *string* as a String.
Len(*string*)	The number of characters in *string*.
LenB(*string*)	The number of bytes in *string*.
LTrim(*string*)	A string, as a Variant, without the leading spaces in *string*.
LTrim$(*string*)	A string, as a String, without the leading spaces in *string*.
Mid(*string, start, length*)	*length* characters, as a Variant, from *string* beginning at *start*.
Mid$(*string, start, length*)	*length* characters, as a String, from *string* beginning at *start*.
MidB(*string, start, length*)	*length* bytes, as a Variant, from *string* beginning at *start*.
MidB$(*string, start, length*)	*length* bytes, as a String, from *string* beginning at *start*.
Replace(*expression, find, replace*)	A string in which one or more instances of a specified substring (*find*) in an *expression* have been replaced by another substring (*replace*).
Right(*string, length*)	The rightmost *length* characters from *string* as a Variant.
Right$(*string, length*)	The rightmost *length* characters from *string* as a String.
RightB(*string, length*)	The rightmost *length* bytes from *string* as a Variant.
RightB$(*string, length*)	The rightmost *length* bytes from *string* as a String.
RTrim(*string*)	A string, as a Variant, without the trailing spaces in *string*.
RTrim$(*string*)	A string, as a String, without the trailing spaces in *string*.
Space(*number*)	A string, as a Variant, with *number* spaces.
Space$(*number*)	A string, as a String, with *number* spaces.

B

continues

Table B.8   Continued

Function	What It Returns
Split(*expression*, *delimiter*)	An array consisting of substrings from a string *expression* in which each substring is separated by a *delimiter*.
Str(*number*)	The string representation, as a Variant, of *number*.
Str$(*number*)	The string representation, as a String, of *number*.
StrComp(*string2, string2, compare*)	A value indicating the result of comparing *string1* and *string2*.
StrReverse(*expression*)	A string consisting of the characters from a string *expression* in reverse order.
String(*number, character*)	*character*, as a Variant, repeated *number* times.
String$(*number, character*)	*character*, as a String, repeated *number* times.
Trim(*string*)	A string, as a Variant, without the leading and trailing spaces in *string*.
Trim$(*string*)	A string, as a String, without the leading and trailing spaces in *string*.
UCase(*string*)	*string* converted to uppercase as a Variant.
UCase$(*string*)	*string* converted to uppercase as a String.
Val(*string*)	The number contained in *string*.

B

INDEX

debugging procedures
    break mode
        entering, 340-342
        exiting, 342
        overview, 339-340
    breakpoints, setting, 341
    compile errors, 338
    data tips feature, 347
    debugging tips and
        techniques, 350-352
    Immediate window
        executing statements
            in, 350
        overview, 348
        printing data in,
            348-349
    Locals window, 344
    logic errors, 339
    overview, 337-338
    Quick Watch feature, 347
    runtime errors, 338-339
    stepping into
        procedures, 343
    stepping out of
        procedures, 343
    stepping over
        procedures, 343
    stepping to cursor, 343
    syntax errors, 338
    watch expressions,
        344-346

Declare statement, 356

declaring
    arrays
        dynamic arrays, 41-43
        multidimensional
            arrays, 44
        one-dimensional
            arrays, 44
    variables, 33-35
        explicit declarations,
            35-36
        implicit
            declarations, 35

default drive,
    changing, 315

default folders
    changing, 315
    referencing, 214

Default property
    (CommandButton
    object), 249

DefBool statement, 356

DefByte statement, 356

DefCur statement, 356

DefDate statement, 356

DefDbl statement, 356

DefInt statement, 356

DefLng statement, 356

DefObj statement, 356

DefSng statement, 356

DefStr statement, 356

Def*Type* keywords, 39

DefVar statement, 356

Delete command (Edit
    menu), 245

Delete method
    Attachment object, 229
    MailItem object, 222
    MAPIFolder object, 217
    Range object, 128-129
    Recordset object, 207
    Worksheet object, 152

DeleteAll procedure, 143

DeleteFolder procedure,
    317-318

DeleteSetting statement,
    307, 357

deleting
    application settings from
        Registry, 307
    controls, 245
    files, 315-316
    folders, 316-318
    records, 207-208

text (Word), 128-129
watch expressions, 346

DeletingARecord
    procedure, 207

Description property (Err
    object), 330

Developer tab,
    displaying, 16

dialog box launchers
    (Ribbon), creating, 289

dialog boxes. *See also* **forms**
    Add Procedure, 20
    Add Watch, 345
    Create Digital Certificate,
        304-305
    Create New Data
        Source, 192
    Customize Keyboard, 9
    displaying, 83-87
    Edit Watch, 346
    Export File, 300
    Import File, 300
    input boxes, 50-51
    Insert Function, 26-27
    Macro, 8-9, 21-22
    Macro Options, 11
    Macros, 8-9
    message boxes
        creating, 45-46
        message styles, 46-48
        return values, 48-49
    Microsoft Office Security
        Options, 302
    Modify Button, 12
    ODBC Microsoft Access
        Setup, 192
    Quick Watch, 347
    Record Macro, 5, 7
    Select Certificate, 305
    Select Database, 192
    Tab Order, 247
    Trust Center, 302-303

dialogBoxLauncher
    element (XML), 289

saving, 148-149
specifying number of
sheets in, 147-148
ThisWorkbook
objects, 146
Workbook object, 146
Worksheet object, 150
accessing worksheet
functions, 139-140
creating
worksheets, 151
methods, 152-153
properties, 151-152
specifying, 150-151

Execute method, 86-87

**executing statements in
Immediate window, 350**

Exit Do statement, 110

Exit For statement, 110

Exit statement, 357

exiting
break mode, 342
loops, 110

Exp function, 61, 365

explicit declarations, 35-36

exponential notation, 37

**exponentiation
operator (^), 55**

**Export File command (File
menu), 300**

Export File dialog box, 300

exporting modules, 300

expressions
data type consistency, 54
date expressions, 68-70
definition of, 24, 53
logical expressions, 66-67
numeric expressions
financial functions,
62-63
math functions, 60-62
overview, 60

operands, 54
operators
arithmetic
operators, 55
assignment (=), 54
comparison operators,
56-57
concatenation, 56
definition of, 54
logical operators,
57, 67
order of precedence,
57-60
overview, 53-54
string expressions, 63-66

**extending selection
(Word), 131-132**

**extensibility of Ribbon,
263-265**

**ExtractLastName
function, 65**

F

**field values, exporting from
Access to Excel, 208**

**Fields property (Recordset
object), 198**

File menu commands
Export File, 300
Import File, 300
Remove, 301

file system
default drive,
changing, 315
file/folder information,
returning
CurDir function, 310
Dir function, 310-312
FileDateTime function,
312

FileLen function,
312-313
GetAttr function,
313-314
files
copying, 315
deleting, 315-316
file/directory functions,
363-364
renaming, 316
setting attributes
of, 318
tracking file usage,
307-309
folders
changing default
folder, 315
creating, 316
deleting, 316-318
renaming, 316
setting attributes
of, 318

FileAttr function, 364

**FileCopy statement,
315, 357**

**FileDateTime function,
312, 364**

**FileLen function,
312-313, 364**

**FileName property
(Attachment object), 229**

files. *See also* **file system**
copying, 315
deleting, 315-316
file/directory functions,
363-364
inserting slides from, 172
MyRibbon.xml file
adding to document
package, 268-269
creating, 267-268
renaming and
opening, 269

On...GoSub, On...GoTo
statement, 358

onAction attribute
(controls), 276

one-dimensional arrays, 44

OnKey method, 142-143

OnRepeat method,
145-146

OnTime method, 144

OnUndo method, 145-146

Open method
Documents
collection, 116
Presentations
collection, 166
properties, 195
Recordset object, 193-196
Workbooks collection,
146-147

Open statement, 358

opening
database connections, 191
Excel workbooks, 146-147
modules, 18-19
PowerPoint
presentations, 166
recordsets, 192-193
with Open method,
194-196
with SELECT
statement, 196-198
with tables, 193-194
windows, 88
Word documents
with Open
method, 116
with RecentFiles
object, 116-117

operands, 54

operators
And, 95
arithmetic operators, 55
assignment (=), 54

comparison operators,
56-57, 80
concatenation, 56
definition of, 54
logical operators
And, 67
Not, 67
Or, 67
table of, 57
Xor, 67
Or, 95
order of precedence,
57-58
controlling, 58-60
table of, 58

optimizing procedures
avoiding data
selection, 319
avoiding
recalculation, 319
hiding documents, 319
loops, 320-321
turning off screen
updating, 319

Option Base 0|1
statement, 358

option buttons, 250-251

Option Compare
Text|Binary
statement, 358

Option Explicit
statement, 351, 358

Option Private
statement, 358

OptionButton object,
250-251

Options object, 73

Or operator, 95

order of precedence
(operators), 57-58
controlling, 58-60
table of, 58

outgoing messages,
handling (Outlook),
219-220

Outlook
attachments
adding to messages,
230-231
Attachment
objects, 229
removing from
forwarded
messages, 229-230
custom rules, 223-224
folders
listing all folders,
214-215
methods, 217
prompting users for,
216-217
referencing default
folders, 214
incoming message
handling, 217
AddItem event,
218-219
custom rules, 223-224
spam, 224-225
logging off, 233-234
logging on, 232
MailItem object
methods, 221-223
properties, 220-221
messages
creating, 225
forwarding, 225
replying to, 225
sending, 226-227
specifying message
recipients, 226
supplementing
reminders with email
messages, 227-228
NameSpace object, 213
Folders property, 214
Logoff method,
233-234

InsertParagraph
method, 127
InsertParagraphAfter
method, 127
InsertParagraphBefore
method, 127
InsertParagraphsAnd
Text procedure,
127-128
Italic property, 126
reading and changing
range text, 126
returning with Range
method, 125
returning with Range
property, 125

Range property, 125

ranges. *See* **Range object**

rate function, 62-63, 365

ReadInboxData procedure,
233-234

reading
application settings from
Registry, 306-307
range text (Word), 126
section settings, 309

ReadReceiptRequested
property (MailItem
object), 221

recalculating worksheets,
140, 319

ReceivedTime property
(MailItem object), 221

RecentFiles object, 73,
116-117

Recipients object, 226

Recipients property
(MailItem object), 221

Record Macro command
(Macros menu), 5-7

Record Macro dialog
box, 5-7

recording macros
Excel macros, 7-8
overview, 3
Word macros, 5-7

records
adding, 205-206
deleting, 207-208
editing, 203-205
finding, 202-203
navigating, 199-201

Recordset object
accessing recordset
data, 198-199
adding records, 205-206
deleting records, 207-208
editing records, 203-205
finding records, 202-203
methods, 199
AddNew, 205-206
Delete, 207
Find, 202
GetRows, 208
Move, 200
MoveFirst, 200
MoveLast, 200
MoveNext, 200
MovePrevious, 200
Open, 193-195
Update, 204
navigating records,
199-201
opening with Open
method, 194-196
opening with SELECT
statement, 196-198
opening with tables,
193-194
overview, 192-193
properties, 195
BOF property, 200
EOF property, 200
Fields property, 198

RecordsetBookmark
Navigation
procedure, 201

RecordsetData
procedure, 199

RecordsetOpenProperties
procedure, 196

RecordsetOpenSELECT
procedure, 197

RecordsetOpenTable
procedure, 193-194

recordsets. *See also*
RecordSet object
accessing recordset
data, 198-199
adding records, 205-206
deleting records, 207-208
editing records, 203-205
exporting from Access to
Excel, 210-212
finding records, 202-203
navigating records,
199-201
opening with tables,
193-198
overview, 192-193

ReDim statement, 42, 358

referencing
Outlook folders, 214
Outlook from other
applications, 231

Registry
deleting settings from, 307
overview, 305
reading section
settings, 309
reading settings from,
306-307
storing settings in, 306
tracking file usage,
307-309

Relationship element
(XML), 265, 269

Rem statement, 358

Remove command (File
menu), 301